Urban Land Economics and Public Policy

Macmillan Building and Surveying Series
Series Editor: Ivor H. Seeley
Emeritus Professor, Trent Polytechnic

Advanced Building Measurement, second edition Ivor H. Seeley
An Introduction to Building Services Christopher A. Howard
Applied Valuation Diane Butler
Asset Valuation Michael Rayner
Building Economics, third edition Ivor H. Seeley
Building Maintenance, second edition Ivor H. Seeley
Building Quantities Explained, fourth edition Ivor H. Seeley
Building Surveys, Reports and Dilapidations Ivor H. Seeley
Building Technology, third edition Ivor H. Seeley
Civil Engineering Contract Administration and Control Ivor H. Seeley
Civil Engineering Quantities, fourth edition Ivor H. Seeley
Civil Engineering Specification, second edition Ivor H. Seeley
Contract Planning and Contractual Procedures B. Cooke
Contract Planning Case Studies B. Cooke
Environmental Science in Building R. McMullan
Introduction to Valuation D. Richmond
Principles of Property Investment and Pricing W. D. Fraser
Quantity Surveying Practice Ivor H. Seeley
Structural Detailing P. Newton
Structural Surveying S. L. J. Mika and S. C. Desch
Urban Land Economics and Public Policy, fourth edition P. N. Balchin, J. L. Kieve and G. H. Bull
1980 JCT Standard Form of Building Contract, second edition R. F. Fellows

Other titles by the same authors
Housing Improvement and Social Inequality P. N. Balchin (Gower)
Housing Policy: An Introduction P. N. Balchin (Croom Helm)
Housing Policy and Housing Needs P. N. Balchin (Macmillan)
Regional and Urban Economics P. N. Balchin and G. H. Bull (Harper and Row)
The Electric Telegraph: An Economic and Social History J. L. Kieve (David and Charles)

URBAN LAND ECONOMICS AND PUBLIC POLICY

Fourth Edition

PAUL N. BALCHIN
Ph.D., B.Sc.(Econ.)
Principal Lecturer in Economics
Thames Polytechnic

JEFFREY L. KIEVE
M.Phil., B.Sc.(Econ.), A.I.A.S.
Property Investment Consultant and Visiting Lecturer
Thames Polytechnic

GREGORY H. BULL
B.A., M.A., Doctorate
Senior Lecturer in Economics
Thames Polytechnic

MACMILLAN
EDUCATION

First edition 1977
Reprinted 1979
Second edition 1982
Reprinted 1983
Third edition 1985
Reprinted 1986
Fourth edition 1988

Published by
MACMILLAN EDUCATION LTD
Houndmills, Basingstoke, Hampshire RG21 2XS
and London
Companies and representatives
throughout the world

Typeset by TecSet Ltd, Wallington, Surrey
Printed in Hong Kong

To Daniel
Elizabeth
Karen
Mark
Paul

and

Richard

British Library Cataloguing in Publication Data
Balchin, Paul N.
Urban land economics and public policy.—
(Macmillan building and surveying series).
1. Great Britain. Urban regions. Real
property. Economic aspects
I. Title II. Kieve, Jeffrey L. III. Bull,
Gregory H.
333.33′7′0941

ISBN 0-333-46377-3
ISBN 0-333-46378-1 Pbk

Contents

Preface to the Fourth Edition

While this book, like the first three editions, is a basic text for students registered on degree courses in Estate Management/Land Economics, Building Surveying and Quantity Surveying, it is hoped that it will increasingly serve as an essential reader where there are degree or diploma courses (or specialisms) in urban economics, urban geography or town planning. In addition, the book should remain an important reader for students preparing for the examinations of the many professional bodies concerned with land – for example, the Royal Institution of Chartered Surveyors and the Royal Town Planning Institute.

Between us we have lectured on courses in land economics and town planning for nearly two decades and have been involved in the preparation of both degree and honours degree syllabuses. We have found that while there is an ever-increasing flow of new literature on urban land economics, often the product of intensive research, the student's problem of a restrictive range of suitable books still remains partly unresolved. By combining theory with the applied aspects of the subject, however, this book is intended to eliminate this deficiency.

In recent years there has been a dramatic change in the economic strategy of government in the United Kingdom – most notably with the adoption and relegation of monetarism and the implementation of programmes of privatisation, not least within the field of property. This edition therefore considers public policy in greater length than in former editions – a facet now reflected in its subtitle and inevitably in the coursework and examination questions of the relevant academic and professional institutions. This alone (apart from more detailed theoretical considerations) distinguishes this book from others of similar title and should make it a more comprehensive and therefore useful text. A further new feature of this edition is the inclusion of a chapter on welfare economics. By placing welfare considerations near the middle of the book, it is hoped that a bridge will be formed between the initial chapters which concentrate mainly on the private market and subsequent chapters which deal with public intervention.

The subject matter of the book progresses from the general to the specific. Chapter 1 is an attempt to provide a background account of population change, the process of urbanisation, the basic features of land as a factor of production and it considers the role of urban land economics. Chapters 2 and 3 seek to explain the rationale of the locational determinants of economic activity. Chapters 4 and 5 deal with property investment, the economics of development and investment appraisal in the private sector. Chapter 6 considers the relationship between welfare economics and land, and examines the question of pollution. Chapter 7 sets out to explore urban decay and renewal – including the constraints of urban transport and public finance. Chapter 8 analyses the problems of housing. Chapter 9 examines land values and public intervention, and chapter 10 looks at the performance and organisation of the construction industry.

In compiling all editions of this book, every effort has been made to ensure that legislative and statistical detail is accurate or at best undisputed at the time of writing. In this edition, to take account of policy development, it has been necessary to add a Postscript on page 344.

We must acknowledge the debt we owe our colleagues past and present who have advised us particularly with regard to amendments to later editions. We would particularly like to thank Professor Ivor Seeley who painstakingly read and edited the initial manuscript and without whose help the publication of this text would not have been possible. We would also like to extend thanks to Christine Marcouyre who helped to type and collate material for this edition, and finally we would like to thank our respective families and particularly Maria and Mildred for the patience which they have shown throughout the preparation of this book.

Paul N. Balchin
Jeffrey L. Kieve
Gregory H. Bull

Acknowledgements

The authors and publishers wish to thank the following who have kindly given permission for the use of copyright material.

P. Cheshire and D. Hay for table 3.5 'Suburbanisation and deurbanisation in Western Europe, 1970–80' [quoted in P. Hall, 'Flight to the Green', *New Society*, 9 January, 1987].

Financial Times for figure 4.3 'Share price movements 1973–87' [*Financial Times*, 24 October, 1987].

Morgan Grenfell Laurie for table 4.2 'Investment media: comparison of real rates of return, 1978–86' [*MLG–CIG Property Index*, 1987].

Every effort has been made to trace all the copyright holders but if any have been inadvertently overlooked the publishers will be pleased to make the necessary arrangement at the first opportunity.

List of Figures

List of Tables

1

Introduction

Urbanisation

An increasing proportion of the rapidly growing world population is attempting to satisfy its economic and social needs and desires in an urban context. The enormous migration of people into cities and towns has produced a very distinct possibility of an uncontrollable urban explosion – an unprecedented increase in population, greater demands on the urban infrastructure, higher rates of pollution and a decrease in the non-material (and in some cases material) standard of life.

There are four major forces determining the pace of urbanisation throughout the world – economic growth and development, technological change, a rapid growth in the world population and a large-scale movement of people from rural areas to cities and from cities to towns. Despite the current recession in most Western industrial countries the world production of goods and services continually increases. As a result of improvements in transportation and the supply of power, production becomes more rather than less concentrated in those locations offering the greatest comparative advantages. These tend increasingly to be large urban market areas – smaller urban settlements declining in relative importance. This trend is compounded by the simultaneous growth of large, often multi-national, companies which with their increasing market dominance and internal and external economies of scale form an interdependent relationship with areas of large population and high purchasing power.

The increased pace of industrial growth commencing in western Europe in the eighteenth and nineteenth centuries has had a direct effect upon mortality. An improved food supply and better living conditions and medicine have all led to a decline in death-rates – in Britain, for example, it fell from 30 per 1000 of the population in 1750 to 11.8 per 1000 in 1986. Yet while birth-rates in industrial countries have also been declining – in Britain from 35 to 13.3 per 1000 between 1750 and 1986 – the rate of fertility has remained very high in many developing countries, often being in excess of 40 per 1000. Recently the population of the world has been growing by about 1.9 per cent per annum, a rate of increase unparalleled in history. Although it took from palaeolithic times to 1850 for the world population to reach 1000 million, by 1925 this number had doubled and by 1962 it had trebled. In 1987, the world population reached 5000 million.

Small urban settlements are incapable, however, of evolving into major cities solely through the process of natural population increase – the migration of people from the countryside is an equally or more important determinant of growth. Apart from the economic 'pull' of towns there is also the 'push' effect of agricultural change such as the establishment of enclosures, land reform or an acceleration in the application of capital-intensive farming. Although the proportion of the working population employed in agriculture in economically developed countries consequently began to decline in the late nineteenth century, the share of civil employment in agriculture has continued to diminish in recent decades (table 1.1).

Table 1.1 *Percentage of active population employed in agriculture in selected advanced capitalist countries, 1955, 1966, 1973 and 1981*

	1955	1966	1973	1981
Italy	40.8	25.2	18.3	13.4
Japan	37.9	22.0	13.4	10.0
France	26.7	17.3	11.4	8.6
West Germany	17.8	10.6	7.5	5.5
Canada	18.0	9.0	6.6	5.5
United States	9.7	5.6	4.2	3.5
United Kingdom	5.4	3.6	2.9	2.6

Source: OECD, *Labour Force Statistics* (various).

In global terms there has been a decrease in the ratio of the overall rural population to the total population, and a reciprocal increase in the proportion of the urban population. Today about 40 per cent of the world population is urban but whereas in rural areas population increase is at a rate of 1 per cent per annum, in towns and cities the growth is on average 3.5 per cent per annum with an even greater increase in developing countries. Even in the ten years 1950–60 the number of cities with populations in excess of 500 000 grew from 158 to 234, and agglomerations with populations greater in number than 2 million grew from 20 to 26 (of which 12 were within the developing countries). In Britain not only did the population increase from 10.5 million to 55 million between 1801 and 1986 but the proportion of the population which was urban grew from 21 to 80 per cent – an increase in both relative and absolute terms. In 1750 there were only two cities in Great Britain (London and Edinburgh) with populations greater than 50 000, by 1851 the number had increased to 29 and by 1981 there were over 150 cities with populations in excess of this size.

As part of this process of urbanisation, industry (and particularly manufacturing) replaced agriculture as the dominant economic activity in terms of employment. But in all advanced capitalist countries since the 1950s, services have increasingly superseded industry as the largest sector (tables 1.2 and 1.3).

There has been a recent tendency for these sectoral shifts in employment to be accompanied by decentralisation.[1] Within the European Community, for example, between 1960 and 1970 the population of non-urban areas grew at a

Table 1.2 *Percentage of active population employed in industry in selected advanced capitalist countries in 1955, 1966, 1973 and 1981 (percentage in manufacturing in brackets)*

	1955	1966	1973	1981
West Germany	45.5 (33.8)	48.2 (35.2)	47.5 (36.7)	43.5 (33.6)
Italy	29.2 (20.0)	36.9 (25.8)	39.2 (28.5)	37.5 (26.1)
United Kingdom	47.9 (36.1)	46.3 (34.8)	42.6 (32.3)	35.7 (26.4)
Japan	24.8 (18.4)	32.7 (24.4)	37.2 (27.4)	35.3 (24.8)
France	36.2 (26.9)	39.9 (28.7)	39.7 (28.3)	35.3 (25.1)
United States	37.6 (28.5)	36.3 (27.8)	33.2 (24.8)	30.1 (21.7)
Canada	34.0 (24.1)	33.6 (23.9)	30.6 (22.0)	28.3 (19.4)

Source: OECD, *Labour Force Statistics* (various).

Table 1.3 *Percentage of active population employed in services in selected advanced capitalist countries in 1955, 1966, 1973 and 1981*

	1955	1966	1973	1981
United States	52.7	58.1	62.6	66.4
Canada	48.0	54.7	62.8	66.2
United Kingdom	46.7	50.1	54.5	61.7
France	37.1	42.8	48.9	56.2
Japan	37.3	45.1	49.4	54.7
West Germany	36.7	41.2	45.0	51.0
Italy	30.0	37.9	42.5	49.1

Source: OECD, *Labour Force Statistics* (various).

faster rate than the population of urban areas, but in the period 1970–75 in Italy, France, Denmark and probably West Germany urban population growth not only remained relatively slow but it also decelerated. The urban populations of Belgium, the Netherlands and Britain, moreover, declined in absolute terms during this period (table 1.4) – a trend particularly indicative of the economic and social malaise affecting the urban areas of north-west Europe.[2] A similar process of decentralisation also occurred in the United States.

Except for averting a catastrophic war or famine, there are few challenges and problems which appear so daunting and intractable as the problems of urban areas. To many the city has seemed synonymous with civilisation, with the height of man's achievement in the arts and sciences, in technology and in administration. To others, especially since the industrial revolution, the city has offered poverty, misery and disease. Yet although economic processes may have brought about distress to millions, economics as a discipline has helped to solve

Table 1.4 *Population growth in urban and non-urban areas, 1960–70 and 1970–75*

	Average annual growth (%)			
	1960–70		1970–75	
	Urban	Non-urban	Urban	Non-urban
Belgium	0.78	4.52	–0.58	3.74
Netherlands	2.97	10.55	–0.35	9.04
Great Britain	1.16	5.06	–0.03	3.45
West Germany	3.41	5.09	n.a.	n.a.
Denmark	3.79	3.81	0.43	3.51
France	3.36	7.55	1.58	7.18
Italy	4.35	2.30	2.51	2.93

Source: L. Van den Berg *et al.*, *Urban Europe: a Study of Growth and Decline* (Pergamon, 1982).

many of the problems of the human condition. But as yet it has not been applied on any scale to these problems within a specifically urban context. In the United Kingdom, this is illustrated by reference to the long boom of the 1950s–70s and its aftermath. In the twenty or more years prior to the oil price shock of 1974, the long boom facilitated the extension of the housing stock and the improvement in the urban infrastructure.[3] But with the adoption of monetarist policy in the late 1970s, a further oil price hike in 1979 and the application of free-market ideology (marked by continuous programmes of privatisation) in the 1980s, it became evident that any further improvement in the urban environment would at best be patchy. Except for small areas of commercial development, the inner cities were increasingly debilitated by deprivation and a resurgent housing crisis, and it was evident that there was a glaring and widening mismatch between, on the one hand, 'need' and, on the other hand, unused land, labour and construction capacity. The plight of our cities was of course intensified by the recession of the national economy in the early 1980s. Unemployment soared from 5.2 per cent in 1979 to 13.9 per cent in 1985 and was very largely associated with deindustrialisation. The pace of deindustrialisation (and a less than compensatory growth of service employment) was not only more rapid than in most other advanced capitalist countries, but it produced new divisions of labour and disparities of growth between cities and suburbs, and metropolitan areas and provincial towns (in addition to a widening 'north–south divide').[4]

The Resource of Land

Urban land shares most of its basic features with land in general. To the classical economist land is defined as being all the free gifts of nature which yield an income. Agricultural land would obviously be included, but so would minerals, water resources and forests with all their natural flora and fauna. Although structures on land have been regarded as part of the factor of production capital, the distinction is of little concern to the urban or land economist. He often finds land and capital so interdependent that separate identification may either be impossible or inconvenient. A lawyer's definition of land is thus more appropriate to his needs – land is 'the surface of the earth together with all the subjacent and super-jacent things of a physical nature such as buildings, trees, minerals'.[5] Land has a number of features which in aggregate are not entirely possessed by other factors, especially if the classical definition of land is accepted. Land is characterised by the following.

The relative fixity of supply

Economists have traditionally argued that the total supply of land is fixed. If one type of use is increased in area (for example, farmland) it will be at the expense of another (for example, forests). But the land economist is not directly concerned with this global definition of land and its implication. He knows that productive land *can* be both increased *or* decreased through man's actions – Dutch polderland and the dustbowls of the United States often being cited as respective examples. He also knows that land can be increased by more intensive use; for example, by constructing a multi-storey office block on a formerly low density residential site (or decreased by a reversion to less intensive use). Yet it must still be accepted that when compared with capital (as an independent resource), labour or entrepreneurship, land is the least flexible factor of production, its supply being comparatively fixed.

No cost of creation

Man has of course the power to increase his own numbers, he can also produce capital and evolve entrepreneurial skill. But he cannot *make* land in its broadest meaning, it was there before him and it cost him nothing to create. But when land is developed costs are incurred. It then becomes like the other factors of production, no longer a free resource.

Heterogeneity

To the user of land each site and building is different, even so land can be classified into a number of economic categories – sub-marginal land having no remunerative use, break-even marginal land, and profit or surplus yielding intra-marginal land.

Yet the boundaries or 'margins of transference' between these different categories of land frequently change. If, for example, the price of cereals increased or the cost of cultivation fell (or both), wheat cultivation might expand from its intra-marginal land into mainly oat areas (normally break-even land for wheat) and these in turn might extend into livestock rearing areas (usually break-even land for oats and sub-marginal land for wheat). Conversely, if cereal prices fell or costs increased (or both) the margins of transference would shift in the opposite direction. In urban areas shifts similarly occur. If office rents and relatively lower residential rents increased or the cost of construction in real terms fell (or both), office use would expand into residential areas and these in turn would extend into agricultural areas, sub-marginal land becoming break-even land and break-even land becoming intra-marginal land. The converse could happen in theory but it rarely does in practice.

Table 1.5 *Diminishing returns to land*

Units of land	Number of men employed (each with equal amount of farm capital)	Total output per year (tonnes of potatoes)	Average output	Marginal output
1	1	8	8	8
1	2	18	9	10
1	3	30	10	12
1	4	44	11	14
1	5	56	11.2	12
1	6	66	11	10
1	7	74	10.6	8
1	8	80	10	6
1	9	84	9.3	4
1	10	86	8.6	2
1	11	86	7.8	0
1	12	84	7	−2

The Law of Diminishing Returns

Nineteenth-century economists, in particular David Ricardo and his followers, believed that land was unlike other factors in that it was subject to the Law of Diminishing Returns. The law states that 'after successive applications of labour and capital to a given area of land, first the marginal output, then the average output and eventually the total output diminishes'. Table 1.5 shows that marginal output increases to 14 tonnes when the number of men employed is raised to four, average output increases to 11.2 tonnes when five men are employed and total output rises to 86 tonnes when the labour force increases to ten or eleven men. Above these levels of output it can be seen that diminishing returns set in.

In a free market economy the producer would employ additional men until marginal output reached its maximum (in table 1.5 four men would be employed producing marginally 14 tonnes of potatoes). If the extra men available were re-employed elsewhere, according to the same criterion there would not only be a marked increase in overall output but each producer would maximise his profits (assuming factor costs per unit of output and product prices remained constant). But the quality of land and capital can be improved and farming skills might become more sophisticated, and in consequence diminishing returns could be delayed. Table 1.5 could equally show diminishing returns of a building development – the number of storeys could substitute for the number of men employed, total rent income could replace total output, and marginal rent and average rent income could substitute for marginal and average output. If construction costs were the same for each storey, a building of four storeys would provide the maximum profit. Yet improved technology and lower real costs of development would enable more storeys to be constructed prior to the onset of diminishing returns.

The absence of a market for 'land'

While in market economies other factors of production can be bought or sold in their own right, in most if not all countries land deals are transactions not in land itself but in interests or rights in, on, under and over land. Since at least feudal times land has been owned only by the Crown or State, and various forms of tenure have been bestowed on individuals, firms, or institutions enabling them to use land subject to various conditions. In English Law these rights in aggregate are known as 'real property'.

Economic or scarcity rent

The word 'rent' originally referred only to the factor of production land – classical economists realising that the comparative scarcity of land produces a return quite different in character from that normally earned by labour or capital.

(i) *Agricultural rents*

Until the early nineteenth century it was generally believed that the price of food largely reflected the rent charged to tenant farmers. It was thought that landlords would charge rents directly in relation to the fertility of the land and that farmers would attempt to pass on these rents to the consumer in the price of farm produce. But in 1817, Ricardo suggested an alternative explanation of the relationship between food (especially corn) prices and rents. Although conceding that rent represented

> "that portion of the produce of the earth which is paid to the landlord for the use of the original and indestructible powers of the soil,"[6]

he argued that food prices determine rents rather than vice versa. Aware of a decreasing supply of corn from the Continent as a consequence of the Napoleonic Wars and the effects of an increasing population, he postulated that "corn is not high because rent is paid, but a rent is paid because corn is high." Ricardo further argued that if either the supply of corn increased with the resumption of imports, or the demand decreased, prices would fall, the demand for land for corn would decrease and rents would consequently diminish. Clearly, therefore, the demand for land was a derived demand. Land was not required for itself but for the value of its product.

Ricardo thus believed that rents were determined by the interaction of supply and demand. Given a fairly fixed supply of farmland, land of high fertility would yield a high marginal output (in response to a constant marginal increase in labour and capital inputs) and would therefore command a high rent – a surplus equal to the marginal revenue of the product less the marginal cost of labour and capital (figure 1.1). Land of low fertility would attract the least demand and therefore command little or no rent.

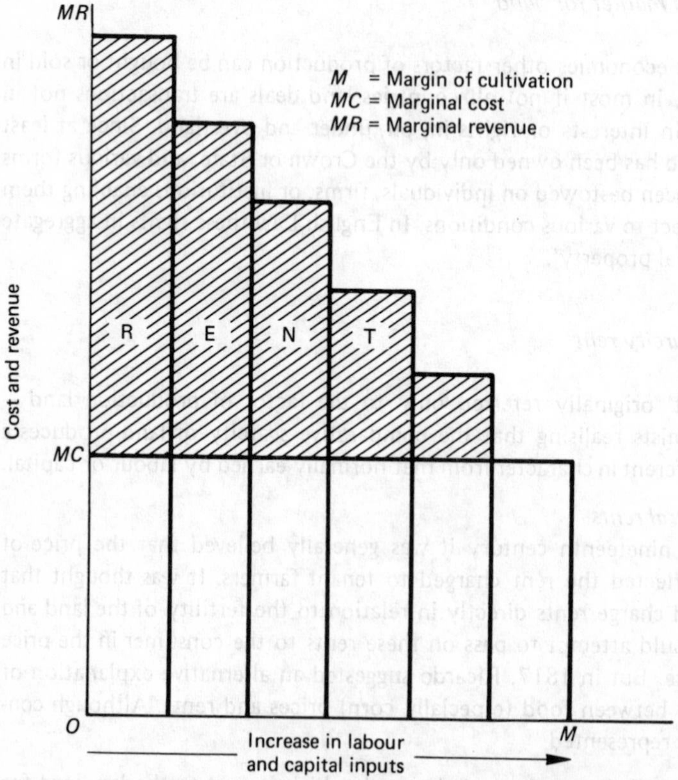

Figure 1.1 *Relationship between labour and capital inputs and rent*

To modern economists the Ricardian concept of rent is inadequate. Although in colloquial terms rent can refer to any regular payment for the hire of a product (for example, a motor car or a television set), in a more specific economic sense the term 'rent' relates to factors of production not perfectly elastic in supply with land as the principal example. The payment for the use of land is known as *commercial rent*, but there are two constituents of commercial rent – *transfer earnings* and *economic* (or *scarcity*) *rent*. Transfer earnings occur because most land is capable of being used for many different purposes and there is competition between various potential interests to secure the right to use it. They are the minimum sums which have to be paid to retain land for its current economic purpose, and if the land has no maintainable use the transfer earning is zero. Economic rent is a payment reflecting the scarcity value of land in excess of its transfer earnings.

Although most farmland contains elements of transfer earnings and economic rent, the proportions vary according to the elasticity of the supply of land. If land were plentiful, supply would be relatively elastic and a high proportion of rent would be in the form of transfer earnings and comparatively little of the payment would be economic rent. But in an intensively farmed area, land would be fairly inelastic in supply, and consequently economic rent would account for a high proportion of total rent. It is not impossible, of course, for some types of farmland to command equal proportions of transfer earnings and economic rent – a situation obtaining if supply were of unitary elasticity (figure 1.2).

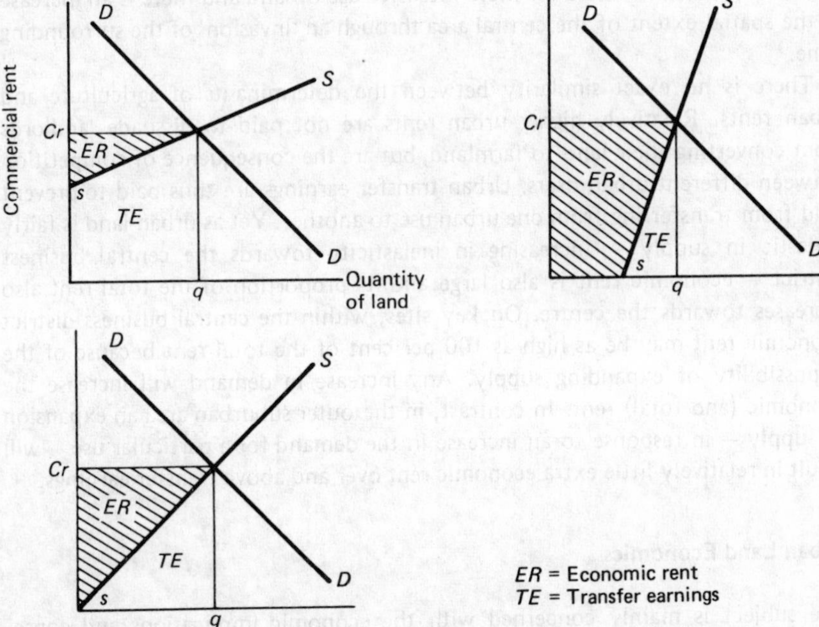

Figure 1.2 *Economic rent and transfer earnings*

If there was a completely free market, land would transfer to its most profitable or *highest and best use*. Each user would be paying more for his land than that which any of his competitors would be willing or able to pay. Every eventual user will pay for land, either an outright purchase price or rent appropriate to the expected profit he can realise from his use of the land. Therefore the capital value of land is determined indirectly by the profitability of its use, and directly by the annual rental value. An example of this is the annual value of farmland being derived from the difference between the cost of production and the revenue from the sale of farm produce.

(ii) *Urban rents*

Whereas in the country the demand for farming land is derived from the demand for farm produce, in towns "the demand for land is a demand for space which can be varied by structural changes through the allied processes of property development, redevelopment and conversion."[7] In contrast to the farmer, the developer may find himself constrained by the relative inflexibility of his capital and labour inputs. Location and siting, while being of only general significance to the farmer, may thus be of crucial importance to developers in urban areas.

Within urban areas land use is subject to fewer changes; location is therefore of greater importance, and advantages and disadvantages of location are more long-lasting. If there is scarcity of land within the central business district and a high level of demand for central sites rents will be high. No instant increase in the supply of land in central areas is possible, although in the long term supply might be increased if there is a more intensive use of land and there is an increase in the spatial extent of the central area through an 'invasion' of the surrounding zone.

There is no exact similarity between the determinants of agriculture and urban rents. Relatively higher urban rents are not paid to dissuade landlords from converting their land to farmland, but are the consequence of competition between different urban users. Urban transfer earnings are thus paid to prevent land from transferring from one urban use to another. Yet as urban land is fairly inelastic in supply – increasing in inelasticity towards the central business district – economic rent is also large and its proportion of the total rent also increases towards the centre. On key sites, within the central business district economic rent may be as high as 100 per cent of the total rent because of the impossibility of expanding supply. Any increase in demand will increase the economic (and total) rent. In contrast, in the outer suburban area an expansion of supply – in response to an increase in the demand for a particular use – will result in relatively little extra economic rent over and above transfer earnings.

Urban Land Economics

The subject is mainly concerned with the economic implications and consequences of the scarcity and choice of essentially urban property rights. Yet despite the recent interest taken in urban land economics, especially in the United States, the discipline is in its infancy. This is because conventional economic analysis cannot easily be applied to an urban situation. The market is absent for many products especially those associated with the urban infrastructure, there are many externalities, and investment decisions are usually undertaken without reference to the urban structure in general and to external scale economies and diseconomies in particular. It is thus difficult or impossible to allocate resources optimally either within the public sector or between the public and private sectors.

Where there are markets (for example, in the case of owner-occupied houses) they tend to function imperfectly. The scarcity or glut of specific uses is common and often transactions do not occur when market prices are offered. The property market is quite unlike the Stock Exchange or a commodity market. It is not organised and there is no central buying or selling place. It consists of an aggregate of a vast number of deals, large and small, involving heterogeneous buildings and sites. The land professions attempt to bring together buyers and sellers generally within a fairly local context.

The complexity of urban life proves an obstacle to the application of economic analysis. There is no satisfactory resource allocation model (with a manageable number of variables) which can determine the optimal combination of factors of production in an urban economy – an economy which changes both over time and in space. Yet economic analysis can and must be applied to the many problems relating to urban land use. The location of economic activity, spatial structure and urban growth, the property market, the processes of development and techniques of investment analysis, welfare considerations, the economics of urban decay and renewal, housing, betterment and land nationalisation, the condition of the construction industry – these and other areas provide the economist with the opportunity to apply his special powers of analysis and to investigate in specific contexts the productive and distributive processes of urbanised society.

REFERENCES

1. P. Hall and D. Hay, *Growth Centres in the European Urban System* (Heinemann, 1980).
2. L. Van den Berg *et al.*, *Urban Europe: A Study of Growth and Decline* (Pergamon, 1982).
3. M. Edwards, 'Planning and the Land Market: Problems, Prospects and Strategy' in M. Ball *et al.*, *Land Rent, Housing and Urban Planning: A European Perspective* (Croom Helm, 1984).
4. D. Massey, 'In What Sense a Regional Problem', *Regional Studies*, 13 (1979).
5. G. C. Cheshire, *Cheshire's Law of Real Property* (Butterworth, 1972).

6. D. Ricardo, *Principles of Political Economy and Taxation* (Penguin, 1971).
7. R. H. Wright, 'The Property Market 1', *The Architect and Surveyor* (January/February, 1971).

2

The Market and the Location of Urban Land Uses

Regardless of the geographical location, origin or size of an urban area a rational pattern of land use evolves. Normally after an assessment of various advantages and disadvantages, the location of any activity is determined either by the desire to maximise (or realise satisfactory) profits in respect of business users of land or to maximise (or obtain acceptable) utility in the case of residential and other non-business users. The urban land use pattern is mainly determined by activities competing for sites through the forces of demand and supply – demand being the quantity of property required at given prices or rents and supply being the amount of property available at those prices and rents.

The demand for land is a reflection of the profitability or utility derived from its use by current or potential users. The greater the benefit to be obtained from using a site for any particular purpose the higher the rent or price the would-be user is willing to pay. Since capital values are derived from annual rental values, so the higher the levels of rents the greater will be the capital values. Just as with any other form of investment, so the prices of property interests rise in anticipation of future increases in rent incomes. Property investors may therefore be prepared to accept low yields or returns in relation to current property income in order to obtain the future benefit of an increased income and the possibility of additional capital gains.

The total supply of land in any country is fixed except in cases of territorial gains and losses or reclamation and dereliction. But the supply of land for different uses can be either increased or decreased. Change in supply occurs when, for example, land transfers from one agricultural use to another, from farming to urban use, from residential to office or retailing use, and from private to public use.

The supply of land for specific uses is comparatively static in the short term. The underlying conditions of supply (the state of construction technology, sources of materials and other factors of production, number and type of public utilities, and the transport system) remain fairly constant. Because supply is slow to react to increases or decreases in demand, it is demand which is the major determinant of rental values and consequently of capital values. In Britain from the 1950s until the late 1980s there was a substantial increase in property values due to the effect of increased demand for urban property upon a more slowly changing pattern of supply. The increased demand was the product of four distinct factors: inflation, credit availability, population growth and increased affluence.

(i) Until the late 1980s inflation not only increased property values in step with the rise in the general level of prices, but because property was regarded as a 'hedge' against inflation, and because of its scarcity in relation to demand, values increased ahead of general price levels. Property therefore became very attractive to developers and speculators.

(ii) The availability of finance from institutional investors, not least from building societies, compounded the rate of increase in the level of effective demand. Interest rates on mortgages barely kept pace with the increased prices of property. After tax allowances on interest payments were taken into account the real financial cost of purchasing property was either very small or nil.

(iii) The population increased over the period mainly as a result of changes in birth- and death-rates, by 1986 being over 12 per cent greater than in 1951 (table 2.1).

Table 2.1 *United Kingdom population 1951–86*

Year	Population (millions)	Birth-rate (per 1000)	Death-rate (per 1000)
1951	50.2	15.8	13.4
1956	51.2	16.0	12.5
1961	52.8	17.8	12.6
1966	54.4	17.9	11.8
1971	55.6	16.2	11.6
1981	56.3	13.0	11.8
1986	56.3	13.3	11.8

(iv) An increase in population by itself would have had little effect upon the level of property values. But this increase occurred simultaneously with an increase in real incomes. These two factors led to an increase in the quantity of demand for property, and to qualitative changes, the result of changing social, economic and cultural characteristics. Changes included the earlier age of marriage and the dispersal of the family unit into separate dwellings with young people leaving home at an earlier age, the demand for improved quality and higher standards of both new and older properties and the demand for second homes – the latter decentralising increased values throughout the country – especially where there was an increase in accessibility resulting from motorway development.

Influenced by changes in the underlying conditions of demand, land within the market transfers to the user who is prepared to pay the highest price or rent (demand and supply for ever moving towards an equilibrium situation). This monetary value will reflect utility in the case of householders and profit levels in respect of commercial and industrial users.

Although the property market can be described as an economic mechanism rationing land between competing and occasionally conflicting users, it is one of the most imperfect markets and one of the most susceptible to change in underlying conditions.

The Inefficiency of the Market

The property market is one of the least efficient markets of all. The imperfect knowledge of buyers and sellers, the 'uniqueness' of each site and building, the strong preference of establishments for existing sites, the unwillingness of some owners to sell despite the certainty of monetary gain, the absence of easily recoverable investment in costly and specific developments, the immobility of resources once they are committed, the possible loss on initial investment, the time-absorbing and costly process of seeking and acquiring new locations, the expense and legal complexity of transferring property, the length and legal rights of property interests, the influence of conservationists, the slowness of the construction industry to respond to changing demand, the monopoly power of planning authorities, property companies, mortgage institutions, sellers of property and the design professions – these are some of the factors which prevent land from transferring smoothly to its most profitable use. The pattern of land use only changes slowly over a long period and at no time is the market in a state of equilibrium with all resources being optimally used.

Even where market prices (as determined by comparable valuation) are offered a transaction may not take place as the owner may weigh non-monetary factors more heavily than monetary considerations.

Despite these imperfections the market still attempts to assert itself, albeit inefficiently. While there is a perpetual state of disequilibrium between demand and supply resulting in either the scarcity or overabundance of different land uses, a change in the demand for a specific use will ultimately have an effect on prices and rents and subsequently will produce a change in supply.

Accessibility and Demand

Profitability and utility are largely determined by accessibility. The greater the accessibility of a location (and the lower the net economic cost of movement in terms of distance, time and convenience), the greater the comparative advantage and the greater the demand for property at that location.

In the case of business use, general accessibility refers to nearness to transport facilities (rail termini, bus stations, motorways), labour, customers and service facilities such as banks and post offices. Special accessibility exists when complementary uses are in close proximity to each other, for example in London lawyers are close to the Law Courts, stockbrokers are near the Stock Exchange, commercial and merchant banking is located adjacently, and the wholesale and retail clothing industry is situated in the Oxford Street area. (Special 'inaccessibility' is desirable when there are repellent uses, for instance noxious heavy industry and new high income housing, or take-away food shops and retailers of luxury merchandise.) The importance of accessibility to residential land is illustrated when the utility of particular sites depends upon monetary factors such as travelling costs to work, schools, shops and public and private open space, and upon non-monetary considerations such as peace and quiet (or the converse), compatible neighbours, fresh air and other less tangible amenities.

The greater the accessibility (general or special) and the greater the relevance of accessibility to the user of land, the higher the value of the land in question. Therefore the pattern of accessibility creates a pattern of urban land use which will be concomitant with the pattern of land values. In addition there is a relationship between accessibility, land uses and values, and the intensity of utilisation. As demand is greatest for those sites with the highest degree of accessibility, the more feasible it is to develop those sites intensively. Users able to put the site to its most productive use would be prepared to pay the highest price or rent to acquire the developed property.

THE URBAN LAND USE PATTERN

There are, of course, wide differences in the land use patterns of different urban areas. Varying topographical features have an effect on land use; so do climatic conditions, past and present social and religious customs, legislation and legal decisions, demand for goods and services including varying consumer preferences, and the policy of local and central government in the supply of public utilities and social services. These variations provide different frameworks within which competition between the existing and potential land users decides the pattern of land use in any urban area. Within these frameworks and subject to the imperfections of the market, the forces of demand and supply provide the means by which land is developed up to its highest and best use. It is as a result of this process that a general pattern of land use has evolved in most urban areas which in the industrialised world comprises the following areal components: the central business district, the zone of transition, the suburban area and the rural–urban fringe.

The Central Business District

Having the maximum overall accessibility to most parts of the urban area, the central business district is the focus of intra-city transport routes. Competition for sites among commercial users raises land values and the intensity of development to a peak. Population increase and economic growth increase densities within the central business district, development usually being vertical rather than horizontal. The central business district becomes a smaller and smaller proportion of the expanding urban area. If a number of urban areas merge into a conurbation, the central business district with the greatest comparative advantage in terms of accessibility will become the most intensively developed centre at the expense of the other centres.

Within the larger central business districts the shopping area is usually separated from the main office area, although office users will produce a demand for more localised retail services. A separate entertainment area may emerge, although the dispersed siting of cinemas, theatres and concert halls, may make it difficult to delineate its boundaries.

The central business district merges almost unnoticed into the surrounding transitional zone, but usually its boundaries are marked by public transport (especially rail) termini reflecting the general absence of the lateral growth of the central business district since the nineteenth century.

The Zone of Transition

In most industrial nations over the last one hundred years an area of mixed use developed around the central business district. This consisted of warehousing and light manufacturing (serving the commercial activities of the central business area) interspersed with transport facilities and residential land. Housing initially would have been for the middle and higher income groups, but generally it has become decayed and dilapidated due largely to its conversion into multiple occupancy low income dwellings. There are also areas of local authority and charitable trust housing much of which is old and in need of renewal. Almost alone, London has some transitional areas (such as Belgravia and South Kensington) which have retained their status as high income enclaves.

The transitional zone is generally beset with many social and economic problems, for example mass deprivation (including homelessness, disease and delinquency). Land might be continually blighted because of the slow pace at which planning proposals are implemented and many landlords (both private and public) may forgo rents keeping their properties empty pending redevelopment. The maintenance or improvement of dwellings may be impeded by rent regulation and vagaries in public policy concerning housing rehabilitation. The zone of transition is often referred to as 'the twilight zone'.

Yet new development within the zone does take place. To some extent the market enables land to be developed to its highest and best use as commercial development takes place along the radial routes towards the suburbs or in areas specifically designated for publicly-assisted regeneration.

The Suburban Area

The predominant use in this area is moderate or low density residential land. Housing is segregated by socio-economic class or ethnically, and there is clustering close to railway stations and the main road foci – the area being dependent upon easy access to the employment opportunities and the general attractions of the central part of the city.

Although there is a scattering of schools, churches, public houses and medical facilities, shops tend to be more concentrated into parades and neighbourhood shopping centres. Where office development takes place on a sufficiently large scale, shopping and other commercial and social facilities may have been comprehensively developed to form an 'outlying business district'.

Since the expansion of motor transport and electricity supply, manufacturing industry has been attracted to suburban locations. Sites adjacent to major routeways are particularly favoured making it easy to distribute goods not only to the urban area but also to the regional or national market. Manufacturers also benefit from relatively low cost sites convenient for further development.

Interspersed with other uses, there are usually extensive areas devoted to golf courses, race tracks, parks, cemeteries, allotments and public open space.

The Rural–urban Fringe

As the density of the surburban area becomes less and the built-up parts become largely residential, public open space is replaced by market gardens or farmland. There may also be extensive 'green belt' areas for the purpose of constraining urban expansion. The rural–urban fringe is mainly a commuter belt, its high income adventitious population now usually outnumbering those engaged in horticulture and agriculture.

URBAN LOCATION THEORY

Location theory not only explains the pattern of land use, but by indicating a solution to the problem of what is the most rational use of land suggests ways in which the current pattern can be improved. Very rarely is an activity's location determined by a single locational requirement, a mixture of interacting influences usually explain each locational decision. A location may only be selected after an appraisal has been made of the advantages and disadvantages of alternative locations for the particular activity.

As the price mechanism largely decides the profitability or utility of goods and services, it subsequently determines the location of activity and the spatial structure of the urban area supplying those goods and services. But although land is developed up to its highest and best use, the process is lengthy and is frustrated by changes in underlying market conditions and by severe market imperfections.

Factor inputs may be equally important in determining location. High levels of accessibility within the central business district are reflected in low transport costs attracting the greatest demand for sites especially from commercial users. Conversely low overall accessibility and high transport costs within the suburban areas and the rural–urban fringe will attract a much lower level of demand especially from commercial users.

There may be some general reduction in the cost of factor inputs due to internal and external economies of scale being realised within a city. Up to a certain population size the economies will become greater. Richardson[1] argued that these will increase at a rate more than proportionate to an increase in population, but it is difficult both to quantify these agglomeration economies or to ascertain the optimum size of a city. He suggested that it would be useful to measure the *per capita* cost of retail and office services and of urban transport facilities, social services and entertainment at different levels of population, and to estimate at what level of population agglomeration diseconomies take over from the agglomeration economies, and when net social costs replace net social benefits.

It has been difficult to devise a location theory about urban land use in general or commercial and industrial land use in particular. Inertia, stability in the occupation of land and the pre-empting of sites result in most urban land being used sub-optimally. Land use models are usually very simplistic as changes in population, technology and transportation continually exert an influence on the built environment. Further pressures come from central area redevelopment and local and central government policy. Often similar types of use are seen to be feasible in different locations within the urban area. For these reasons it is difficult to suggest where optimal locations should be. It is probable that there may be several optima for the same use and that these locations are continually changing.

The rationale of current theory can be traced back to Heinrich von Thünen's hypothesis. In 1826 in the light of empirical evidence von Thünen[2] postulated that around a 'central' town, rural land of constant fertility assumed different forms, land use diminishing intensively in inverse relationship to increased distance from the town. The land use pattern outward would comprise the following concentric belts: horticulture and dairying, silviculture, intensive arable rotation, arable with long ley, three-field arable and ranching (figure 2.1). Although in part influenced by practicality, for example milk could not be transported any distance to the market prior to refrigeration (therefore dairying would be close to the town), land in greatest demand would be that land as near as possible to the market on account of low transport costs. The highest rent would be gained for this advantage and the highest value output per hectare would accrue. In the outer belt there would be little demand for land because of high transport costs, rent would be low and the value of extensive production would be correspondingly low.

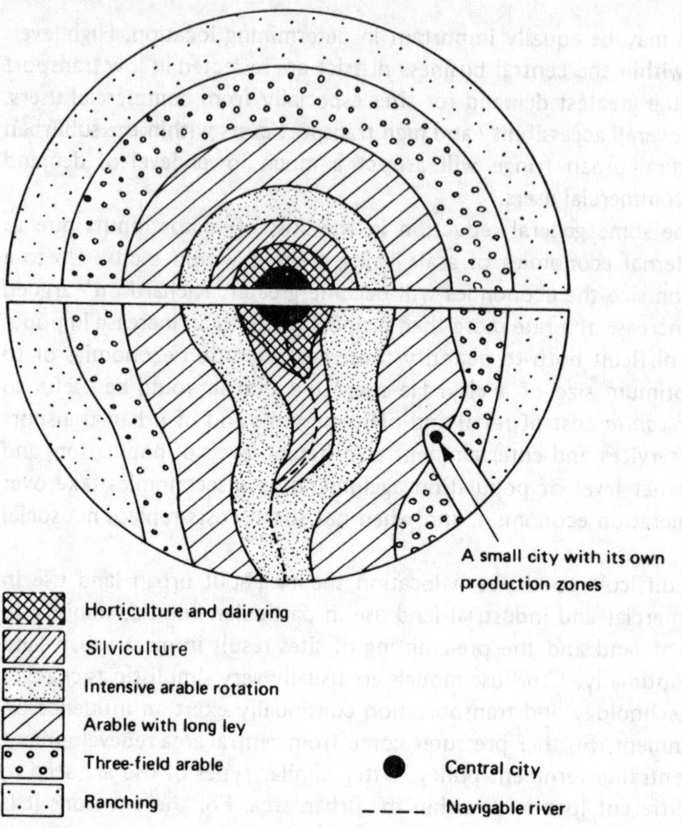

Figure 2.1 *Von Thünen's model of agricultural land use*

The overall land use pattern might be modified by the existence of a navigable river. In contrast to fairly high transport costs over land, costs of river transport are low especially for bulky commodities. The river would have the effect of extending the different land uses almost parallel along its course. A further modification might occur if a small city with its own production zones is located within the land use pattern of the main settlement.

Although the von Thünen model has been criticised because it assumed unlikely conditions such as production taking place around an isolated market and soil being of constant fertility, it nevertheless established a distance–cost relationship which has recently become the basis of urban location theory.

In the twentieth century, neo-classical theory became concerned with rent as an allocative mechanism. In the 1960s Alonso[3] evolved an approach to urban location theory based on the principle that rents diminish outward from the centre of a city to offset both lower revenue and higher operating costs not least transport costs. A rent gradient would emerge consisting of a series of bid-rents which would exactly compensate for falling revenue and higher operating costs. Different land uses would have different rent gradients (figure 2.2), the use with the highest gradient prevailing. Thus, competitive bidding between perfectly informed developers and users of land would determine the pattern of rents throughout the urban area, and would allocate specific sites between users so as to ensure that the 'highest and best' use obtained – that is, land would be used in the most appropriate way to ensure the maximisation of profit.

In figure 2.2 use *a* prevails up to a distance of two kilometres from the central business district, from two to five kilometres use *b* is dominant, and beyond five kilometres use *c* prevails. A change of use could be expected to take place through the price mechanism when one gradient falls below another. Although the Alonso model does not specify the type of land use associated with each bid-rent gradient, it must be assumed that on the edge of the urban area there is a separate agricultural rent gradient. It has been suggested[4] that outwards from the built-up area the proportion of the total value of land attributable to agriculture rises – until agricultural values exceed urban values and so dictate the predominant land use (figure 2.3). Inwards, speculative values increase as urban development becomes imminent and agricultural values become blighted.

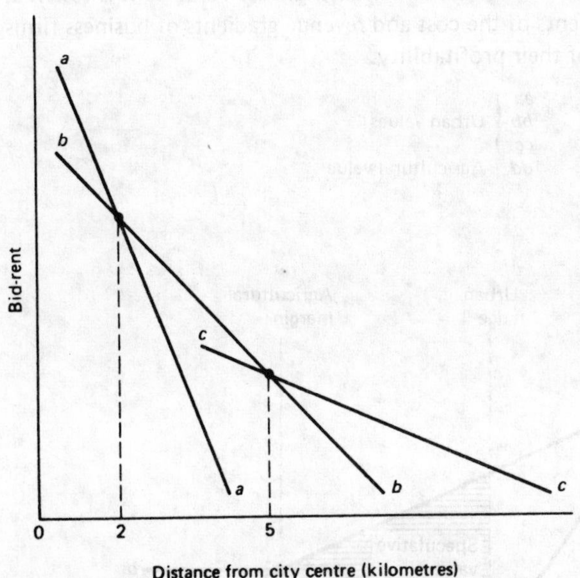

Figure 2.2 *Alonso's bid-rent–distance relationship*

The Alonso theory has been subject to much criticism. First, it can be argued that the information available to the developers and users of land is very incomplete and this alone produces an imperfect market. The theory fails to take account of the very distinctive nature of buildings and their use, for example, once offices, shops and factories have been built they cannot be moved or easily converted into other uses – there is considerable inertia resulting in sub-optimal use over time. Likewise, many large properties may not be suitable for subdivision or sub-letting at current use when demand for the complete property decreases.[5] It is also argued that since commercial, industrial and residential property is not homogeneous, varying in age, size, design, layout and location, each parcel of land is unique. This often provides the owner with a considerable degree of monopoly power which can be particularly exploited in urban areas. Alonso fails to take account of public sector land and ignores the external or spillover effects of specific land uses on other property. Alonso's theory is clearly a very idealised view of reality, but it has some merit in that it attempts to demonstrate the nature of the land market and emphasises the notion of efficiency in the use of urban land. If it can be assumed that public policy has a very variable effect upon the pattern of urban land use and values, then the bid-rent theory cannot be dismissed as an irrelevance – particularly if it is also assumed that even an efficient market in private urban property cannot be equated *per se* with a socially optimal pattern of land use.[6]

Because the Alonso model is general, it is necessary to consider separately the locational determinants of commercial and industrial use. To do so it is essential to identify the componenents of the cost and revenue gradients of business firms and to indicate the basis of their profitability.

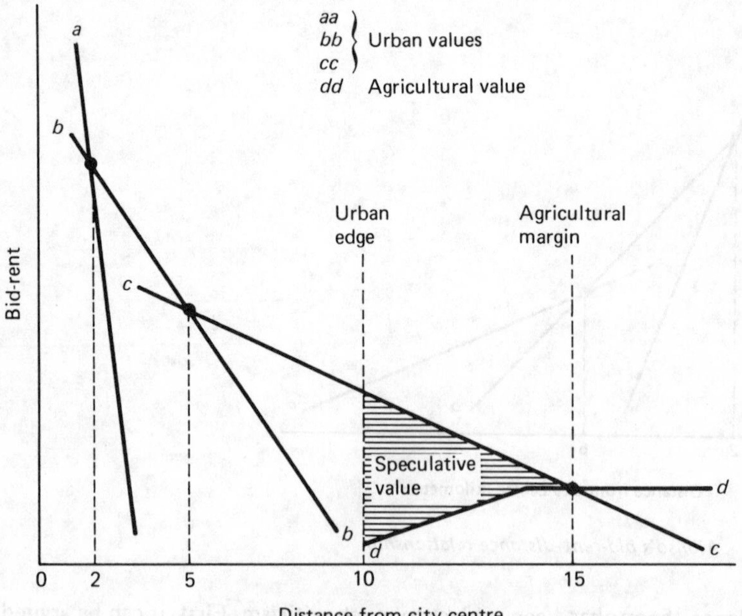

Figure 2.3 *Urban, speculative and agricultural values*

Costs

The price and rent of land fall with increased distance from the central business district though the gradient is rarely smooth. Wages are likewise higher in the centre – local demand for labour being greater than local supply. Also, personal costs of commuting need to be offset by higher remuneration, but this might also apply to travelling to decentralised employment. Transport costs are more of a reflection of accessibility than distance. Locations close to junctions, nodes and termini are particularly favoured, maximising proximity to suppliers and markets. Although retailing is still generally attracted to the lowest overall transport cost location of the central business district, decentralised shopping centres are being developed following road improvement and increased car ownership. Modern manufacuring industry relies increasingly on heavy road vehicles for long distance transportation and incurs lower transport costs on the fringes of cities than at more central locations. Capital costs (interest charges) are generally uniform and have little effect on location.

Revenue

Retailing revenue is determined by the size of the shopping catchment area or hinterland, not just in terms of population but in terms of purchasing power. The distribution of the day-time population and points of maximum transit (where people cluster together) are also important. In the case of offices the spatial distribution, number and size of client establishments determine revenue.

In general, revenue is thus greatest within the central business district and so are aggregate costs. But as the distance from the centre increases, whilst revenue falls, aggregate costs (after falling initially) rise in suburban locations and beyond. This is mainly due to the upward pull of transport costs, which are no longer offset sufficiently by economies in the use of land and labour. Only within fairly short distances from the central business district are commercial users able to realise high profitability.

Costs, Revenue and Decentralisation

So far in this discussion it has been assumed that rents generally diminish outwards from the centre of an urban area, and in a Ricardian sense reflect a centrifugal reduction in population density and the level of economic activity. However, since the late nineteenth century, both the population density and employment gradients have been flattening-out as a result of decentralisation[7] – in Western Europe population out-migration preceding employment change, and in the United States employment change pre-dating population out-migration. Rent gradients have also flattened-out but not always to the same extent because of imperfections in the property market. The monopolistic ownership of central area land and restrictive planning policies have kept rents at a high level in the urban core long after the process of decentralisation commenced. An implication of decentralisation is therefore that costs do not necessarily fall continuously from the central business district and neither does revenue. Indeed, both costs and revenue may begin to rise outwards as firms increasingly decentralise to exploit spatially expanding markets.

Profitability

To maximise profits firms need to locate where they can benefit from both the greatest revenue and from the lowest costs. But there are no single locations where this can be achieved in absolute terms. Nevertheless in an attempt to realise maximum revenue, specialised functions and activities serving the urban market as a whole might continue to locate centrally; firms requiring large sites and those attempting to reduce costs of overconcentration will be attracted to the suburbs. Firms locating close together to benefit from complementarity will incur lower costs because of external economies and enjoy higher revenue due to joint demand. Outlying business districts may be at least as attractive as the central business district in terms of profitability and more attractive than the relatively high cost and low revenue locations of the suburban belt in general.

But there is a high degree of inertia, most firms not operating at maximum profit locations. As with the level of output, firms find it difficult to adjust their locations to the optimum. A satisfactory rather than ideal location is usually the best that can be achieved. The pattern of location moreover is stabilised by zoning and land use controls.

Retailing Location and Development

Retail efficiency is highly dependent upon location, and within a location highly dependent upon site. Within short distances one site may be very superior to another. Often the selection of the right site may mean the difference between business success and failure. The number and type of shops which can locate profitably in an urban area is very limited and is dependent upon the determinants of revenue (see above) and the degree of competition among retailers for a portion of that revenue. Retailers may wish to break down mass markets into segments (*market segmentation*), and respond differently to variations in the social class, age and lifestyle of consumers; and increasingly retailers are undertaking *niche-marketing*, attempting to satisfy the very specialised needs of relatively high-income, credit-worthy and closely-defined groups of consumers.[8] Low-income shoppers, on the other hand, are being catered for less and less in terms of new shopping development.

Shops (which in the UK had a total floorspace of 83 million m^2 in 1986) can be broadly classified into five categories.

Convenience shops

Customers purchase goods from these shops fairly regularly at short intervals spending only a very small proportion of their net weekly incomes. Although retail turnovers and rents per m^2 are low, convenience shops are viable with only a small catchment area, a low consumer purchasing power and a small floorspace – say less than 280 m^2. Newsagents, tobacconists and confectioners, grocers, bakers and greengrocers are examples of shops in this category.

Over the last two decades, convenience shops have generally been unable to withstand competition from larger retailers; for example, the number of independent grocer shops in the United Kingdom fell from over 56 000 in 1971 to 47 000 in 1983 and their share of grocery turnover nationally plummeted from 42 to 21 per cent. There has, however, been a renewed interest in the development of local convenience retailing.[9] Small shops are proving viable if they remain open up to ten (or more) hours a day, seven days a week, are located close to the focal point of residential areas (particularly in the outer suburbs of Greater London and elsewhere in high income areas of the South-east) and cater particularly for pedestrian and impulse shoppers. Development (and refurbishment) has recently been undertaken by specialist companies (for example, Cullens and Misselbrook and Weston), voluntary groups (such as Spar and Mace), the Cooperative Wholesale Society and petrol stations (notably those operated by BP) – rather than by independent traders. It is anticipated that up to 6000 convenience stores of this type will be trading by the mid-1990s.

Shopping shops

Goods are purchased from these shops less regularly and at longer intervals with shoppers spending a higher proportion of their net weekly incomes. Turnovers and rents per m^2 will be higher than in the case of convenience shops, but larger catchment areas and a greater purchasing power will be necessary. Examples of shops in this category include clothes shops, ironmongers, hairdressers and some soft furnishing stores.

Speciality shops

Customers buy goods at very irregular and lengthy intervals and may spend a multiple of their net weekly incomes. The turnover and rent per m^2 of this category of shop can be very high and profitability may be dependent upon a very large catchment area and a high purchasing power. Jewellers, furriers, and furniture, antique and musical instrument shops fall into this category of retailing.

Department and multiple stores

In one building a department store will be concerned with convenience, shopping and speciality activity. Increasingly key-traders (Marks & Spencer, Boots,

W. H. Smith and Woolworth) are extending their range of merchandise assuming many of the functions of department stores.

Service shops

These shops are often workshops and sometimes partly wholesale premises. Turnovers and rents per m^2 are usually small. Even though customers may spend a multiple of their net weekly incomes they do so at very irregular intervals thus making a service shop dependent upon a large catchment area with a high purchasing power. Examples of shops of this type include furniture renovators and re-tread tyre dealers.

This classification of shops can be incorporated into the hierarchy of shopping centres, the structure of the hierarchy being as follows:

The central shopping area

This approximately coincides with the central business district except where there is exclusively office use. Generally shops co-locate with offices. Office employees are often the principal customers, and retailers may specialise in supplying offices with stationery, machinery, fittings and furniture. Moreover, as shops very rarely utilise space above the ground floor (except in the case of department and multiple stores) office use at higher levels ensures that valuable sites can be developed to their maximum.

Some large cities may have more than one central shopping area. It may be linear or nuclear in form. Except for service shops all the other categories of retailing are well represented. Department stores and key-traders may locate solely in the central shopping area because of this area having the maximum accessibility to the largest catchment area and greatest purchasing power. Customers may be attracted from all regions of the country or from abroad.

Within the central shopping area the relationship between retail turnovers and rents per m^2 is particularly pronounced. There is little inertia and, with the exception of the major retailers, shops are continually changing use as increasing demand raises rent levels. In central London, for example, only one shop in five in 1986 had the same trader in occupation that it had 20 years earlier, while multiple shops increased their occupancy of retail premises in Oxford Street from 33 to 40 per cent (1983–86). There was also an increase in menswear, fashion and footwear shops in the West End from 31 to 42 per cent of retail properties (1966–86).[10] The 'turnover-rent gradient' may slope steeply or gradually away from the key or '100 per cent' sites, but in general as distance from the key sites increase shops change in use from being department or multiple stores to women's clothing, jewellery, furniture and grocery shops. Corner sites are especially favoured where window display is important, for example in the case of footwear and menswear (figure 2.4). Throughout the central shopping area turnovers and rents are usually higher on the side of the

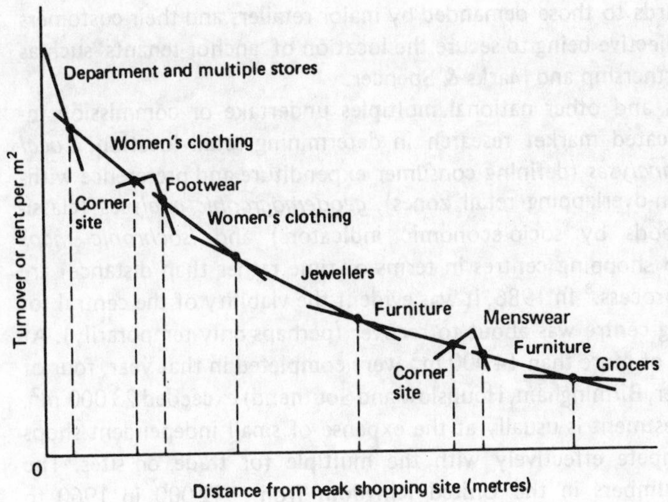

Figure 2.4 *Hypothetical turnover or rent gradient within a major shopping centre*

street which receives the most sunshine, this being the northern (south facing) side in the northern hemisphere.

With the redevelopment of bombed city centres after the Second World War, the central shopping area became increasingly important in the 1950s and 1960s mainly because of the economies of scale associated with the growth of multiple stores, the wider range and larger stocks of goods that can be carried when turnovers are high, the rise in rents forcing out small independent retailers, and the effective end of resale price maintenance after the Resale Prices Act 1964. In the 1970s planning authorities continued to concentrate new retail investments in city centres rather than on the periphery. Either in the form of large regional shopping centres of 46 000 m^2, or smaller centres of up to 23 000 m^2, these developments could blight not only other shops within the same city if central positions suddenly became off-centre locations but also other shopping centres in the regional or sub-regional hierarchy. By the 1980s, however, the average size of the town centre scheme was decreasing and was significantly less than the out-of-town development. In 1986, the *average* floorspace of town centre schemes under construction, with planning consent and proposed, ranged from only 11 600 m^2 to 13 200 m^2, whereas the average floorspace of out-of-town shopping centres at all stages of development ranged from 22 500 m^2 to 40 700 m^2.

Central shopping areas are currently posing considerable problems for investors and retailers. The purpose-built centre — first developed in the 1960s to consolidate urban shopping — is in danger of being forsaken by the major national retailers who increasingly favour decentralised locations. Institutional investors in town centre shops, experiencing a decline in the value of their investments, are thus attempting to redesign, remodel and refurbish their properties to raise standards to those demanded by major retailers and their customers — an important objective being to secure the location of 'anchor tenants' such as the John Lewis Partnership and Marks & Spencer.

Anchor tenants and other national multiples undertake or commission increasingly sophisticated market research in determining retail location. *Local expenditure zone analyses* (defining consumer expenditure and preference within a system of non-overlapping retail zones), *geodemographic analyses* (classifying neighbourhoods by socio-economic indicators) and *isochronic maps* (showing access to shopping centres in terms of time rather than distance) are each used in this process.[8] In 1986, it was evident the viability of the central (or suburban) shopping centre was about to recover (perhaps only temporarily). At least eight schemes of more than 14 000 m^2 were completed in that year, four of which (in Colchester, Birmingham, Hounslow and Southend) exceeded 23 000 m^2.

City centre investment is usually at the expense of small independent shops which cannot compete effectively with the multiple for trade or sites. The decline of shop numbers in the United Kingdom from 542 000 in 1960 to about 360 000 in 1987 indicates the vulnerability of the small shop. In view of the fact that most major shopping development schemes are undertaken by a partnership of a local authority and a property company, it is remarkable how little the proposals are subject to public scrutiny. The United Kingdom is, however, still over-provided with retail space, though much of it is in the wrong place. It is clear that the traditional High Street has become increasingly obsolescent and unappealing because of a confusion of architectural styles, the inappropriate floorspace and layout of shops, and the problems of traffic congestion, parking and shelter. National multiples may soon be no longer satisfied with their town centre shops — redesigned and refurbished every two to three years — and instead employ, once and for all, the easier option — decentralisation.[8] It is important, however, not to exaggerate the scale of the problem. Town centre floorspace in the United Kingdom in 1986 amounted to 77 million m^2, while out-of-town floorspace in the same year was as little as 249 000 m^2 (or only 3.2 per cent of the total). Central shopping areas will thus continue to dominate retailing well into the twenty-first century.

Ribbon shopping

This extends along the main radial roads outward towards or beyond the suburban shopping centres. There will be the greatest concentration of shops in the direction of the most densely populated or highest income areas. Generally, department and multiple stores are absent and the only speciality retailers are motor traders — convenience and shopping shops predominate. From central areas outward, accessibility, turnovers and rents diminish, although gradients are not smooth and small peaks occur near suburban centres.

Ribbon shopping development is faced with numerous problems. The distribution of shops may be over-extended for convenient shopping, motorists may face parking restrictions, there may be no recognisable shopping centre (though key-traders may be located in 'hot spots'), traffic or even physical barriers divide shopping frontages, and there may be many redundant shops occupied by non-retail uses.

Suburban centres

These are usually of recent growth although their origins may be old, in some cases dating from medieval times. The larger suburban centres may be part of an outlying business district with shops relating to offices in the same way as in the central business district. There are signs of substantial expansion where access to the central shopping area is poor, and where the suburban population and its purchasing power is high. In many cases car parking and servicing facilities are comparatively good. The same type of shops that are found in the central shopping area will be located in the surburban centre, although turnovers and rents per m^2 will not be as high.

Neighbourhood centres

These will either be in the form of small parades of shops or small shopping precincts dependent on a restricted catchment area and a fairly low purchasing power. Turnovers and rents per m^2 are relatively low. Convenience shops will be profitable, though shopping or speciality shops will be less viable. Yet even in neighbourhood centres compound trading is ousting the small independent retailer.

Local corner shops

Though tending to disappear, the corner shop will remain if it can truly retain its convenience function. The catchment area is small and the required purchasing power is very low. In consequence turnovers and rents per m^2 are also very low.

Decentralised shopping facilities

These consist of the activities of most types of shops – convenience, shopping, speciality – perhaps in a number of different buildings under different leases possibly with one retailer dominating: alternatively the activities may be concentrated in one building operated by one firm. Out-of-town shopping centres were first developed in the United States – where there were 2000 centres in 1956 (increasing to 28 500 by 1985) – but in recent years decentralised shopping has expanded in Europe especially in France and Western Germany, but less so in the United Kingdom.

Increased congestion and reduced accessibility have rendered retailing less and less profitable in the central areas of many cities in the United States, motivating the development of shopping centres in out-of-town locations. But in Europe it is improbable that central shopping areas have reached the same level of congestion and subsequent decline – yet the viability of decentralised centres and stores has been recognised in spite of the continuing (and often increasing) profitability of central area locations.

There are the following types of decentralised shopping facility:

(1) Out-of-town shopping centres – complexes of shops dominated by department stores with catchment areas of at least 250 000 people. In the United Kingdom by 1980, despite a number of applications, only the Brent Cross development had been permitted – a centre of 74 300 m^2. (It is often argued, however, that Brent Cross is not an out-of-town development at all, but rather a strategic suburban shopping centre.) Similar restrictions were placed on developments of this scale in France and West Germany.

By 1986, only the Metrocentre at Gateshead had been added to the list of major out-of-town developments, while the Park Gate Centre at Rotherham was in the process of construction. However, developers had announced plans to build a further 43 major out-of-town centres in Britain, each of 37 000 m^2 or over – a total floorspace of 2.3 million m^2 (table 2.2). (There were also proposals to develop over 40 smaller out-of-town centres of between 10 000 m^2 and 37 000 m^2.) Some of these proposals will be withdrawn if they risk being eclipsed by competing developments, while others may fail to receive planning permission.

Table 2.2 *Proposed major out-of-town shopping developments in Great Britain, 1986 (December)*

Location	Shopping centre	Motorway access	Developer(s)	Floor-space '000 m^2
South-east				
Dartford	Bluewater Park	M25/M20	Shearwater/ Blue Circle	125
Grays-Thurrock	Dolphin Park	M25	Town & City	121
	Lakeside	M25	Capital & Counties	107
Hook	Elmbridge Park	M25	London & Edinburgh Trust	93
Orpington	Hewitts Park	M25/M20	Prudential	84
Wraysbury	Runnymeade Centre	M25	ARC Properties	81
Southampton	Test Valley	M27/M271	Taylor Woodrow Property/Barker Mill Family Trust	80
Maidstone	Leybourne Grange	M2	Ideal Developments	74

Table 2.2 *continued*

Location	Shopping centre	Motorway access	Developer(s)	Floor space '000 m²
Luton	Sundon Springs	M1	Brookmount Estates/ Blue Circle	54
St Albans	Bricket Wood	M1/M25	Town & City	46
West Midlands				
Wednesbury	Sandwell Mall	M5/M6	Color Properties	204
Dudley	Merry Hill Centre	M5	Richardsons	139
Birmingham	Fort Shopping Town	M6	George Harris & Associates	116
Walsall	Walsall CEGB Centre	M6	Carroll Group	99
Wolverhampton	Wolverhampton Racecourse Park	M54	Regentcrest	93
Walsall	Walsall CEGB Centre	M6	Cameron Hall	46
Solihull	Monkspath Business Park	M42	Standard Life Assurance	37
Greater Manchester				
Manchester	Westside Park	M56	Prudential	116
Eccles	Barton Docks	M62/M63	J. & J. Fee	93
Stockport	Springpark	M56	Springpark Securities	93
Trafford	Barton Dock	M62/M63	Manchester Ship Canal Co./Peel Holdings	93
Rochdale	Kingsway Industrial Estate	M62	J. & J. Fee	74
South Yorkshire				
Sheffield	Meadowhall	M1	Paul Sykes Developments	120
Rotherham	Parkgate Centre	M1	Stadium Developments	93
Sheffield	Oakes Park	M1	Henry Boot	93
South-west				
Exeter	Skypark	M5	Exeter Park Estates	60
	Exe Vale	M5	Shearwater/SW Area Health Authority	59
	Metro Centre West	M5	Cameron Hall	37
	Monkerton Road	M5	Michael Baker (Property Services)	37
	Oak Marsh Farm	M5	Carkeek	37
	Sowton Industrial Estate	M5	Exeter Building Co.	37
Central Scotland				
Bathgate	Landmark Centre	M8	Landmark Properties	93
Strathclyde	Motherwell	M8	Highland Developments	93
Edinburgh	Hermiston Gate	—	Miller Group	37
	Maybury Park	—	Edinburgh DC/Wimpey/ Marks & Spencer/Asda	37

Table 2.2 *continued*

Location	Shopping centre	Motorway access	Developer(s)	Floor-space '000 m²
Avon				
Avonmouth	Royal Portbury Dock	M5	Heron Group	93
Bristol	Cribbs Causeway	M4/M5	J. T. Baylis	58
	Project Retail 2000	M4/M5	Prudential	44
North-east				
Gateshead	Metrocentre	–	Cameron Hall	121
Teesside	Metro Tees	–	Cameron Hall	37
West Yorkshire				
Leeds	Cherwell Grange	M62	Evans of Leeds/Yorkshire Water Authority	47
	Pudsey	M62	Mountleigh	47
East Midlands				
Leicester	Centre 21	M1	Penwise Developments	65
South Wales				
Newport	Tredegar Park	M4	Cameron Hall	47

Source: *Chartered Surveyor Weekly* (various).

(2) Edge-of-town centres – complexes of shops dominated by supermarkets or variety stores with catchment areas up to 100 000. Planning permission has been more readily forthcoming than in the case of out-of-town centres.

(3) District shopping centres – relatively smaller complexes of shops dominated by convenience trades, with catchment areas rarely in excess of 10 000.

(4) Hypermarkets – large free-standing stores of up to 23 000 m² combining food trades with a variety of cheaper household goods. They may contain banks, restaurants, hairdressers and other service trades. Although hypermarkets have proliferated in France and Western Germany, only four were permitted in Britain up to 1978 (in Caerphilly, Eastleigh, Irlam and Telford).

(5) Superstores – also large free-standing stores but with only up to 7000 m² of floor area. Similar to giant supermarkets, they concentrate on food and household goods. In contrast to hypermarkets, a large number of superstores have been developed in the United Kingdom in recent years, often as nuclei of new town shopping centres or on inner city sites. Retailers such as Asda, Fine Fare, Tesco and Woolco have been notable in this field, and the number of superstores increased from about 200 in 1980 to 340 in 1986 taking nearly 30 per cent of the retail market. Further expansion in the late 1980s–early 1990s is certain. In 1986, for example, Tesco planned to open a further 29 superstores (on average each with a floorspace of 3252 m²) – increasing its total to more than 150 (or nearly half) of the nation's superstores. The growth in the number of superstores is particularly rapid in London. Whereas in 1980 there were only 5 superstores in

the capital, by 1987 the number had increased to 22, and planning permission had been secured for a further 27 – all in excess of 2500 m^2. Since each store is likely to provide about 350 new full time and part time jobs, local authorities have been reluctant to withhold planning permission despite protests from small shopkeepers. Outside urban areas, however, applications for planning approval have often been rejected. From 1970 to 1985, of the 189 superstore appeals, two-thirds were rejected largely on the grounds of countryside protection, environmental damage and location in the green belt.

(6) Retail warehouses – are normally large single storey buildings of up to 6500 m^2 (although there are plans for units of over 9000 m^2). There have been three stages in their development since the early 1970s. *First generation* units were relatively small converted warehouse buildings (rarely in excess of 2300 m^2), often located in industrial estates, and mainly concerned with DIY, carpets and furniture. *Second generation* units occupied prominent main road locations and provided adequate car parking. *Third generation* development consisted of retail warehouse parks – planned and purpose-built sites for clusters of warehouse 'shops' with scale economies such as shared car parking and advertising. Since the 1970s, Sainsbury's, W. H. Smith and Woolworth have absorbed some of the earlier warehouse operators, and together with other national multiples have operated from their own purpose-built warehouses – becoming more selective in their choice of sites. It is likely that there were 750 000 m^2 of retail warehouse floorspace in the United Kingdom in 1986, but further growth was dependent upon a continuing increase in consumer spending, a further growth in car and home ownership, a retained interest in this sector by the major retailers, and of course planning consent.

Decentralised shopping development in the 1980s made considerable strides. It benefited from a consumer boom of unusual length and magnitude – starting in 1983 and continuing for at least four years (in 1987 alone, consumer spending in real terms rose by 5.8 per cent – the largest rise since 1972). There were significant reductions in direct taxation, there was large scale credit expansion and wages rose significantly faster than inflation. Shop rents likewise increased ahead of inflation reflecting soaring retail profitability (particularly in 1986 and 1987). Apart from a favourable macroeconomic climate, however, decentralised shopping also requires the following conditions: a high car-owning population and ideally a high proportion of families owning at least two cars, a large proportion of married women employed making it necessary for shopping to take place mainly once a week and at one point, a high proportion of households owning deep-freezers, a highly developed ring-road system making adjacent locations as accessible to as large a catchment area and as high a purchasing power as is enjoyed in the central shopping area, the availability of large and inexpensive sites for the development of shopping facilities and spacious car parks, and the availability of finance and development expertise.

Like central shopping areas, decentralised facilities generally benefit from high accessibility, but unlike central areas, rents per m^2 are initially low. Although turnovers per m^2 may also at first be low, the very large retail floor areas result in a high level of total profitability. Consumers also benefit because internal economies of scale are passed on in relatively low prices, and lower travel costs might be incurred on shopping journeys.

But there are a number of obstacles in the way of decentralised shopping development. In Britain land values in outer urban locations may not be very much cheaper than in the central shopping area or existing suburban centres, ring roads are far less developed in Britain than in say the United States or Western Germany – central areas retaining the highest level of accessibility in the urban area; two-car families still account for a very small proportion of shoppers, urban land (even on the fringe of the built-up area) is scarce and out-of-town shopping may be considered wasteful of land especially if there are already large scale supermarkets in suburban areas, and governmental policy may be opposed to the further development of out-of-town centres. Under the Town and Country Planning (Shopping Development) Direction 1986, local authorities are obliged to consult with the Secretary of State for the Environment before granting planning permission for developments in excess of 23 325 m^2. The government, however, appeared to be adjusting its stance towards out-of-town development. In 1986, for example, the Secretary of State declared that development should not be stopped merely on the grounds that it might compete with something else (existing retail provision), but later in the year, the Department of the Environment (DOE) began to oppose out-of-town development in the green belt and subsequently ordered that any scheme of more than 23 325 m^2 would need to be centrally vetted. Despite much opposition from retailers in established shopping centres, there was little evidence by 1987 that decentralised retailing development had had a harmful effect on the viability of traditional shopping locations. But with the rapid opening of new out-of-town centres and superstores in the late 1980s, decentralised shopping is increasingly accounting for a greatly increased share of the retail market to the detriment of the High Street. It would thus seem that the government needs to do more to vet schemes in excess of 23 325 m^2. It has been suggested that the DOE must study the accumulative impact of these developments, and also should vet slightly smaller schemes since these could have a major impact on catchment areas. The DOE must recognise that local authorities may be unable to gain an overview of proposals (if some are within and some are outside their boundaries), and that a few local authorities may wish to adopt a soft option by appearing to create employment by approving out-of-town schemes regardless of the cost to town centres.

Local authorities, however, usually pursue a cautious approach to out-of-town proposals. Developers are normally obliged to undertake *impact assessments* (IAs) in support of their planning applications, but invariably IAs show that the potential effect on town centres will be minimal. While the Secretary of State had not defined what was an acceptable impact, the 1986 Direction stated that in assessing the impact of a scheme, "the vitality and viability of a nearby shopping centre as a whole" should be considered. The impact could, in reality, be enormous. The scale of shopping schemes out-of-town (in terms of floorspace) in 1986 was on average at least twice that of town centre schemes and at least half of all new shopping floorspace in the United Kingdom was out-of-town by the mid-1980s (table 2.3). According to the John Lewis Partnership (JLP), if 92 000 m^2 of out-of-town development is undertaken and turnovers amount to £1870 per m^2, then the total turnover of the new centre would be equivalent to that of a town centre the size of Exeter, Stockport or Watford. Out-of-town development could also have an unfavourable impact on the modernisation of many city centres. JLP reported that there was not enough demand (despite the consumer boom) in the late 1980s to support both out-of-town developments and the renewal of High Street shopping centres – a view shared with Tesco.

Table 2.3 *Out-of-town and town centre shopping development in Great Britain, 1986*

Stage of development	Average floorspace of development (m^2)		Total retail floorspace being developed (m^2)	
	Out-of-town	Town centre	Out-of-town	Town centre
Underconstruction	23 319	11 600	248 980	178 374
With planning consent	22 482	13 192		
Proposed	40 692	12 450		

Source: Hillier Parker, *Shopping Schemes in the Pipeline*, 1986.

The abolition of the Greater London Council and the metropolitan county authorities in 1986 had a serious effect on the strategic planning of shopping centres in their areas. Faced with 13 proposals for out-of-town shopping development, the Association of Greater Manchester Authorities (aware that the defunct Greater Manchester Council's structure plan had aimed to strengthen existing town centres) commissioned Roger Tym and Partners to advise on these intended developments.[11] Their advice was that if the proposals went ahead they would jeopardise proposed town centre developments since there was insufficient projected consumer expenditure to support both forms of development. Similarly, the structure plan of the former West Midlands Council had emphasised the need to redevelop existing centres. But faced with edge-of-town shopping proposals, seven West Midland boroughs commissioned Drivers Jonas to undertake an impact study on these proposals.[12] The study showed that only by ignoring the effects of two approved centres at Merry Hill and Sandwell could a further 60 000 m^2 be supported by 1991.

In justifying new out-of-town proposals, developers argue that there is enough growing demand to support both town centre and out-of-town shopping provision. Developers also point out that whereas out-of-town centres facilitate bulk-buying by car-borne shoppers, town centres accommodate a wide range of specialist shops and are more accessible to pedestrians – and as such are complementary rather than competitive. In historic cities, out-of-town centres can usually divert traffic away from the centre, easing congestion and parking problems, and as such could be welcomed by city centre retailers.

Impact assessments, however, are not only very unreliable (different assessments could, for example, show a 10, 25 or 40 per cent impact on trade) but are very narrow. They do not take into account broader considerations such as the impact on the utilisation of energy. It might be pertinent, for example, to question whether at a time when future supplies of cheap oil are unpredictable it is rational to develop a new kind of shopping dependent very greatly on the extensive use of the private motor car, and to bear in mind that such developments are highly regressive, in so far as the low-income consumer will probably not own a car and will be disadvantaged by a diminishing number of accessible shops.

The rise of the shopping centre

The distinction between individual shops and shopping centres is diminishing. This is because of the growth of compound trading, the tendency towards one-stop shopping and the increased use of franchises within stores. These trends have been brought about by economies of scale, changing shopping habits due to more married women in employment, improved storage of food (by refrigeration) and the increased use of private cars. In assessing the value of a shop location it is essential to have regard to the centre in which it is situated. The relevance of the centre to a specific shop depends on whether the trade is receptive (that is, it receives trade from incidental or impulse shoppers) or self-generative (it attracts intending shoppers). The former group may be situated anywhere in the centre where it can tap trade, but self-generative trades are often gregarious for competitive or complementary reasons.

Shopping centres are footloose. In London, for example, the centre of shopping moved westward from St Paul's churchyard in the seventeenth century, to the Strand in the eighteenth century, to Piccadilly and Regent Street in the early nineteenth century, and to Oxford Street by 1900. In each period the centre was the point of maximum accessibility, and as the means of transport changed there was a relocation of the transport node. As in the past, the future pattern of shopping will be determined largely by the pattern of transportation, and there is likely to be a continuation of current trends – the decline of small businesses and the falling number and increased size of shops. The pace at which this takes place will not only be dependent upon the rate of economic growth but upon government policy concerning monopolies and consumer protection, and upon planning policy at a local and central level. Alternatively, with the increased decentralisation of population, electronic shopping from home could evolve or there might be a re-emergence of the small independent shop in the small country town or village. This would reflect a changing demand and a reaction against the ever-increasing scale of both central and out-of-town shopping centres.

Office Location and Development

Offices are of two kinds – those attached to factories and those which are independently sited. In the case of the former, location will be dependent upon the factors responsible for the location of factories (these will be considered later in this chapter), but in the latter, location is dependent upon general accessibility and in particular upon special accessibility to complementary firms and the offices of clients. Even so, location may be fairly flexible and the site might not be as important as in retailing. Office functions moreover do not have to be tied to the ground or lower floors of a building.

Independently located offices (with a total floorspace in the UK of over 46 million m^2 in 1985) can be classified into the following groups.

The head offices of major commercial and industrial firms

To benefit from accessibility and from a 'prestige' address, firms have demanded more and more office space within the central areas of cities and are attracted more to large rather than small cities – London being of foremost importance. In 1938 there were 8.8 million m^2 of office space in Central London, in 1966 the figure had increased to 16.7 million m^2, and by 1976 the area exceeded 18.7 million m^2. In the United Kingdom office jobs as a percentage of the total work force increased from 24 to 32 per cent, 1960–70, and the percentage growth in office employment was five times the increase in employment generally – an increase much greater than in most other countries including those with higher gross national products (GNPs) *per capita*. Office rents simultaneously increased, rising from about £15 per m^2 in the 1950s to £165 per m^2 in the City of London in 1973. This contrasted with rents of up to £45 per m^2 in other cities. By 1987 rents reached nearly £470 per m^2 and £420 per m^2 in the City and West End respectively. Taking occupancy costs (rent, rates and service charges), only Tokyo had higher outgoings than the City of London in 1987 – £720 per m^2 as opposed to £650 per m^2. Costs in downtown New York were £440 per m^2, £430 per m^2 in Paris and £230 per m^2 in Frankfurt. Suburban London and the South-east continued to increase their appeal with, for example, Windsor and Slough (adjacent to the M4) attracted rents of over £162 and £153 per m^2 respectively, and Redhill/Reigate and Crawley (close to the M25 and M23) commanded rents of over £125 and £102 per m^2. In other regions rents were a lot lower, for example, £79 per m^2 in Bristol and Birmingham, £69 in Manchester, £56 in Liverpool, £51 in Sheffield and £44 in Newcastle-upon-Tyne and Plymouth. With such enormous regional disparities in rent, it is not surprising that 70 per cent of all new office investment in the United Kingdom in 1986 was in London.

By affording high rents and rates, office users usually push out alternative uses except perhaps ground-floor retailing. High rents and rates are paid because of the intensive use of the floor area and because of substantial external economies of scale (such as access to labour, material and service inputs, and where offices collectively provide a large market for advertising, accounting and legal services – each consequently supplied at low unit cost). Where earning capacity is dependent upon being sited in a specific area, users are simply willing to incur the expense. Firms place a premium on locations providing the maximum opportunity for face-to-face contact and maximum degree of access to information. As it is practicable to construct multi-storey offices (in contrast to shops), those sites occupied by offices will be the most intensively developed and most valuable sites within the urban area.

But eventually the central business district becomes saturated. Further vertical development is too costly and, except for minor instances of infilling and redevelopment, horizontal expansion is impossible due to the lack of sites. Decentralisation thus offers the only possibility for an expansion in office space and the process has been adopted in most capitalist countries. In the United States, for example, 87 per cent of major firms were located in the central business district in 1956, but this proportion decreased to 71 per cent by 1974[13] and continued to decline into the 1980s. In the United Kingdom, following the Control of Offices and Industrial Development Act 1965 office development became strictly controlled. Office Development Permits (ODPs) were required for all office development in the South-east and Midlands where the proposed floorspace exceeded 3000 ft^2 (279 m^2) and in Central London there was a complete ban on office development. Although ODP limits were subsequently raised in 1967 to 10 000 ft^2 (929 m^2) outside the Metropolitan Area, to 10 000 ft^2 within the region (exclusive of Greater London) in 1969, and to 10 000 ft^2 in London in 1970, the effect in these years was to raise office rents substantially because of the inadequate supply of new development. Between 1965 and 1970 rents of new and old offices in central London increased by five- and four-fold, respectively (in contrast to increases of 39 and 23 per cent in the respective rents of new and old offices in Manchester and Liverpool). Were it not for economic uncertainty and financial stringency, the Greater London Council's policy of restricting office development in Central London in the mid-1970s would have similarly produced a further soaring of office rents.

Encouraged by the Location of Offices Bureau (established in 1963), and influenced by expiring leases, premises due for demolition and the need for more space (and to a lesser extent by rising rents and rates, higher wages, labour scarcity and travel inconvenience), many firms have moved all or most of their office requirements out of London. General administration, routine accounts, records and technical departments have been decentralised since it became recognised that the need for face-to-face contact had been exaggerated, but small reception departments usually remained (and many firms doubled up on their use of office space) within the central area. Between 1963 and 1977 over 2000 office-using firms left Central and Inner London accounting for about 145 000 jobs, yet suburban areas or towns within the South-east were usually preferred to other locations in Britain. Concentrated decentralisation in the South-east made possible the retention of contacts between firms withouth them needing to incur the high direct costs of locating in London.

The pattern of decentralisation has clearly been at the expense of provincial locations. Whereas, for example, the outer South-east increased its share of company headquarters from 7 to 15 per cent of the national total between 1968 and 1983 (a gain of 114 per cent), the North-west decreased its share from 8 to 5 per cent, Scotland from 5 to 4 per cent and the North from 4 to 2 per cent. The concentration of company headquarters in one region (the South-east) is in complete contrast with many other capitalist countries such as the United States and West Germany where head-offices are widely distributed.

Within the Assisted Areas of the North and West, decentralised offices were induced not only by the absence of the need to obtain an ODP, but after 1973 by government grants paid to employees who moved with their work and rent grants for periods of three to five years. Loans were also available at concessionary rates for normal capital needs, interest relief grants could be claimed, removal grants up to 80 per cent of cost were provided, and the government offset up to 80 per cent of the redundancy pay commitment of firms relocating. Under the White Paper, *Regional Industrial Development*, 1983, some service sectors previously excluded from regional development grants (RDGs) (for example, advertising agencies, credit-card companies, cable television and football pools) now qualified for assistance. Regional aid was to be allocated largely in the form of RDGs (which were limited to a cost of £10 000 per job) or as job grants (of £3000 per job).

By 1977 the economic plight of the inner cities (not least Inner London) was recognised. The Department of the Environment therefore altered the terms of reference of the Location of Offices Bureau to attract office development to the inner cities rather than exclusively to decentralised locations. The Inner Urban Areas Act 1978 further emphasised the importance of offices to the inner cities. But decentralisation was finally rejected in July 1979 when the incoming Conservative Government (favouring a *laissez-faire* approach) abolished ODPs and closed down the Location of Offices Bureau. An office boom in Central London was anticipated. Despite some major developments in the early 1980s, by the middle of the decade big increases in demand pushed up rents in Central London ahead of the rate of inflation – a trend dramatically boosted by the deregulation of the City's financial markets in 1986 (the 'Big Bang'). Deregulation created an intensified demand for office space from conglomerates, solo firms, companies with futures determined by the Financial Services Act of 1986, and from spin-off accountancy and legal services. Most importantly was the strong demand for offices (such as those being developed in Broadgate and redeveloped in London

Wall) built to sophisticated specifications to house the electronics of the Big Bang. By mid-1987, rents in the City were already exceeding £465 per m^2 and had increased by over £90 per m^2 since December 1986. Even small office suites were now commanding £370 per m^2.

There were substantial fears of shortages of office space in Central London. Normally, the vacancy rate in the United Kingdom is never much higher than 8 per cent (in the United States it often exceeds 30 per cent), but by the mid-1980s this was drastically reduced. Whereas in January 1983 there were 4.1 years of new office supply in Central London, by January 1986 this had plummeted to only two years and in 1987 it was estimated that while supply amounted to 240 000 m^2, demand had soared to 353 000 m^2. This shortage was exacerbated by older offices being taken out of use for redevelopment or refurbishment. The immediate effects of this inadequacy of space were: the increased degree of pre-letting, particularly to the banking and financial sector (by 1987 over 70 per cent of total floorspace under construction in the City was pre-let); the increased extent to which firms acquired the freehold of their offices (this was particularly the case among foreign operators, not least Japanese companies); and an inflationary impact on the West End office market where rents rose to £418 per m^2 in Mayfair in 1987.

As for the 1990s, most commentators argue that shortages will remain and could damage London's role as a world financial centre. Shortages might even become more severe if Japanese firms move into London on an increasing scale. However, there are indicators that supply might begin to bulge in the early 1990s. A number of very large developments are likely to be completed, for example, the later phases of Broadgate and all of London Wall. Most importantly, the 930 000 m^2 of office space to be developed at Canary Wharf in the London Docklands should become available – and at rents of only £260 per m^2 (at 1987 prices). The impact on the City office market will be substantial, particularly as the scheme is geared to the needs of banking and finance – a very vulnerable sector after the collapse of share prices in October 1987 (see chapter 4).

Offices of professional institutions

Though central locations are desired, maximum or special accessibility is less important than in the case of business firms. Nevertheless prestigious sites are sought after. Accountancy, architectural, medical and surveying institutions may pay fairly high rents or own valuable properties adjacent to parks or in squares or crescents of historic interest.

Offices of small professional firms and branch offices of commercial organisations

Accessibility to a residential population is important, thus location in the high street of a suburb or small town is appropriate – sites close to a railway or tube station being particularly attractive. Whereas building societies, banks and estate agents prefer ground-floor situations, solicitors and accountants often utilise office space above shops. Generally turnovers and rents per m^2 are only moderate to low.

Local government and civil service offices

In the nineteenth century and earlier, town halls and civil service departments occupied central locations to signify the importance of the function of government. But except where comprehensive redevelopment has occurred in recent years, and where costs of development are shared with commercial interests, local and central government offices have tended to be located on less costly sites within the urban area, although there are many examples of civil service departments having taken the lead in decentralising offices to the Assisted Areas or to the overspill towns. Over 55 000 civil service jobs were dispersed to offices outside London between 1963 and 1975, and following the recommendations of the Hardman Report[14] it was announced in 1974 that a further 31 000 civil service posts would be moved from London mainly to the Assisted Areas. But with cuts in public expenditure the dispersal programme was postponed in 1979.

Accessibility may be an exaggerated reason for offices in general being attracted to central areas. Tradition may have played a substantial part in firms choosing city centres as a base for their activities, and while leases continue inertia militates against decentralisation. The use of the telephone, telex and the increasing employment of computers provide the same degree of accessibility between firms almost regardless of location. Nevertheless the centre of a city has for generations been both a market place and a social meeting place and it is unlikely that the central area of a town will cease to be attractive as a major location for offices.

Industrial Location and Development

The development of road transport, the use of electricity and the availability of large and relatively low cost and spacious sites in suburban areas have encouraged manufacturing industry (which in total occupied 230 million m^2 of floorspace in 1985) to move out from central areas to locations on the periphery of cities. Inertia nevertheless exists. Some firms may have a traditional preference for central sites, or external economies of agglomeration may compensate the internal diseconomies of cramped sites and often obsolete and multi-storey factory premises. Once a firm is located in a particular place it may eventually find difficulty in disposing of its old factory buildings, it might be reluctant to establish additional space elsewhere because of technical difficulties of splitting production, and it may be unwilling to incur the disruption of a move.[5] In recent years, however, deindustrialisation has had a very major impact on manufacturing and its location.

Between 1979 and 1986, the gross domestic product (GDP) of the United Kingdom grew by an average of only 1.4 per cent per annum, and over the whole period GDP increased by only 11 per cent. Manufacturing output, however, in 1987 was 4.9 per cent *lower* than in 1979. This poor performance was in part due to a comparatively low level of investment.[15] In 1985, total investment in the United Kingdom was only 17.2 per cent of the GDP, while in manufacturing the rate of investment in 1986 was 24.8 per cent *below* that of 1979. Low growth and low investment had a serious impact on the United Kingdom's export capability. In 1986, while the balance of payments deficit of the United Kingdom amounted to £1.1 billion, the manufacturing deficit soared to £5.4 billion (compared with a surplus of £5.5 billion in 1980), and the United Kingdom's share of world manufacturing trade decreased by 18 per cent below its 1979 level. It is consequently not surprising that there was a marked decrease in employment over the years 1979–86. The total number of employees in the United Kingdom fell from 22.6 million in June 1979 to 21.2 million in December 1986 – a decrease of 6 per cent, but in manufacturing employment the number plummeted from 7.1 million to 5.1 million (June 1979 to March 1987) – a fall of 28 per cent. The most dramatic and serious indicator of deindustrialisation, however, was the massive increase in unemployment. From 1 141 000 in 1979 the number of unemployed rose to 3 020 000 by April 1987, an increase from 5.0 to 11.1 per cent of the total workforce. By international standards, the economic performance of the United Kingdom was appalling (table 2.4). It could be argued, however, that the shedding of labour has led to a faster growth of productivity in the United Kingdom than in any other major industrial country. But there is little economic benefit in achieving higher productivity if *production* has re-

Table 2.4 *Indicators of economic performance in selected advanced capitalist countries, 1979–87*

	Increase in GDP 1979–86 (%)	Investment as a percentage of GDP 1985 (%)	Change in employment 1979–86 (%)	Increase in unemployment 1979–86 (%)	Unemployment 1987 (February) (%)
Japan	32.0	27.5	+13.7	0.9	3.0
United States	17.0	18.6	+14.3	0.8	6.6
West Germany	13.0	19.5	+ 0.4	4.8	8.0
Canada	20.0	18.6	+12.4	2.2	9.6
Italy	14.0	18.2	+ 0.9	3.1	10.7
France	11.3	18.9	0	5.1	11.0
United Kingdom	11.0	17.2	– 6.3	6.1	11.1

Source: OECD, *Economic Outlook* and *Main Economic Indicators.*

mained stagnant and with unemployment costing the taxpayer £21 billion a year (at 1987 prices) in welfare payments and lost taxes.

The failure of the United Kingdom to secure a rate of growth and net exports sufficient to achieve full employment, and particularly the contraction of manufacturing industry and loss of manufacturing jobs, have of course not been confined to the period since 1979. In absolute terms, both industrial and more specifically manufacturing employment reached their peak in 1966 but in relative terms they peaked in 1955 (table 2.5). By international standards, the United Kingdom has experienced a comparatively high rate of decline of manufacturing employment and at an accelerating rate (table 2.6). This might be partly explained by the United Kingdom increasingly concentrating on the production and export of services rather than manufactured goods, but must also be attributable to the failure of macro-economic policy over the year,[15] for example, the effects of stop-go measures from the 1950s to the 1970s and monetarism post 1979.

Table 2.5 *The decline of industrial and manufacturing employment in the United Kingdom, 1955–84*

	Percentage share of total employment		Number of employees (million)	
Employment	1955	1984	1966	1984
Industrial	47.9	34.0	11.5	7.0
Manufacturing	36.1	26.0	8.7	5.4

Source: Based on Ministry of Labour and Department of Employment data.

Table 2.6 *Changes in manufacturing employment in selected advanced capitalist countries, 1955–83*

	Percentage share		Change 1955–81	Annual percentage change		
	1955	1981		1955–66	1966–73	1973–83
Japan	18.4	24.9	+6.4	3.9	2.9	–0.4
United States	28.5	21.7	–6.8	1.3	0.7	–0.4
Canada	24.1	19.4	–4.7	2.4	1.4	–0.4
Italy	20.0	26.1	–6.1	1.0	2.0	–0.9
West Germany	33.8	33.6	–0.2	1.2	0.2	–1.9
France	26.9	25.1	–1.8	0.8	0.6	–1.9
United Kingdom	36.1	24.6	–9.7	0.4	–1.2	–3.1

Source: OECD, *Labour Force Statistics* (various).

In spatial terms, contemporary deindustrialisation became apparent first in the 1960s in London and the other conurbations – old geographical bases of nineteenth century industry. In the 1970s, the Development Areas again became stagnated, having been centres of depression in the 1930s. But from the late 1970s, the West Midlands – the industrial heartland of Britain (and the growth area of engineering and vehicle assembly in the 1950s–60s) – suffered from severe unemployment and the other indicators of deindustrialisation.[16]

It might be assumed that deindustrialisation is synonymous with an increase in vacant floorspace, with an increase in supply in relation to demand and with falling rents. However, a high proportion of factories (vacant or occupied) are outmoded (40 per cent were built before 1945), are multi-storeyed and have little external space for storage or expansion or vacant land adjacent to site.[5] Although in 1985 there were nearly 12 million m^2 of vacant factory floorspace on the market for sale or rent (about 3 per cent of the total stock), this may be inadequate to meet demand despite deindustrialisation. Fothergill *et al.* have shown that although manufacturing employment decreased dramatically in the period 1967–85, the demand for factory floorspace has increased since employment densities decreased from 36 to 21 workers per 1000 m^2 (1965–85) (table 2.7) and are likely to continue to decrease.[5] There was, however, only a limited amount of space for the physical expansion of industry in London and the conurbations, therefore most growth was elsewhere – a marked urban–rural shift being evident (table 2.8).

Table 2.7 *Changes in manufacturing employment and floorspace in England and Wales, 1967–85*

	Manufacturing employment (000s)		Change (%)	Floorspace (million m^2)		Change (%)	Floorspace per employee (m^2)	
	1967	1985		1967	1985		1967	1985
North-west	1216	693	–43	48.0	42.9	–11	39.5	61.9
Yorkshire and Humberside	813	502	–38	31.4	28.4	–10	38.6	56.6
West Midlands	1162	682	–41	34.0	36.9	+ 9	29.3	54.2
North	450	288	–36	10.9	14.3	+31	24.2	49.7
Wales	311	202	–35	6.8	10.0	+47	21.9	49.5
East Midlands	621	479	–23	19.1	23.4	+23	30.8	48.9
East Anglia	174	176	+ 1	5.8	8.3	+43	33.3	47.2
South-west	423	347	–18	11.1	15.3	+38	26.2	44.1
South-east	2316	1519	–34	53.2	52.7	– 1	23.0	34.7
England & Wales	7485	4888	–35	220.1	232.2	– 6	26.9	47.5

Source: Department of the Environment, *Commercial and Industrial Floorspace Statistics: Statistics for Town and Country Planning.*

Table 2.8 *Location of industrial floorspace in England and Wales*

	Manufacturing floorspace (million m²)		Change (%)
	1967	1985	
Rural areas	16.5	25.1	+52.1
Small towns	44.3	57.0	+28.7
Large towns	29.7	32.8	+10.4
Free-standing cities	37.2	38.8	+ 4.3
Conurbations	65.8	58.0	−11.9
London	26.7	20.5	−23.2
England and Wales	220.1	232.2	+ 5.5

Source: Department of the Environment, *Commercial and Industrial Floorspace Statistics; Statistics for Town and Country Planning.*

Fothergill *et al.* warn that as the economy (eventually) recovers, spare capacity will be utilised and vacant premises will become occupied.[5] Far more floorspace will be required, they argue, but they foresee bottlenecks in the development process particularly in London and the conurbations. Whereas, for the most part, the depressed regions have the greatest supply of available land for industrial development, London and the conurbations are disadvantaged with regard to the quantity, quality and price of industrial sites (table 2.9). With the economic upturn, therefore, the industrial prospects of London and the conurbations will remain bleak (unless these areas are able to attract small and medium firms with modest site requirements), and as before the burden of industrial adjustment would be borne by the inner cities. Inter-regionally, too, there are major disparities in the demand and supply of vacant factories and industrial sites. With regard to both rents and land prices there has been a growing north–south divide (tables 2.10 and 2.11), particularly as the demand for high tech buildings has substantially pulled up the price of sites in the South-east close to the motorways (especially the M4 and M23).

Nationally, there are thus serious problems relating to the supply of industrial property. In the mid-1980s there was a low rate of new investment in factory floorspace, a substantial mismatch between the property requirements of firms and the sites they occupied, little likelihood of industrial regeneration in London and the conurbations, and in general an uncoordinated and unregulated supply of industrial property.

According to Fothergill *et al.*, if it were assumed that manufacturing output were to increase by 3.5 per year (by means of a 3 per cent increase in productivity and a 0.5 per cent increase in employment), then 3.5 per cent more floorspace would be required each year.[5] Also taking into account demolitions and factories no longer suitable for use, the total additional floorspace required

Table 2.9 *Available industrial land in Great Britain, 1982*

	Ha	per 1000 employees
Wales	3550	15.0
Scotland	6350	13.0
North	3850	11.3
South-west	2650	7.0
East Anglia	1250	6.9
Yorkshire and Humberside	3850	6.8
East Midlands	3400	6.5
North-west	2850	3.6
West Midlands	2600	3.3
South-east	3200	2.0
Rural areas	7000	10.7
Small towns	11 200	7.0
Large towns	4850	6.4
Free standard cities	5100	5.4
Conurbations	4650	3.6
London	750	1.2
Great Britain	33 500	5.7

Source: S. Fothergill *et al.*, *Property and Industrial Development* (Hutchinson, 1987); Local authorities.

Table 2.10 *Industrial rents and rental growth in Great Britain*

	Rents per m² 1986 (£)	Average annual rental growth, 1982–86 (%)
London	35.77	5.1
South-east	28.06	4.5
South-west	19.60	5.5
West Midlands	16.44	0.3
Scotland	15.51	0
Wales	14.49	−0.5
East Anglia	14.31	0.5
North-west	14.03	−0.7
East Midlands	13.38	−0.3
Yorkshire and Humberside	13.19	0.5
North	11.80	−0.2
Great Britain	21.37	2.4

Source: Hillier Parker, *Industrial Rent and Yield Contours*, 1987.

Table 2.11 *Prime and high tech industrial land values in Britain, 1980–86*

Location	Prime values 1980 (£'000 per ha)	Prime values 1986 (£'000 per ha)	High tech values 1986 (£'000 per ha)
Maidenhead	740/865	1360/1480	1853/2471
Crawley	618/680	988/1174	1730
Watford	680/740	927/1050	1483/1730
Southampton	297	432/494	680
Bristol	247	309/432	494
Birmingham/Coventry	124/185	185/247	272
Manchester	124/222	124/185	247
Leeds	49/185	124/185	222
Cardiff	49/99	62/99	148

Source: J. D. Organ, 'Retail and residential competition hike industrial land prices. *Estates Times Supplement* (March, 1987).

would amount to 190 million m^2 (or 12.5 million m^2 per year). This would necessitate an annual investment of £2.5 billion (at 1980 prices), £1 billion more each year than in the early 1980s. Half of the 190 million m^2 would be needed in new units (as opposed to extensions/refurbishments), but this would require 31 600 ha. Although the amount of land available for industrial development is probably in excess of this, not all of it (suggest Fothergill *et al.*) is "in the right place, available at the right time, of the right size and the right price." This is particularly the case in London and the conurbations. Elsewhere (such as in the Green Belts) restrictive planning policies limit the supply of land.

Since it would be a tragedy if the possibilities of sustained economic growth were thwarted by a shortage of industrial buildings and land, public policy (argue Fothergill *et al.*) must ensure that investment funds are available for industrial property development, and that the mismatch between the demand and supply of both buildings and land is eliminated.[5] In this context, it is necessary for the policies of the Department of Enterprise and Department of the Environment to be coordinated, but also there must be the maximum degree of partnership between the public and private sectors.

Public sector developers could play an important part in supplying the required industrial floorspace. English Estates, the Scottish Development Agency, the Welsh Development Agency, the New Towns Development Corporations and the local authorities have all been instrumental in regenerating the depressed areas and in aiding decentralisation. It is unlikely that the private sector – if left to itself – would have promoted growth so effectively. Currently, urban development corporations and local authorities are involved in regenerating the inner city (chapter 7). There is an urgent need for these bodies to facilitate national economic growth by tackling (in their areas) the problem of industrial buildings and land. Fothergill *et al.* argue that the problem of land supply must be solved if the inner cities are to attract a larger share of manufacturing growth.[5] They argue that local authorities should redesignate land currently reserved for other uses and that the cost of clearance, demolition and reclamation should be more heavily subsidised. The government should also subsidise rents on publicly owned land or they should be willing to sell such land to industrial developers at subsidised prices.

Small firms – occupying buildings of say less than 500 m^2 – numerically dominate the stock of factory space (more than 65 000 units of this size account for over half the total number of industrial premises in Britain). While most small premises were supplied by speculative developers, many local authorities in partnership with the private sector have played a significant part in the formation and growth of small firms in recent years – an involvement which clearly needs to be continued.

Regional policies have an effect on the pattern of urban land use and need to be examined. Since the Distribution of Industry Act 1945 industrial development in London and the South-east and in the Midlands has been restricted by the government being generally unwilling to grant industrial development certificates (IDCs) to firms wishing to expand. Throughout most of the period since 1945 IDCs were required when proposed factory development involved floor space in excess of 5000 ft^2 (465 m^2). In contrast IDCs were freely granted for expansion within the development areas of the north and west of Britain. Under the Industry Act 1972 IDCs were not required in the development and special development areas, but in the intermediate areas IDCs were necessary for expansion in excess of 15 000 ft^2 (1395 m^2). In South-east England they were needed for development over 5000 ft^2 (465 m^2) and elsewhere over 10 000 ft^2 (929 m^2) – the threshold rising in 1976 to 12 500 ft^2 (1162 m^2) and 15 000 ft^2 (1395 m^2) respectively.

As part of a general policy of attempting to eliminate regional imbalance (especially in terms of unemployment levels) the government since the Special Areas legislation of the 1930s has made loans, grants and tax allowances available to industrialists developing in the depressed regions. Throughout most of the 1970s manufacturers in the Assisted Areas were able to claim regional development grants (RDGs) of 20–22 per cent for new industrial buildings, plant and machinery, and could write off for tax purposes 100 per cent of their capital expenditure on new plant and machinery and 44 per cent of the construction costs of new industrial buildings. Firms were also encouraged to increase or at least maintain their employment of labour by means of Regional Employment Premiums which were up to £3.00 per employee per week in the mid-1970s. The result of these policies is that the quantity of industrial development around cities in the South-east and Midlands probably has been far less than would have been the case if market forces had been permitted to operate freely. Conversely there is more new industry around cities in the Assisted Areas than would have occurred otherwise. Regional policies have also had a qualitative effect on industry in the South-east and Midlands, manufacturing is taking place in many small and duplicate factories and workshops which have been developed within the IDC exemption limit. This otherwise might have been concentrated in larger buildings – manufacturers then not having to forego internal and external economies of scale.

As part of their dual commitment to monetarism and *laissez-faire* industrial policy, the Conservatives on their return to office in 1979 reduced planned regional aid from £842 million to £540 million (at 1980 prices), 1979–83 (cutting RDGs in development areas from 20 to 15 per cent and withdrawing them completely in intermediate areas); rolled back the boundaries of the Assisted Areas so that they would contain only 27.5 per cent of Britain's working population (as opposed to 44 per cent before); and relaxed IDC controls – the threshold rising generally to 50 000 ft^2 (4645 m^2) with IDCs no longer being required in any of the Assisted Areas. In 1982 IDCs were abandoned altogether. This was at a time when regional unemployment was soaring. Whereas nationally unemployment increased from 5.3 to 13.1 per cent (1979–84), in the North it increased from 8.3 to 18.1 per cent, in Wales from 7.3 to 16.2 per cent and in the North-west from 6.5 to 16.0 per cent. Although £20 billion had been spent on regional aid, 1964–83, creating 500 000 jobs (at a cost latterly of £35 000 per job), stark regional disparities remained. The White Paper, *Regional Industrial Development*, 1983, recommended that policy should be more selective and cost-effective (in accountancy rather than social terms). In 1984, planned regional aid was subsequently cut from £700 million in 1982–83 to £400 million (at 1983 prices) by 1987–88. RDGs were limited to a cost per job of £10 000, or alternatively companies could claim employment grants of £3000 per job. It was one thing, however, to promote greater efficiency, but quite another matter altogether to cut *total* expenditure on aid at a time of soaring unemployment – with potentially disastrous effects on the depressed areas. In 1988, even the above grant limits were replaced by a more selective form of assistance – steering aid particularly to small firms.

By the late 1980s, the complexity of regional assistance and the lack of coherence and integration of policy were of increasing concern to the developers and users of land. The RICS[17] therefore proposed that: a centralised advisory service be set up to channel information and advice to the business sector; there should be an emphasis on the maintenance of the infrastructure in the depressed areas; environmental improvement should become a marketing tool in attracting industry; inter- and intra-regional mobility of labour should be facilitated; and that an English Development Agency (modelled on the Scottish Development Agency and Welsh Development Agency) should be established to promote opportunities in the depressed areas and to further development.

Residential Location

Housing constitutes the largest urban land use (in some towns over 50 per cent of the total area) and may account for over 25 per cent of personal expenditure.

There is a great variety of types of housing but most residential land is fixed in area and location. Forced out of areas of good business accessibility, housing land is less frequently redeveloped compared with other uses, but marginal changes may have important economic and social ramifications. Although there is a relationship between personal income, place of employment and place of residence, this relationship is subject to different and conflicting interpretations. There are basically three explanations of the rationale of private-sector housing location.

Travel cost minimisation theory

It has been argued that if travel costs to work are nil or very low, householders will be prepared to pay the highest rents or prices for accommodation. Through the working of the price mechanism this would imply that the rich live very close to the central business district and the poor live in less expensive outer areas. But the converse is generally true. Low income earners live close to their work (usually within the inner areas of cities) to minimise their cost of travelling, rents are mainly regulated, and housing densities are high. As incomes rise, there has been a tendency for people to live further away from their work in areas of lower density and more expensive housing. Moreover, the outward spread of cities would only be compatible with travel cost minimisation if employment was simultaneously decentralised and this usually does not take place.

But the theory is valid to some extent. Although house prices may be very high in the commuter belt, residential values per m^2 tend to diminish outwards from the central area as competition from business uses gets less. Both in the cases of the unregulated furnished tenancies in the 'twilight' areas in inner London (up to 1974) and the exclusive leasehold properties in Belgravia and Mayfair, values could only be as high as they are because of the very large demand from persons unable or unwilling to incur high travel costs to gain access to employment and the other facilities of inner and central London.

Travel cost and housing cost trade-off theory

This assumes that householders of the same income group are prepared to pay over a period the same real aggregate cost of travel and housing. If travel costs rise there will be a migration to areas of lower priced housing, if travel costs fall the movement will be to more expensive housing. This hypothesis suggested by Wingo[18] implies that residential values will be very high close to the central business district and low in the outer suburban areas or beyond.

But although there is an inverse correlation between site values and travel costs around many cities, for example, London, the same is not true of house prices and travel costs. High income commuters do not have to trade-off travel costs and housing costs – they can afford both, the rich may prefer to live in the commuter belt where they can benefit from a better environment and open space and where they can segregate themselves from lower socio-economic groups, and it may only be within the outer areas of cities that sites are available for the construction of new and expensive houses. Motorways, moreover, may make outer locations more accessible from the central business district than many inner suburban locations.

In the Metropolitan South-east, the absence of trade-off is clearly demonstrated. Although the average price of dwellings in Greater London peak at the centre, for example, at £107 000 in Westminster, £105 000 in Kensington and £91 000 in Camden (in April 1987), average prices in the outer suburbs are normally higher than in the inner urban areas. In Richmond and Harrow, for example, average prices were respectively £93 000 and £77 000 – appreciably more than in the neighbouring but more central boroughs of Hammersmith and Brent.[19] Also, whereas in Greater London, the average price of all dwellings was (only) £43 600 (in April 1985), in Surrey, Buckinghamshire, Berkshire and Hertfordshire prices were respectively £54 700, £50 300, £47 900 and £47 800.[20] These differences suggest that, in general, households will pay extra for the space and environmental attributes of detached houses and bungalows in rural areas, compared with the more centrally located terraced houses and flats which dominate the London housing market.

Even if there were an inverse correlation between house prices and travel costs, however, it is unlikely that householders would trade-off. Housing expenditure (including rates as well as mortgage interest payments) and travel costs change frequently but households may only alter their location at intervals of five or more years. There is usually a long time-lag before householders react to changing costs, and there is a high degree of immobility as non-economic reasons may outweigh economic considerations in determining locational choice. The main reasons why householders change residence may be due more to a change of job, marriage or a change in the size of family than to a changing relationship between travel costs and house prices. It is completely unrealistic to assume that a householder is free to locate anywhere from the central business district to the outer commuter belt. His choice is fairly restricted and the point on the housing cost curve will be determined largely by mortgage availability.

A trade-off model of the above sort is least satisfactory in explaining residential location within a conurbation where there may be several central business districts and a complex pattern of commuting. Patterns and relationships will also be distorted by the decentralisation of employment. Nevertheless the trade-off hypothesis has been extended by Evans[21] who suggested that if the demand for household space increased, the household might move further out from the centre; but if the household's income increased and the demand for space remained constant, the household might move nearer the centre (the increase in the rate of pay and the resulting increase in the valuation of travel time could mean that the total saving in travel costs would offset higher house prices). Therefore when incomes increase there are two opposing forces influencing locational choice. The actual direction of change, if any, will depend upon the relative strength of these two opposing forces. Evans further suggested that following a general increase in pay, higher income households out-bid lower income groups both on the periphery of urban areas and in the inner cities, in the latter case often by means of 'gentrification' (chapter 7). The resulting pattern of household distribution (a more than proportionate number of high-income households in both inner and peripheral areas and a more than proportionate number of lower and middle-income groups in between) is well marked in British conurbations, particularly in Greater London and the Home Counties, as the data above demonstrate.

Maximum housing expenditure theory

This states that income and the availability and conditions of mortgage finance (including the effects of tax allowances) determine residential location. The theory is based on the assumption that house-buyers will attempt to acquire a house as expensive as they can afford with the maximum mortgage which they can raise in the area of their choice. But although house-buyers may seek a property over a wide area, transport costs may be a relatively minor consideration and may be variable in relation to the distribution of houses within a specific price range. Environmental and social factors (and the prospects of capital appreciation) are likely to be a much greater influence over choice. This hypothesis evolved by Ellis[22] and Stegman[23] implies that there is no overall relationship between income, travel cost/time and place of work, and that there is no effective trade-off.

In formulating policies, central and local government need to know why people live in a certain area, what types of houses should be constructed and in which locations, how significant are journey-to-work considerations, how far is it desirable to decentralise employment, how should investment in either improved transport (to the central and inner areas) or in residential environmental improvement be decided, and if regional growth points are likely to provde a preferable environment and facilitate a more efficient transport system how should investment decisions be made. Richardson[24] suggests that if it is thought that there is a trade-off between housing expenditure and travelling costs then policy should concentrate on reducing travelling costs to work and/or developing high density housing in the inner areas of cities. Alternatively, a policy of decentralising employment would benefit particularly low income householders in the outer suburbs. But if it is found that environmental conditions influence householders more than travelling costs, policies would need to concentrate on providing satisfactory residential environments rather than on reducing the cost of the journey to work.

REFERENCES

1. H. W. Richardson, *Urban Economics* (Penguin, 1971).
2. H. von Thünen, *Der Isolierte Staat*, 1826; English translation by C. M. Wartenberg, *Von Thünen's Isolated State* (Pergamon, 1968).
3. W. Alonso, 'A Theory of the Urban Land Market', *Papers and Proceedings of the Regional Science Association*, 6 (1960); *Location and Land Use* (Harvard University Press, 1964); 'A Reformulation of Classical Location Theory and its Relation to Rent Theory', *Papers and Proceedings of the Regional Science Association*, 19 (1967).
4. R. Sinclair, 'Von Thünen and Urban Sprawl', *Annals of the Association of American Geographers*, 57 (1967); R. Goodchild and R. Munton, *Development and the Landowner. An Analysis of the British Experience* (George Allen & Unwin, 1985).
5. S. Fothergill *et al.*, *Property and Industrial Development* (Hutchinson, 1987).
6. G. Keogh, 'The Economics of Planning Gain' in S. Barrett and P. Healey (eds), *Land Policy: Problems and Alternatives* (Gower, 1985).
7. P. Hall, 'A Problem with its Roots in the Distant Past', *Town and Country Planning* (February, 1985).
8. J. Carr, 'Malls laugh as the high streets die', *Observer* (28 June, 1987).
9. P. Jones, 'Small Shops, big implications', *Town and Country Planning* (June, 1986).
10. Hillier Parker, *Central London Shops Survey*, 4 (January, 1987).
11. P. Cheeseright, 'An awful lot of shopping in Manchester', *Financial Times* (6 March 1987).
12. P. Cheeseright, 'A shop-around for the West Midlands Planners', *Financial Times* (20 March, 1987).
13. I. Alexander, *Office Location and Public Policy* (Longman, 1979).
14. *The Dispersal of Government Work from London*, Cmnd 5363 (HMSO, 1973).
15. B. Rowthorn, 'De-industrialisation in Britain', in R. Martin and B. Rowthorn, *The Georgraphy of De-industrialisation* (Macmillan, 1986).
16. R. Martin and B. Rowthorn, The Geography of De-industrialisation (Macmillan, 1986).
17. Royal Institution of Chartered Surveyors, *A Fresh Approach* (RICS, 1986).
18. L. Wingo, *Transportation and Urban Land* (Johns Hopkins University Press, 1961).
19. Nationwide Building Society, *Local Area Housing Statistics*, No. 15, London Boroughs, December 1986.
20. Nationwide Building Society, *Local Area Housing Statistics*, No. 4, London and the Home Counties, April 1985.
21. A. W. Evans, *The Economics of Residential Location* (Macmillan, 1971).

22. R. H. Ellis, 'Modelling of Household Location – A Statistical Approach', *Highway Research Record*, 207 (1967).
23. M. A. Stegman, 'Accessibility Models and Residential Location', *Journal of the American Institute of Planners*, 35 (1969).
24. H. W. Richardson, *Urban Economics* (Penguin, 1971).

3

Spatial Structure and Urban Growth

The ability of activities to compete for sites depends upon whether they have the means to benefit from accessibility and complementarity within the urban framework. But economic conditions, population, other land uses both public and private, and the size of the urban area continually change subjecting the urban land market to forces of perpetual adjustment.

The underlying influences upon urban growth are both national and regional. At a national level the size and rate of growth of the gross national product (GNP) *per capita* determine the quantity and quality of urban land use activity. Yet the less industrialised the country, the greater the potential rate of urbanisation, while countries with high GNP *per capita* may witness a decline in their city centres and an increased rate of suburbanisation and decentralisation. Nationally, non-economic forces reinforce economic factors. Population growth and migration to urban areas ultimately tend to increase living standards and to lower death-rates. Technological development likewise raises real incomes and affects the urban land use pattern, for example, improved construction techniques allow the development of taller buildings and new production methods might necessitate larger buildings on the periphery of cities. Government intervention, even where it is minimal, imposes a national influence over urban growth. But if the government is concerned with such issues as the nationalisation of development land, the taxing of increased values and strategic planning rather than with merely controlling, say, public health or building standards, the degree of influence is substantial and the economic consequences immense.

Regional or local economic, social and political factors may result in some cities growing more rapidly than others. An area may be endowed with expanding industries and, because of greater job opportunities and other attractions, there may be a net inward migration of population. Conversely other areas may be disadvantaged by declining industries, an out-dated infrastructure and an outward migration of population. The structure of local government and the impact of its policies may or may not be favourable to the growth or improvement of the urban area.

Urban Rent – Land Values – Density

Urban growth alters not only the pattern of land use and land values, but the intensity of site use. As the supply of land in an urban area is fixed in the short term this will create scarcity. Commercial users will double-up and may operate less efficiently, households may have to live in shared dwellings. Only in the medium and long term will business and residential development extend the city outwards. In the meantime rising rents will increase the degree of competition for sites within the existing built-up area.

The medium- and long-term supply of land is elastic provided that there is an absence of constraints such as green belt controls, use-restrictions and assuming the availability of transport. With the extension of the radius of the urban area the supply of land increases in geometric proportions, and if the demand for sites is relatively inelastic any increase in demand should cause site values and rents to fall. But it would be wrong to assume that outward-decreasing site values and rents are due to higher transport costs, and that higher values and rents inward are due to a saving in transport costs. Urban rent is determined by productivity (or profitability) which is highest at the place of maximum accessibility, that is, the central business district. Even if general accessibility began to diminish when congestion in the centre increases to severe levels, values and rents may continue to rise if sites benefit from some form of special accessibility. In the same location within the urban area, large sites may be more valuable than small ones as economies of scale can be realised even if the site is used for many uses.

Land value gradients vary from city to city, and because of higher incomes and internal and external scale economics, peaks are generally higher in larger cities. But the rate of fall in value is not the same for every use. Competition among commercial users in the central business district produces a very steep slope, but further out the slope becomes gentler as competition diminishes. The residential gradient is very gentle as values may be adversely affected in the inner areas of cities on account of small sites. The gradient may be flattened-out by decentralisation and the diffusion of journey destinations. Smaller peaks may be found at suburban route foci and especially in outlying business districts.

Values continually change because of changes in general and special accessibility. Planning controls, especially those concerning residential and commercial densities, may modify the gradient and green belts might create local areas of scarcity and so raise values. Rating differences between local authorities also affect gradients. Where there is an absence of industry (for example, in high income residential areas) a high rate poundage could depress residential values, but this might be more than offset by the appreciating effect of amenity.

There is of course a general reduction in population density with an increase in the radial distance from the inner areas of cities (although the central business district may have an almost complete absence of a residential population). In the case of older cities where employment and housing evolved centrally, the density gradient can be quite steep, whereas in cities of recent origin there is a greater dispersal of commercial, industrial and residential use and the gradient may flatten out and comprise numerous outer peaks. If the public transport system is highly developed in the inner areas of cities and if there are social customs such as workers returning home for lunch, gradients will be very steep. Although gradients of the day-time population density or of net residential densities may produce smoother slopes, it is probable that the gradient of gross population density is a preferable measure of urban structure.

THEORIES OF URBAN STRUCTURE

Although the character of the physical structure and population of cities is heterogeneous, the city is a unit of social behaviour. It is also an aggregate of smaller homogeneous areas all focusing on the central business district. The spatial structure of a city is a product of centripetal forces of attraction and congestion, centrifugal forces of dispersion and decongestion, and forces of areal differentiation. Many theories of spatial structure and urban growth are unsatisfactory because they fail to take sufficiently into account suburbanisation, decentralisation, the development of sub-centres, greater flexibility of location, improvements in technology and transportation, and the effects of central and local government policies. It tends to be the more complicated theories which have lost their credibility, and ironically it is the earliest and simplest ones which are still valid, however loosely.

The Concentric Zone Theory

This emerged from a study of Chicago by Burgess[1] and was essentially an application to urban land use of von Thünen's earlier theory relating to rural land around a city (page 19). It was suggested that any city extends radially from its centre to form concentric zones and that as distance from the centre increased there would be a reduction in accessibility, rents and densities. Land use would assume the following forms outward: the central business district, a zone of transition, an area of factories and low income housing, an area of higher income housing and a commuter zone (figure 3.1). There would also be declining proportions of recent immigrants, delinquency rates and poverty and disease, as distance increased from the centre. The concentric zone theory is compatible with Alonso's theory on rent (page 20). Where rent gradients intersect there would be a change of use to that activity which could afford to pay the higher rent. In figure 3.2 rent gradient *a* could coincide with the central business district, category *b* with the transition zone, categories *c* and *d* with low and high income housing and category *e* with the commuter zone. In the central business district the gradient would be steep due to intense competition for sites, but would be very gentle in the outer zones.

The concentric zone theory allows for underlying conditions to change continually. Natural population increase, in-migration, economic growth and income expansion will all result in each zone within the urban area 'invading' the next

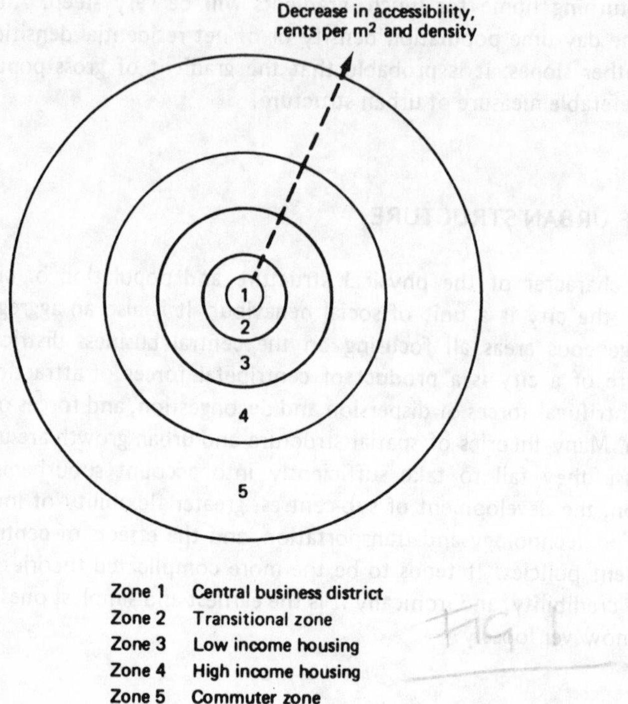

Figure 3.1 *The concentric zone theory*

outer zone (figure 3.3). But there may not be a simple transformation in land use outwards. As the central business district expands the locational advantages of central sites might diminish, the transitional zone (awaiting redevelopment) might become more and more a twilight area, and as suburban populations increase new outlying business districts may evolve. There are further effects upon the spatial structure as traffic flows become more complex in response to decentralisation.

Many criticisms can be made of the theory. Land uses within many parts of the urban area are heterogeneous – shops, offices, factories and housing may all be located close to each other although they may have potentially different site and locational requirements; and there may be many possible locations for different activities which do not all conform with the idealised model. Accessibility may be a relatively unimportant consideration for many uses especially housing, and commercial users may find that it may be disadvantageous to agglomerate if there is an opportunity to corner an undeveloped market. Decentralised shopping centres and offices may further distort the pattern, and the central business district might experience a decrease in rents and density following the reduction in its accessibility through congestion. The concentric zone

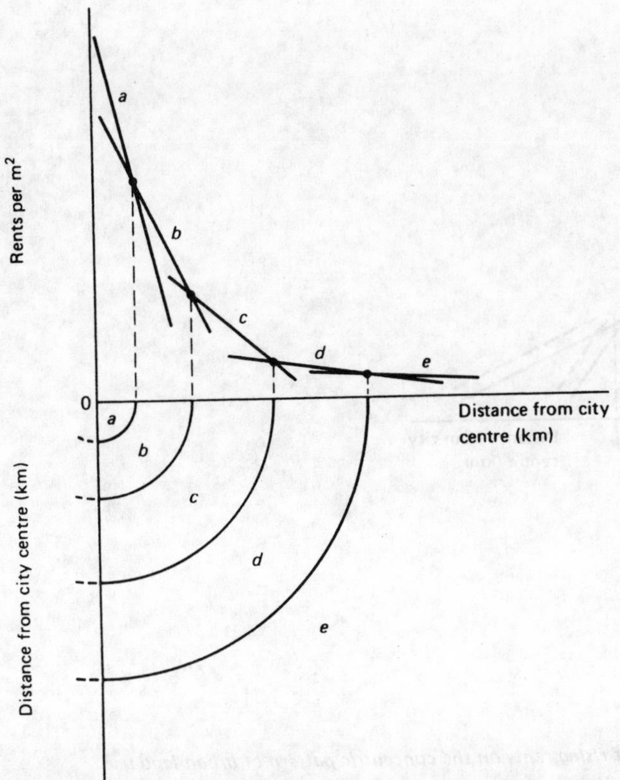

Figure 3.2 *Rent gradients and the concentric pattern of urban land use*

model also ignores physical features, takes little account of industrial and railway use, and disregards the effect of radial routeways upon land values and uses. It is more likely that a star-shaped pattern of land use will emerge; travel time rather than transport costs often being more important as a determinant of use. An axial development model (figure 3.4) modifies the concentric zone pattern, taking into account the effect of routeways. The assumption of a single focal point remains though maximum accessibility need no longer be found at a central location.

However, even in its modified form the concentric zone theory is little more than descriptive, showing how, rather than why, urban growth takes place. It is deterministic and assumes that social groups have to accord with a specific urban structure. Its greatest weakness is that it assumes that there is a free or perfect market, it ignores imperfections (such as locational inertia, sub-optimal use and long leases) and takes no account of planning controls. It disregards the purchasing of sites for future development with current use being retained at a sub-optimal value. But the pattern of urban land use is not wholly irrational and is not subject to an incomprehensible welter of paradoxes and anomalies. The con-

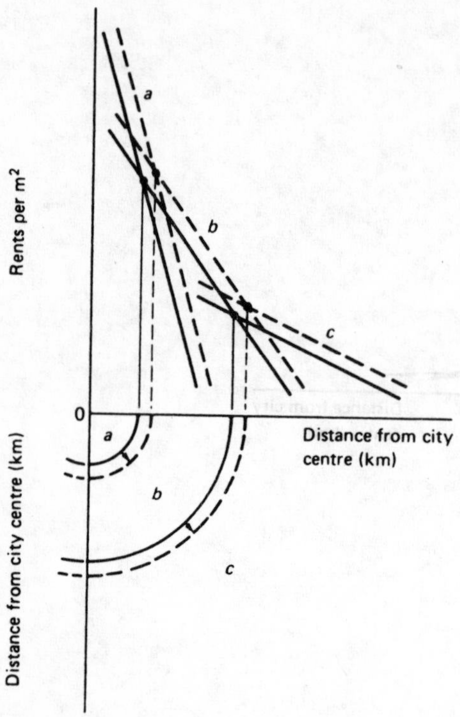

Figure 3.3 *The effect of rising rents on the concentric pattern of urban land use*

centric zone theory is illuminating; it shows that, in general, accessibility, rents and densities diminish with increased distance from the central business district and that the process of invasion is responsible for changing land use.

Sector Theory

This theory, as presented by Hoyt,[2] propounds that growth along a particular transport routeway takes the form of land use already prevailing and that each sector of relatively homogeneous use extends outwards from the centre (figure 3.5). Compatible land uses would lay adjacent to each other (for example, warehousing and light manufacturing, and low income housing) and incompatible uses will be repelled (for instance high income housing, and warehousing and light industry). Residential uses will tend to be segregated in terms of income and social position and will expand in different directions in different parts of the city. As with the concentric zone theory there is a process of invasion as economic and population growth takes place. When the inner areas are abandoned by high income households they are infilled (usually at a higher density) by lower income households.

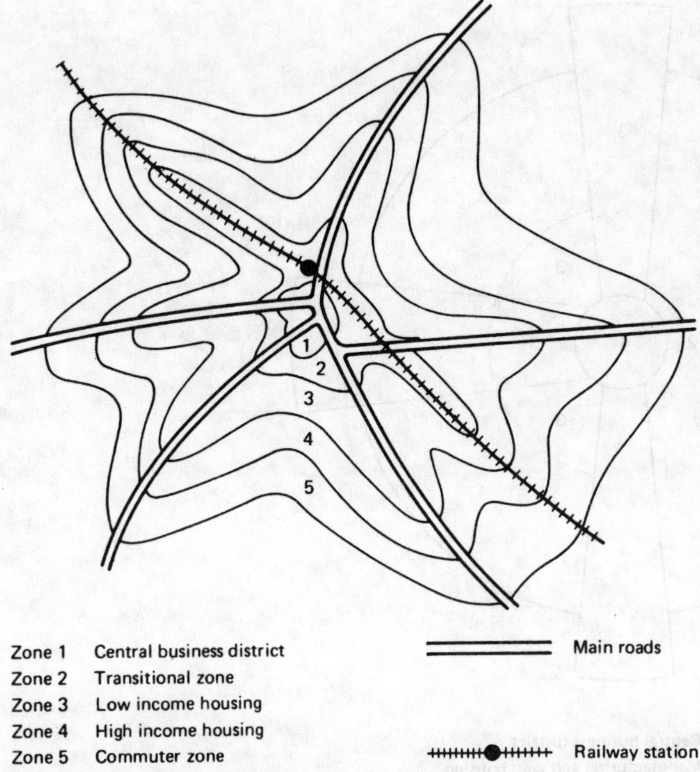

Figure 3.4 *The axial development theory*

The criticisms of the theory are broadly the same as those made of the concentric zone theory and so are the merits. But whilst recognising the relationship between accessibility, land use and values, and densities, Hoyt believed that the interdependence of these variables expresses itself differently in terms of the spatial structure of the city.

Concentric Zone – Sector Theory

Both the previous theories were developed in the United States following studies undertaken by a number of cities, the concentric zone theory being related to Chicago. But Mann[3] produced a hybrid model of the structure of a hypothetical British city – an urban area large enough to have distinct internal differentiation, but not too large to exhibit the complexities of a conurbation. The main additional feature is the existence of commuter villages separated from the built-up area of the city (figure 3.6).

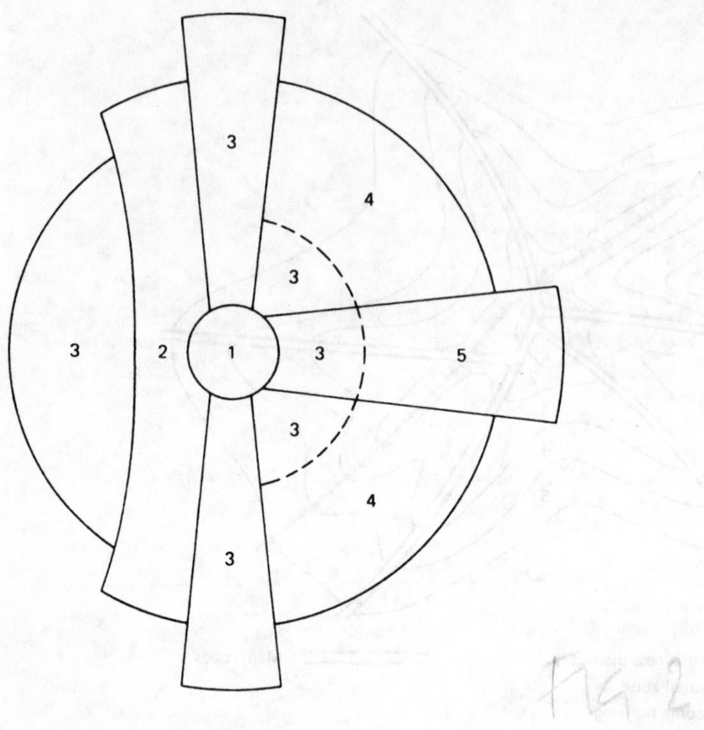

Sector 1 Central business district
Sector 2 Manufacturing and warehousing
Sector 3 Low income housing
Sector 4 Middle income housing
Sector 5 High income housing

Note: The diagram assumes a prevailing wind from the east. The manufacturing sector is thus located to the west of the high income housing sector. In the United Kingdom the reverse conditions usually apply.

Figure 3.5 *The sector theory*

In considering theories of urban growth it has been assumed so far that zones or sectors 'invade' each other generally outward, low income housing moving into the high income housing area and the latter expanding into the commuter belt. But with increased costs of commuter travelling the inner areas of cities have again attracted higher income households – invasion and 'gentrification' taking place inward. If, simultaneously, the central business district expands outwards the area of low income housing will be squeezed between two invading forces. Increased occupancy of the remaining low income dwellings, migration to country towns or homelessness will be consequently compounded.

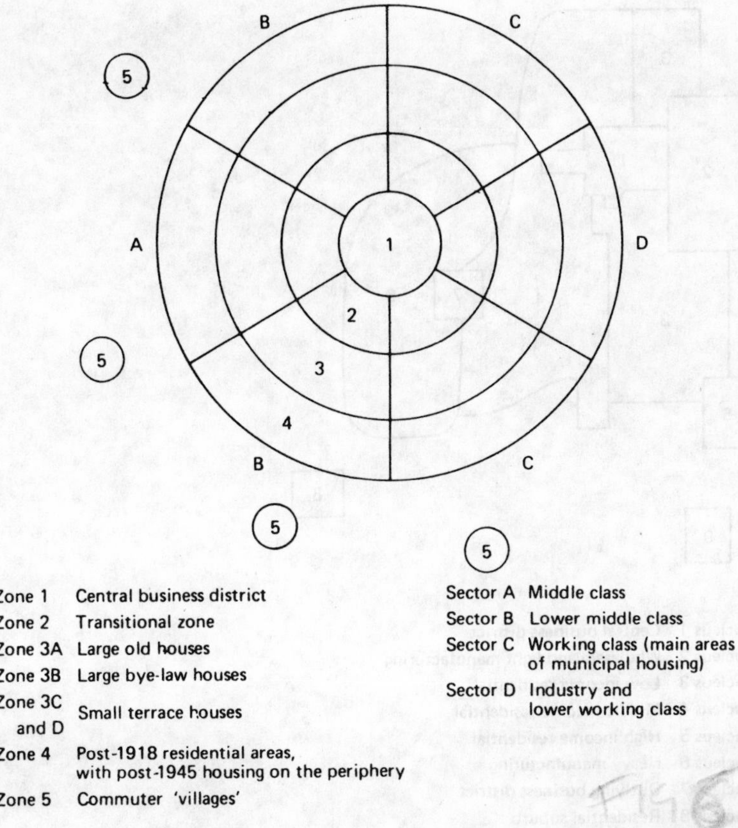

Figure 3.6 *The structure of a hypothetical British city*

Multiple-nuclei Theory

Unlike the theories of urban growth considered so far which have all assumed that cities grow from one central point, the multiple-nuclei theory produced by Harris and Ullman[4] in the United States is based on the assumption that urban growth takes place around several distinct nuclei. The nuclei could include the first urban settlement (probably a market town), a nearby village, a factory, a mine, a railway terminal or waterside facility. Ultimately they would be integrated into one urban area largely agglomerated by residential use and intra-city transportation. The original nuclei would help to determine current use, for example the market town might become the central business district, the village an outlying business district, the factory site might evolve into an area of wholesaling and light manufacture, and the mine or waterside facility could become an area of heavy industry (figure 3.7).

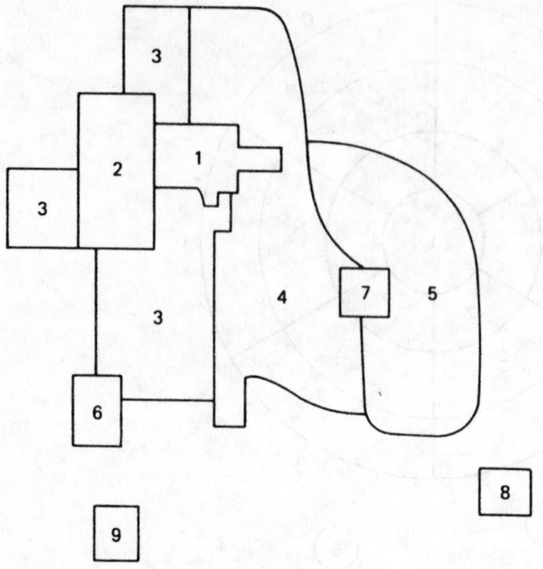

Nucleus 1 Central business district
Nucleus 2 Wholesale and light manufacturing
Nucleus 3 Low income residential
Nucleus 4 Middle income residential
Nucleus 5 High income residential
Nucleus 6 Heavy manufacturing
Nucleus 7 Outlying business district
Nucleus 8 Residential suburb
Nucleus 9 Industrial suburb

Notes: (i) The diagram assumes a prevailing wind from the east.
(ii) It is assumed that land use boundaries coincide with the main traffic routes of a 'grid-iron' street pattern.
Neither of these conditions are applicable to cities in the United Kingdom.

Figure 3.7 *The multiple nuclei theory*

Within the urban area compatible uses are attracted to each other – for example, low income residential land would be close to wholesaling and light manufacturing and near heavy industry, and the medium and high income residential areas would surround the outlying business district. Incompatible uses would remain far apart, for example, high income housing and heavy manufacture. The number of nuclei would be generally greater in large urban areas than in small cities and there would be a greater degree of specialisation within each nucleus.

The multiple-nuclei model initially related to cities within the United States where grid-iron road patterns separated land uses geometrically. But less regular

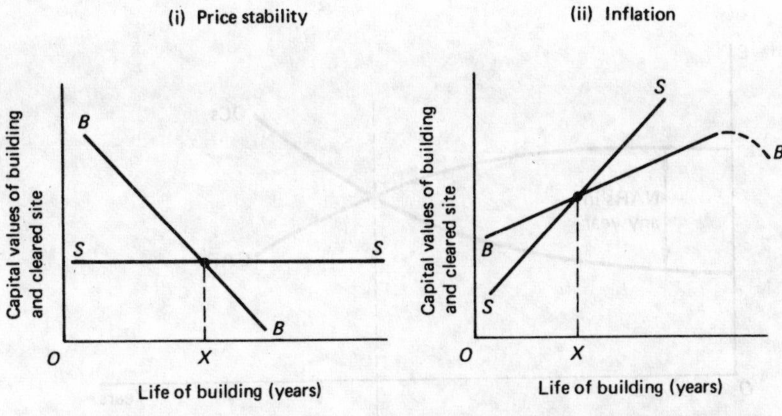

Note: *BB* = capital value of building and site in existing use
SS = capital value of cleared site in its best alternative use

Figure 3.8 *The maximum economic life of a building*

route patterns and use boundaries in other countries do not invalidate the basic principles of the theory.

Theories of urban spatial structure are as much descriptive as analytical. They explain how cities change their form, and very rarely will a single theory be adequate in this task. The concentric zone theory, while recognising that the transitional zone experiences deterioration prior to eventual redevelopment, ignores the same trend occurring elsewhere – for example, on the rural-urban fringe. None of the theories explains satisfactorily the significance of sub-centres to urban growth, and none gives sufficient attention to agglomeration; most ignore the important changes which occur within the central business district and which affect the urban area as a whole and, perhaps more importantly, all fail to consider the process of decentralisation.

The Development of Individual Urban Sites

Whichever of the theories of urban spatial structure is being considered, it is assumed that land uses invade each other and that there is a varying pace of renewal. Changing property values are both a cause and consequence of these processes. Urban property has two basic values – the capital value of buildings and sites in their *existing use* and the capital value of cleared sites in their *best alternative use*. In a period of price stability, the capital value of the building and site in existing use falls as the building becomes obsolete or wears out, but the value of the cleared site in its best alternative use remains constant (figure 3.8(i)). During inflation both values increase although the capital value of the cleared site for the best alternative use would probably rise more quickly than the capital value of the building and site in existing use – the latter value eventually declining (figure 3.8(ii)).

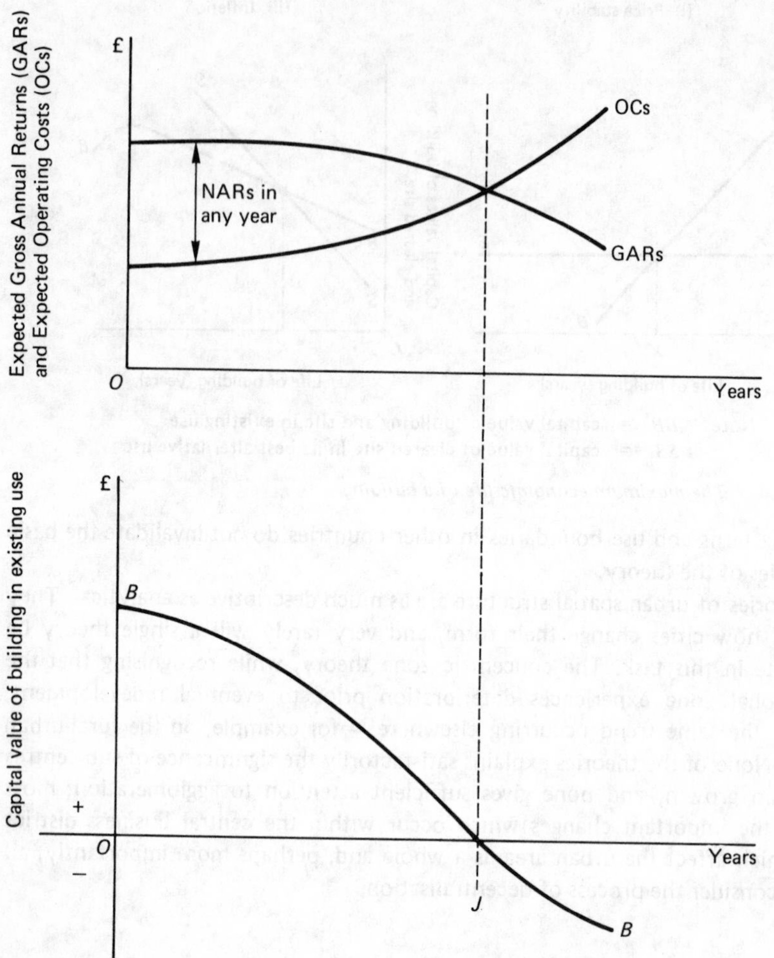

Figure 3.9 *Net annual returns (NARs) and capital value of a building in current use over time (price stability assumed)*

Sites and buildings transfer to new owners either through the sale and purchase of the freehold or at the end of a lease – the property changing hands because buyers can pay more for its use than the existing occupants. If redevelopment is not contemplated the price paid for the property will be equal to the current capital value of the future flow of net benefits anticipated from its use.

This is illustrated in figure 3.9. In the upper diagram expected operating costs (OC) are shown as rising over time as outgoings on repairs and maintenance increase in later years. By contrast, expected gross annual returns (GARs) – based on estimates of total annual rent – may eventually fall in real terms as competition with other developments increases or as the initial building becomes increasingly obsolete relative to changing user demands. Net annual returns

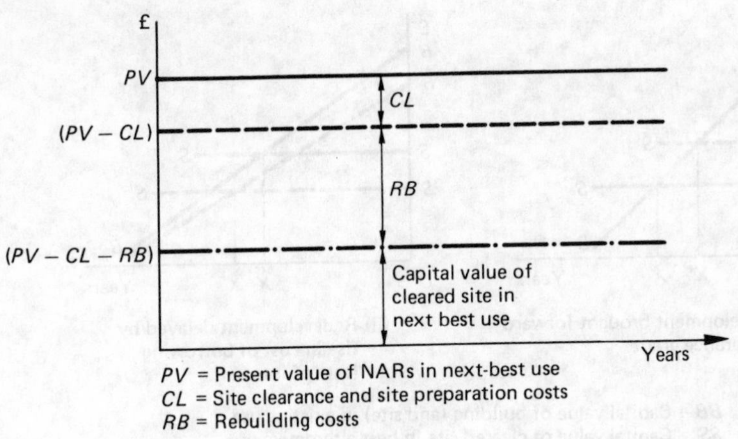

Figure 3.10 *Capital value of a cleared site in new use upon redevelopment*

(NARs) for any year are given by the difference between GARs and OCs for that year. After *J* years, NARs fall to zero.

The lower diagram in figure 3.9 shows the capital value of the building – derived from future capitalised NARs – declining over time. This occurs since as we move closer to point *J*, there are fewer NARs remaining to be discounted to their present value. After *J*, capital value actually becomes negative, hence if redevelopment is not contemplated, the site and building would be abandoned and left derelict at this point.

However, when redevelopment is proposed, the capital value of the cleared site in its alternative use must exceed the capital value of the building and site in its existing use. To the developer, the capital value of the cleared site is determined by the present value of the site in its new use less the cost of clearing the site, any land preparation costs (for example, drainage) and the cost of rebuilding. This is illustrated in figure 3.10. It can also be seen that any increase (decrease) in clearance and preparation costs (*CL*) or rebuilding costs (*RB*) will push down (up) the capital value of the cleared site – other things (such as rent) being equal. Although the capital value of the cleared site is shown as remaining constant at whatever point in time the redevelopment is contemplated, in practice shifts may occur over time because of changes in demand or supply factors; for example, technological change may lower the cost of rebuilding, or changes in demand (such as towards out-of-town retailing) could influence expected rents, or again public subsidy could reduce site clearance costs.

As shown in the following diagrams, redevelopment will occur (at point *X*) as the capital value of the cleared site in its next best use comes to exceed the capital value of the building in its current use. Two examples of economic changes which may influence the timing of redevelopment are given in figure 3.11. In the left hand diagram a clearance grant is shown as raising the capital

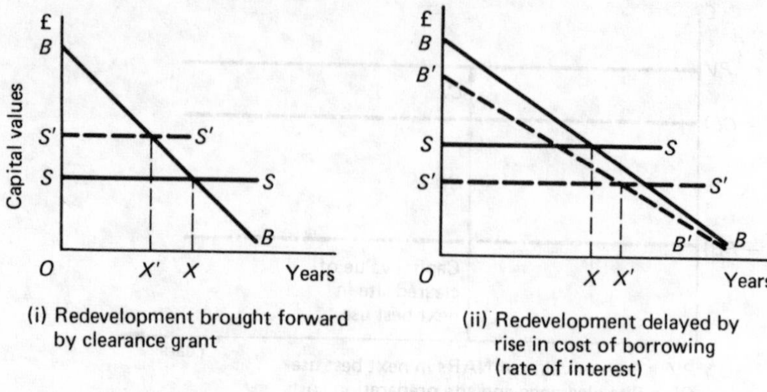

Figure 3.11 *Factors influencing timing of development*

value of the cleared site and bringing forward redevelopment from *X* to *X'* years. In the right hand diagram, a rise in the rate of interest lowers both the capital value of the existing building (since future net earnings are capitalised at a higher rate) and the capital value of the cleared site – to *B'B'* and *S'S'* respectively. However, the current use is marginally favoured by this change, putting off redevelopment from *X* to *X'* years. This occurs for several reasons:

(i) the higher interest rate is applied to fewer net annual returns in the case of the existing building (this is why *BB* and *B'B'* converge towards later years of project life); (ii) the next best alternative use will, in addition, incur higher development costs because of the higher cost of borrowing. Conversely, a fall in interest rates will tend to bring forward the pace of redevelopment.

When redevelopment occurs it will usually be to a more intensive use and, assuming planning consent, to higher buildings. There are economic limits to height. On the supply side, the state of building technology could mean that sub-ground conditions are unsuitable. Increasing costs occur as additional storeys are added because of the necessity for increased hoisting and more costly foundations. There is an increasing percentage of unremunerative space which needs to be devoted to servicing and maintenance of buildings. On the demand side there may be limits although penthouses command high values. Basically the developer may go on adding storeys until the marginal yield from the additional storey is equal to the marginal cost of providing it subject to statutory approvals and structural considerations. Beyond this point further storeys would be unprofitable. For housing developers terraces of narrow fronted housing achieve higher density and lower site costs. Stone[5] contends that the real costs of providing and maintaining dwellings rise more rapidly than the requirement for land falls; hence the real costs per hectare of land saved increase with the number of storeys. Frequently the use of high density development is advocated as a means of housing more people nearer the centre of the city and nearer their work; however, additional space must be made available for local shopping and other facilities, this increases the amount of land required and hence reduces the numbers that can be housed near the centre.

In figure 3.8 redevelopment should take place after X years *ceteris paribus*. But because of the durability of buildings (and often because of their architectural merit or historic interest) redevelopment might not take place until the buildings are structurally unsound. In other cases inaccurate valuation of the cleared site or building (or both) may create inertia. The multiplicity of interests, properties being retained by their existing owners for non-monetary reasons, and the length of leases and legal rights of tenants may also inhibit the redevelopment of a site. The continued use of the building after X years therefore implies that the land is being used inefficiently or sub-optimally, although it must be recognised that non-economic or indirect influences may be important.

The transitional zone, in particular, has been kept in a state of obsolescence through government controls over offices and manufacturing industry. Apart from planning permission being required, new office development (especially in London) was restricted by the need for developers to acquire office development permits (ODPs). ODPs were no more readily granted for offices in the transitional zone than in the central business district, thus retarding the outward growth of commercial uses into the inner areas of cities. The need for industrial development certificates (except in the Assisted Areas) likewise inhibited the development of factories either in the transitional zone or on suburban sites, thereby not only slowing down the redevelopment of 'twilight' sites but impeding decentralisation within the urban region.

On the rural–urban fringe the direct value of agricultural or horticultural activities may be considerably less than the capital value of sites. Redevelopment again may be restricted through planning controls not least by green-belt restrictions. In both urban and rural areas when the capital values of buildings fall below the capital values of cleared sites, the possibility of the nationalisation of development land and the taxation of increased values might deter development – sub-optimal use consequently resulting.

The micro-economic aspects of the change (or lack of change) in the use of individual sites is consistent with macro-economic explanations of the urban structure and the theories of urban growth. Firey[6] argued that although accessibility and the capital value of sites diminish outward from the centre of the city the rate of fall in site value is not the same for each use. There is a greater rate of decline of those uses most dependent on accessibility, namely the commercial uses of the centre. Where the site value of one use becomes less than that of another, change to the higher value will eventually occur. In figure 3.12 commercial use will replace residential use when the distance from the city centre becomes less than X km. Any remaining residential sites within the central area will probably be redeveloped as commercial properties.

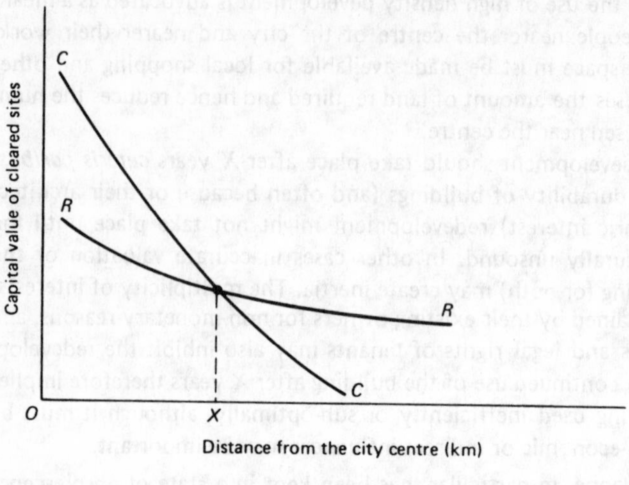

Note: *CC* = commercial site values
RR = residential site values

Figure 3.12 *Site values of competing uses*

Firey's hypothesis of site value is closely related to Alonso's theory of rent (page 20). Both approaches help to clarify the rationale of the numerous models of urban structure discussed earlier in this chapter, and the theories of urban growth offer explanations of why the underlying determinants of the capital values of cleared sites and buildings fluctuate – the values reflecting the levels of economic activity, technological application and government policy.

THEORIES OF URBAN GROWTH

Urban economics is in its infancy and therefore cannot be expected as yet to produce satisfactory models to explain urban growth. The complexity and diversity of urban growth, social and cultural influences (in addition to economic forces) and inadequate data make the economist rely heavily on demographic variables and persuade him unavoidably to equate an increase in population with an increase in urban growth. It must not be assumed, however, that population growth can immediately be related to an increase in welfare – congestion, a higher cost of living and poorer housing could be direct results of an increase in the urban population, and even if the GNP *per capita* rises following increased urbanisation, this could be attributed to higher incomes being realised in rural areas.

It is important to draw a distinction between the dynamics of spatial structure (discussed earlier in this chapter) and the theories of urban growth. The former attempt to explain how cities grow, and the latter (now to be considered) help to identify the reasons why urban areas grow (or decline).

Central Place Theory

Christaller[7] hypothesised that the distribution of centralised services accounts for the spacing, size and function pattern of urban centres. On the assumption that urban settlements locate on a uniform plain, centralised service centres would be distributed regularly within a systematic pattern. Market areas or spheres of influence would take the form of a hexagonal mesh. This would avoid either certain areas not being served, or other areas being served by overlapping hinterlands – consequences of a pattern of circular market areas. The main function of each town would be to supply goods and services to the countryside – town and country being interdependent.

A hierarchy of centres would evolve. Towns with the lowest level of specialisation would be evenly spaced and surrounded by their hexagonally-shaped market areas. For each group of six towns there would be a larger city with more specialised functions which would also be located an equal distance from other cities with the same degree of specialisation. Such cities would have larger hexagonal hinterlands for their own specialised services. Even larger and more specialised settlements would have larger market areas and be situated at an equal distance from each other. Christaller believed that the lowest ranked centres were likely to be located 7 km apart. Settlements of the next highest rank would serve three times the area and three times the population. Thus they would be situated 12 km apart ($\sqrt{3} \times 7$). Likewise, the market areas of centres of the next rank would again be three times larger (table 3.1, figure 3.13). Since the number of settlements at successively lower ranks follows a geometric progression (1, 3, 9, 27, . . .) the pattern is referred to as a $k = 3$ hierarchy. Towns within the hierarchy would grow as a result of an increase in the production of goods and services to satisfy an increased demand from a growing population within their zones of influence but generally they would remain within their rank and the rule of three would persist.

Christaller recognised that the hierarchy would be modified by long-distance trade, by routeways and by administrative functions. Towns influenced by these factors would have larger populations than their local market would imply and would be part of a $k = 4$ or even $k = 7$ hierarchy. Settlement generally would tend to be clustered along routeways and be larger at route junctions. Large-scale manufacturing industry would also have an agglomerating influence increasing population out of proportion to the size of the immediate service hinterland.

The central place theory is criticised as it is dependent upon the evolution of settlement on a uniform plane – Christaller largely ignored variable topography. The influence of manufacturing industry both past and present and below a large scale is also discounted, the production of goods and services for distribu-

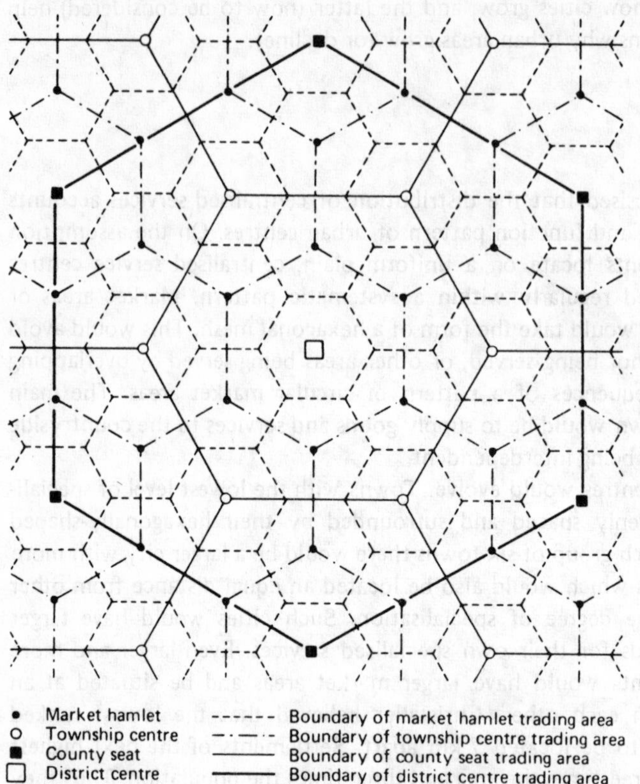

Figure 3.13 *Christaller's theory of the arrangement of central places*

tion to other areas is not considered, local specialisation is ignored, and it is not appreciated that growth generates the internal needs of cities (for example, schools, hospitals and general service and manufactured requirements). Neither the growth of industrial suburbs or outlying business districts fits in with the central place theory, and there is no consideration of the effect upon the size of towns of a large in-migration of labour. Christaller has been criticised on the basis of empirical data. Although the theory concerned urban settlement in Saxony, neither the geometric scheme of spacing nor the regular order of ranking of central places in that region can be found.

But the central place theory is useful in that it stresses the relevance of the market area to the size of a town's population and it introduces the idea of the urban hierarchy. It has led to the introduction of the 'rank–size rule' which states that the population of a given urban area tends to be equal to the population of the largest city divided by the rank of the population size into which the given urban area falls, the population of settlements thus being arranged according to the series $1, \frac{1}{2}, \frac{1}{3}, \frac{1}{4}, \ldots 1/n$. If plotted on a graph this produces the result exhibited in figure 3.14.

Table 3.1 *The urban hierarchy in South Germany (after Christaller)*

Market centre	Distance apart (km)	Population	Tributary area size (km^2)	Population
Market hamlet (*Markort*)	7	800	45	2 700
Township centre (*Amtsort*)	12	1 500	135	8 100
County seat (*Kreistadt*)	21	3 500	400	24 000
District centre (*Bezirksstadt*)	36	9 000	1 200	75 000
Small state capital (*Gaustadt*)	62	27 000	3 600	225 000
Provincial head capital (*Provinzhaupstadt*)	108	90 000	10 800	675 000
Regional capital city (*Landeshaupstadt*)	186	300 000	32 000	2 025 000

Source: E. L. Ullman, *American Journal of Sociology*, 46 (1941) 857.

Whereas the central place theory was idealistic, not being derived from empirical information, the rank–size rule is based on the study of actual population data. Yet generally the rank–size rule is in accord with the central place theory. Both imply that there are very few large cities, and although Christaller's urban hierarchy would produce a stepped arrangement of population sizes whereas the rank–size rule shows a smooth progression of settlements through the ranks, this divergence is largely illusory. Christaller's theory is most relevant to small rural areas and to the lower ranks of the hierarchy, whereas the rank–size rule is particularly relevant to a large area – possibly a whole country. Because of regional variations in the degree of industrialisation, the development of transport services and administrative structures, a series of stepped hierarchies merge together to produce a relatively smooth population curve blurring the edges of individual hierarchical systems. The rule depends upon the assumption of a stable relationship between the populations of central places and the population of the market areas served by them. The principal weakness of the rank–size rule is that in most countries the largest city is larger than the rule would suggest.

Central place theory and rank–size rule provide an efficient basis for administering urban regions and for allocating resources. Investment decisions must take the urban hierarchy or rank–size into account if the desired private or social returns are to be realised.

Based on empirical studies made in 1938 Smailes[8] suggested that the urban hierarchy in England and Wales comprised seven ranks of settlement, that is,

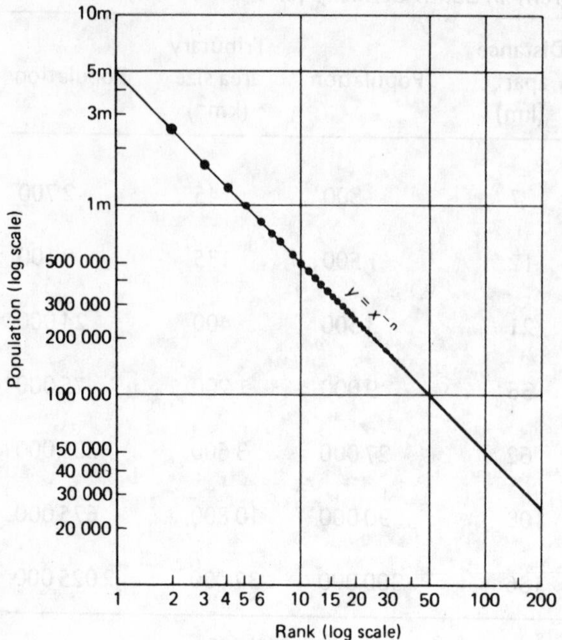

Figure 3.14 *The rank–size rule: the hypothetical population of cities in relation to their ranking*

major cities, major towns, towns, sub-towns, villages, and hamlets. To qualify as a fourth rank 'fully-fledged' town an urban settlement would need to possess at least three banks, a Woolworth store, a secondary school, a hospital, a cinema and a weekly newspaper. Settlements which did not possess this complete range of services were categorised as sub-towns or villages. In contrast, a city would have all the services of a town and would also possess department stores, specialised hospital services and an evening newspaper. A major city in addition would have the regional offices of private firms and government departments; and when the research was being undertaken, a major city would also have its daily morning newspaper and a civic university. But Smailes was not prepared to identify market areas and recognised that the location and spacing of urban settlements showed no hexagonal pattern.

Smith[9] using a much larger number of indicators of urban rank than Smailes had used in his 1938 classification, showed that the urban hierarchy in England and Wales had remained very stable. Of the 606 urban centres, only 138 rose in rank and 78 declined. Change occurred mainly among the lower order centres especially in the north, but the south and east were particularly stable due to the dominance of London.

In research recently funded by the Royal Institution of Chartered Surveyors and the Economic and Social Research Council,[10] it has been shown that the hierarchy of shopping centres in Britain changed little over the period 1961–84. Comparing 1984 data of the number of multiple branch shops with the 1961 and 1971 Censuses of Distribution, it was evident, however, that six major regional centres emerged which in the 1960s had only district rank or did not exist at all (table 3.2), seven major regional centres evolved which ranked as only minor regional centres in 1971, and certain centres attractive to tourists and high income shoppers appeared to have increased their importance as retail centres. Some centres inevitably declined, notably 22 London suburban centres and a few towns in the North of England and Scotland.

In the United States central place theory has been further developed. Berry and Garrison[11] suggested that the concepts of 'range' and 'threshold' control the distribution of central places. The range of a good or service is the distance over which people are prepared to travel to obtain that product, and the threshold is the minimum amount of purchasing power necessary to support the supply of a good or service from a central place. The range of a product is limited at the upper level by the degree of competition from other central places supplying

Table 3.2 *The changing hierarchy of shopping centres in Britain, 1961–84*

Centres		Rank order 1961	1971	1984	Number of multiple branch stores
Regional centres emerging by 1984	Brent Cross	—	—	72	34
	Harlow	207	119	78	32
	Fareham	228	204	86	31
	Milton Keynes	—	—	87	31
	Basingstoke	—	136	90	30
	Basildon	210	121	91	30
Minor regional centres in 1971 becoming major regional centres by 1984	Peterborough	106	100	34	45
	Warrington	97	108	59	37
	Torquay	101	131	62	36
	Blackburn	110	99	67	35
	Staines	149	146	89	30
	Kirkcaldy	130	142	94	30
	Kilmarnock	115	134	95	30
Tourist shopping centres increasing in importance	Chester	38	34	14	63
	Exeter	39	42	18	58
	Bath	54	54	25	53

Source: R. Schiller, 'A ranking of centres using multiple branch number', *Estates Gazette* (23 March, 1985).

the same product, and at the lower level by the threshold necessary to permit it to function. As more specialised products require a larger threshold they usually need a more extensive range, therefore it is logical for an urban hierarchy to evolve based on the degree of specialisation of central places.

The central place theory and considerations of urban rank have been generally concerned with towns as service centres. But Pred[12] argued that (at least in the United States) the rate of development of a city is functionally related to the diversification of its manufacturing sector, and that city size depends largely on the number and extent of its overlapping hinterlands.

Urban Base Theory

Unlike the central place theory which was concerned with the distribution of products from an urban centre to its hinterland, the urban base theory involves a consideration of demand from anywhere outside the boundaries of the settlement.

The more a city specialises the more it destroys its self-sufficiency. Urban growth will thus depend upon the urban area's ability to export goods and services to pay for its imported needs. The production of goods and services for export is known as a 'basic' activity and the output of products for distribution solely to the urban area itself is referred to as a 'non-basic' activity. According to the theory the growth of an urban area depends upon the ratio of basic to non-basic activities – the higher the ratio the greater the rate of growth. Non-basic industries will be dependent upon the basic sector, employees in the latter activity providing much of the demand for the products of the former.

The theory assumes that once the underlying economic, technological and social structure of a country has stabilised, the basic–non-basic ratio of an urban area and the ratios of these activities (separately or combined) to the total population remain constant. If there is an injection of basic employment into the town eventually non-basic employment will have to increase to meet the higher local demand for goods and services, and the total dependent population will also increase. Thus any temporary instability resulting from an initial increase in basic employment will be eliminated through an upward adjustment in both non-basic employment and total population (table 3.3). The extent of the overall change will therefore be at a multiple of the initial injection of basic employment.

The urban base theory also suggests that if an urban area loses some basic employment, less non-basic employment will be required and the town's population will decline at a multiple of the initial withdrawal of basic employment.

Many criticisms have been expressed regarding the validity of the theory. There is unlikely to be a constant basic–non-basic ratio for an urban area even if the overall underlying conditions remain fairly stable. Total non-basic activity increases in relative importance as urban areas increase in size, and individual

Table 3.3 *The basic–non-basic equilibrium*

	Number	I Initial equilibrium ratio to basic employment	Number	II Disequilibrium ratio to basic employment	Number	III Eventual equilibrium ratio to basic employment
Basic employees	10000	1.0	12 500	1.0	12 500	1.0
Non-basic employees	15 000	1.5	15 000	1.2	18 750	1.5
Total employees	25 000	2.5	27 500	2.2	31 250	2.5
Total population	50 000	5.0	55 000	4.4	62 500	5.0

basic and non-basic activities may experience economies of scale (and possibly eventual diseconomies) thereby altering ratios. Undue importance is attached to basic employment; non-basic employment may sometimes be more important in determining economic activity in an urban area, and while the theory argues that non-basic employment is dependent upon basic employment the reverse is often true. Well developed non-basic activities will attract basic industry which will be dependent upon the non-basic activities' ability to supply goods and services, capital, ancillary labour and developable land. The theory only suggest what might happen if there is a change in basic activity, it gives no indication of what future changes may be anticipated in an urban area. But a major weakness is that it ignores the importance of imports. If all of the increase in export earnings of basic activities was spent on imported goods and services there would be no increase in demand for the products of non-basic industries. Any application of the urban base theory (or one where non-basic activities were assumed to be dominant) would involve the difficult problem of first defining and then identifying basic and non-basic activities and employment, since industries, institutions, firms and employees may not demarcate between production for the local market and production for export.

Nevertheless although the numerical aspects of the theory are unrefined, in many urban areas (especially in medium and small towns) changes in overall economic activity and in population depend largely upon changes in basic activity. The theory also shows that there is a multiplier effect following initial injections (or withdrawals) of activity. In general it should be assumed that there is interdependence between basic and non-basic activities and that the multiplier of each activity is different and varies over time and over different population and income levels.

Keynesian Theory

Whereas the urban base theory concentrated upon urban employment, additions to the level of employment and multiplier effects upon the total population, the flow of money theory is essentially concerned with the economic growth of an urban area expressed in monetary terms. It involves the assessment of the effect upon total income of the circular flow of money between producers and consumers, export earnings and import expenditure, investment and savings and public spending and taxation (figure 3.15).

This approach developed with regard to the national economy by Keynes[13] in the 1930s identifies money inflows as export earnings, the earnings of externally-employed factors, and national government expenditure; money outflows are identified as import expenditure, payment for externally-owned factors (used by producers located in the urban area) and national government taxes. Investment and saving may or may not be retained for use within the town, but net investment is an injection into the money flow, whilst net savings would be a withdrawal.

The income of the urban area would grow if there was an increase in the circular flow of money between producers and consumers, money inflows exceeded money outflows, and investment exceeded savings. If the opposite trends occurred the income of the urban area would decline.

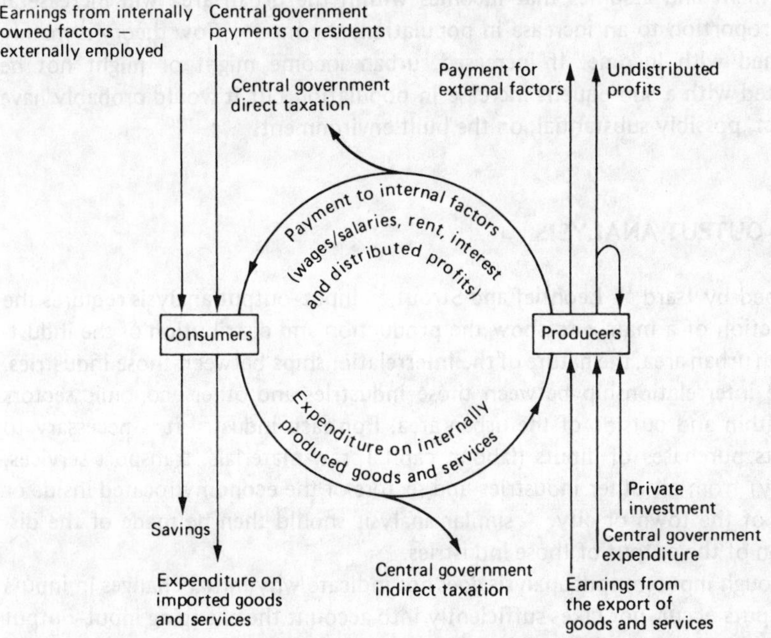

Figure 3.15 *Money flows circulating around, injected into and withdrawn from an urban area*

A multiplier would result in any initial increase (or decrease) in income having a more than proportionate effect on the eventual urban income. The greater the marginal propensity to consume (MPC) or the smaller the marginal propensity to save (MPS) the larger the eventual increase in income. The extent of the multiplier is measured accordingly:

$$K = \frac{1}{1 - \text{MPC}} \quad \text{or} \quad K = \frac{1}{\text{MPS}}$$

where K is the multiplier. (Note: the marginal propensity to consume and the marginal propensity to save are the additions to consumption and savings resulting from an increment of income expressed as fractions of that income.)

Although the money flow theory of growth is as relevant to an urban area as it is to a national economy its weakness is that data at a local level are largely unavailable and that even if information were to hand the theory would not predict when a change in variables would occur. But like the urban base theory it suggests that there is a causal relationship between the export activities of an urban area and its rate of growth, and that basic and non-basic activity are mutually dependent. While the urban base theory is primarily concerned with employment and assumes that incomes within the urban area will increase at some proportion to an increase in population, the money flow theory is mainly concerned with income. If increased, urban income might or might not be associated with a subsequent increase in population but it would probably have an effect, possibly substantial, on the built environment.

INPUT-OUTPUT ANALYSIS

Developed by Isard,[14] Leontief and Strout,[15] input–output analysis requires the construction of a matrix to show the production and distribution of the industries of an urban area, the nature of the interrelationships between those industries, and the interrelationship between those industries and other economic sectors both within and outside of the urban area. For each industry it is necessary to know its purchases of inputs (labour, capital, raw materials, transport services, property) from all other industries and sectors of the economy located inside or outside of the town or city. A similar analysis should then be made of the distribution of the output of those industries.

Although input–output analysis does not indicate why initial changes in inputs and outputs occur, nor takes sufficiently into account the changing input–output relationships resulting from technological improvement, its use is pertinent to the understanding of urban growth. By showing the dependence of one industry or activity on all other industries and activities it allows the chain of repercussions stemming from a change in that industry or activity to be traced through until the adjustments necessary to restore stability have been made. This is of relevance to government policy since at a central and local level it can encourage, deter or prohibit industrial development.

Location Theory

There is an obvious link between urban growth and industrial location. The creation of new employment is usually the chief determinant of a city's expansion. But the ability of an urban area to attract employment depends upon its relative locational advantages and disadvantages concerning revenue and profit potential, costs of production, external economies, infrastructure and social or cultural characteristics.

Czamanski[16] produced a location theory model of urban growth separating industries within an urban area into three categories: geographically-orientated industries, complementary industries and urban-orientated industries. The first are very mobile and are influenced by factors such as the market, the source of materials, and break of bulk locations; complementary industries require the presence of other industries especially those geographically orientated; and urban-orientated industries have evolved purely to satisfy the demand of the city. The theory relates total population to employment in each sector, but an increase in population is related particularly to growth in employment in the geographically-orientated industries.

A problem of categorising industries and employment arises and it is difficult quantitatively and over a period of time to relate population growth to an increase in employment in a specific industry.

SIZE, URBAN GROWTH AND OTPIMALITY

Urban areas gradually evolve over time but when they reach a 'minimum threshhold level' growth becomes rapid and self-generating. However, the minimum threshold level varies over time and between regions and countries according to socio-economic conditions, the level of technology, and the nature of institutional systems.

Large cities benefit from substantial external economies of scale and provide large pools of labour, capital and entrepreneurial skill. The larger the city the more it is self-contained and viable as there is less dependence on basic (export) activities. Its producers incur lower average transport costs than are found in other urban areas relying more on basic production. Inertia and the self-perpetuating momentum of geographical concentration compound the underlying cost advantages of a major urban area – the external economies of the firm being co-locational with the urbanisation economies of the city. These latter and general economies attract factors of production which in turn increase the scale of production and the size of the city, thereby further producing external economies.

Assuming that administrative and business skills and the level of technology remain constant, and that government policy is not aimed at restricting urban growth, the average aggregate costs of production and municipal services will tend to diminish until a 'minimum cost population' is reached and then diseconomies of scale will be experienced.

But in the long term administrative, economic and technological application becomes more sophisticated, so at successive stages of urban development it is not only possible to delay the onset of diseconomies of scale but to establish new and lower cost situations (in real terms). Yet even on this long-term basis diseconomies eventually appear.

It is difficult or impossible to quantify both short- and long-term average aggregate costs and to estimate the minimum cost population. But the rate of urban growth will tend to slow down when scale diseconomies such as the rising cost of land, labour and transport are incurred. It is doubtful however whether rising environmental costs by themselves reduce the rate of growth, and business firms may be less concerned with rising costs than with their level of revenue and profitability.

The optimum size of an urban area (that population level and magnitude of land use which maximises the net product and utility per head of population with given resources, technology and social conditions) may not only be difficult to determine but may be of limited use as a concept. Cities cannot be considered in isolation. They are part of a regional, national or even wider economic framework which for its own efficient functioning does not require each urban area within it to be of optimum size.

Although the populations of many large cities are falling, this is attributable both to governmental decentralisation policies and to market forces. In advanced capitalist countries it is unlikely, however, that government policy alone puts a break on urban growth if optimal levels of population and economic activity are exceeded. Market forces have to be relied upon to help bring about a halt in growth and a decentralisation of activity. Yet when cities do decline they do not decrease in population below their 'urban size rachet' – a number equivalent to that obtaining at their most recent threshold level.

The decline of urban population should be seen as the final stage in the process of urbanisation. The stages theory of urban growth shows – in terms of population mobility – how urban development passes through successive stages of growth and contraction. In the first stage (*urbanisation*), agricultural labour is attracted to fast-growing industrial cities. In the second stage (*suburbanisation*), improved transportation facilitates the out-migration of an increasing number of households from the urban core while the core continues to attract in-migration from rural areas and elsewhere. By the third stage, suburbanisation continues but the core areas decline in population. In the final stage (*deurbanisation*), even the suburban areas experience population decline as households out-migrate to satellite towns and villages. Britain passed through stage one during the Industrial Revolution from the late eighteenth to mid-nineteenth centuries, stage two in the late nineteenth and early twentieth centuries, stage three from about 1950 to the early 1960s, and has subsequently been passing through the final stage.

In the 1960s and 1970s, the process of deurbanisation accelerated.[17] The population of the urban cores of several West European countries decreased more quickly (or grew more slowly) in the period 1970–75 compared with the years 1960–70 (table 3.4). The number of towns and cities deurbanising 1975-80 showed a marked increase over the rate of deurbanisation over the whole period 1970–80, while (except for France) the rate of suburbanisation declined – presumably as urban areas had reached the final stage in their development (table 3.5).[18]

In the period 1980–84, the annual decline in the population of Britain's main urban areas ranged from, for example, 0.8 per cent in Inner London and

Table 3.4 *Population change in urban cores – Western Europe, 1965–75*

	Percentage change per year	
	1960–70	1970–73
Netherlands	–0.21	–1.52
Belgium	–0.83	–1.23
Great Britain	–0.55	–0.92
West Germany	+0.03	n.a.
Denmark	–0.21	–0.81
France	+0.46	–0.49
Italy	+0.98	+0.11

Source: L. Van den Berg *et al.*, *Urban Europe: A Study of Growth and Decline* (Pergamon, 1982).

Table 3.5 *Suburbanisation and deurbanisation in Western Europe, 1970–80*

	Number of towns and cities			
	1970–75		1975–80	
	Suburbanisation	Deurbanisation	Suburbanisation	Deurbanisation
United Kingdom	42	21	31	30
West Germany	33	14	19	27
Italy	50	15	41	23
Benelux	32	2	31	4
France	50	2	57	7

Source: P. Hall, 'Flight to the Green', *New Society* (9 January, 1987).

Cleveland, 0.7 per cent in Merseyside, 0.6 per cent in the West Midlands, 0.5 per cent in Greater Manchester, 0.4 per cent in Tyne and Wear, and 0.3 per cent in South Yorkshire. Deurbanisation continued apace, both as households out-migrated to satellites (since there was a lack of accommodating space in suburban areas) and more fundamentally in response to the structural decline of the basic industries of the main urban areas (such as cars, engineering, steel and ships).[19] In contrast to the United States and Japan, the decline in manufacturing employment has taken place more rapidly than the growth of jobs in the service sector. This is particularly evident in the major *functional nodal cities* (for example, Birmingham, Glasgow, Liverpool and Manchester – although in the latter two cities even service employment has decreased in recent years albeit at a slower rate than the decline in manufacturing employment).[20]

In the same period (1980-84), the fastest growth of population generally occurred in the rural and coastal counties of Southern England – annual increases ranging from, for example, 1.5 per cent in Dorset, 1.3 per cent in East Sussex, 1.1 per cent in West Sussex, 0.9 per cent in Somerset, 0.8 per cent in Buckinghamshire and 0.7 per cent in Cambridgeshire, Norfolk, Suffolk and Devon. Within these counties, as is the case throughout much of Western Europe, small cities have continued to experience both economic and population growth. Many of these cities, such as Cambridge, Norwich and Exeter, have easy access to motorways, stable labour relations, space for expansion and pleasing environments and consequently have been successful in attracting manufacturing industry. These cities, however, are essentially *regional nodal centres* (administrative and service centres for largely rural hinterlands) and have increasingly accommodated service industry since rents and wages are generally lower than in the major cities; and being traditional centres of local government and further and higher education, find little difficulty in attracting information technology, financial and professional services and retailing.[20] The manufacturing jobless of these cities have not directly benefited from these trends. Newly located manufacturing industry is capital- (rather than labour-) intensive and high tech, and like much of the service sector, recruits its workforce from ready-trained migrant labour and commuters ('yuppies' and 'gentrifiers') with very mixed effects on the local economy. Some provincial cities have a special appeal to tourists and the retired, amplifying their service base. It has been suggested that all over Western Europe, a reversion to the medieval settlement pattern is taking place – but one harnessed to new technology rather than to agricultural exchange. If this interpretation of population and urban development trends is correct, the major cities will need to evolve new functions or face terminal decay.

In addition to deurbanisation, *peripheralisation* is having a substantial impact on the viability of urban areas throughout Europe.[20] Although, in absolute terms, most deurbanisation has occurred within Western Europe's 'Golden Triangle' (an area bounded by Dortmund, Birmingham and Milan), the inner core of this triangle – centred on Amsterdam, Frankfurt and Paris – has been little affected by this process, while the peripheral areas have deurbanised the most. Indeed in relative terms, some cities outside of the triangle, for example, Belfast, Glasgow, Liverpool and Manchester, have experienced the greatest population losses. Ranking the largest functional urban regions (FURs) in Western Europe on the basis of migration, employment, income and travel variables, recent research has shown that while the thriving cities or FURs (notably those in West Germany and to a lesser extent in France) have recently improved their economic performance, the problem FURs (found mainly in Italy and the United Kingdom) have performed increasingly badly – with disparities widening over the period 1975-83.

It must be clear from the above analysis that even if it were possible to determine the optimum size of an urban area, it would only remain at that size for a short period of time. As the town or city passed through different stages in its development, attracted or discarded functional or regional nodal activity, and increasingly benefited or suffered from the degree to which its location was central or peripheral, so the optimum size would continually fluctuate. At best it would provide a moving target for urban planners and a far from predictable local context for fiscal policy.

REFERENCES

1. E. W. Burgess, 'The Growth of the City', in R. E. Park *et al., The City* (University of Chicago Press, 1925).
2. H. Hoyt, *The Structure and Growth of Residential Neighbourhoods in American Cities* (Federal Housing Administration, 1939).
3. P. H. Mann, *An Approach to Urban Sociology* (Routledge & Kegan Paul, 1968).
4. C. D. Harris and E. L. Ullman, 'The Nature of Cities' in P. K. Hatt and A. J. Reiss (eds), *Cities and Society* (The Free Press, 1951).
5. P. A. Stone, *Urban Development in Britain: Standards, Costs and Resources, 1964–2004, Vol. 1, Population Trends and Housing* (National Institute for Economic and Social Research, Cambridge University Press, 1970).
6. W. Firey, 'Ecological Considerations in Planning for Urban Fringes', in P. K. Hatt and A. J. Reiss (eds), *Cities and Society* (The Free Press, 1951).
7. W. Christaller, *Die Zentralen Orte in Suddeutschland* (Fisher, 1933).
8. A. E. Smailes, 'The Urban Hierarchy in England and Wales', *Geography*, 29 (1944).
9. R. D. P. Smith, 'The Changing Urban Hierarchy', *Regional Studies*, 2 (1978).
10. R. Schiller, 'A Ranking of Centres Using Multiple Branch Numbers', *Estates Gazette* (23 March, 1985).
11. B. L. J. Berry and W. L. Garrison, 'Recent Development of Central Place Theory', *Papers and Proceedings of the Regional Science Association*, 4 (1958).
12. A. R. Pred, *The Spatial Dynamics of U.S. Urban–Industrial Growth 1800–1914* (M.I.T. Press, 1966).
13. J. M. Keynes, *The General Theory of Employment, Interest and Money* (Macmillan, 1936).
14. W. Isard, *Location and Space Economy* (M.I.T. Press, 1956).
15. W. Leontief and A. A. Strout, 'Multiregional Input-Output Analysis' in T. Barna (ed.), *Structural Interdependence and Economic Development* (Macmillan, 1963).
16. S. Czamanski, 'A Model of Urban Growth', *Proceedings of the Regional Science Association*, 13 (1964).
17. L. Van den Berg *et al., Urban Europe: A Study of Growth and Decline* (Pergamon, 1982).

18. P. Cheshire and D. Hay, see P. Hall, 'Flight to the Green', *New Society* (9 January, 1987).
19. P. Hall, 'Flight to the Green', *New Society* (9 January, 1987).
20. P. Hall and P. Cheshire, 'The Key to Success for Cities', *Town and Country Planning* (February, 1987).

4

The Property and Investment Markets

PROPERTY INTERESTS

Fundamentally the subjects of real property transactions are not the land and buildings themselves but interests in rights over land, which in aggregate are known to English law as property.[1] Land is merely the medium in which property rights subsist. The greatest bundle of rights in property is the 'fee simple absolute', an unencumbered freehold estate free from any sub-interest. Freehold rights are however not unlimited; they will be subject to the provisions of planning and other legislation. The freehold interest may be purchased subject to obligations entered into by the previous owner. For example, a property may be purchased with an existing tenant who has a leasehold interest. The freeholder has purchased the right to receive rent from the tenant, the right to regain possession at the end of the lease, and then to use the property within the constraints of planning or local authority regulations. The durability of real property enables more than one interest to exist; in particular, ownership and right of use may be separated.

A leaseholder may use the building subject to conditions laid down in return for which he agrees to pay a specified rent. Many alternative forms of leasehold interests may be created by the freeholder. He may grant a building lease on condition that a building is erected on the site. At the end of the lease – normally 99 years – both land and buildings revert to the landlord. The rent agreed, the ground rent, may be nominal or a 'peppercorn rent' not necessarily representing the full value of the land; thus in addition to the rent a capital sum may be paid. The sum paid as rent or as capital will depend on various factors, especially tax. Where rents are chargeable against taxable income, whereas capital payments are not, the tenant may prefer a higher rent to any capital payment. An alternative arrangement is where the ground rent is reviewed periodically and related to site value, an arrangement beneficial to the freeholder.

The range of possible interests in property is exceedingly diverse: the head-lessee may be entitled to sub-let, grant his own leases and state the obligations and rights of the sub-lessee. Freeholders may borrow through a mortgage with the freehold as collateral; the mortgagee will have rights and interests in the freehold until the mortgagor clears the debt. In default of repayment, the mortgagee may exercise his right to foreclose and force the sale of the interest in order to repay the debt.

The Property Market and Price Determination

The property market deals in rights and interests in land and buildings; transactions involving heterogeneous units of high value in many submarkets – shops, offices, houses – reflect variations in buyers, sellers, local knowledge and unique locational factors. The market has no formal organisation or central agency or institution like the London Stock Exchange or Lloyds.

The property market is very imperfect; nevertheless there is an underlying rationale arising from the effectiveness of market price in allocating resources between different users. Transactions occur between sellers and buyers of property, and in the long run rights and interests will be controlled by those users who bid the highest price for these interests.

A property may be purchased either for own-occupation or for investment. If the former the purchaser's return is in occupational benefits; if the purchase is for investment, the return may be as an annual rent or as a capital gain following a successful planning application either changing the use or density of existing use.

Assuming rational behaviour, the investor will be seeking to maximise returns in profitability or satisfaction from either own-occupation or investment. The decision to rent or purchase will depend upon the current level of rents, interest rates, the availability of credit, expectations about future trends, and personal financial factors. If anticipated rents are less than interest charges the owner might be induced to sell rather than rent, unless there is a prospect of capital gain. Similarly a potential purchaser will compare interest payable on borrowings and their availability with rents payable. The opportunity cost of capital must be considered whether renting or buying.

When a potential user decides to rent rather than purchase, he must offer a rent high enough to induce the owner to let; the greater the potential profitability and utility to him of use of a building, the higher the rent he will offer. Similarly, the potential purchaser will bid a price determined by expectations regarding likely profits from ownership of that building. Bids will reflect the different expectations. Owners will similarly differ on how much they should receive for giving up interests in their property.

Real properties are heterogeneous and this adds to the complexity of supply and demand analysis. The market price of real property reflects economic assessments on the part of various buyers and sellers regarding anticipated net income and profitability.

Whether renting or purchasing, the investment aspect is present; the essence of investment is the giving up of a capital sum in return for income over time. The purchaser or potential occupier needs to discount the stream of anticipated income and benefits from the property to a present value at the appropriate rate of interest, probably the marginal cost of financing the project and according to present income and capital, the degree of risk and the likely return on capital in alternative investments with similar risks. Potential occupiers or purchasers will consider differing advantages from occupations so that each will arrive at a different place influenced by the price and availability of substitute properties. For any property interest there will be a maximum price which buyers will be prepared to pay. Similarly potential sellers will value their interests and establish minimum prices influenced by the selling prices of comparable properties, expectations regarding future price changes, economic policy and prospects, and the cost of equivalent reinstatement elsewhere. Thus, deals will occur provided potential buyers have maximum prices above the minimum prices of potential sellers. Where the buyer's maximum price is above the seller's minimum price, the price fixed will be determined by the competition among buyers and their expectations as against the number of properties on offer and the expectations of sellers.

If there were only one potential buyer of a particular property with a maximum price higher than the seller's minimum price, the market price will be fixed somewhere between the two points of bargaining. The two prices fix a limit on the possible movement of market price at any time; the situation may change as expectations or conditions within the property market vary. The stronger the seller's bargaining position, the closer the market price will be to the maximum price; the weaker his position, the closer the price will be to the buyer's maximum (or seller's minimum).

Thus prices within the various submarkets will be determined by the various maxima and minima determined by prospective buyers and sellers bidding against each other. Equilibrium prices may be reached at which the amount of real property offered for sale is taken up by buyers; however, a characteristic of the property market as a whole and of submarkets such as private housing is that it lacks the flexibility to clear itself. At times property remains unsold because the minimum price asked by owners is higher than the maximum price of bidders. That the property remains unsold may bring about an adjustment in the owner's minimum price or buyer's maximum in a subsequent market period. Alternatively the owner may keep to his price hoping that buyers will raise their maximum price as perhaps economic conditions change. In the depressed housing markets of 1974 and 1981 in the United Kingdom, many new houses were not sold because developers' minimum prices exceeded the limit of many prospective buyers. Within the commercial property market, prevailing uncertainty adversely affected many sales. The Centre Point office block in London, completed in 1966, remained largely unlet until 1980 because the minimum rental demanded by the owners exceeded the maximum rental bid by potential occupiers.

Any potential buyer of real property is likely to view several properties before making a purchase, and a potential seller will await a number of bids before making a sale. However, few persons are able to investigate all alternatives; where a potential buyer lacks information or buys too quickly he is more likely to pay a price which may be higher than the market level generally. Similarly, the potential seller lacking information or making a hurried sale will receive a lower-than-the-market price. Where a potential seller purchased a property in boom conditions and is under no pressure to vacate, he may hold out for a price that will cover his expenditure even though conditions may have changed fundamentally. This situation commonly prevailed in the United Kingdom residential market between 1974 and 1976. Conversely, where the original owner dies, his heirs may consider the property as a windfall and sell quickly for a lower price than they might otherwise have obtained.

The imperfection of the property market is especially significant in sub-markets, such as for land. A plot in a similar area may be bought or sold at different prices according to the expertise or lack of experience of the buyer. Herein lies the chance of making a speculative profit because one person is more astute than the market in anticipating future trends. If perfect knowledge were available as to future events regarding land, there would be no opportunity for speculative gains because all future potential and therefore value would be fully and accurately discounted to the present. Speculative gains can only be made in an imperfect market. Similarly when there are few sales involving a particular type of property and where buyers and sellers are not fully informed, relative skill in bargaining is significant in determining price. Market imperfections may mean a heavy reliance on professional middlemen, leading to monopoly power.

The typical method of conducting transactions in the property market is by private treaty between buyer and seller. The price will be determined by the offer and counter-bid process described. The transaction is likely to be carried out discreetly through the medium of professional middlemen. Because of market imperfections the seller will not know exactly what price he will obtain; the final selling price of a real property is rarely revealed. A more open method of buying and selling real property is through auctions which are used where there is great uncertainty as to property values because of unique factors or where the market conditions are so fluid as to produce rapidly changing values. Auctions were particularly popular in the United Kingdom between 1971 and 1973 and again between 1985 to 1987 when prices increased sharply and sellers wished to ensure that they received a current, higher price. Conversely in a buyer's market, auctions are normally a less attractive method of selling although the transaction is completed in a much shorter period than under private treaty.

Auctions are also used for sales by special bodies such as public trustees. If the necessary minimum price required (the reserve) is not reached, the property may be withdrawn and possibly put up for sale at a later date. Another method used where market conditions are exceptionally unstable or where the property is unusual is the tender; potential buyers are invited to submit a sealed bid by a set date. The seals are not opened until this date and, provided the tender is acceptable (the reserve is reached), the highest bidder secures the property. The tender may secure the highest possible price for the seller as potential buyers will tend to put in a maximum bid without having the advantage of knowing competitors' bids as at an auction; also buyers will not have the opportunity normally of resubmitting a tender. There are also many other transactions between divisions of a large company or members of a family, completely sheltered from the market processes and where prices will be determined by quite unique features.

Typically only a very small proportion of real property of any type is on the market at any one time. Because of the durability of buildings, the inelasticity of supply for relatively long periods, institutional and legal factors, change is slow and at any moment of time the market is in a state of disequilibrium.

Institutions and the Property Market

Although some insurance companies commenced building up property investment portfolios in the 1930s, a feature of the post-1945 property market in the United Kingdom has been the extent of institutional involvement. Insurance companies, pension funds and other major institutions have acquired interests mainly in prime shops and offices and modern industrial property. The institutional preference for property has reflected expectations relating to the extent to which it is believed that rents, and therefore capital values, will increase faster than the rate of inflation. Property has been seen as a secure, long-term investment that maintains earning power in real terms in spite of inflation. Between 1962 and 1980 property capital values (offices, shops and industrial) increased from base 100 to 880. The *Financial Times* actuaries all share index increased from 100 to 227; the retail price index increased from 100 to 462. Thus commercial property values in real terms increased from 100 to 194, despite a very sharp fall in rentals in real terms between 1974 and 1977.[2]

However, the period 1980–85 saw relatively stagnant growth with virtually no rental growth in real terms. Subsequently between 1982 and 1983 capital values fell, the only exception being shop rents which continued to outpace both offices and industrials. Average annual real rates of returns from property, 4.8 per cent between 1977 and 1987, were inferior to equities, 13.0 per cent, although better than gilts, 3.5 per cent.[3] Consequently instiutional investment in the United Kingdom property declined from 1982 (see table 4.1) as the performance gap between property and equities continued to widen as share markets entered a long bull market which lasted to 1987 (see table 4.2). With lower inflation, instiutional investors could disregard the security offered by property and concentrated their efforts on short term gain with privatisation issues and the expansion of the Unlisted Securities Market ensuring a ready supply of investments. With a booming owner occupier market, 1986–87, insurance companies extended their interests into the residential market by incorporating networks of established estate agencies able to offer a range of financial services. The potential for profit in the cross-fertilisation between the financial sector and the buying and selling of houses was clear.

Before 1970, insurance companies had been virtually the sole institutional investor in property as from the 1950s they steadily acquired property assets as values accelerated. By the late 1970s, land and property portfolios were 19 per cent of total investments compared with 11 per cent in 1964. There was heavy emphasis towards prime areas of central London and other large UK cities. Over 50 per cent of total property holdings were invested in offices with the balance in commercial property. Despite a reduction in real terms, insurance company property assets in the UK totalled £22 billion by 1986 compared with £13 billion held by pension funds. Indicative of a downturn in property investment was the rise in property disposals measured by the turnover rate. This increased to 4.7 per cent by 1986 compared with 1.5 per cent in 1980.[4]

Table 4.1 *Institutional investment into property, 1973–86 (£ million) (not deflated)*

	1973	1976	1979	1982	1984	1986
Insurance companies	307	449	628	1059	744	877
Superannuation funds	248	513	498	797	674	306
Property unit trusts	57	71	90	57	47	–55
Other financial institutions	52	152	80	151	132	59
Total	664	1185	1296	2064	1597	1187

Source: *Money into Property* (Debenham Tewson & Chinnocks, 1987).

Pension funds have invested in property since 1955 although only in the early 1970s was there significant large investment. By 1980, over 13 per cent of total investment was in property. Public-sector funds were investing close to one-third of their cash flow in property on behalf of approximately 12 million people in occupational schemes. Some funds carried out their own developments and also invested in property in the EEC and USA. Generally, funds invested in existing freeholds with less than 10 per cent invested in new buildings.

Low inflation and rising equity markets in the 1980s placed funds in a strong position at a time when early retirement and redundancy reduced their liabilities. By the mid-1980s, property represented only 3 per cent of investment funds with significant property disposals occurring. The turnover ratio increased to 5.9 per cent compared with 1.5 per cent in 1980. Fifty-five per cent of investments were in UK equities and 20 per cent overseas.

The actual flow of institutional money into property has been largely determined by the supply of suitable prime properties. The institutional dominance in the market for existing property, especially in the higher price ranges, is con-

Table 4.2 *Investment media: comparison of real rates of return, 1978–86 (percentages)*

	1978	1979	1980	1981	1982	1983	1984	1985	1986	Annualised rate Dec. 1977 to Dec. 1986
MGL–CIG *Property Index*	11.4	3.8	4.2	2.8	2.2	4.2	5.0	3.0	6.5	4.8
Offices	–	–	–	–	–	–	–	–	–	4.3
Retail	–	–	–	–	–	–	–	–	–	8.1
Industrial	–	–	–	–	–	–	–	–	–	2.8
Pooled Property Funds	10.8	4.9	2.3	1.7	3.5	2.8	4.1	2.6	4.2	3.8
FT Actuaries Property Share Index	3.9	3.8	25.5	–6.4	–10.1	28.4	18.1	2.4	20.4	8.8
FT Actuaries All Share Index	nil	–5.7	17.6	1.4	22.8	22.4	26.2	14.2	22.9	13.0
FT Actuaries All Stocks Index	–8.4	–10.4	3.8	–6.7	34.3	7.9	4.1	6.0	7.5	3.5
FT Actuaries Index-Linked All Stocks Index	–	–	–	–	10.7	–4.6	0.9	–4.2	3.0	1.0*

*Annualised rate for the period 1982–86

Source: *MGL–CIT Property Index* (Morgan, Grenfell Laurie, 1987).

siderable. For both insurance companies and pension funds there is a correlation between the size of the fund and the percentage invested in property. Smaller funds face a narrower investment choice and are likely to continue as net sellers of property assets. Generally, the larger funds with heavy weighting in Central London and other prime locations have been able to maintain good returns from their property portfolio.

By the mid-1980s, the institutions were investing approximately 12 per cent of their funds into property compared with 22 per cent into government securities and 45 per cent into UK company equities. Twenty per cent of investment was overseas – the ending of exchange controls in 1979 resulted in an increase in the proportion of funds invested overseas, particularly into North America and Japan. There has been a considerable decline in real terms in property investment from the 1981 peak.

In the late 1960s, the property bond and the property unit trust developed. The property bond enabled a person with limited capital and income to purchase a stake in commercial buildings through regular premiums which are used by life assurance companies to buy a portfolio of properties. The portfolio is divided into units which are then allocated to the policy holder proportionate to the premium. The first property bond was launched in 1966[5] and by 1980 funds exceeded £1000 million. The property bonds are dominated by the two largest companies which account for some 56 per cent of the market, with assets in the United Kingdom, Europe and North America. Most funds are backed by a major insurance company. Only a small proportion of portfolios are committed to development and generally no more than 10 per cent of assets are committed to any one property.[4]

The property unit trust (PUTs), first launched in 1966, is more limited in its appeal, being restricted originally to pension funds too small to be able to invest directly in a well-balanced property portfolio, but later spreading to local authorities and charities. The trusts have provided a tax efficient channel through which smaller institutions are able to invest in property without having to pay capital gains or corporation tax to which the trusts are not liable. By the early 1980s, the ten largest trusts controlled portfolios valued in excess of £1000 million including a specialised trust investing in agricultural land. The stagnant growth of the property market during 1982 to 1986 saw the PUTs generally in decline with a significant net outflow of funds, resulting in a net surplus of disposals with a virtual ceasing of overseas investment.

Among other institutions, significant in the property market are the Church Commissioners, since 1945 major investors in real property. The value of properties owned was over £1000 million by 1986, comprising 44 per cent offices, 15 per cent residential investments (the Commissioners are one of the largest private landlords in London), 22 per cent agricultural holdings, and the balance in shops and industrial investment. They were also actively involved in redevelopment schemes valued at millions of pounds.

Until 1957 there was no separate property section listed on the London Stock Exchange because it was not considered to be sufficiently important. The ending of building licensing and the 100 per cent development levy in 1954 together with the vast acreages of land available in city centres for redevelopment made conditions ideal for property development, and many new property companies came to the stock market for a full listing. By 1986, Land Securities Investment Trust, the largest property company, had assets exceeding £3000 million. Small investors benefited as shareholders in property companies which provided a hedge against inflation and gave a higher degree of income security than from most other equities.

Much of these huge funds were channelled into commercial property, mainly into modern office blocks, 100 per cent shop sites and modern industrial units. Residential investments have been avoided as being too subject to statutory interference. As commercial rents have risen, especially in London, so have capital values, making property an even more attractive investment. Underlying the strong pressure on property as an investment is the unique nature of land and property. Land as a whole is perfectly inelastic in supply; in any location its supply is finite, it is subject to government controls and restrictions over planning and use. Thus the supply of accommodation for one particular use such as offices, in the short term, cannot easily be expanded. This applies especially to cities surrounded by green belt and already densely occupied. Because supply is inelastic, a small increase in demand will result in a proportionately much greater increase in price. Thus the prospects of capital gain will compensate for relatively low current yields.

Government and the Property Market

Despite the Conservative Party policy of general deregulation since 1979, a feature of the property market has been the extent to which governments interfere with the market mechanism and allocation of property interests between different users. Essentially government measures influence effective demand and supply of real property; some measures increase demand by raising the bids of potential purchasers and by encouraging new purchasers into the market. In the United Kingdom, house purchasers are able to offset mortgage interest charges against taxable income. This subsidy encourages potential purchasers to raise bid-prices above the level which would have existed in the absence of this scheme, thus raising market price. Similarly, schemes such as option mortgages, or deferred interest mortgages to first time buyers, all increase effective demand. Demand will be reduced and bid-prices lowered if concessions are withdrawn or reduced. The limitation of tax relief on owner occupier mortgages (£30 000 since 1983) or the abolition of this relief might be expected, other things being equal, adversely to affect the sale of houses as effective demand would be reduced. Equally, the abolition of higher tax rate relief would have the same effect.

This effect is illustrated in figure 4.1. Existing demand and supply is shown by *DD* and *SS* with an equilibrium price of *OP*. If governments reduce the amount of mortgage interest allowable against taxable income, demand shifts to D_2D_2 and equilibrium price is OP_2. Conversely, if the government grants building societies a lump sum to subsidise mortgage rates at the present level or to reduce mortgage interest rates, demand will shift to D_1D_1 and price will rise to OP_1 (other things remaining equal).

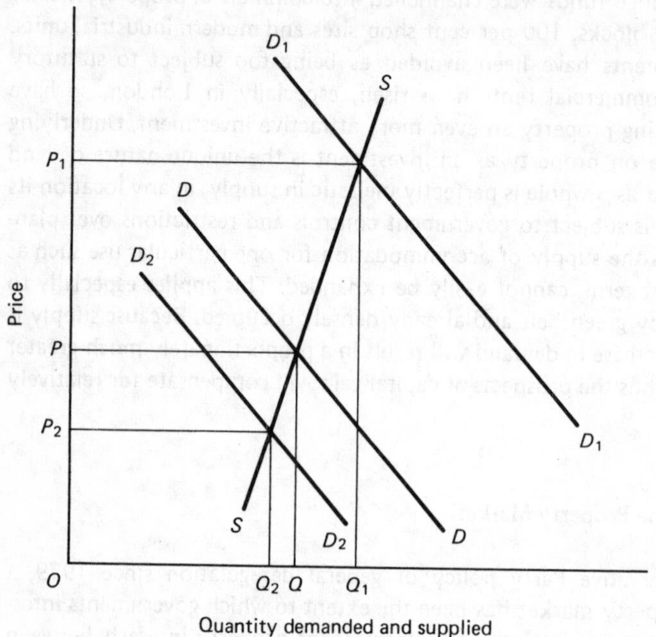

Figure 4.1 *Demand and supply of owner-occupied houses and changes in tax relief*

The supply of real property is equally influenced by government intervention. Landlord–tenant legislation in the United Kingdom since 1915 has strengthened the position of tenant against landlord. For example, security of tenure has been coupled with control of rents for all but the luxury sector of the unfurnished rented market. Thus owners of rented properties have preferred to sell in the uncontrolled owner–occupier sector when properties become vacant rather than relet. Similarly developers have preferred to build houses for sale rather than for renting. Thus persons seeking rented accommodation are faced with diminishing supply and excess demand at the controlled rent. Consequently the allocation of the accommodation is determined not by market forces but through point schemes in the public sector and through premiums in the private sector. Unsatisfied demand in the controlled sector is forced on to the uncontrolled sectors, owner-occupied housing and furnished flats (until the Rent Act 1974) contributing significantly to the upward movement of prices.

In the uncontrolled sector there will be a shift of the demand curve *DD* to D_1D_1. The unsatisfied demand in the controlled sector results in an increase in demand for furnished flats and owner-occupier houses where the supply *SS* will be relatively inelastic. The result is a price increase from *OP* to OP_1 in figure 4.2. The effect of the Rent Act 1974 granting furnished tenants security of tenure was to shift the supply for furnished accommodation to S_1S_1 thus increasing market price to OP_2 and widening still further the gap between market rents and controlled. Taxes such as inheritance tax may increase the supply of real property being offered for sale in any period if land has to be sold to meet duty. Taxes such as betterment levy have the effect of reducing the supply of land to the market as owners anticipate that the tax will be abolished or the rate reduced if they delay selling until a later date. Similarly any tax on development, such as the Development Land Tax 1976, reduces the supply of developed property. Planning decisions and legislation which limits the type of development and the

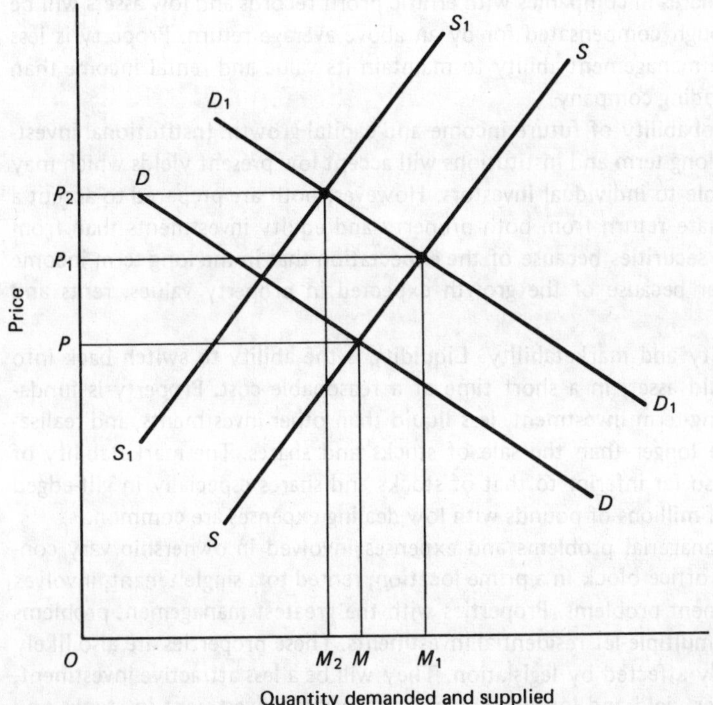

Figure 4.2 *Demand and supply in the uncontrolled sector of the housing market*

density or location of that development have fundamental effects on land values and consequently on the supply of land and buildings. The 100 per cent tax relief for all commercial buildings in Enterprise Zones together with rate-free periods and relaxed planning regulations acted as a powerful stimulant to development and was a major factor in the dramatic regeneration of the Isle of Dogs in London's Docklands in the mid-1980s.

PROPERTY AS AN INVESTMENT

Investment is the giving up of a capital sum in return for income to be received over time. The durability of property and the ability to separate ownership from use means that property is an ideal medium for investment. However, there are alternative investments, for example, in ordinary shares and fixed interest stocks. The investor needs to assess certain fundamental general principles which apply to investment generally.

(1) The present and future stability of his capital. He will avoid situations where there is a possibility of civil disturbance or war.

(2) The prospects for regular and secure income. Investments in buildings of limited life, shares in companies with erratic profit records and low assets will be avoided although compensated for by an above average return. Property is less dependent on management ability to maintain its value and rental income than the average trading company.

(3) The probability of future income and capital growth. Institutional investment is very long term and institutions will accept low present yields which may be unacceptable to individual investors. However, both are prepared to accept a lower immediate return from both property and equity investments than from fixed interest securities because of the expectation that in the long term income will be greater because of the growth expected in property values, rents and dividends.

(4) Liquidity and marketability. Liquidity is the ability to switch back into cash, the liquid asset, in a short time at a reasonable cost. Property is fundamentally a long-term investment, less liquid than other investments, and realisation will take longer than the sale of stocks and shares. The marketability of property is also far inferior to that of stocks and shares especially in gilt-edged where deals of millions of pounds with low dealing expenses are common.

(5) The managerial problems and expenses involved in ownership vary considerably. An office block in a prime location, rented to a single tenant, involves least management problems. Properties with the greatest management problems are probably multiple-let residential investments. These properties are also likely to be adversely affected by legislation. They will be a less attractive investment, sell on a higher yield and lower relative capital value. Investment in stocks and shares involve little management expenses and unit trusts enable the small investor to derive benefits of professional management.

(6) Protection against inflation: persistent inflation, accelerating in the 1970s, carried property values generally far above the general level of prices. The supply of property has been inelastic against ever-increasing effective demand from institutional and other investors. There has been decreased demand for fixed income investments; consequently capital values have fallen and yields have risen, reflecting that the real value of fixed income falls over time. Investors have preferred to purchase a building or asset with a low current income but with the prospects of rent reviews which ensure that real income is maintained. How far property is a protection against inflation is determined by the rental provisions in the lease. Increasingly, property investors have secured concessions on rent review periods; the accepted normal period has been revised downwards from thirty-five years to seven and even five years in a twenty-one year lease. Alternatively, escalated rents are agreed before the lease is signed or a turnover rent, especially popular in the United States, based on annual turnover. Rents may be indexed to the cost of living as in many EEC countries. Increasingly, tenants will be offered short renewable leases. Inflation in the post-1945 period has brought the reverse yield gap. Traditionally, fixed interest yields have been lower than the yield on ordinary shares because of the security of income while equity dividends are dependent upon the profitability of firms and may therefore fall to zero. With accelerating inflation the average yield on equities has fallen below that on fixed interest stocks. By 1981, the reverse yield gap was over 8½ per cent, emphasising investors' preference for future income and capital growth over high fixed current income.

(7) Tax: rates vary according to status as individual, corporation, pension fund or charity. The latter two institutions are not liable for corporation or capital gains tax and can therefore aim for either high income or capital growth. Individuals paying high rates of tax on income may prefer to invest in low-yielding assets with the prospects of capital gains where the rate of tax is lower. Companies too may prefer to invest in low-yielding assets with potential for capital appreciation against which they will be able to borrow.

The rational investor will consider all factors. The net attractiveness of the investment will be reflected in its yield. The higher the risk, the less protection against inflation; the less the prospect of capital gain, the greater will be the current income required to compensate. This pattern is general throughout the investment market whether property or stocks and shares.

Property yields do not exist in a vacuum; there is an interrelationship between yields from different property investments. Similarly there is a relationship between yields in different sectors of the stock market. Clearly there is also a relationship between property and all non-property yields, each reflecting assessments of present and future risk characteristics of the different investments.

The general level as compared with the pattern of yields in a sector is fundamentally influenced by the state of the economy and by government economic policy. The minimum lending rate (MLR) at which the Bank of England was prepared to lend money to the money market was broadly the key to the level of yields until 1981. It was then replaced by base rate. When MLR (Bank Rate to 1972) was increased, so too were most other rates, borrowing became more expensive throughout the economy and yield consequently increased. Between June 1972 and December 1973, MLR was increased from 5 to 13 per cent, establishing a new high plateau for interest rates which lasted to the mid-1980s. Yields on all fixed interest investments rose. In 1975, the yields on long-dated gilts rose to 17 per cent while capital values fell. Yields on all property investments increased – though less dramatically. Prime offices selling on a 3.7 per cent yield in November 1972, a post-war low, were on offer at approximately 7 per cent by December 1974; consequently property capital values fell sharply. Conversely, the resilience of prime property as an investment was shown between 1978 and 1980. Average bank base rates increased from 8½ to 16½ per cent. Prime office yields remained relatively stable at around 5 per cent while yields on both fixed interest stocks and equities increased as capital values fell.

Assuming rational behaviour, the potential investor will consider each property on offer in comparison with other property and non-property investments. Fundamentally, property and non-property interests are competing for investment yields. A price movement in one sector will affect demand for investment in the other.

Differences between Property and Non-property Investment

The essential differences between property and non-property investment derive from the unique characteristics of the property market. The absence of a central institution, imperfection of knowledge and the uniqueness of individual properties lead to problems of valuation and marketability not faced by stock market investors. In addition there are other significant factors:

(1) Investment in property necessitates the employment of professionals such as surveyors and solicitors. This increases the expenses of property transactions and also delays completion; the title to each individual property interest will need to be proved before any sale can take place. With stocks and shares it is not essential for an investor to employ professional advice although many may choose to do so especially if large sums are involved.

(2) Unlike stocks and shares, property cannot be purchased direct in small units and it is therefore out of the question for the small investor; most direct investment in property is by institutions. The small investor may obtain an indirect stake in property through investing in shares of property companies or being a policy holder with an insurance company. Direct investment in property, with a portfolio spread and management expertise, has been the great attraction of property bonds.

(3) The property market may often be vulnerable to legislation. Residential rent controls, taxation of development gains and betterment, and the freezing of commercial rents under the Prices and Incomes Policy 1972–74 are examples of

public intervention which affect both incomes from real property and investment values. The refusal or grant of planning consent can destroy, create or redistribute wealth.

(4) Generally the income on real property can only be adjusted periodically, typically in the United Kingdom at the end of a lease or when a rent reversion is due. Therefore incomes from property investments tend to adjust more slowly to changing conditions than income from comparable investments, and higher yields may be necessary to compensate. Generally the nearer in time to a reversion and the larger its extent in relation to current income, the more it will influence the yield in a downwards direction. The advantage of property investment is that the date when income variation may take place is known with relative certainty. This does not apply to investment in equities where future income is uncertain; hence the commercial property rent freeze brought great uncertainty into the property sector.

CYCLES: THE PROPERTY MARKET BOOM AND COLLAPSE, 1972–75, AND THE PROPERTY BOOM, 1986–87

In a boom the government may stimulate effective demand, share prices rise, and yields fall, anticipating growth in dividends and capital gains. Within the property market, rents increase, yields fall and capital values increase. In a recession, effective demand will be curbed as confidence ebbs with tighter monetary and fiscal measures. Incomes, employment and share prices fall and on the stock markets yields rise. Property investors, attracted by higher yields, may consider switching outside property as will institutions with new money to invest. Property sales slow down, prices fall and yields rise. The process will continue until a new equilibrium is reached in which investment funds have been recycled to yield maximum utility to investors.

Between 1969 and 1970 a severe credit squeeze and falling confidence resulted in stock market values declining by approximately 30 per cent. The property market reacted differently. Institutions, disenchanted with equities and fixed interest, poured funds into property. Thus while share prices fell, underlying property values were maintained and in many cases sharply increased. A similar pattern was repeated through 1973. Stagflation, international economic and political crises precipitated a disastrous slide in share values. The property market, although affected by high record interest rates and general economic uncertainty, stayed relatively firm although the number of transactions was reduced and prime yields moved marginally upwards partly as a reaction to the 50 per cent surge in office rents in London between 1972 and 1973. The demand for agricultural land continued to boom and property bonds continued to be popular with small investors.

It was not until 1974 that the great post-war property boom really collapsed. The boom of the early 1970s, fuelled by a combination of inflation and an imbalance between the supply and demand for space, gathered impetus as governments imposed and maintained restrictions on new developments. The apparently inevitable increase in property values created a situation in which property companies indulged increasingly in deficit financing whereby the income from the property purchased fell far short of the interest on the borrowings used to fund the purchase. Clearing, merchant and secondary banks provided as much as 100 per cent of the finance for a scheme. A combination of uncertainty over the duration of the rent freeze, penal interest rates and the prospect of fiscal measures to curb development profits hit the property market. Values fell and with them secondary banks whose fortunes were intimately connected with the property sector. Major property groups collapsed. It was necessary for the Bank of England and major clearing banks to launch a lifeboat operation to save widespread collapse as it became apparent that many secondary banks would have a deficit of net tangible assets, if valued on a break-up basis, because of the fall in property values. There was grave concern that property bonds, many of which down-valued their units, might suffer from heavy withdrawals. Such turmoil in the financial system would ultimately have an indirect effect on industry and foreign confidence in the City of London would be undermined.

In Central London and in the provinces, rents fell by at least 20 per cent from the peaks reached in 1973. The implications for property values were grim. The attractions of a reversionary situation (with the possibility of increased income when the present lease ends) had in any case been undermined by the establishment of a rent control precedent; now they were virtually extinguished by the possibility that future leases might be made at rents lower than at the present time. For many property development companies there was also the question of how existing loans were to be serviced if expected increase in rent failed to materialise. Many British developers, in the face of an uncertain market, the Community Land Act, which threatened to eliminate many of the attractions of private development, and spiralling costs, abandoned schemes. The situation was worsened by approximately £2700 million of property overhanging the market as a result of the collapse of major property groups.

However the collapse of the property market was relatively small compared with the catastropic fall in share values as measured by the *Financial Times* All-Share Index which fell to 60 in December 1974 following an unprecedented steep fall in values from a high of 230 in 1972. This crash was worse than that which preceded the great depression of the 1930s (figure 4.3).

A result of the 1974-75 collapse was that many property companies were forced to sell off many of their portfolios of investment properties to financial institutions in order to improve cash flows. Consequently, the role of the property company as an investor declined leaving development as its principal function so far as prime sites were concerned. The Bank of England 'lifeboat' scheme organised the orderly sale of vast amounts of property to the institutions in order to pay off debt. Even so, several property companies went into liquidation and most had to reduce their portfolios substantially. Between 1973 and 1977 the

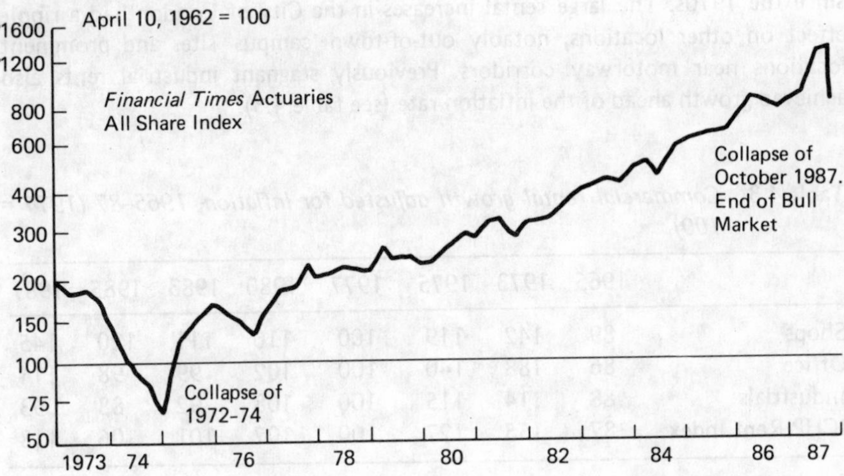

Figure 4.3 *Share price movements, 1973–87*

institutions acquired some £4000 million of property, of which £2000 million can be attributed to acquisitions under the 'lifeboat' scheme, much of this being in offices. These massive institutional acquisitions reached a peak of about 21 per cent of total investment in 1974. The institutions were operating in a buyers' market at this period, although subsequently a reduction in the supply of good-quality property forced yields downwards. The lesson of the mid-1970's crash was that even in a depressed market institutional funds flow and need to be invested and that in a crisis the attraction of property is in its tangible asset backing, and also that a business defaults on rent only as a last resort.

Leading property indices indicated that between 1977 and 1984 adjusted for inflation there was little real growth in commercial rents.[6] Shop rents had risen in real terms by about 10 per cent but both office and industrial rents had fallen in real terms. Over this period, property investments had not yielded the returns achieved by other investors in equities or fixed interest stocks. The possible over-supply of offices and the continued economic recession contributed to the concern. Briefly, there was discussion that property had lost favour as an inflation hedge compared with government issued index-linked stock. It was suggested that the prospect of a lower rate of inflation might remove part of the rationale for property investment. Essentially, rental growth was unlikely to accelerate until there was a sustained increase in economic activity with improved levels of profitability.

The property boom of 1986–87 was based on rising real incomes, tax cuts, an inflation rate of 4 per cent and an acceleration in economic growth. Together with a shortage of prime sites, rental values for shops were higher than at any time since 1973 in real terms. Office rents too achieved a rental growth not seen since the 1970s. The large rental increases in the City of London had a ripple effect on other locations, notably out-of-town 'campus' sites and prominent locations near motorway corridors. Previously stagnant industrial rents also achieved growth ahead of the inflation rate (see table 4.3).

Table 4.3 *Commercial rental growth adjusted for inflation, 1965–87 (1977 = 100)*

	1965	1973	1975	1977	1980	1983	1985	1987
Shops	89	142	119	100	116	111	120	145
Office	86	188	140	100	102	99	98	114
Industrials	88	114	115	100	108	92	88	93
ICHP Rent Index	87	155	127	100	107	101	106	118

Source: ICHP *Rent Index*, 1987

As capital and rental values increased there was concern that there might be a repeat of the 1973–74 boom and collapse. There was concern that bank lending to property companies was rising, that London office rents were escalating and that speculative development sites were changing hands at contract stage. However there were significant differences. Bank lending to property companies may have equalled the 1974 peak in real terms but in 1973–74 property loans equalled 25 per cent of the banks' total lending; in 1987 it represented only 6 per cent. Banks generally vetted developers and their projects carefully, yet Big Bang brought many speculative schemes forward that were dependent on a continuing rental boom and rises in capital value. Increased competition among lenders reduced bank margins on property loans and possibly resulted in them taking more risks than were prudent.

Much of the sharp rises in London property values and office rents came from organic growth in the financial and service sectors. In London and the City in particular, the deregulation of financial markets with Big Bang meant additional demand from an influx of foreign banks and security houses. The expansion of domestic credit and the rising stock market added to demand. The type of space required by financial and professional firms changed; existing buildings could not provide the size of units or infrastructure needed by large international and national organisations. Hence this additional pressure on the limited suitable space resulted in London rentals increasing by 35 per cent in the City core and by 70 per cent in some fringe areas. Even so, rents were only 60 per cent of 1973 levels in real terms. The long lead times on development causes short-term imbalances which lead to periods of fast rental growth which slacken when the new supply comes to the market (see the discussion on Development cycles in chapter 5). It was anticipated that at least 20 million square feet of office space would be built in the City and Docklands by 1989. The massive development at Canary Wharf on the Isle of Dogs would add 9 million square feet.

In October 1987, the long bull market in equities which had lasted since 1975 ended. Share prices in London fell by 30 per cent in a week (see figure 4.3). The collapse of share prices was worldwide – in Hong Kong prices fell by 33 per cent in a day. The dramatic collapse of the stock market emphasised the volatile nature of equities after Big Bang. It was likely adversely to affect the occupational demand for expensive new office space in the City of London and Docklands from international financial companies and ancillary services. Developers who had pre-let or pre-sold were relatively secure; speculative developments were vulnerable as were over-geared property companies with optimistically valued assets. Any falls in property values and rises in yields were, however, likely to attract financial institutions back into direct property investment, thus providing support for property values. The relative stability and security of property would once again be revealed.

REFERENCES

1. D. R. Denman, *Land in the Market*, Hobart Paper (Instiute of Economic Affairs, 1964).
2. *An Analysis of Commercial Property Values* 1962–1979 (Michael Laurie & Partners, 1980).
3. *The MGL–CIG Property Index* 1978–86 (Morgan Grenfell Laurie, 1987).
4. *Money into Property* (Debenham Tewson & Chinnocks, 1987).
5. P. R. A. Kirkman and D. C. Stafford, 'The Property Bond Movement 1966–74', *National Westminster Bank Quarterly Review* (February, 1975).
6. *ICHP Rent Index* (Hillier Parker, *Investors' Chronicle*).

5

Economics of Development and Investment Appraisal

THE NATURE AND TYPES OF DEVELOPMENT

Development is the process of carrying out works involving a change in the physical use or in the intensity of an existing use of land or buildings. Development may be a lengthy process from the original conception to change the existing use, to survey, design, estimates, preliminary discussion with various public bodies, land acquisitions, to the formal application for planning consent. Constant appraisal of the cost implications of the scheme and financial arrangements are necessary until successful completion.

There are two main categories of developers: public including local authorities, and private including property development companies and other institutions. There are significant differences in objectives and also legal status. Public developers only have received special privileges including extensive powers of compulsory purchase under legislation such as the Community Land Act 1975 (abolished 1980) – ultimately the public statutory duty. Much public development is non-profit-making or only semi-commercial, such as the building of libraries. Public developers take a longer, wider view than a private developer. The most economic development, given constraints, will be that showing the greatest return in terms of aesthetics or function to the community for the minimum capital invested. A local education authority must consider trends in the growth of the child population over the next decade; a highway authority may consider road proposals which cannot be achieved for twenty years. The indirect costs and benefits of the scheme in relation to other activities will be carefully appraised.

Private development is essentially profit motivated. The unity of the environment and its quality, externalities and the interplay of social, political and economic factors will not be considered. A function of planning authorities is to make private developers bear some of the indirect costs created by imposing planning conditions. It is clear that there can be divergence between the aims of planning authorities and private development.

Many developments are complex and costly. The risks are great, especially for speculative developments, as fundamental changes may occur in the market before the scheme is successfully completed. Many schemes fail because of unforeseen factors which have an adverse effect upon the initial calculations of the developer. Adverse legislation and changes in economic policy which may bring higher taxes and interest rates make marginal projects unprofitable; costs of labour and material may soar. Losses may occur because of unexpected capital expenditure, problems with underground services, or additional work needed to satisfy town planning requirements. Inadequate research into income and prices of existing houses may mean provision of dwellings for which the demand is limited, resulting in unsold buildings. Schemes fail because too high a price has been paid for land in anticipation of increases in prices continuing. There are four basic ingredients to a successful development: a well located site, purchased at the right price, correct financing and sufficient expertise to carry out the development.

SITE SELECTION

The acquisition of the site is usually the developer's first major commitment to the development project; from the limited land which is available, the ideal site satisfying all requirements can rarely be found. It may take a private developer many years to assemble a city centre site. In selecting sites, therefore, the developer must usually compromise in his requirements. A multiple store can rarely sacrifice location, a hypermarket may sacrifice location in order to obtain more space; an office requires a central location, a single-storey factory needs space. Price may be the crucial factor but each site has its own characteristics which will influence its suitability for development for a particular purpose.

Space

Requirements will vary greatly with the type, number of units and size of development proposed, the density of building allowed and whether any extensions to the scheme are likely.

Physical Characteristics

Industrial development requires a reasonably level site. Housing may be developed on sloping sites but this involves extensive earthworks and more expensive foundations. A cleared site will be preferred as site clearance involves additional expense. The subsoil should have reasonable load-bearing capacity and the site should be free of soil pollution and from the possibility of flooding.

Public Utility Services

Developers require some or all services available, or to be made available. Private installations are expensive both to provide and to operate. Industrial developments are especially demanding in their requirements for essential services. Inability to provide essential services at an economic cost may effectively prevent development from taking place.

Accessibility

A location and environment suitable to a housing development and nearness to shops and schools may not suit an industrial development requiring access to labour, raw materials and markets. Offices may require a central city location for external economies, the prestige of a central city address, and the possibility of better communication with other parts of the country. Out-of-town locations with access to motorway or ring-roads will also be demanded.

Legal Aspects

The leasehold or freehold interest needs to be acquired. There may be easements, restrictive covenants or public rights of way. It may be possible to overcome them: by payments, offering alternative ways, or setting aside outmoded restrictive covenants. Public authorities may more easily overcome such impediments and have the power of compulsory acquisition. In addition, permission must be obtained from various public authorities, who may impose restrictions on the use and development of the site.

(a) *Planning authorities:* structure and local plans will indicate the uses to which the site may be put and the permitted densities. They will indicate how adjoining areas are to be developed and the location and extent of major public works, such as new roads; planning authorities may impose requirements as to design or materials or make preservation orders on trees which can possibly restrict the form and extent of development. There are often delays in obtaining planning permission which is required for most forms of development unless it constitutes *permitted development*.

(b) *Highway authorities:* under the Highway Act 1959 a developer is normally required to submit plans of any new streets for approval. Authorities may prescribe improvement lines restricting development between the improvement line and the street. Building lines may also be prescribed beyond which no building will generally be permitted. In both cases the developer loses part of his site for profitable development.

(c) Until 1982, *Department of Trade and Industry* (DTI) permission was required for Industrial Development Certificates. Where certificates were refused by the DTI, no right of appeal existed and the local planning authority was unable to grant planning permission for the project.

(d) *Department of Environment* (DOE): office development permits were required until 1979, and where these were refused, planning permission would not be granted. The DOE lists buildings of special architectural or historic interest which cannot be demolished or altered so as to seriously affect their character without obtaining local planning consent. A listed building can create a major difficulty in a development scheme.

(e) *Building requirements:* local authorities are responsible for ensuring that all building work is carried out to certain minimum standards of construction. For most of England and Wales the requirements are laid down in the Building Regulations. Even comparatively minor alterations and improvements require consent.

FINANCIAL CALCULATIONS FOR PRIVATE DEVELOPMENT AND THE PRICE OF LAND

Thus, prior to the purchase of a site a developer must know what development will be permitted and to what density. He also needs a financial appraisal including a projection covering building costs, finance charges and the likely rent or selling price of the completed development. It will indicate the feasibility of the scheme and is likely to include the following.

The Gross Development Value (GDV)

The anticipated value of the development on completion may be calculated for commercial property on an investment basis on the estimated total annual rent accruing from the development less the cost of outgoings. The net annual income is capitalised by multiplying by an appropriate year's purchase to obtain the GDV. The choice of multiple may create problems; the valuer advises on the basis of his knowledge of the market and current practice. However, there is no definitive method of valuation and much of it is intuitive. There is a fundamental difference between the valuer and the quantity surveyor, the latter being more cost conscious and working with tangible cost data.

The problem of valuation assumed a particularly acute form between 1971 and 1974 with sharper than normal movements in investment yields. For example, in early 1971 the yield on prime properties was around 6 per cent, by December 1972 yields had touched a post-war low of 3.75 per cent, indicating a sharp rise in the value of developments and completed buildings. The reverse occurred during 1974–76 when, plagued with uncertainty and financial collapse, the market in investment property came to a virtual standstill. Properties may be valued reflecting their future trading or redevelopment potential. A housing developer will estimate his GDV on anticipated selling prices in the area based on local knowledge. Values will vary with location, environment, character of the development and changes in the economic conditions.

Building Costs

Building unit rates are often computed per square metre of floor area to assess the total building costs of the development. A quantity surveyor's knowledge of cost analysis and data will be essential. Sharp increases occurred in building costs between 1973 and 1975 (weak demand conditions resulted in developers' inability to pass on these cost increases to purchasers). Sharply increased costs in the late 1970s saw housebuilders increasing their prices as demand allowed.

Professional Charges

The cost of specialist skills must be considered. The architects' and surveyors' fees cover the preparation of all drawings and contract documents, survey and supervision and financial arrangements for the contract. A large development organisation is likely to have its own 'in-house' design staff to carry out basic work, employing consultants to obtain variety and to cope with peak periods. It can also provide cost guidance and feedback from experience. It deals with abortive and *ad hoc* investigations and speculative work. It can advise on the appropriate fee for outside consultancy work. Legal costs are incurred on the purchase of the site, to buy out easements, to close rights of way and to prepare leases. Agents carry out research in an area and fees will be incurred on advertising and disposing of the property. This will be influenced by the number of units in the development; special fees may be negotiated where there is clear repetition of work. Approximately 2 per cent of the GDV may be allowed for agency and legal fees and 10 per cent or more of the value of building work for architects' and surveyors' fees.

Cost of Finance

To purchase a site a developer will either borrow or he will use his own capital. The interest paid or the revenue foregone should be charged to the development from the date of purchase of the site to when the completed building is let or sold. Building cost finance is usually calculated at market rate on one half of the building costs for the full contract period, or the full costs for half of the contract period. For only a limited period will the contractor make full use of the funds available. Interest rate changes are a major development risk unless long-term finance with an institution has been arranged. A sharp rise can change a profitable scheme into a loss-making one.

The developer's profit is the return for the entrepreneurial risk-taking function, risk involving rising costs, falling rents, changing legislation and the inability to dispose of property on completion. The amount will depend upon the size and type of development, the degree of risk and gearing and the time before completion.

Thus the price a developer can afford to pay for a site is restricted. On the one hand the rent or sale price of the finished development is determined by the market in relation to the size and quality of the building, and on the other side the price offered for the site is determined by the market in relation to its location and current demand. The developer must assess all costs of construction and finance against the likely selling price; since the stock of buildings is large compared with the annual amount of building, the market price for new building is determined more by demand than the costs of construction. The price-bid for the site should enable the developer to cover all costs including profits; it must also be sufficient to make it worth while for the owner to sell. Thus the maximum available for site expenditure will be a residual cost after all other expenditures have been taken into account. There is a relationship between the size and quality of a building and the price it will fetch. It may be worth spending more on a building if as a result it will sell for a higher price. The expected price of a building therefore implies a given size and standard; the development will only be worth while if it can be built within the price constraints including land acquisition costs.

Table 5.1 illustrates a developer's budget for five terraced two-bedroom houses assuming a selling price of £60 000 each and interest charges of 15 per cent on maximum borrowings of £200 000 for six months with a total development period of one year, yielding a useful profit of £45 000. However, a 20 per cent increase in building costs to, say, £192 000 together with a lengthening con-

Table 5.1 *Developer's budget*

	£	£
Gross Development Value (GDV)		300 000
Building costs		
Costs of labour, plant and site overheads	160 000	
Costs of materials, subcontractors' fees	24 000	
Interest charges at 15 per cent	15 000	
Total development expenditure	199 000	
Developers' profit, say 15 per cent of GDV	45 000	
Maximum available for site acquisition	56 000	
	300 000	300 000

struction period due to problems on site increasing interest charges to £25 000 might change this profitable scheme into a loss maker. Difficulty in disposing of all the houses at the price anticipated might also jeopardise the scheme.

OPTIMAL DEVELOPMENT

Since a relationship exists between the size and quality of a building and the price or rent it can command, we need to examine more closely the question of whether it is worth spending more on a building if, as a result, it will sell for a higher price.

In order to maximise site-bid, development of a site should continue as long as the addition of an extra unit of capital increases GDV by a greater amount than it adds to the total cost of development. This situation is analysed graphically in figure 5.1. The figure assumes a given use (such as offices) and standard of construction. The horizontal axis measures – in units of £1000 – the quantity of capital in the form of all construction and development expenditure applied to the site, including an allowance for normal profit. The cost of a unit of capital is measured on the vertical axis. We assume for simplicity that the cost of an

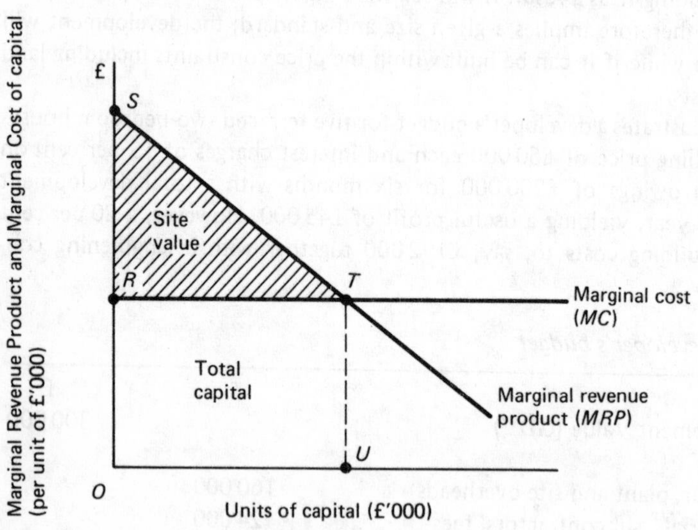

Figure 5.1 *Optimal site development and site-bid*

additional unit remains constant, hence the marginal cost (MC) curve forms a horizontal straight line. The MC curve will be higher the greater the level of interest charges and the longer the capital is tied up in the development.

The marginal revenue product (MRP) curve shows the amount by which total returns (that is, GDV) are increased by the addition of one extra unit of capital. This estimate, as we saw earlier, could be based either on annual rental less outgoings or anticipated selling price on completion. MRP is shown as declining as total capital applied to the site increases, illustrating the process of diminishing marginal returns to a fixed factor (that is, land). This may occur for several reasons: greater height may involve substantial additional expenditure on foundations or car parking, lifts and fire escapes may be required, and construction costs may also rise. Rents on higher floors may also diminish, especially with retailing.

The optimum level of development is at point *T* where *U* units of capital are applied to the site and where the MRP of an additional unit of capital just equals the marginal cost of that unit. The total cost of capital is given by *ORTU* (that is, £*OR* per unit x *OU* units), whereas total returns or GDV is given by *OSTU*. The difference between the two is *RST*, representing the surplus or maximum amount left over once costs are deducted. It is also the maximum sum the developer can bid for the site – at a higher or lower level of capital investment, maximum site-bid would fall below *RST*.

Factors influencing Site-bid

Maximum site-bid will rise if either the MRP curve rises or the MC curve falls (and vice versa). A rise in the MRP curve could occur if: (1) the value of the finished product rises, (2) capital productivity rises, for example, through technological advance, or (3) there is a fall in the price of any inputs, such that a unit of expenditure on capital results in a higher level of output (and higher MRP given a constant price for output). A fall in the marginal cost curve could arise if: (1) the interest rate falls, (2) there is a reduction in the construction time such that capital is tied up for a shorter period, or (3) with reduced risk, a loan on more favourable terms can be achieved. In practice, changes influencing any of the above factors are likely to affect different types of development in rather different ways, perhaps favouring some land uses relative to others.

Different land uses (such as offices, retailing, housing) will result in different site-bids because of differences in capital intensity (for example, offices may use more floors than retailing) and differences in the occupier's profitability from use of floor space – for example, High Street retailing as opposed to residential uses. If there were no controls over land use, then competition would ensure that a particular site would go to its highest and best use – that is, the use providing the highest possible site-bid. Although the developer would clearly like to pay less than this, competition between developers should ensure that each puts in a maximum bid in an effort to obtain the site. However, even among similar development schemes (for example, housing) different site-bids may result; although this may be due to differences in efficiency as between developers, it is important to recognise that it may also result from qualitative differences in layout, density levels or even construction standards.

In practice, the planning process may restrict the type of use to which land may be put, or limits may be placed on the maximum permissible height of the building – thus restricting the amount of capital which may be applied to the site. Also, location will significantly affect the profitability of any particular land use.

Finally, MRP will decline at different rates in different land uses; for example, while office users may be largely indifferent to high rise buildings, housing developers may find that as total capital and housing densities increase, so this may reduce the anticipated selling prices of all and not just additional units. Where units of capital are large and indivisible (for example, successive floors in office blocks) MRP declines in a stepwise fashion. This is shown in both figure 5.2 and table 5.2, which also illustrate the point that rising costs result in higher capital requirements for successive floors.

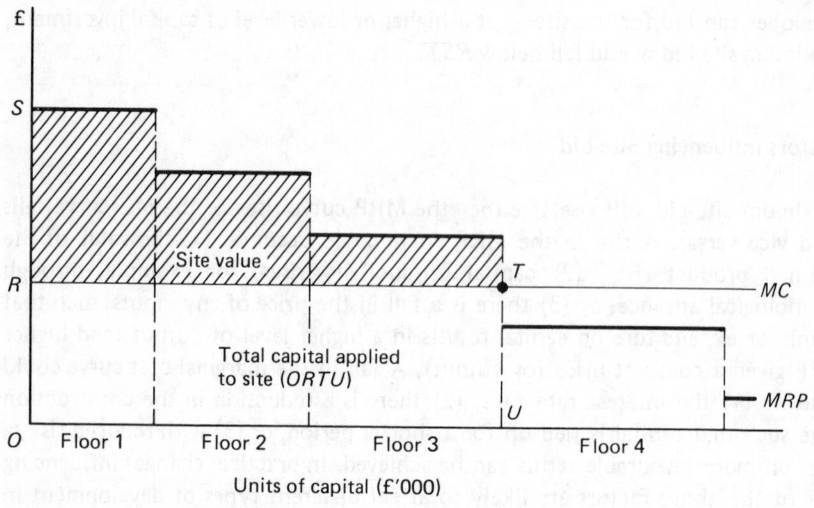

Figure 5.2 *Multi-storey development*

Where several uses are considered together, the analysis becomes more complex. For example, increased site value may result from the addition of ground floor shops to a residential block of flats (see figure 5.3).

On a larger scale, city centre or out-of-town shopping and leisure developments will require very careful consideration in order to obtain the correct mix and location of activities and facilities (for example, parking and access to public transport) to achieve a maximum value for the available site.

Table 5.2 *The cost, revenue and site value of a hypothetical office development**

Floor	Capital outlay per floor (marginal cost) (£)	Rent per floor (marginal revenue product) (£)	Residual (site) value per floor (£)
4	95 000	70 000	−15 000
3	75 000	80 000	5 000
2	60 000	90 000	30 000
1	50 000	100 000	50 000
Totals to third floor	Cost 185 000	GDV 270 000	Site value 85 000

*Present value.

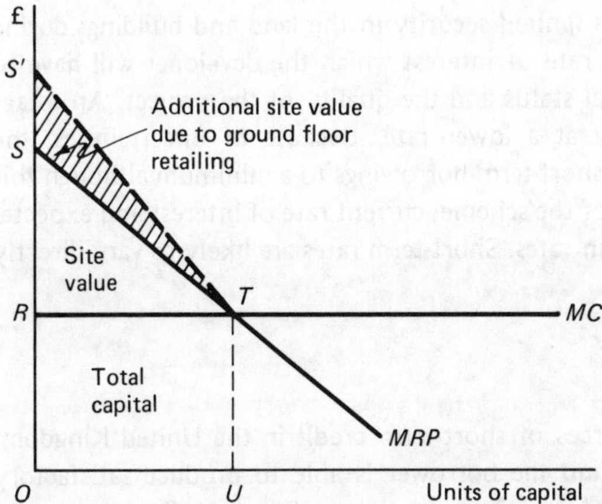

Figure 5.3 *Maximisation of site value for given capital investment*

SOURCES OF FINANCE FOR DEVELOPMENT

The type of finance required will depend on the development period and whether it is intended to retain the interest as an investment or to sell it. If the latter, the developer will need medium- or short-term finance, probably from the banks, for site acquisition and to cover construction costs. Long-term investment, generally the aim of property development companies in the United Kingdom, involves borrowing against the security of the development or creating an interest which may be sold to an institution. Because a development company frequently retains its investment, its financial structure is somewhat unusual. Revenue is mainly rents and premiums paid for rent concessions. For a company to expand, it needs to raise equity capital or borrow. Since most development companies do not trade but merely retain property, accumulated unrealised assets may change in value without affecting the profit and loss account, although they are reflected in the balance sheet. This distinction is significant as property companies have been accused of making exorbitant profits from changes in the market values of their unrealised permanent investments. Programming expenditure is crucial to planning the development so that capital remains unproductive for as short a period as possible. There are significant differences between private and public developers' source of finance; the latter will be discussed later.

Short- and Medium-term Finance

This is generally available for maximum periods of up to five years. It may be relatively expensive as there is limited security in the land and buildings during the construction period. The rate of interest which the developer will have to pay depends upon his financial status and the quality of the project. An established company may borrow at a lower rate. Because of uncertainties, the developer will prefer to keep short-term borrowings to a minimum although this will depend upon the length of the scheme, current rate of interest and expectations regarding future trends in rates. Short-term rates are likely to vary directly with changes in base rate.

Clearing banks

These are the traditional sources of short-term credit in the United Kingdom. Provided projects are sound and the borrower is able to produce satisfactory collateral, funds may be available at 2–5 per cent above base rate. Banks generally loan up to 70 per cent of the value of the scheme and normally do not require equity participation. Sometimes an arrangement fee is charged, usually 1 per cent of the facility arranged. With stable rates of interest this is a satisfactory and relatively cheap way of raising funds.

Removal of controls over bank lending in 1971 saw the banks as major lenders to property companies. Between 1971 and 1975, bank advances to property companies increased over sixfold. This rapid and very large increase was a factor in the general destabilisation and collapse of the property market in the mid-1970s. Following the collapse, the clearing banks drastically reduced their commitments even to the well-established companies and from 1975 to 1979 were net disinvestors to property developers. With the property boom of 1986-87, bank lending on new development accelerated so that by mid-1987 total loans to property companies and developers exceeded £5 billion or 4½ per cent of total advances. This was some 40 per cent lower in real terms than the peak lending to the sector of the mid-1970s. Residential mortgages substantially exceeded loans to property companies.

Merchant and secondary banks

These were an important alternative source of short-term finance for property development until the financial crisis of December 1973. Groups with large equity backing such as listed property companies or larger private development companies were favoured.

Secondary banks were responsible for much of the new money between 1972 and 1974, and the concentration of debt on banks with a low capital base was a major factor in the subsequent collapse. Some banks lent incautiously and the collateral available from the property company was often inadequate. Gearing among property companies was very high and the proportion of short-term debt on variable interest rates was too high to withstand the abrupt change in economic conditions.

Interest rates were higher than those charged by the clearers but were sometimes fixed for up to two years. Funds were generally available for development but often on an equity participation basis. This often suited the developer since risks were shared and he paid out only realised profits. An established developer was able to borrow as much as 100 per cent of his development expenses often on the basis of a revolving credit of a maximum amount being available for up to two years. The bank had the right to approve specific projects on which it agreed to provide all development costs. The developer was obliged to offer all proposals to the bank which could call for properties to be revalued, and if the value was below the total costs incurred the bank might call for additional security or for the loan to be redeemed. As a result of the failure of several 'fringe' banks in 1974, the merchant banks became much more cautious in their lending to property companies – between 1975 and 1978 calling in over £600 million in loans.

In the mid-1980s the merchant banks were again active, although their role was largely confined to investment banking and underwriting. Lending to property companies as a percentage of merchant banks total advances fell to 8.4 per cent during 1986.

Foreign banks

Since the 1960s, foreign banks in the United Kingdom have shown remarkable growth rates in the volume of business and also in numbers. By the early 1980s there were around 200. With 'Big Bang' in 1986 this increased to over 400 banks in London alone. By 1987, foreign banks accounted for over £3.7 billion of loans, about 30 per cent of total loans to property companies.[1] North American, West European, Australian and Japanese banks predominated. Unlike the clearers, foreign banks were prepared for longer-term involvement, often in particularly large or complex development schemes. Most of these banks were subsidiaries of large parents based overseas and for whom they conduct foreign business; they thus have huge resources. Their rates are often cheaper than those of merchant and clearing banks and they have been prepared to loan 80 per cent on a suitable project. Large loans were syndicated among other banks with only a small proportion of the total value held by the initiating bank.

Syndication

Syndicated loans have been a feature of the mid-1980s. Syndication allows a single bank to arrange an advance that exceeds its normal size limit and then to reduce the bank's exposure by inviting others to participate. Risk reduction allied to higher returns on very large projects have encouraged such arrangements. The increased activity in sharing debt among the banks has created new opportunities for borrowers and lenders alike. Syndication also allows smaller banks to participate in high-quality development that would normally be beyond their loan limits.

Limited recourse loans

Limited and non-recourse lending was an innovation of the late 1980s.[1] Property companies were able to arrange special-purpose loans confined to an individual project. The exposure of the parent company is limited should any difficulties subsequently arise. A subsidiary or joint venture company is usually created for the specific development and the capital structure organised so that the sponsor company has less than 50 per cent equity. The evolution of this practice indicates the borrowing strength and degree of security offered by major development companies.

Trade credit

This is significant for most developers. It is the time interval between receiving plant and materials and paying for these. Trade credit, often 30 days, is therefore a useful source of working capital free of interest. Delays in payment may effectively reduce the capital required to fund a contract, although too long delays in payment may undermine the commercial confidence in the company. As interest rates have risen so builders' merchants have restricted both the credit amount and period allowed for payment, which might adversely affect cash flow for some developers.

Long-term Finance

The mortgage

Traditionally, funds were borrowed over 20–30 years at a fixed rate of interest and repaid at the end of the term. However, inflation and rising interest rates have disadvantaged the lender: capital has depreciated in value and has earned a rate of interest substantially less than the market rate. Average interest rates have tended to increase; average Bank Rate was about 3.5 per cent between 1946 and 1959, while MLR averaged over 9 per cent between 1976 and 1986. Consequently mortgages are now repaid by annual instalments over the period of the mortgage. The lender thus recovers his capital over the term of the loan and may reinvest it at current rates; however, he still has no protection against inflation. The disadvantage to the borrower of repayment by annual instalments is that though interest may be charged against taxable income, capital payments cannot. In addition, income from the property may be insufficient to provide for both interest and capital, and there may be a negative cash flow. Generally, no more than 70 per cent of the value of the security may be borrowed by mortgage.

An alternative to the straight mortgage is the mortgage debenture. Funds are advanced against the security of a particular property, but in addition the lender has a charge over all assets of the company. Should it be necessary to enforce repayment of the loan by selling the security and an insufficient sum is realised, the lender can claim on the other assets to liquidate the balance of the debt. Repayment of the mortgage debenture is at the end of the loan period. The lender has a fixed interest investment with a substantial security but no hedge against inflation. With real interest rates in the 1980s at exceptionally high levels, debentures and mortgages lost favour with developers as a means of financing projects.

A variation is the convertible loan stock. The lender has an option to purchase ordinary shares in the company at some future date at a fixed price in proportion to the amount of loan stock held. If the lender does not take up his option, he continues to receive interest at an agreed rate until the redemption date. The lender thus links the advantages of a fixed interest stock with protection against inflation. A further variation is where debenture holders receive both a fixed rate of interest and also part of the profits after the developer has received a fixed return on the total costs of development. These trends reflect the increasing sophistication of lenders in protecting their funds against the ravages of inflation.

The sale and leaseback

This method has increasingly been used since the 1960s as interest rates increased. The developer, having orginally acquired the site and erected buildings, sells an interest to an institution which then grants a lease to the developer. Thus the developer continues to have the use of the property while obtaining funds to finance another scheme. Initially, leases were as long as 99 years at a rent representing a percentage return to the institution for the acquisition of the interest. The rents are subject to reviews; the tendency has been for the reviews and leases to be at ever shorter periods (reflecting inflationary pressures). Whereas in the 1950s a 50-year interval was not uncommon, by the 1980s reviews were often at 5- or 7-year intervals, while leases were for 25–35 years.

The advantage to the institution of the sale and leaseback is that the security of both income and capital is good. The transaction is not normally concluded until the property has been developed and let. The main types of development involved are prime commercial properties. Shops are especially favoured as their location is usually in central thoroughfares where site value is very high. The investor is relieved of management obligations since the development company takes the lease on full repairing and insuring terms. Under sale and leaseback, the developer may obtain 100 per cent of the value of the asset as compared with two-thirds with a mortgage – although the larger the sum raised the less the security of the purchaser, who will therefore require a higher yield. The disadvantage to the development company is that having disposed of a substantial part of its assets it only retains a relatively small profit rent; it has to meet a substantial head rent before it takes its profit. Should the developer wish to sell his profit rental to raise capital or to pledge it for security for temporary finance, it will be capitalised at a higher rate of interest (less year's purchase) than the rate at which the total income might have been capitalised for raising a mortgage.

A variation on the sale and leaseback is the rent charge. The developer retains the freehold or leasehold of the building but grants the institution a charge on the property for as long as the developer's interest subsists. Rent charges can be made subject to periodic reviews in exactly the same way as rent under a lease. The stage at which the developer can obtain long-term finance, which is much cheaper than short-term, is critical. He must produce a scheme which can be presented to an institution for long-term funding with the risks and unknowns reduced to a minimum.

Various types of leaseback arrangement have evolved, the difference mainly centring on the split of the initial rental income, and subsequent rent increases, between the institutions and the development company. With 'geared leaseback' the institution typically takes the major share of the initial rent (say 70 per cent) plus a small proportion of subsequent rent increases, so that over time its share of the total income declines, and that of the developer increases. With 'ungeared leaseback' their respective shares remain fixed over time; but with the institutional portion guaranteed, the return to the developer can be severely affected if some floor area remains unlet. With the 'reverse leaseback' the institution agrees to purchase a long lease and sub-lets back, enabling the developer to retain the freehold and therefore the certain and marketable bottom slice of income.

Where a developer is building for investment, it is sometimes possible to combine short- and long-term finance. Some institutions are prepared to finance development during the building period. On completion, rent is calculated at an agreed percentage on the total costs of developments. This method of finance is normally only available to well-established developers.

Joint companies

This is an arrangement by which the financing institution and the development company hold shares in agreed proportions. The institution acquires the site and grants a lease to the joint company at an agreed percentage of the total costs of the development. The hedge against inflation for the institution is provided by the equity stake in the joint company. In some cases the site owner becomes a participant, thus effectively creating a similar position to the local authority-private developer partnership where the local authority freeholder, in addition to the ground rent, requires a share in the equity, and the financing institution requires similar equity participation.

A problem of any large company is attracting entrepreneurial talent to its structured organisation. Several large property companies have backed new developers by providing them with finance, generally by forming joint companies in which the developer has the major shareholding while the public company retains financial if not voting control. The developer is free of financial problems while the public company vets the principles of each scheme. Projects too small for the public company are likely to be offered to the joint company.

Share issues

Companies quoted on the Stock Exchange are able to raise long-term capital by additional share issues. Existing shareholders may be given prior rights to subscribe for further shares. These rights enable shareholders to purchase new shares in proportion to their existing holding, and thus their voting power is not diluted. In addition, the rights' issue is made at a privileged price lower than the current market price of existing shares. Many development companies have preferred to increase their gearing, by increasing fixed interest borrowings, rather than to dilute the equity base of the company. However, with higher interest rates, many have resorted to rights' issues with historically low levels of dividend yield and high stock market prices.

Smaller development firms are able to raise funds through 'Juning markets' – the Unlisted Securities Market (USM) and the Over-The-Counter Market (OTC). In both cases the expenses of quotation and the demands for a track record are less rigorous than on the main London Stock Exchange. The USM started in 1980. A USM quote gives advantages to existing shareholders in a private company, enabling them to release part of their investment without any change in control, and allows funds to be raised for company development. A quote gives the potential to use marketable securities for future acquisitions. The company must normally have been trading for at least 3 years and at least 25 per cent of the equity must be available to ensure a spread of shares. OTC shares are quoted by licensed dealers who make the market in the shares.

Among medium-size development companies, internally generated funds may be critical to growth. It is only the large companies that are able to arrange a sophisticated financial strategy to meet changing needs; financial constraints still apply but the large company has a much wider range of options open.

The Business Expansion Scheme

The Business Expansion Scheme (BES) was introduced in 1983, originally the Business Start Up Scheme, as an incentive for taxpayers to invest in unquoted British companies at an early stage in their development. The principal advantage to investors is that they get tax relief at their highest marginal rate for investing in qualifying companies. If held for five years, any gains are free from Capital Gains Tax. Although investment in purely property asset-backed schemes and in agricultural land lost their exemptions, several development companies did use BES as a means of raising equity capital.

Unitisation

By 1986 it was anticipated that a further source of funding would be created by unitisation. Shares or units in single property investment schemes would be traded on the London Stock Exchange. Three new property investment vehicles – Property Income Certificates (PINCs) Single Asset Property Companies (SAPCOs) and Single-Property Owned Trusts (SPOTs) – were proposed.[2] Any of these schemes would be able to offer units directly to the public and to ensure 'tax transparency' – that is, investors should have any income and capital gains produced by their units taxed as if they had invested directly in property. Pension funds were expected to be major purchasers of the units. The Financial Services Act 1986 provided the framework for the legal establishment of these schemes.

It was anticipated that the new markets would add to the range of long-term funding available to developers. Large projects, in particular, would benefit by providing opportunities to a wider range of investors. Smaller funds would have a wider choice and opportunities to invest in schemes beyond their normal scope; market makers would ensure the liquidity hitherto lacking in property investment. Uncertainties related to the size and type of scheme to be offered, the problems of an after market and at what price the new units would trade. Other criteria included adequate investor protection, a ban on insider dealings and access to data and information on buildings. It was likely that the creation of a liquid market in property units would have implications for the quality of building maintenance and the construction industry.

PROPERTY DEVELOPMENT AND INVESTMENT OVERSEAS

With freer capital and money markets, an increasing amount of development and investment overseas has been undertaken by British companies and institutions, particularly in the EEC but also in North America and Australia. The movement overseas developed in the 1960s, peaked in 1973 and then declined. Relatively high yields and good growth prospects initially attracted institutions. Typically, in 1972 Abbey Life Property Bond purchased Tour Madou, an office block in Brussels, which yielded 7 per cent as compared with the 4–5 per cent yields on comparable property in London.

British property companies did not venture overseas until the early 1960s. They concentrated upon domestic expansion as boom conditions prevailed from 1954 onwards.

However, increasing competition for available sites meant higher prices and lower yields. Other factors inhibited the pace of development and made developers look overseas, first to Belgium and then to other EEC countries.

(1) Development controls became increasingly more stringent. Planning permission was becoming longer and more difficult to obtain with the appeal process both time-consuming and costly, thus increasing the risks and the costs of development. Industrial development certificates and office development permits restricted the location of development.

(2) Public sentiment in Britain tended to be increasingly anti-property development. As property values seemed to rise at a faster rate than other assets, property developers became the object of widespread unpopularity. Legislation tended to be politically rather than rationally motivated. Rent controls and freezes had disastrous effects on property investment. Its ownership and development was made less attractive by tax changes: corporation and capital gains taxes and in 1967 a betterment levy. There was the threat of the nationalisation of development land, a wealth tax, and local authorities' increasing awareness of the profitability of central areas for redevelopment.

Thus for the British developer there were attractions in development overseas.

(1) Opportunities to participate in growth-oriented economies in which both income *per capita* and investment opportunities would be greater than those in the United Kingdom.

(2) Risk could be more widely spread.

(3) Unfulfilled demand for modern commercial and industrial developments.

(4) A strong local currency likely to give further capital appreciation compared to sterling.

(5) The necessary infrastructure in EEC countries, the availability of adequate legal, accounting and tax advice on development and the problems of non-resident controlled company. Banks were prepared to lend for property investment and development and competent professional advice and ancillary services were available. There was also the existence of a legal and tax structure not opposed to or penalising property companies.

(6) There were few native property development or investment companies with the expertise of the British companies.

Initially the concentration was on office development such as in Paris and Brussels, but this has broadened into residental and also speculative industrial and warehouse development. Traditionally, in most EEC countries industrialists own their own premises but, as with the office market a letting market emerged, especially around Paris and Brussels. The gradual acceptance of letting in areas where it has previously been unfamiliar is one major result of growing international influence in EEC property markets. A factor was the increasing tightness of finance during the late 1960s; many industrialists began to see the wisdom of selling their existing premises and renting a building modified to their special requirements. Shopping development came later, because local companies were well established. British groups acquired shop investments in major cities such as Amsterdam, and out-of-town shopping centres were developed near Paris. Until 1973 there was a growing scale and widening of the geographical spread of investments, often away from the established centres and into new countries such as Germany, Spain and Italy.

The overseas property boom came to an abrupt halt in 1974. Many companies had as many projects as they could handle; also, because of the increased competition, there had been a drop in investment returns. More fundamental were the effects of the international financial blizzard which brought a rise in interest rates and credit restrictions in most of Europe and North America. For example, whereas in the early 1970s banks in Belgium would grant long-term loans at around 8 per cent interest rate, by the mid-1970s rates had increased to 13 per cent and few banks were willing to make loans. Mortgages were limited to 55 per cent of the value of a project compared with 70 per cent previously. Most foreign development companies depended upon local finance. For example, in France a developer might purchase land or buildings with short-term funds from local banks negotiated on the basis of guarantees from British banks or other institutions. Sometimes 100 per cent of funds could be negotiated locally.

Dependence upon short-term financing in countries such as France was a major weakness. Ideally a development company aims to reach a situation where the yield from rents exceeds the costs of financing a project. In practice, there are situations in which costs are higher than the yield and a negative cash flow emerges which requires additional financing and thus the company is in a vulnerable position. In 1973, legislation in France ended the position whereby foreign companies could raise 100 per cent finance locally. In 1974, the United Kingdom government ended the annual ration of £1 million of official exchange currency available for any EEC investment. This effectively prevented any large transfers of capital from the United Kingdom to Europe. At the same time the difficulties of raising finance for British companies was compounded by domestic liquidity difficulties and the general decline in value of their collateral security with the slide in the British property market during 1974–75. In many cases, companies were forced to sell properties on a falling market to ease the situation.

The worldwide tightening of credit facilities coincided with the tightening of planning measures and building controls in various EEC countries. In Belgium there was a 12-month postponement of most new building projects; work on non-essential schemes was delayed, severely affecting new office development; there were proposals for property taxes to be levied on new office buildings. Increasing awareness of external environmental factors led to closer scrutiny of potential schemes submitted by developers.

Thus the outlook for British developers overseas, especially in Europe, was uncertain. On the positive side, the sharp decline in building, following measures such as the control on the growth of offices in the Paris region, boosted lettings and earlier fears of a temporary glut of office space and a subsequent fall in rents in centres such as Brussels diminished by the late 1970s. The companies with the major liquidity problems withdrew, leaving only the strongest to survive. There was the need for new buildings of all types and the EEC countries with fast-increasing national incomes and potential growth situations could afford them. The strong inflow of international funds created a property market which did not exist before the British incursions. Several British property groups countered local measures against overseas companies by seeking European partners, and included their investments in continental quoted companies.

So far as the real estate profession is concerned, there are signs of improving standards; many French property companies, for example, only employ graduates as development executives. The Fédération Nationale des Constructeurs Promoteurs considered the possibility of introducing examinations. The efficient British company that really knows the market in which it operates, develops co-operative schemes with a local company or British agent and arranges its long-term finance soundly, will still emerge as a major force overseas, particularly in North America, where there has been growth in the number of estate agents from Britain opening offices.

Major economic recession unprecedented in post-war history affected all EEC countries from 1979. Many countries experienced negative real growth between 1980 and 1982 while unemployment in the EEC increased to more than 30 million. Real interest rates stimulated by high US rates rose to post-war peaks. United Kingdom developers and investors freed by the abolition of exchange controls looked further afield to the USA, Australia and Singapore.[3] This trend continued into the late 1980s.

THE DEVELOPMENT CYCLE

The production of commercial buildings and particularly office floor area has proved a very profitable activity since the Second World War because of the difference between the capital value of a completed building and its development costs. The capital value is determined by the rental income and the acceptable yield from investment in property. It is fluctuations in profitability compounded by the long lag between site acquisition and completion of a scheme which create successive cycles of development. The floor area produced in each cycle supplies two markets; the user market for occupiers of office space and the investment market in which financial institutions acquire prime property as long-term assets. The interaction between supply and demand affects rent levels in the user market, and yields and capital values in the investment market. There has tended to be a declining rate of growth in office and industrial activity but an increasing growth in investment demand because of the returns from property investment and the growing weight of institutional funds.

It is the cyclical nature of development which provides the crucial link between profitability in the property sector, the user market and the investment market. The cycle of development proceeds as follows:

(1) The upward pressure of demand leads to increasing rents in the user market and declining yields in the investment market as existing space is taken up.

(2) Capital values rise, so increasing the potential profitability of development.

(3) Developers are encouraged to initiate schemes (although it may be some time before they are completed).

(4) If demand continues to grow, available space will continue to decline and new schemes will be initiated.

(5) The first wave of developments reach the market and there is potential over-supply from the volume of schemes started.

Although the boom appears to be at its height, the profitability of new schemes is much reduced but only when the over-supply actually materialises does development activity slacken off. By this time the volume of newly developed space coming on to the market causes rents to stabilise or fall, yields to rise and capital values to fall. Development then continues at a low level until the supply of available space has declined sufficiently for the cycle to begin again.

There have been three major property booms in the United Kingdom since the Second World War. The boom of the late 1950s and early 1960s and also that of the early 1970s followed the pattern set out above. The boom of 1986–87 appeared likely to be followed by over-supply of space by 1989–90.

Analysis of the development cycle in the City of London by Richard Barras[4] shows significant differences between the first and second post-war booms, both in terms of conditions in the user and investment markets and the consequent extent of floor area redevelopment. In the immediate post-war years there was strong user demand for an increase in the stock of office space because of war damage, low levels of inter-war office building and high rates of growth in office-using activity. Much early development took place on war-damaged sites and the total supply of floor area grew rapidly, often on prime sites close to the City's banking core.

In the second boom, redevelopment of the existing secondary office stock was the dominant activity. Since the best sites in the core were already occupied by prestige offices, the larger redevelopment schemes were forced into the ring around the core.

Regarding cyclical fluctuations in profitability, it is clear that development conditions are most favourable in the early stages of a boom. Because of the time lag between the start and completion of a scheme, conditions decline to their least favourable for schemes started when the boom appears to be at its height. This explains why developers continue to initiate schemes when hind-sight suggests that conditions are not so favourable. Also, typical valuation practice seems to encourage a short-sighted view of development profitability since the potential capital value and construction costs of a scheme are often derived from current rents and costs rather than based on appropriate future estimates. This is particularly significant in that there is a long-term trend for construction costs to take up a decreasing share of development value, leaving an increasing share for site cost and development profit. This is principally because rents and capital values have, on average, been growing faster than construction tender costs. Between 1962 and 1977, capital values rose on average at 13 per cent per year, while construction costs rose about 10 per cent per year.[5] The annualised rate of return on property averaged 13.7 per cent between 1977 and 1987.[6]

INVESTMENT APPRAISAL

Continuing government intervention, changing economic policies, higher inflation, mounting interest rates and building costs and the growing scale of development projects have made the investment decision increasingly complex. All business decisions are made against a background of uncertainty about the future based upon assumptions regarding future needs and an evaluation of all facts, administrative, legal and economic, relating to the viability, social and political acceptability of a scheme.

In reaching a decision the developer may need to choose between alternatives and will need to be equipped with techniques that assist him in his choice. Each alternative will possess a range of respective costs and benefits, some of which can be quantified in money terms, and others 'intangibles' which will probably not be considered by a private developer but will be by a public body. (These special factors will be discussed under cost–benefit analysis in chapter 6.)

The increasing use of computers and operational research, together with increasing need for long-term planning, have contributed to the greater use of rational methods of investment appraisal. Using the relevant techniques a firm can identify the most profitable of a number of projects and after considering constraints, risk and uncertainty make an objective choice.

Conventional Methods of Investment Appraisal

Many investment decisions are taken on the basis of entrepreneurial hunches and experience which do not take sufficient account of the timing of profits derived from the investment, neither do they fully consider all costs and revenues deriving from the project. Two methods of investment appraisal of this type are (1) pay-back method and (2) average rate of return.

Pay-back method

This is a crude form of investment criteria used particularly for smaller projects. The pay-back (PB) is defined as the period it takes for an investment to generate sufficient net profits, after tax, to recover its initial capital outlay in full. Generally, the shorter the period in which the original capital outlay is expected to be recouped (the shorter the PB) the more favourable will be the firm's attitude. PB recognises that earlier returns are preferable to those accruing later and it will have justification when later returns are particularly uncertain. The major weaknesses of the PB method are that it fails to measure long-term profitability since it takes no account of the cash flows beyond the PB period. It also takes no account of the timing of cash flows within the PB period.

Average rate of return method (ARR)

This is the ratio of net profit after tax to capital. However, net profit can be either that made in the first year, or the average made over the lifetime of the project. Similarly capital can be taken as either the initial sum invested or as an average over time of all capital outlays over the life of the project. The process tends to be arbitrary and will give an inaccurate method of investment appraisal which might lead to the selection of projects yielding a sub-maximum return. The result depends on the number of years chosen and it takes no account of the timing of the cash flows.

DISCOUNTING AND THE TIME VALUE OF MONEY

Both ARR and PB fail to take into account that earnings vary over the life of the project and that a sum of money today is worth more than the same amount at a later date. Money has a time value; a given sum now is worth more than an equal and certain sum at some time in the future. This is so even without inflation if the rate of interest is positive because the sum of money now can be invested to earn a rate of interest and accumulate to more in a year. Alternatively the same sum now can be used to reduce borrowings and so avoid interest payments. Thus, if faced with the choice of £100 now or £100 in one year's time, the rational choice would be to take the £100 now. That sum could be invested, let us assume, at a risk-free market rate of interest (say 10 per cent) and would have grown to £110 at the end of the period, $£100 \times (1 + 0.10)^1$, £121 in two years, $£100 \times (1 + 0.10)^2$, £133.1 in three years, $£100 \times (1 + 0.10)^3$. Thus if a sum of money (P) is invested at a rate of interest (r), the sum arising (S) after n years is given by the formula: $S = P\,(1r + r)^n$. Similarly, it can be seen that the offer of a certain £133.1 in three years' time is equivalent to the offer of £100 now. The present value or worth of any sum S due to be received in the future can be calculated by discounting the future sum at the appropriate rate of interest using the formula

$$P = \frac{S}{(1+r)^n} \quad \text{for example } P = \frac{£133.1}{(1+0.10)^3} = £100$$

The present value of any future sum of money is dependent upon two factors: how far in the future the sum is and how high is the rate of interest. The further in the future the sum is or the higher the rate of interest or discount used, the less is the present value of that future sum. Using this discounting technique the potential investor can thus derive an exchange rate for cash flows over differing periods, enabling a rational comparison to be made. The two major techniques are the internal rate of return (IRR) and the net present value (NPV). These are based on the same theoretical approach and lead to identical decisions. Both methods involve the calculation year by year of the net cash flow (NCF) expected from the project, that is, the cash receipts and cash expenditures over its life. Once the cash flow has been estimated and discounted to present values by the appropriate rate it is possible to calculate both the present value and the yield on the development.

Net Present Value

The NPV or earnings profile of a project is the sum of the present values of future cash flows for all years during the project's life. Basically receipts and expenditures falling earlier are more significant than those occurring later; all foreseeable effects on other projects within the business must be incorporated in the calculations. Thus the effects on cash flow should be presented in the form of a timetable showing the estimated effects on outflows and inflows in each of a number of successive accounting periods.

To determine the NPV of a proposed development, the forecast net of tax cash flows are discounted to the time of the initial capital outlay. The rate of interest used to discount will tend to be the opportunity cost of the capital employed, the rate of return that could be earned by investing the money in the next best alternative, or the firm's marginal rate of financing. The NPV method calculates profitability by subtracting the present values of all expenditures when they occur from the present value of all revenues when they occur. Any project that has a positive present value, that is greater than zero, is viable and the one revealing the highest NPV is in purely financial terms the most profitable. It is possible that political, social or environmental factors make it less attractive. In addition the most profitable solution could entail a capital expenditure beyond the borrowing powers of the developer concerned. However, all budgetary implications are exposed. Since all capital expenditure is included in the cash flow and an interest charge equal to the cost of finance to the company is implicit in the discounting process, no separate provision for depreciation or other capital charges is required. It will be apparent that the NPV of the project will vary with the rate which is used to discount the future cash flow. The lower the discount rate the higher the NPV and conversely the higher the discount rate the lower the NPV. If the cash flows sum to zero the return on the investment will be exactly equal to the discount rate, it is a marginal investment. In this context clearly discount rate and interest are synonymous. If the present values of all expected net flows discounted to the base year at the appropriate rate of interest give a negative NPV the project should not go ahead.

The operation of this technique is shown in table 5.3 with the example of an investment of £15 000 with anticipated annual income of £4000 over the next five years. The firm's cost of capital is 10 per cent. In this example the NPV is positive and at the rate of discount used the scheme will add to the wealth of the company; the return is greater than the 10 per cent cost of capital involved.

Internal Rate of Return (IRR)

The yield or rate of return of a project is the rate of interest which if used to discount the cash flow would make the NPV exactly zero. A project is worth while if its yield is greater than the firm's required rate of return. Thus the method employs the present value concept but seeks to provide an evaluation procedure that avoids the difficult choice of a rate of interest. Instead, it sets out, by trial and error, to establish a rate of interest that makes the present values of all expenditures incurred in a project equal to the present values of all revenues gained. That is, it determines the discount rate which reduces the NPV

Table 5.3 *The calculation of net present value*

Year	Net cash flow (NCF) (£)	Discount factor (DF) (10 per cent)	Present value (NCF × DF) (£)
0	−15 000	1.0	−15 000
1	+ 4000	0.9091	+ 3 636
2	+ 4000	0.8264	+ 3 306
3	+ 4000	0.7513	+ 3 005
4	+ 4000	0.6830	+ 2 732
5	+ 4000	0.6209	+ 2 484
		NPV =	163

to zero. When calculated, this interest rate is known as the 'yield' of the investment. Having worked out the IRR, or yield, for each alternative, they should be compared with the cost of borrowing the capital. Any project or alternative having a higher return than the cost of borrowing is fundamentally 'profitable' and the highest return will be most financially attractive. As with NPV, the IRR will generally be higher if the bulk of the cash flows are received earlier than later. Using table 5.3 for NPV, IRR will be equal to 10.4 per cent (table 5.4).

Table 5.4 *The internal rate of return*

Year	Net cash flow (NCF)	Discount factor of 10.4 per cent	Present value (NCF × 10.4 per cent)
0	−15 000	1.0	−15 000
1	+ 4 000	0.9058	+ 3 623
2	+ 4 000	0.8025	+ 3 282
3	+ 4 000	0.7432	+ 2 973
4	+ 4 000	0.6732	+ 2 693
5	+ 4 000	0.6098	+ 2 439
		NPV =	0

Internal Rate of Return and NPV

The relationship between the IRR and NPV methods can be seen in figure 5.4. An initial capital outlay of £15 000 generates revenues of £4000 in each of the ensuing five years. The present values of the positive cash flows arising from the project have been estimated for a range of interest rates. The difference between the present value curve and the initial capital outlay at any rate of interest represents the NPV of the project and thus the intersection of NPV and the

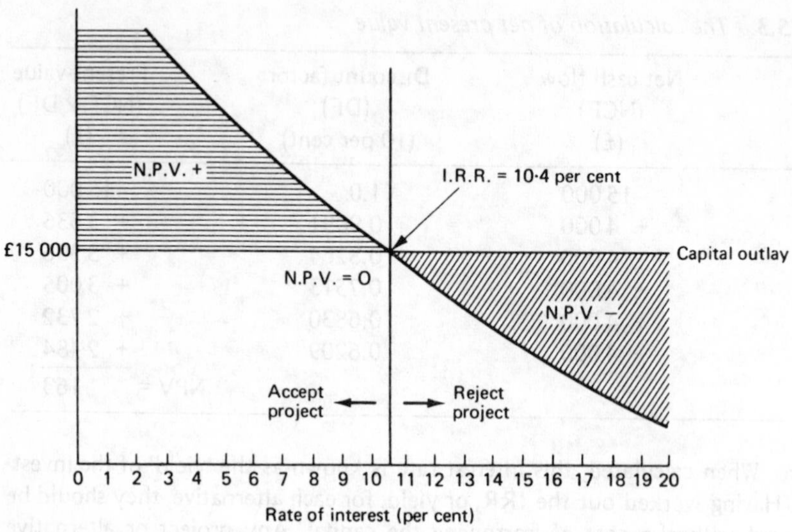

Figure 5.4 *Present value of income and expenditure*

capital outlay gives the IRR. Therefore if a company's cost of capital is less than the IRR, the project would add to the firm's worth (NPV is positive) and should be accepted: if it is higher than the IRR, the project would not be profitable (NPV is negative) and should not be accepted.

No method of evaluation is ever precisely accurate. The purpose of investment appraisal is to examine all likely eventualities, given all the known and relevant data, in order to select the most probable solution. Where both NPV and IRR techniques are employed, the results will often be identical; there will also be situations in which different decisions will be indicated. This may be so when trying to decide which is the most profitable of two mutually exclusive projects (see table 5.5).

Using the NPV method, Project B appears more profitable than Project A; while using the IRR method, A appears favourable to B. Different results are obtained because neither of the discounting methods makes allowance for the total capital involved in a project, nor for the time for which the capital is ex-

Table 5.5 *Optimal investment criteria*

Project	Initital capital outlay	Project life (years)	Annual cash flow generated	NPV @ 9 per cent	IRR (per cent)
A	–500 000	5	140 000	44 544	12.5
B	–750 000	5	207 000	55 147	11.8
B–A	–250 000	5	67 000	10 603	10.8

posed to risk. However, by comparing the incremental cash flows that would result from carrying out Project B instead of Project A (that is B–A) with the extra capital cost required, a NPV and IRR for B–A can be obtained. Then if the return on the extra capital is deemed to more than compensate for the risks involved, Project B should be carried out rather than A.

This highlights one important advantage of the IRR method. The risks associated with the project are largely dependent on the quantity of capital involved and the length of the project. By showing a rate per unit of capital per unit of time of the project, the IRR shows the margin over the cost of capital that is being obtained in return for risk taken. It also avoids the controversial decision of selecting an interest rate.

Thus, once working hypotheses have been formed, techniques of investment appraisal can be used to predict the profitability of alternative courses of action. In some cases sophisticated appraisal techniques will be unnecessary. In relatively small developments decisions may be taken in the light of experience and market factors. In fact the principles of NPV and IRR underlie conventional valuation methods which frequently compute the profitability of the scheme by calculating the gross development value from the completion costs to the present. Variation can be allowed for by adjusting the capitalisation factor (years' purchase) or by setting aside sums for contingencies.

In effect discounted cash flow analysis (DCF) differs only in being more sophisticated and risk-conscious in its consideration of time, and more flexible in investigating the possible range of variance in the factors underlying the investment decision. It is evident that costs, interest rates, schedules and rents can alter in the course of a development. DCF can be refined by the introduction of risks and uncertainty testing.

Uncertainty and Probability Theory

Uncertainty is defined as a situation in which neither the outcome of an event is known, nor the number of possible outcomes, their values or the probability of their occurrence. Risk is defined as a situation where the outcome lacks certainty, but the number of possible outcomes, their value and their probability of occurrence is known. It is largely with risk that development appraisal is concerned.

The evaluation of any plans, or developments, requires the measurement of the constituent factors forming the scheme, together with an estimation of their future performance. Such estimates depend largely upon an interpretation of what has happened in the past, and since the pattern of past events is never exactly repeated, future predictions can at best be imprecise approximations.

Sensitivity Analysis

It is necessary to list and examine the possible range of likely outcomes by using sensitivity analysis. This can take the form of estimating the worst and best possible outcomes of the project's cash flow. Decisions based on these extreme estimates tend to be misleading. A more precise approach is to define all the critical variables contained in the project and affecting its profitability – building costs, rents and the cost of borrowing – and to investigate their range together with the probability of their achieving any particular value in that range. The span of likely results occurring when these variables are combined and their consequent estimates of probability for alternative schemes can then be calculated. Consider a development proposal with three key variables which each have a 50 per cent probability of the 'best estimate' being correct, and which yields a return of 10 per cent. Assuming none of the factors are mutually determined, there is only a 12½ per cent chance of the 10 per cent return being obtained $(0.50)^3$, and thus an 87½ per cent chance of the return being either above or below 10 per cent. The greater the number of variables, and the less certain their performance, the lower the degree of reliability.

Assume a development project with three basic variables: construction costs of £200 000; the rental return estimated at £32 000; and a discount rate of 8 per cent. Calculations are made assessing the effect on the NPV of variations in the value of the variables. For example, it may be calculated that NPV becomes negative if construction costs increase by 5 per cent, if expected rents were to be 5 per cent short, or if the rate of discount is increased by 16 per cent. By testing of this nature it will be seen that the scheme is more sensitive to changes in construction costs and rents than to changes in the discount rate.

Ideally the probability of the respective variables should be obtained from prior empirical investigation. In practice it may be necessary to substitute subjective opinions which may be relatively inaccurate. Probabilities may be estimated from the statistical records and sensitivity variants obtained from experience or sampling. The larger the number of variables the more difficult becomes the appraisal. With the use of computers it is possible to process the simulation of multiple combinations of values and variables, and their relative returns and probabilities.

The list of returns and resulting probabilities can then be expressed graphically as a histogram plotting returns against probabilities, producing a risk/return profile. This approach is valuable where there are many variables with wide possible ranges, or where it is desirable to assess the characteristics of alternative investment proposals. One critical factor is the level of investment. In comparing alternative projects, it is possible that one project, while producing a favourable return, entails a considerably higher capital investment and the risk involved at this level might militate against selection.

Thus in the financial evaluation of alternative plans the treatment of risk and uncertainty presents problems. The methods of appraisal discussed present no clear-cut answer, but both probability theory and sensitivity analysis provide a useful and significant improvement on conventional techniques. The presentation of data in the form of risk/return profiles is of considerably greater value than a single rigid estimate of the project's viability. Increasingly these techniques are being used in financial development appraisal in both private and public sectors. Conventional techniques are inadequate in their treatment of time and risk; they produce a too simplistic view of a problem.

REFERENCES

1. *Money into Property* (Debenham Tewson & Chinnocks, 1987).
2. 'Unitization: Threat or Opportunity?', *Estates Gazette* June 6, 1987).
3. P. R. A. Kirkman and D. C. Stafford, 'The Property Bond Movement 1966–74', *National Westminster Bank Quarterly Review* (February, 1975).
4. R. Barras, 'The Development Cycle in the City of London', *C.E.S. Research Series* 36.
5. R. Barras, 'The Returns from Office Development and Investment', *C.E.S. Research Series* 35.
6. *MGL–CIG Property Index 1978–86* (Morgan Grenfell Laurie).

6

Welfare Economics, Land and the Environment

One only needs to cast a glance at urban activities to realise the degree to which actions are encouraged or constrained in some way in an attempt to bring about a more efficient allocation of resources: control of urban traffic flows, subsidies to public transport, planning controls and limits on permitted housing densities – to name but a few. In addition, public sector infrastructure projects (such as roads, bridges, airports) will generally affect the well-being or welfare of a large number of individuals, and since many of these benefits (and costs) are of a non-monetary nature, economic theory must provide the means to assess such changes.

In the private sector only, direct monetary costs and benefits (revenue) determine the profitability or otherwise of increased output and investment. In the public sector, all (not only monetary) costs and benefits for *all* individuals affected by an investment must in some way be evaluated. Welfare economics, then, is the study of how such economic changes can be assessed in terms of the welfare implications that affect individuals in society.

Welfare economics helps to address such problems as how to evaluate costs and benefits of a non-monetary nature, how to assess social benefit when no charge is made for a public facility (such as parks, open spaces, monuments) and how to adjust for market failure – for example, when decisions are made in the private sector or by private individuals which fail to reflect costs imposed on others (such as urban traffic).

In the first place, it is necessary to consider how we can define and compare the welfare, utility or well-being of individuals in society. Secondly, the measurement and assessment of levels of welfare and changes therein must be addressed. Thirdly, the question of whether the free market can always be relied upon to maximise the well-being or welfare of society must be considered. Fourthly, the means by which the public sector evaluates the welfare implications of investment projects (cost–benefit analysis) must be looked at closely. Lastly, the case for public control over the urban environment must be examined, with reference to examples.

THE CONCEPT OF ECONOMIC WELFARE

Few people would argue with the observation that as an individual's consumption of goods and services increases so his well-being, satisfaction or economic welfare might also be expected to increase. In practice, this could occur either because of a rise in the individual's income (with prices of goods and services unchanged) or because of a fall in the price of some goods and services consumed by that individual (assuming the individual's income remains unchanged). Of course, the individual's increased consumption of, say, cigarettes might conceivably do him some harm, but in general it must be assumed here that the individual knows best. In other words, his change in welfare must be measured as he himself values it – that is, in relation to what he is willing to pay to achieve a particular pattern of consumption. Problems arise, however, when we try to go further. For example, how is the welfare of different individuals to be compared? If it is realised that different individuals will generally have different capacities for deriving satisfaction from a unit of expenditure, the problem of making interpersonal comparisons of welfare becomes apparent.

To take a simple problem, how is a move from a situation where all the population have real incomes of £100 per week to one where half the population have £200 per week and the rest nothing to be assessed? Both yield the same overall monetary value for society but with very different distributional consequences. While traditional measures of national output or consumption suffer from these (and other) problems of interpretation, we can for the moment fall back on another criterion for assessing economic changes which provides a more widely acceptable starting point.

In an attempt to remove the problem of interpersonal comparisons in assessing changes in social welfare, Vilfredo Pareto (1848–1923) suggested the following criterion: any economic change can be ambiguously said to improve social welfare only if at least one member's welfare increases while no other individual's welfare diminishes. Changes which satisfy this criterion are termed 'Pareto improvements' or 'gains'. This proposition is illustrated in figure 6.1.

The vertical and horizontal axes measure the level of satisfaction or utility of two individuals *A* and *B*. At the initial position *r* the welfare levels of *A* and *B* can be seen by reading off the corresponding points on the two axes. Alternative situations *s* and *t* correspond to different bundles and distribution of goods between *A* and *B*. They yield situations where one individual is better off while the utility of the other individual is unchanged. However, at a position such as *u* both individuals are better off. In contrast, at *v* both are worse off. Of all these changes, *s*, *t* and *u* all conform to the criterion for a Pareto improvement. In fact, any position between *s* and *t*, within the shaded area, also conforms to this criterion.

In practice, situations are clearly likely to arise where although one or more individuals may suffer from a change, a great many others may in fact gain. Kaldor[1] and Hicks[2] suggested that as long as the gainers from such a change

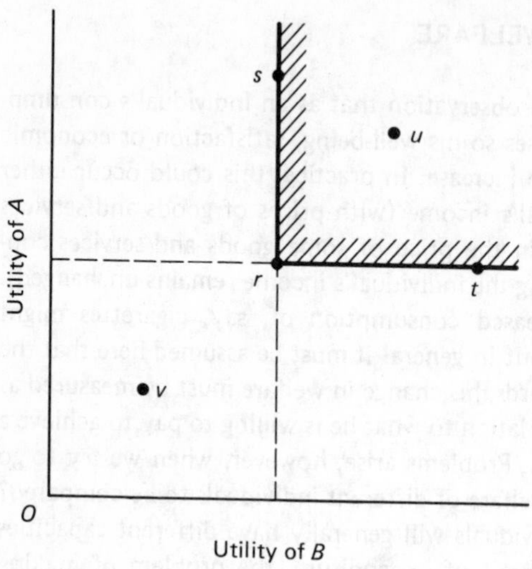

Figure 6.1 *Pareto gains and losses*

could fully compensate the losers and themselves remain better off, the change could produce a net welfare gain for society in line with the Pareto criterion. Kaldor went on to suggest that the job of the economist was only to point out when such a gain was possible, the actual process of compensation being another matter – political, legal or interpersonal in nature. Such changes could then be termed *potential* Pareto improvements, and the concept is clearly more attractive and operational than one where no one should lose out from any project.

Again, the point can be illustrated using the same diagram as previously, but assuming this time that output is fixed and corresponds to a particular bundle of goods which may in principle be distributed in a variety of ways between individuals *A* and *B*. Line *11* illustrates this proposition (figure 6.2) and combinations of welfare between the two consumers may occur anywhere along this utility possibility curve depending on the distribution of goods. Similarly, *22* represents possible outcomes resulting from alternative distributions at a higher level of output.

The actual position of the individuals along any utility possibility curve or frontier such as *11* or *22* will be determined by the distribution of income between them. However, this will have been determined by the level of production itself, since the consumers are also the owners of factors of production within the economy. In sum, given the ownership of factors, any level of output automatically determines factor rewards and therefore the distribution of income. The latter in turn determines what goods the individuals may purchase and consequently their respective levels of welfare. If, for example, there is a move from *11* to *22*, it may be found that the two individuals move from a point such as *a* on *11* to one such as *b* on *22*. Individual *A* is clearly worse off at *b*

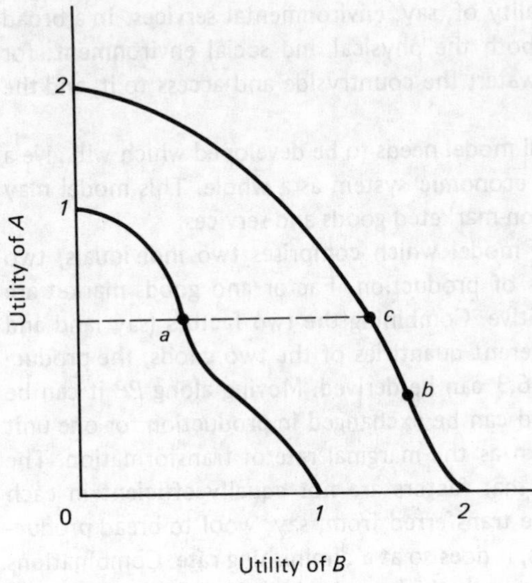

Figure 6.2 *Potential Pareto improvements*

since the income distribution and relative prices have moved against him. Nevertheless, a Pareto gain is possible: *B* could in principle take a cut in consumption along *22*, donate goods to *A* and thus raise *A*'s welfare back to his pre-change position at *C*. According to the Hicks–Kaldor criteria then, the change from *a* to *b* would be approved as a potential Pareto gain.

Of course, in the absence of lump sum taxes on beneficiaries such as *B*, there is no way of actually compelling *B* to compensate *A* (unless somehow *B* has infringed *A*'s property rights). Clearly it is no good relying on *B*'s altruism to solve this problem, but without payment of compensation a Pareto gain remains only a possibility rather than an established event.

The problem of how to measure costs and benefits of an intangible nature will be dealt with later. For the moment we need to look at how, in general, non-priced benefits and costs relate to the present notion of social welfare and changes therein.

WELFARE, EXTERNALITIES AND PUBLIC GOODS

In relating measures of welfare to output of goods and services in the economy, such as Gross National Product (GNP), we are implicitly assuming that the welfare of individuals and societies is dependent on the consumption of *marketed* as opposed to *non-marketed* output. Hence, such measures of economic welfare will largely avoid valuing the quality of, say, environmental services. In a broad sense these include aspects of both the physical and social environment; for example, the quality of air and water, the countryside and access to it, and the right to peace and quiet.

First of all, however, a general model needs to be developed which will give a view of the components of the economic system as a whole. This model may then be adapted to include also non-marketed goods and services.

We shall start with a simple model which comprises two individuals, two marketed goods and two factors of production. Factor and goods market are assumed to be perfectly competitive. Combining the two factors (say land and labour) in the production of different quantities of the two goods, the production frontier *PP* given in figure 6.3 can be derived. Moving along *PP* it can be seen how many units of one good can be exchanged in production for one unit of the other good. This is known as the marginal rate of transformation. The concave shape of *PP* illustrates that factors are not equally efficient in each sector, so that when resources are transferred from, say, wool to bread production, although the latter increases, it does so at a diminishing rate. Combinations of the two goods (here bread and wool) which are to the left of *PP*, such as *r*, are clearly *possible* but also *inefficient* and correspond to sub-optimal use of the two factors.

The two consumers' preferences for the two goods available are given by the series of social indifference curves, *SIC*. Higher curves denote higher levels of

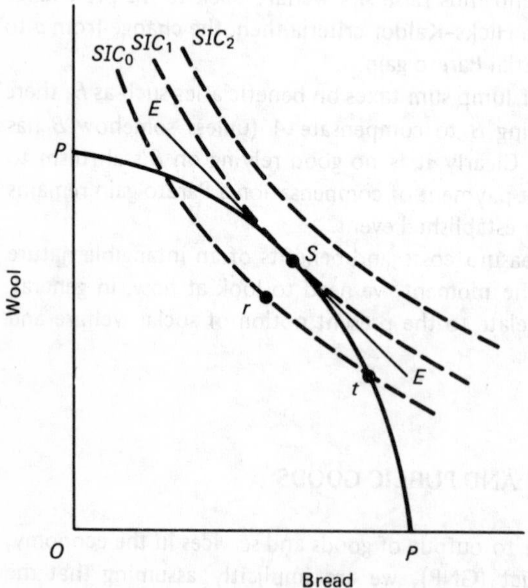

Figure 6.3 *Welfare maximisation: a simple model*

welfare for *both* consumers. Points along each curve denote bundles of the two goods between which the two individuals are indifferent (that is, yield identical levels of welfare).

For the two individuals to maximise welfare, production and consumption must occur at *s* which corresponds to the highest attainable *SIC*. At this point, SIC_1 is at a tangent to the production frontier, and the slopes of both curves are therefore the same (*EE*). This indicates that the rate at which goods are exchanged in production along the production frontier (marginal rate of transformation) is equal to the rate at which the individuals wish to exchange the same goods in consumption (marginal rate of substitution). These rates are in turn equal to the market price ratio of the two goods *EE*, which can therefore be viewed as the price ratio under conditions of welfare maximisation. A point such as *t*, while being *technically efficient* in the sense of being on the production frontier, is *economically inefficient* in terms of welfare maximisation. This can be seen either because it corresponds to a lower level of social welfare, SIC_0, or because the marginal rates of substitution and transformation differ; specifically, at the margin, society would prefer to exchange bread for more wool in consumption even if the relative price of wool rises (as occurs when we move from *t* to *s*).

Unfortunately, imperfections in the functioning of the free market may in practice prevent a position such as *s* being reached. There are several potential sources of market imperfection which affect good or factor prices; they include monopolistic control of production, various distortions in factor markets and the non-pricing of certain resources. It is principally the latter which is of most concern for present purposes. The non-pricing of certain resources (for example, environmental services) is in practice quite common and results because production (or consumption) in one sector of the economy can have a negative influence on production (or consumption) in another sector, without any corresponding monetary (or other transfer) taking place. Such non-market effects are called 'externalities' and these will now be considered in more detail.

Externalities

Externalities can be defined as benefits or costs which accrue to an individual, group, or firm as a direct result of *consumption* or *production* by another individual, group, or firm for which no price is paid or no payment is received. In the following discussion we shall deal mainly with *negative* externalities that involve non-market costs between individuals/firms, individuals/individuals, or firms/firms. *Positive* externalities involving non-market benefits also exist and their analysis is simply a mirror image of the former.

Let us assume that, still in the context of the previous model, we have a case of 'production on production' externality. Assume that two goods are produced, beer and leather, and that the factory producing leather dumps toxic waste products into the river, resulting in the beer factory downstream having to treat its water supply which is required for brewing. The resultant increase in costs for the brewery may well be in excess of the cost if the waste had been treated initially at the tannery.

Let us assume this is the case and that for only a very small extra cost the leather firm could eliminate its waste – although quite clearly it will not do so unless there is some legal or financial constraint imposed. If the amount of labour available is fixed, we can illustrate the output possibilities in the two industries as in figure 6.4.

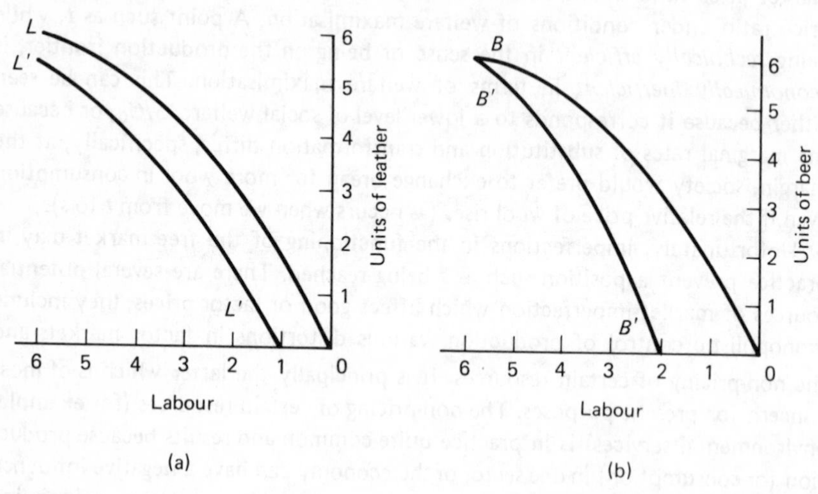

Figure 6.4 *'Production on production' externalities*

Lines *OL* and *OB* show the output possibilities for each industry considered *separately*. They show, for example, that if six units of labour are employed in each industry, a total of six units each of leather and beer may be produced. However, since we have assumed that leather production imposes a negative externality on beer production, we need to establish the outcome when *both* industries are considered *together*. This situation is illustrated by *B'B'* and *OL*; leather production is unchanged (*OL*) but beer production is now lower for any number of labour units employed (assuming for simplicity that some units are employed in eliminating the source of the problem). As illustrated, *OB* and *B'B'* touch at a certain point. This is because we have assumed fixed resources (say six units of labour), so that the point of intersection of *B'B'* and *OB* corresponds to zero production of leather, where all units are employed in beer production.

The final line, *L'L'*, illustrates the position in the leather firm where costs of removing the toxic waste are taken into account. For simplicity it has been assumed that this involves a fixed cost of diverting one unit of labour towards some alternative method of waste removal.

The production frontier facing this society for any combination of employment between the two industries can now be derived. In figure 6.5 *SS* illustrates the production frontier when leather production is uncontrolled, and *S'S'* illustrates the case when the leather firm undertakes waste removal. The latter represents the 'true' production frontier reflecting the *social* (as opposed to the

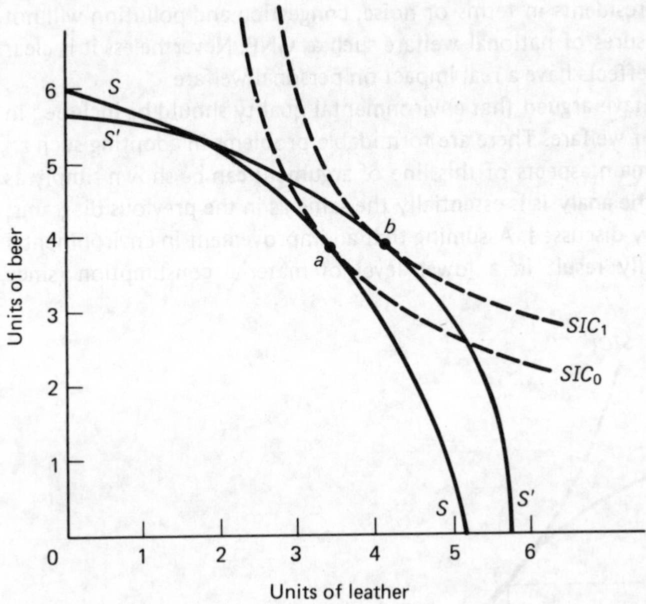

Figure 6.5 *Production frontiers and the internalisation of external costs*

private) marginal rate of transformation, but will clearly only be reached if the leather producer has some incentive (or duty) to control waste disposal. Only if this occurs is society able to reach a higher social indifference curve SIC_1 which in this case also results in higher production levels of *both* goods (from *a* to *b*). In the presence of externalities (as discussed previously) such a move can be achieved by setting an appropriate tax on the firm or group which generates the externalities (more details will be given later). This process is referred to as '*internalisation*', that is, the setting of a market price on otherwise non-priced costs (or benefits). In this case only if the external cost is made internal to the leather firm will optimal decisions regarding output and pricing be made in the economy.[3] As a result, social welfare can be maximised at point *b*,.

One final comment on this example is that we have not included any estimation of the possible benefits accruing to other users of the river (for example, from fishing, bathing, etc.). If such benefits exist then the policy will clearly have resulted in both a greater production volume and an improved level of environmental quality. For other types of externality, such as those which impinge directly on the individuals' consumption of, say, environmental benefits, the analysis is complicated because such consumption does not generally rate in any standard monetary measure of national welfare. For example, while the construction of a new airport will bring measurable economic benefits, the disbenefits to nearby residents in terms of noise, congestion and pollution will not be included in measures of national welfare such as GNP. Nevertheless it is clear that these external effects have a real impact on personal welfare.

Several authors have argued that environmental quality should be included in national measures of welfare. There are formidable problems in adopting such an approach, but the main aspects of this line of argument can be shown simply as in figure 6.6. Since the analysis is essentially the same as in the previous diagrams, it will only be briefly discussed. Assuming that an improvement in environmental quality will generally result in a lower level of material consumption (since

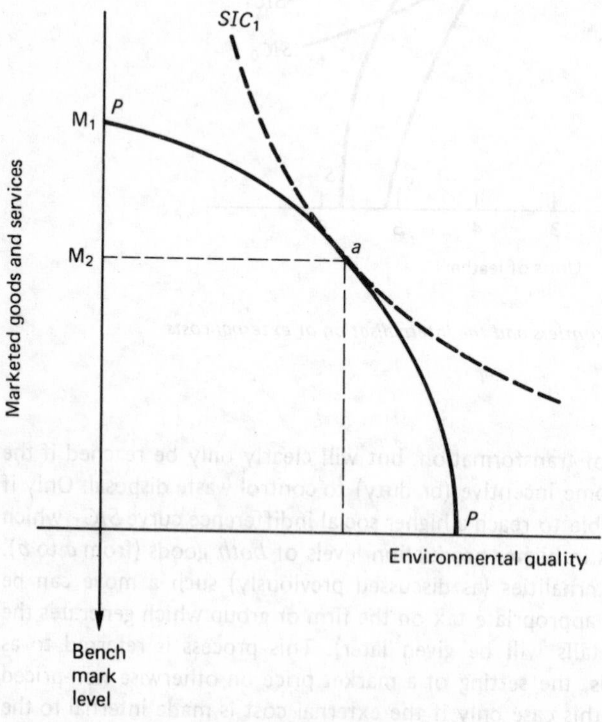

Figure 6.6 *Environmental quality and the production frontier*

resources may need to be diverted from the market sector) and vice versa, society's set of choices can be defined along the frontier *PP*. If environmental benefits are given no weight in this system, then it is likely that maximisation of production of marketed goods and services would lead to an extreme position such as M_1. If individuals however, place value on environmental quality (which it is assumed they cannot express via the market), the point which maximises society's welfare is in fact at *a* and SIC_1. At this point, however, measurable income has fallen to M_2!

The problem then is one of evaluating such non-monetary gains and losses and expressing them in monetary terms. This will be discussed directly, but before doing so there is another important category of goods the provision of which involves externalities. Such goods are known as *public goods.*

Public goods

The reference to 'public' implies anything from a group of individuals to a locality or region, country or group of countries. A pure *public* good has characteristics which are opposite to those of a pure *private* good. The latter are *rival* in the sense that consumption of the good by one person precludes its consumption by another person or persons (for example, a shirt). Following from this, it is clear that the greater the demand by consumers, the more units of the good must be produced and the more resources must be devoted to the production of these units.

Private goods also have the characteristic of *excludability* – a unit or units of the good can be consumed by one person to the exclusion of others, and consumption of the good affects the welfare of no other individual. The latter condition implies an absence of externalities.

In contrast, 'pure' public goods are both *non-rival* and *non-excludable*. They are non-rival in the sense that one unit can satisfy more than one consumer, implying that no additional resources are required as the number of consumers rises. Public goods are non-excludable in that once provided, it is impossible to exclude anyone from consuming them – in other words the effects of providing the good are automatically extended to the whole community. As such, the good is associated with (positive) externalities (such as street lighting). Perhaps the most obvious example is national defence. The decision by government to provide defence automatically extends the benefits to all, regardless of whether or not they have contributed to its expense (non-excludable). Also, the cost is essentially the same however many people are covered by defence (that is, non-rival). In practice, few goods are 'pure' public goods. Many goods, however, share certain public good characteristics.

One of the key points in common shared by public goods is that provision would either not occur or would be sub-optimal if left to the free market. This problem arises because, since provision automatically benefits everyone, it is in the interest of the individual to understate his preferences and avoid payment.

In other words, individuals would attempt to 'free-ride', that is, avoid payment while still enjoying the benefits of the good. If this is true for each individual, then, taken as a whole, society may not provide the good even if it is in everyone's interest to do so. Of course, it is possible that one or more individuals who rate the good very highly in their scale of preferences might be prepared to foot the bill. One problem here is that the good may then reflect only the preferences of these individuals and be underprovided relative to the preferences of the rest of the community.

Clearly, also, no producer would wish to undertake marketed production of the good, since it would be impossible to prevent individuals consuming the good without paying (non-rival).

In contrast, the state will often be in a better position to estimate the demand for public goods, undertake their provision and organise payment via taxation. Nevertheless, problems may remain – in particular, some individuals may be taxed too highly relative to their valuation of the good while others may be taxed too lightly. However, in the context of a large number of public goods, individuals may find that excess taxation for some public goods may be offset by undertaxation relative to their preferences for others.

While the case for supply via public institutions may appear clear cut in the case of 'pure' public goods, it has been shown that many goods exhibit only some public good characteristics. Is there then equally a case for public supply of these goods? For example, while environmental resources such as air quality, water quality, peace and quiet, and open spaces are largely public goods in the sense that once provided they are widely available, they may nevertheless be rival and excludable in the sense that spatial opportunities for their consumption may differ. Facilities such as open spaces in urban areas may become congested so that additional users reduce the benefits to existing users. In particular, residential immobility may mean that different groups in society have unequal access to environmental resources. If income were evenly distributed and households perfectly mobile, spatial differences in access to environmental resources might not matter. Individuals with low environmental preferences could continue to live in, say, decaying inner cities while those with high environmental preferences could choose to live in more peaceful locations with greater access to environmental resources. Other things being equal, substantial local differences in environmental services would eventually become capitalised in different property values. Since, however, assumptions relating to income distribution and housing mobility are probably not met, the likely result is that residents living in low environmental conditions are not so much those who place low values on such resources as those who cannot afford to move or who cannot find similar accommodation elsewhere.

Another important example of 'impure' public goods involves goods where, although it is possible to exclude consumers, it would be inefficient or sub-optimal to do so. Examples of such goods are public roads, museums, bridges and parks. Here, as long as there is no congestion of the facility there is no additional cost, either in provision or to other users, of adding one more consumer. In principle a toll or other charge could be made, but such a charge (assuming no congestion) would lead to a lowering of welfare. This point can be illustrated by considering a major tunnel project.

Assume, firstly, that the welfare benefits of the project – that is, the sum total of the potential users' willingness to pay – can be accurately measured from the demand curve for the good in question.[4] It will also be assumed that the social (or opportunity) cost of the project is accurately reflected in the actual costs involved, measured in monetary terms, and that overall, the total benefits of the project outweigh the total costs.

In the present case, the demand curve for tunnel crossings could be estimated from analysis of existing traffic flows in the area plus some estimate of traffic likely to be generated by the new facility. A social cost–benefit analysis would also include indirect benefits (or costs) of the project such as reduction on congestion elsewhere, but for purposes of simplicity such effects will be ignored in the present case.

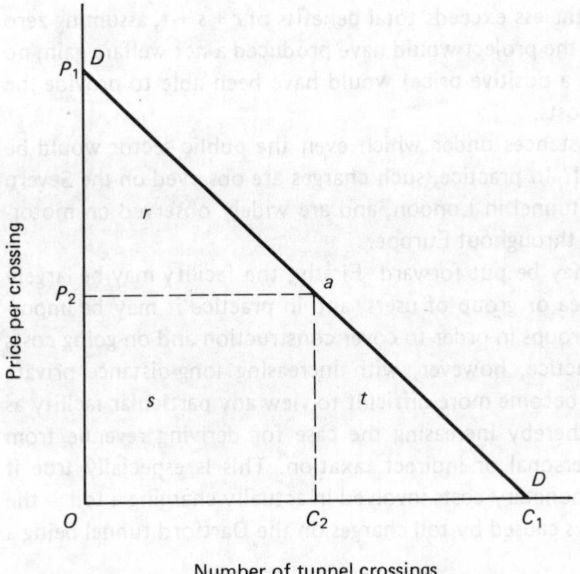

Figure 6.7 *Demand curve for tunnel crossings*

The estimated demand curve is given by *DD* in figure 6.7. It shows that at a zero price per crossing C_1 crossings would be undertaken, while at a charge of P_1 no crossings at all would be undertaken. If the tunnel is provided publicly at zero user cost, then the total welfare gain (willingness to pay) is given by the area under the demand curve *DD*. If, however, the tunnel is provided and run by private individuals who charge a toll, the result will be different. Assuming revenue maximisation is desired, the private supplier will charge a toll such as P_2 per crossing. In this case only C_2 crossings will be undertaken, and C_1–C_2 crossings will have been dissuaded by the toll. The benefit derived from C_2 crossings is given by the areas r and s which represent the willingness to pay for these crossings. However, the actual revenue received is only area s (that is, $P_2 \times C_2$). The remaining area, known as the *consumer surplus* (area r) represents the difference between willingness to pay and the amount actually paid for the service.

It is immediately evident that the reduced number of crossings results in a lower level of consumer benefit – that is, area $r + s$ in contrast to area $r + s + t$ where no charge is made. Although revenue of area s is obtained by the tunnel operator, this is of no allocative importance; the tunnel would otherwise have been financed via taxation, and charging a toll merely constitutes another form of payment. Area t, however, is of allocative significance as it represents a lowering of welfare because fewer crossings are undertaken with a toll. A further feature is of note: if the total cost of the project had been estimated to be just above $r + s$ (which nevertheless exceeds total benefits of $r + s + t$, assuming zero user cost), then although the project would have produced a net welfare gain, no private supplier (charging a positive price) would have been able to provide the tunnel, assuming similar costs.

Are there ever circumstances under which even the public sector would be justified in charging a toll? In practice, such charges are observed on the Severn Bridge and the Dartford tunnel in London, and are widely observed on motorways, bridges and tunnels throughout Europe.

Several explanations may be put forward. Firstly, the facility may be largely specific to a particular area or group of users, and in practice it may be impossible to distinguish such groups in order to cover construction and on-going costs through taxation. In practice, however, with increasing long-distance private travel and haulage it may become more difficult to view any particular facility as region or area specific, thereby increasing the case for deriving revenue from road taxation or even personal or indirect taxation. This is especially true if there are important non-monetary costs involved in actually charging a toll – the congestion and long delays caused by toll charges on the Dartford tunnel being a case in point.

Secondly, it is possible that excessive use of the facility will itself result in non-monetary costs – for example, too many visitors may result in damage to historic monuments or may affect the enjoyment of other visitors. If the facility becomes congested, causing damage, delay or other forms of externality, then a charge in proportion to the damage and inconvenience caused becomes justified, since it is now no longer the case that the good can be enjoyed by everyone, irrespective of the number of users.

A final and important category of public goods involves goods which, although mainly rival and excludable, nevertheless exhibit important external benefits. Such goods (known as merit goods) include health, education, housing, public libraries and fire services.

In principle these goods could all be provided by the private sector but, because of externalities, private provision would result in sub-optimal supply. Additionally, it may be felt that public provision at low or zero user cost is preferable to private provision, since even if the latter is subsidised, there may nevertheless be individuals who are too poor to afford even this. Moreover, the possible 'costs' of non-consumption by the individual may be high or so severe that public provision at zero user cost is considered indispensable (for example, the fire service).

There exist numerous types of activity which exhibit actual or potential externalities. While the case for direct public control does not extend equally to all such activities, indirect control in the form of taxes and subsidies can often achieve the desired result of optimal resource allocation.

HOUSING, EXTERNALITIES AND PUBLIC POLICY

Consider urban housing improvement where property-on-property type externalities exist. In such cases, properties are generally run down and in need of renovation. This will involve substantial financial outlay for long-term improvements such as re-roofing, rewiring, plumbing and glazing, as well as for shorter-term but more 'obvious' improvements such as redecorating. If all properties in the area were renovated then it is likely that property values would rise sufficiently to at least compensate owners for their expenditure on major maintenance items. However, if only one or a few owners undertake the investment, their property values alone might not increase sufficiently to compensate them if the area as a whole remains undesirable. Worse than this, if the area was already in a state of cumulative decline, house owners who invested might find they had done so in an asset that was actually declining in real value.[5] In this situation, nothing may persuade house owners to undertake major or even more minor repairs.

The problem, of course, is that while everyone may gain from joint action to improve an area, the benefits derived from housing renovation are substantially *non-excludable* in the sense that external benefits to other householders (who do nothing) occur in the form of an improved neighbourhood and, hence, property values. The 'residential environment' therefore can be said to have public good characteristics, and in consequence faces problems of sub-optimal provision. Many households are likely to 'free-ride' and enjoy the benefits of an improved environment (and higher property values) without undertaking investment. Yet if everyone does the same, no renovation will occur even though all may want it. This situation is referred to as the 'Prisoner's Dilemma'.[6]

One solution is for improvement grants to be concentrated on areas of greatest housing decay. This would provide confidence in an area and encourage owners to undertake improvements which they might not otherwise contemplate for the reasons just discussed. As long as the overall benefits to residents exceed costs to the state in subsidy and administration, plus the renovation costs paid by residents themselves, then the project will have produced a net improvement in social welfare.

Alternatively, or in addition, the state or local government could undertake selective compulsory purchase followed by renovation and eventual sale or letting on to the residential market. Lastly, with wider use of compulsory purchase powers, wholesale redevelopment of an area may be contemplated.

Whichever solution is chosen, some form of public intervention is clearly required to ensure that existing residents do not lose out. The latter may suffer if, for example, excessive private redevelopment in more intensive uses (such as offices) occurs, or if over-extensive housing redevelopment causes large-scale residential displacement. If housing improvement programmes simply push existing residents into even more precarious housing conditions, then the change can hardly be described as a 'Pareto improvement'.

Public intervention in housing supply provides a further example. The case for public provision of subsidised housing has traditionally rested on three main arguments. Firstly is the argument for redistribution in kind, which assumes that certain groups in society, for a variety of reasons, are likely to under-consume housing and remain ill-housed in spite of quite high levels of public spending on income support. Secondly, and linked to the first argument, is the view that society must ensure that a minimum standard of housing consumption is established and maintained. Although other reasons may exist (such as, to avoid overcrowding), the principle one may be that poor housing standards represent an environmental health risk. Public supply of low-cost housing may thus be seen partly as an alternative to controlling standards at the lower end of the private housing (and rented) sector. Thirdly, since a system of income subsidies alone may be unable to tackle regional and local shortages of adequate housing for low-income families, it may be thought necessary to intervene on the supply side to provide sufficient housing of suitable standard directly, at an affordable and controlled cost to residents.

The problem associated with a 'pure' income subsidy to tenants can be illustrated by comparing income transfers with price subsidies, such as low-cost housing provision. In figure 6.8, point '*a*' on the Budget line *CC* gives the initial position of the low income household. At this point it is achieving its highest possible level of welfare given its (non-subsidised) budget constraint. It is consuming H_0 housing and G_0 other goods at this point.

Assume that the government wishes to achieve a minimum standard of housing consumption equal to H_1. If it provides an income subsidy it will need

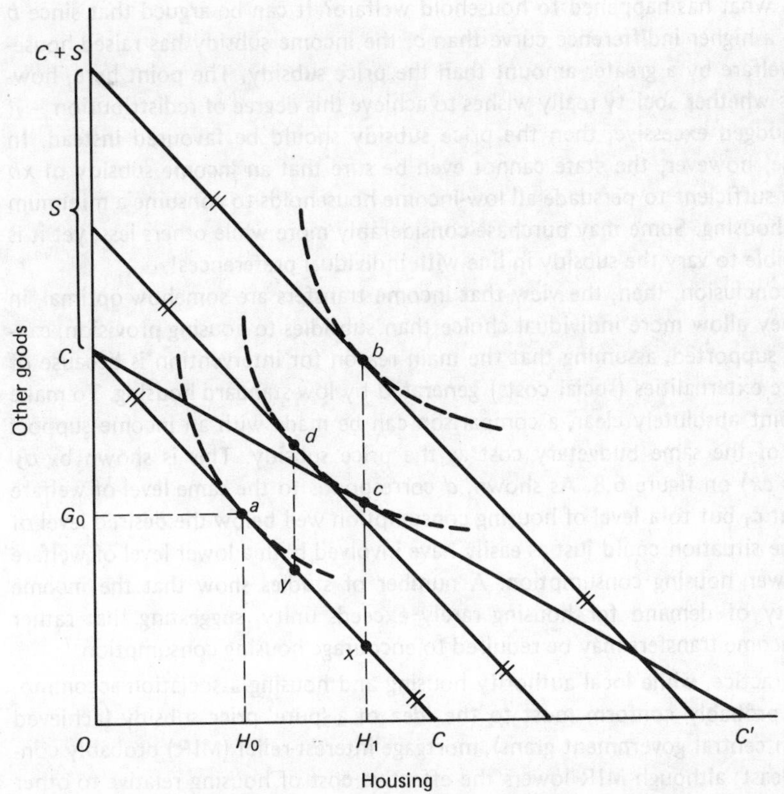

Figure 6.8 *Housing subsidies and the consumption of housing services*

to raise the household's income level to $C + S$ to achieve this ($C + S$ is parallel to CC but vertically above it by the level of subsidy). The household now maximises welfare at point b on the new budget line $C + S$. Note that if the pattern of household indifference curves had shown less preference for housing as income rose, then the degree of subsidy 'S' required to achieve H_1 would have been much greater.

Alternatively, the government could lower the relative price of housing to CC' (say via public provision) and could then enforce a minimum standard of housing H_1. Suppose this is what happens and compare this situation with the alternative of an income subsidy discussed earlier. By providing H_1 housing at a reduced cost to the household of CC', the total cost to the state is given by the vertical distance between CC and CC', that is xc. The cost of the income subsidy which would be required to achieve the same objective is given by the vertical distance between C and $C + S$ and is equal to S or xb. It can be seen that xb clearly exceeds xc, illustrating the point that the least-cost method of achieving a target level of housing consumption is via direct provision/price subsidy.

But what has happened to household welfare? It can be argued that since *b* lies on a higher indifference curve than *c*, the income subsidy has raised household welfare by a greater amount than the price subsidy. The point here, however, is whether society really wishes to achieve this degree of redistribution – if *xb* is judged excessive, then the price subsidy should be favoured instead. In practice, however, the state cannot even be sure that an income subsidy of *xb* will be sufficient to persuade all low-income households to consume a minimum of H_1 housing. Some may purchase considerably more while others less, yet it is impossible to vary the subsidy in line with individual preferences!

In conclusion, then, the view that income transfers are somehow optimal, in that they allow more individual choice than subsidies to housing provision, cannot be supported, assuming that the main reason for intervention is because of negative externalities (social costs) generated by low-standard housing. To make this point absolutely clear, a comparison can be made with an income support policy of the same budgetary cost as the price subsidy. This is shown by *dy* (equals *cx*) on figure 6.8. As shown, *d* corresponds to the same level of welfare as point *c*, but to a level of housing consumption well below the desired level of H_1. The situation could just as easily have involved both a lower level of welfare *and* lower housing consumption. A number of studies show that the income elasticity of demand for housing rarely exceeds unity, suggesting that rather large income transfers may be required to encourage housing consumption.[7]

In practice, while local authority housing and housing association accommodation probably conform most to the idea of a 'pure' price subsidy (achieved through central government grant), mortgage interest relief (MIR) probably conforms least; although MIR lowers the effective cost of housing relative to other goods, it also has a 'perverse' income effect, lowering the relative price of housing *more* for *higher* income groups (because of higher marginal tax rates). Moreover MIR does nothing to help those on low or variable incomes who could not in any case obtain (sufficient) mortgage finance.

It should finally be noted that while in the United Kingdom public sector low-cost housing is mainly achieved through direct subsidies to local authorities (see chapter 8), in several European countries similar aims have been achieved through the quasi-public sector – including cooperatives, housing associations and municipal housing corporations, which have received public subsidies in return for maintaining quality levels, a given proportion of low-income tenants and approved rents.

COST-BENEFIT ANALYSIS

In the private sector, investment decisions are made with reference to the market mechanism on the basis of estimated monetary costs and benefits (see chapter 4). Cost-Benefit Analysis (CBA) is basically an extension of these investment appraisal methods with modifications to make them suitable for project appraisal in the public sector. The main distinction is that public sector CBA attempts to account for all the costs and benefits which affect the welfare of individuals including those of a non-monetary nature. To facilitate comparison and assessment it is usual for such non-monetary costs or benefits to be somehow translated into monetary terms.

From the 1960s onwards, the CBA technique was extended to cover a wide range of applications, including water resource management, motorways, nationalised industries, airport locations, forestry, recreational facilities and a wide range of urban investment projects. While individual projects may pose specific problems, there are a number of considerations which are common to most.

(1) The first of these concerns the notion that projects in the public sector should be capable of achieving a potential Pareto improvement in social welfare. That is, expected social benefits should exceed expected social costs (all appropriately discounted to present values). Here social benefits involve any gain in welfare resulting from the project, including intangible – that is non-market benefits (for example, investment in public transport may produce benefits in the form of lower congestion, accidents, noise and pollution). Furthermore since many public facilities (such as parks) are provided free of charge to users, social benefit, determined by willingness to pay (WTP) criteria, may have to be estimated indirectly. Various methods exist and may involve one or more of the following:

(i) Consideration of demand for similar facilities elsewhere for which charges are made (such as historic monuments).

(ii) Extensive questionnaire analysis of potential users. Although the problem here is that in the case of public goods where 'free-riding' occurs, individuals may deliberately understate their preferences.

(iii) By implication from observed behaviour – for example, with recreational facilities (for example, in the Lake District) demand may be observed to fall with increasing distance from the facility. Willingness to pay can be imputed from the additional travel costs (in time and money) that users are observed to incur as distance increases.

Social costs will include any intangible costs (such as environmental damage, noise, nuisance and congestion) as well as the construction and on-going costs of the project – reflecting the production foregone (that is, opportunity cost) when resources are moved to the public sector. Concerning the latter, two problems may arise. Firstly, if there is imperfect competition in the supply of goods (or factors) used in production or construction, then market price may exceed marginal cost – that is, the true cost of the good to society. Seen in another way, if the project's purchase of input X increases the output of a monopolist supplier, the relevant opportunity cost relates to the marginal cost of extra resources hired and not to the observed (and higher price) charged by the monopolist. Similarly, if workers being employed on a project would otherwise have remained unemployed then hiring them at the going wage will not result in a reduction of output elsewhere in the economy – hence the marginal cost to society is in fact less than the wage rate paid to the labourer.[8] It can be noted that the net cost to the Exchequer will also be lower than the wage rate in this case, since the government benefits from lower unemployment and social security payments and receives higher direct and indirect taxes.

Secondly, market prices may require adjustment to take account of indirect taxes (subtracted) or subsidies (added) or because market prices may not adequately reflect social costs (for example, farmers may be unaware that their farming techniques are impoverishing the soil). However, while consideration should always be given to the need for adjusting market prices, in practice it may not always be feasible to do so; in many cases it may be too difficult or costly to obtain the necessary information with a good degree of accuracy.

(2) The second set of considerations concerns the evaluation of non-market gains and losses. Here it is useful to distinguish two categories of intangibles. The first is where, although no direct market exists, there is nevertheless an indirect (or surrogate) market in other goods which is in some way influenced by the intangibles in question. The process of defining such alternative markets is known as shadow-pricing. For example, although there is no market for peace and quiet, if individuals buying and selling houses are observed to place higher or lower valuations on similar properties in quieter or noisier situations, then resulting differences in house values can be taken to represent the willingness to pay for peace and quiet. However, it is necessary to isolate all other factors influencing property prices; for example, although house prices may fall near motorways or airports, there may exist locational advantages which would tend to work the other way. Hence, basing an analysis solely on observed price variations may tend to produce an underestimate of the willingness to pay for peace and quiet. Also, while individuals may be good judges of peace and quiet, they may be less likely to have full information about other environmental effects (such as lead pollution) – but even if they did, it is unlikely that the full effects would be reflected in the housing market since many households may not have a real choice of relocating elsewhere. Overall, then, the presumption is that intangible costs of an environmental nature are likely to be partially, but not fully, reflected (or internalised) in the property market.

Another example is the valuation of travel time which has been widely applied in transport studies, where time savings may account for by far the largest category of benefit deriving from motorway or road schemes. A distinction is made between time savings in work-time and those in leisure-time. Concerning the former, hourly earnings (plus some savings on overheads) may be taken to represent production gained from the time saving of one hour (or *pro rata*), assuming that the wage rate is an adequate reflection of the workers' marginal product. One problem here is that, in practice, large rather than small time savings are more likely to result in productive work, and in reverse, longer travel times (for example, by train or aircraft) may not always result in lost production if, for example, businessmen are able to work while travelling. Time savings during leisure time could, theoretically, be valued at a similar rate, since if workers are able to choose their hours of work then, at the margin, they should be expected to value an hour's work at an equivalent rate to an hour's leisure. In practice such choice is rarely available, hence an alternative approach to the evaluation of leisure time must be sought. For example, if an individual is observed to choose a faster but more expensive means of travel in preference to a slower and cheaper alternative, then as long as no other factors (such as comfort) come into play, his willingness to pay for time saved on the faster route in terms of the cost difference can be measured. Using this method, various studies have suggested that leisure-time values are proportional to travellers' incomes, at around 25 per cent of the latter, although considerably higher or lower values cannot be ruled out.[9]

It is likely that, in practice, an individual's valuation of leisure time may vary from case to case and depend on many other factors, including frequency, length of trip and means of travel. Nevertheless, travel-time evaluation has played an important role in many studies, including the Roskill Commission Study on the third London airport and the Victoria Line Study.[10] In the former, although the Foulness site produced the lowest estimates of noise-nuisance cost, the procedure adopted resulted in these benefits being vastly outweighed by its more distant location because of the high valuation placed on travel time savings of relatively high-income air passengers. In the Victoria Line Study, the valuation of travel time proved less contentious. Since the new line would benefit passengers (over and above the revenue collected) it was reasonable to assume that users would have been willing to pay for the extra convenience (and time saving) of a direct line. Furthermore, since congestion would be reduced elsewhere in the transport system, some estimate of time savings here was essential.

A second category of intangibles involves those for which no efficient surrogate market exists. The Roskill Commission Study just mentioned, for example, placed no value on the loss of wildlife or preservation of countryside because of the difficulty of valuation. Yet even in these circumstances, a residual approach may be adopted. If a dam project, for example, is expected to produce an excess of measurable benefits over costs of £2 million, decision-makers can at least come to some conclusion as to whether they consider this figure is sufficient to outweigh the loss of countryside and recreational amenities. The attractions of this approach may, however, be reduced if many intangibles exist.

(3) Distributional issues represent the third major consideration. Even if a project is expected to produce an excess of social benefit over social cost, there may still be some objection that the criterion of a potential Pareto improvement tells us nothing about *who* gains and *who* loses. In other words, as it stands, the criterion carries no distributional weight; it cannot, for example, help us to decide between, say, two projects where the first benefits everyone by £10 and the second benefits only the richest by £20 and all others suffer losses – since both could achieve a potential Pareto gain. It is worth stressing at this point that the distributional question does not arise when compensation is actually made, since the welfare of any losers is maintained and, overall, there is still a net

improvement in social welfare (in theory by transfers from gainers who still remain better off). In contrast, when compensation is not made – which is in fact common because of the impracticality of lump-sum transfers – the distributional question becomes a key issue.

Clearly, individual monetary assessments of gains or losses (in terms of WTP) are likely to be strongly dependent on the level of personal incomes. It follows that project assessment will therefore tend to place relatively much weight on the demands (or costs) of those on high incomes and relatively little weight on the demands (or costs) of those on low incomes. For example, strict adherence to WTP criteria might suggest that road projects in urban areas should be located nearer to low-income housing than high-income housing, since the latters' WTP assessment of noise nuisance (reflected in house values) could generally be expected to exceed the formers'.

If no adjustment of the WTP evaluation of gains or losses is made, then projects are implicitly being assessed on criteria that reflect the existing distribution of income. As Pearce has suggested, this is tantamount to saying that those who have been rewarded once (via higher earnings) should be rewarded once again in the choice of public projects. In contrast, in the above example one might wish to argue that a more widely acceptable assessment of noise nuisance would tend to put rather more weight on the number of individuals involved and the level of noise in alternative schemes than on the higher WTP of high-earning groups. A move in this direction could be achieved by weighting WTP assessments of intangible costs. Hence values obtained for higher-income groups could be 'scaled down' while values for low-income groups could be 'scaled up'. To achieve this, one suggestion – by analogy to the principle of 'one man one vote' in politics – has been to adjust each economic 'vote' (that is, monetary assessment of WTP) so that it reflects what individuals would vote if their incomes were equalised. A simple method would be to divide average income for the country by the income for the group in question. For example, if average income is £100 per week then the appropriate weight for income groups earning £200 per week would be 0.5 and for income groups earning only £50 per week the weight would rise above unity to equal 2. Another method suggested has been to observe the weights implicit in past government decisions concerning public spending or taxation. For example, higher marginal tax rates on high earners could be taken to imply that society places lower weights on gains to such groups. This view is strengthened if it is assumed – with rising incomes – that the marginal utility of income diminishes, so that in general, an extra £1 of income for a poor person will raise his total utility (or welfare) by more than would an extra £1 accruing to a rich person.

The arguments in favour of adopting weighting procedures are undoubtedly strong since the main aim is to integrate considerations involving both efficiency and distribution. Failure to do so could result in glaring inconsistencies (for example, it might suggest that environmentally damaging projects should be located in 'poor' rather than in 'rich' localities). While it is possible that the weighting procedure would still sanction projects which made the rich richer and the poor poorer, weighting at least ensures that efficiency criteria will have been balanced against distributional considerations.

Although as we have seen, distributional issues are less important when compensation occurs, even here many problems remain. In particular, compensation may often understate the nuisance caused – for example, houses will be valued at market prices which totally neglect any element of consumer surplus (that is, benefit exists in excess of the market price which an owner will derive from a particular dwelling or location).[11] Additionally, compensation is paid not by the beneficiaries themselves but out of general taxation. Although the cost to an individual taxpayer is minute, when multiplied over numerous projects distributional effects may be significant, especially if costs must be met by taxpayers, many of whom may be on low incomes themselves.

In conclusion, given the choice between two alternative projects producing the same net welfare gain to society, the appeal is clearly greater for the one where fewer people are to be made worse off. In practice, such handy alternatives are rare; hence in assessing public projects, planners should, at the very least point out the size and allocation of gains and losses together with recommendations concerning the feasibility of compensation.

(4) The fourth major consideration concerns the discount rate, the choice of which involves investment, savings and consumption decisions over time. All savings decisions involve the 'sacrifice' of less consumption today in exchange for the promise of consumption at a higher level tomorrow. This is achieved by means of investment which places today's resources into production which will yield results only at some date in the future. The decision of just how much saving and investment society should undertake today can be illustrated as in figure 6.9.

Consider the simplest case of a single individual in a 'Robinson Crusoe' world who is faced with fixed material resources.[12] His savings/investment decision over two time-periods (t_1 and t_2) concerns how much of his time and effort (in t_1) he should spend on projects (say, farming) which will yield a return in the next period (t_2). Spending his time in this way, however, involves Crusoe in a form of 'saving' since he will have less time to spend on activities (such as, say, collecting fruit) which yield an immediate benefit. This choice is illustrated by CC' which is Crusoe's *production frontier* (or production possibility curve). At the limit, he could consume nothing in t_2 but OC in t_1, or consume nothing in t_1 but (provided he did not starve), OC' in t_2. In general, OC' can be expected to exceed OC because of technical advance and use of capital-intensive production techniques; in Crusoe's case, by developing irrigation in t_1 he may ensure higher food output in t_2 than if he had attempted non-irrigated planting for consumption in t_1.

While Crusoe could achieve any combination of consumption levels given by CC', he will in practice choose that combination which gives him most benefit. This in turn will depend upon his relative preference for consumption in t_2 as

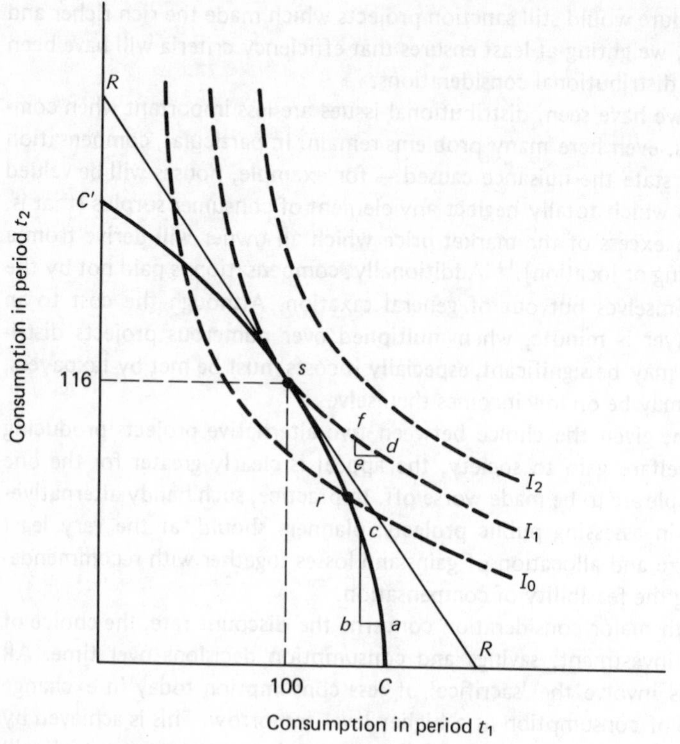

Figure 6.9 *Savings and investment decisions over time*

against consumption in t_1. Crusoe's indifference curves, three of which are shown on figure 6.9, each tells us the combinations of consumption in t_1 and in t_2 which provide him with identical levels of satisfaction. As usual, higher indifference curves represent higher levels of welfare. In this case Crusoe would reach his highest indifference curve by being at point *s* on *CC'*. This corresponds to consumption of 100 units in t_1 and 116 units in t_2. But in period t_1, if consumption accounts for only 100 units this means that remaining resources ($C - 100$) must have been invested for future consumption. In other words, $C - 100$ represents both the level of saving and investment that occurs in t_1.

Point *s* is unique in that it equates the *time preference* of the individual with the marginal profitability or efficiency of avilable investment opportunities. These two rates are identical only at point *s*, and this is shown because the two curves (*CC'* and I_1) have the same slope (they are tangential) at this point. To show the importance of this, consider the two small triangles *abc* and *def. ab* and *de* represent one unit less of consumption in t_1. Considering I_1, it can be seen that (at the margin) Crusoe is indifferent between losing *'de'* in t_1 as long as he is rewarded by *ef* in t_2. But looking at the corresponding segment of the production frontier, it can be seen that the investment opportunities facing him are so good that he can achieve *cb* (which is greater than *fe*) by foregoing a unit of consumption in t_1. The reader should convince himself that the same conclusion applies to all units sacrificed in t_1 as Crusoe moves back from *C* to *s*. After this point the marginal efficiency of investment falls below Crusoe's rate of time preference. Only at *s* are these two rates identical and equal to *RR*. If *RR* represents points on the two axes of 200 units in t_1 and 220 units in t_2, then the rate of discount in the economy is such that 220 units in t_2 will have a present value (that is, in t_1) of 200. It can easily be seen that, in this case, the actual discount rate which will produce this result is 10 per cent. That is, given the discounting equation

$$\text{PV} = \frac{S}{(1+r)^n}$$

where PV = present value of a sum *S* which accrues *n* periods hence, if r = discount rate (fractional) then

$$\text{PV} = \frac{220}{(1+0.1)^1} = 200$$

Projects which yield a higher rate of return than 10 per cent (those to the right of *s* along *CC'*) will be accepted, and those with rates of return below 10 per cent (left of and above point *s*) will be rejected.

There are a number of features of the real world which very much complicate the above description of the Crusoe economy. In reality, there exist many individuals making separate investment and savings decisions and these may not always coincide. There are numerous types of investment, long-term and shorter-term investments, high-risk and low-risk investments, and consequently a variety of interest rates depending on the credit risks involved and the degree of liquidity.

In view of these considerations, it may be asked whether decisions on savings and investment made by individuals will necessarily prove optimal for society as a whole. For example, while individuals may 'know best' about their own welfare, can they realistically be expected to take a longer-term view involving future generations? If not, then society as a whole – which has such responsibilities – may need to adjust the 'market'-derived discount rate in making its own decisions about whether, and how much, to invest.

In order to investigate these issues, figure 6.9 can easily be transformed so that *CC'* now represents the production frontier facing society and I_1 represents the *social* indifference curve (that is, the consumption patterns between which society is indifferent). Once again, at *s* the *social rate of time preference* (STP) given by the slope I_1 equals the *marginal efficiency of capital* given by the slope of *CC'*. The latter is often referred to as the *social opportunity cost* (SOC) of capital, meaning the amount of current resources which has to be given up (or is displaced) to produce a unit of consumption in the future. In practice, it is taken to be represented by the rate of return on marginal projects in the private sector.

Clearly, the only point on the diagram where these two rates, SOC and STP, are equal is at *s*. Any other point will correspond to a sub-optimal level of investment and savings. The question facing the public sector, then, is how to determine the appropriate discount rate to apply to its own decisions regarding public investment. The problem here is that while the marginal efficiency of capital (MEC) or SOC rate is, in principle, observable, the social time preference rate is not – at least directly. This would not matter too much if there were no dispute concerning the equivalence of the SOC and STP rates. The general presumption, however, is that the observable 'market' rate is likely to exceed the STP rate at *s* so that the economy is in fact at a position such as *r* on the figure, corresponding to lower levels of investment, savings and welfare.

In the first place, market interest rates reflect the *private* rate of return rather than the *social* rate of return on investment. The latter is likely to be higher than the former because of spill-over effects from one sector to another which raise the productivity of labour and other factors of production elsewhere. Yet only the private rate of return will enter into individual investment decisions. As a result, levels of investment and savings in the economy may be too low (that is, discount rate too high).[13]

By itself, company taxation would also cause the market rate to diverge from the STP rate at *s*, since for a firm to pay *RR* per cent to its creditors it must in fact earn a rate of return on its capital in excess of *RR* per cent.[14]

In addition, as Pigou[15] has argued, market rates reflect the fact that individuals are 'myopic' and have an irrational preference for present consumption. If this is indeed that case, then use of market rates reflecting 'myopia' will tend to penalise the assessment of benefits which accrue at some distant point, perhaps to future generations.

For public sector projects of a long-term nature, the choice of a 'market'-derived test discount rate may, for these reasons, prove particularly objectionable. Pearce,[16] for example, illustrates this problem in the context of evaluating risks associated with storage of nuclear waste. Say it is known for certain that an event causing £10 billion in damage at current prices will occur in year 500. Discounting at 10 per cent using the above formula gives a present value of only 25 pence to the incident! More generally, the implications of this 'scaling-down' effect stretch far and wide to virtually all aspects of longer-term environmental importance.

Finally, the "market rate reflects the inability of the private sector to 'pool' risks across many projects (and taxpayers) in the way the public sector is able to do. As such market rates will reflect a positive 'risk premium' which will be higher the greater the lack of risk-pooling by institutions in the private sector."[17]

In practice, however, the opportunity cost approach – based on commercial rates of return – appears to have dominated thinking on public sector discounting. From 1969 onwards the Treasury test discount rate for public sector investment was set at 10 per cent. Currently, the minimum required rate of return stands at 5 per cent. It should be noted, however, that this represents a real rate of return with costs and benefits being expressed in real (that is, inflation-adjusted) values.

In defence of the SOC approach it is sometimes argued that setting a lower discount rate (reflecting STP) would redirect resources from the private to the public sector since the latter would only need to secure a lower rate of return. Against this it can be argued that the cost of borrowing for the government (that is, the yield on long-term government securities) is in fact lower than for the private sector, reflecting the fact that lending to the government involves no element of risk (that is, it is 'gilt-edged'). While public sector projects are not themselves riskless, a slightly lower rate than for the private sector would be justified since, as has been seen, a lower element of risk is inherent in public sector investment as a whole.

Perhaps the strongest argument for adopting a SOC approach is in the case where private sector output and investment compete directly, and could be displaced by public sector investment (for example, in haulage). In this event one might wish to ensure that the public sector does at least as well as any private sector projects it displaces.

However, the assumption underlying the SOC approach – that because of increased competition for available savings, public sector investment in some sense 'crowds-out' private sector investment – is not entirely without criticism. Firstly, since government revenue comes mainly from taxation (rather than borrowing), it is not only savings but also consumption which is displaced. If individuals are not content with the rate of return on public investments financed in this way (perhaps reflecting STP), it is up to them to change it via the democratic process. Secondly, with growing capital mobility it is increasingly difficult to argue that domestic investment is significantly restrained by the level of domestic savings (the United Kingdom, for example, has traditionally been a net exporter of investment funds).

In contrast, the main argument in favour of the STP rate is that it more fully reflects the rate at which society as a whole is prepared to trade present for future consumption.

There thus appears to be no clear-cut answer to the choice of discount rate and it has even been suggested that a compromise approach would be to choose a rate that reflects both SOC and STP. In practice, a variety of rates is often used in sensitivity testing. This is certainly a useful addition to CBA methods, given not only that STP and SOC rates are perceived to differ but also that estimates of either can vary over time. For example, in the late 1970s real interest rates were actually negative. Equally, estimates of the STP rate are sensitive (and positively related) to future expected growth rates. In the final analysis, it is important to recognise that the outcome of using a higher SOC-derived rate will affect not only the level of public investment but also its direction – penalising public sector projects where benefits are intrinsically long term in nature.

Conclusion

While CBA raises many conceptual and operational problems – particularly regarding the valuation of benefits and costs and the choice of discount rate – it has nevertheless established itself as a useful technique. It may not be as exact a technique as might be wished but it does at least provide the decision-maker with a rational framework, and it allows systematic examination of all aspects of a scheme, including intangibles which would not be allowed for in any purely private appraisal. This is an essential part of public sector investment; simply ignoring non-market effects does not make them go away, since even if CBA is not undertaken, any decision to go ahead or abandon a project carries an implicit statement about the present value of the social costs and benefits involved.

As Lichfield's Planning Balance Sheet approach (PBS)[18] has shown, the technique can be an important aid in the planning process, making clear the types of cost and benefit involved and the groups who are affected. In this approach the community is divided into categories (for example, producers and consumers) and the costs and benefits are calculated for each sector. The totals for the various sectors are then added to establish whether the scheme as a whole produces a net benefit or cost. Many of the items in the planning balance sheet relate to non-monetary costs and benefits; these may often be measured in physical or time units or, where they cannot be quantified in any way, are listed as intangibles. The PBS approach has the advantage of making clear not only the net social benefit of alternative projects but can also point to their distributional consequences.

For the urban planner, while CBA is a potentially useful aid to planning decisions it does not avoid the need to make value judgements in the comparison of intangibles arising from alternative projects and in the overall conclusions to be drawn from the assessment of costs and benefits. However, as long as such value judgements (for example, relating to distributional effects) are made clear, the analysis cannot be accused of 'subjectivity'.

CBA is least useful where the benefits of a project are intrinsically difficult to value. For example, if security considerations or perhaps the long-term development of an area are of overriding importance, then decision-making becomes a political issue. Similarly, where projects may have major irreversible consequences it can be argued that no decision should be made which severely limits the opportunities or options available to future generations. In contrast, CBA is perhaps most useful where a single project or only a few alternative projects are involved and where the range of intangibles is not too wide to make comparison difficult. In practice, it is often the case that once decisions are made in principle (for example, Roskill Commission on the Third London Airport), CBA is then brought in to facilitate the choice between alternative projects.

POLLUTION

Economic growth has produced[19]

> "the most notorious by-product of industrialisation the world has ever known . . . the pollution of the air and rivers with chemical wastes . . . the destruction of wild life by the indiscriminate use of pesticides, the changeover from animal farming to animal factories, and visible to all who have eyes to see, a rich heritage of natural beauty being wantonly and systematically destroyed – a heritage that cannot be restored in our lifetime."

The problem of controlling externalities caused by pollution is, if anything, more important and also more complex than has been the case in the past. Central government control dates back as far as 1863 when public outcry against emissions of hydrochloric acid gas from the alkali industry led to the Alkali Act of that year. Subsequently, control of industrial processes not covered by this act was granted to local authorities under the Public Health Acts; however, the emphasis was clearly not on prevention since action could only be taken if nuisance could be proved.

Following the great London smog of 1952, the Clean Air Act 1956 gave local authorities positive powers to control smoke, dust and grit emissions from combustion processes. These and subsequent acts have ensured improvements in urban air quality and substantial reductions in both smoke and sulphur dioxide emissions into the air.[20] Major industrial processes where there is a risk of toxic emissions or technical difficulties in control are additionally covered by the Health and Safety at Work Act 1974 and are under control of the Industrial Air Pollution Inspectorate (soon to be merged to form a central Inspectorate of Pollution). However, the powers to control the pollution emissions of many industrial processes (those which are left out of the scheduled processes under the control of a central Inspectorate) will unfortunately remain retrospective since the only legislation applicable remains the nuisance provisions of the Public Health Acts.[21]

But while some of the old-fashioned environmental problems of smoke and dust appear to be largely under control, scientific and public concern has shifted to the effects of toxic chemical pollutants, often at low-level concentrations. In particular, emissions of carbon monoxide and hydrocarbons have increased while emissions of nitrogen oxides have not declined.[20] Other pollutants such as lead and photochemical oxidants such as ozone have only been monitored more recently and at relatively few sites, but there is growing evidence to suggest that at elevated levels the effects may be injurious to humans and plant life.

In the urban context, primary atmospheric pollutants can react in the atmosphere to produce secondary pollutants such as photochemical smog – seriously affecting major cities, particularly Los Angeles and Tokyo, and many other cities under certain atmospheric conditions. The smog is formed by the photochemical action of sunlight on pollutants, mainly nitrogen oxides, aldehydes and certain hydrocarbons (from motor vehicles and industrial sources) which react to produce elevated levels of photochemical oxidants and visibility-reducing haze. Chemical reactions of this type are very complex (ozone, for example, may interact with other pollutants) and may occur over long periods of time as air masses are transported over long distances. The effects of secondary pollution are not therefore restricted to urban or industrial areas but in many cases take a wider geographical dimension.[20] A further example is that of acid deposition, which begins when sulphur dioxide and nitrogen oxide emissions – largely from power stations, industry and motor vehicles – are oxidised in the atmosphere to form sulphuric and nitric acids. The resulting acidic deposits are often transported across national frontiers, and are generally recognised as being a major cause of much of the recent damage to forests, lakes and rivers in Scandinavia, West Germany, France and Switzerland.

Other types of pollution (such as mercury and cadmium) – sometimes discharged into rivers or estuaries – pose special problems in that they are bio-accumulative and can become concentrated via the food chain, progressing, for example, through various forms of aquatic life as far as birds (as well as humans) feeding on poisoned fish. In such cases the effects of pollution are uncertain in magnitude and liable to occur at some distance or point in time from the initial emission. Moreover, since the effects are cumulative, reduction of emissions may not swiftly result in improved quality of the receiving environment. To achieve this, extensive clear-up of previous pollution may be needed. However, pollution problems do not always involve urban or industrial activities; for example, the over-use of nitrogen fertilisers by farmers in East Anglia and surrounding regions is blamed for the exceptionally high nitrate levels in drinking water that affect over a million people in that area.[22]

Finally, since some pollutants are considered very dangerous even in low concentrations, nothing short of a total ban on import and use may be considered reasonable (for example, brown and blue asbestos, previously used in the building industry). For other types of pollutant where exposure costs could be high (such as radiation or dioxin), the risk of exposure is fortunately minute if adequate precautions are taken. Nevertheless, the risk evaluation – derived from the probability of an incident occurring multiplied by the damage costs inflicted – may actually be high if low risk is offset by high potential damage costs. Locating such activities away from densely populated areas would be sensible (that is, would lower the risk evaluation), but regular monitoring may nevertheless be required.[20] Similarly, with the recently discovered problem of radioactive radon gas found in some homes, a reasonable suggested move would be to ensure that the problem is recognised when new housing is being sited and designed.[20]

An example will illustrate the alternative policy approaches to pollution control.[23] Assume that *A* is a firm discharging its waste products into a river and that *B* is a town downstream of *A* through which the river passes. Figure 6.10(i) shows how *A*'s marginal benefit curve, *MB* (that is, marginal revenue – marginal

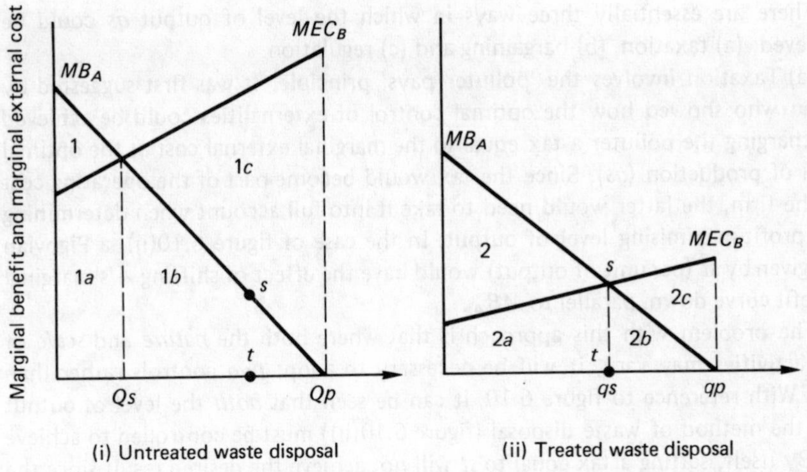

Figure 6.10 *Private benefits and social costs in production: the optimum level of pollution control*

cost) falls as output rises. If *A* were under no constraints it would maximise profits by operating at output *Qp*. The figure also shows *B*'s marginal external cost curve resulting from the effects of the river pollution. This is seen to rise from left to right since, with higher output and pollution, the town may experience higher water purification costs and may be unable to use the river for recreational purposes. If water quality deteriorates further, it may well become a nuisance for nearby residents. If *A* operates at output *Qp*, it can be seen that the total external cost inflicted upon *B* is given by the area under the *MEC* curve – that is, 1*a* + 1*b* + 1*c*. Similarly, the total benefit to *A* is given by area 1 + 1*a* + 1*b*.

Figure 6.10(ii) illustrates the case where the firm has undertaken steps to treat or reduce its waste disposal into the river. This has the effect of reducing the firm's marginal benefit curve (since marginal costs are now higher), but since, for any level of output, pollution is now lower, there is a substantial reduction in the town's marginal external cost curve. Operating at its profit-maximising output (*qp*) *A*'s total benefit is now slightly lower at 2 + 2*a* + 2*b*, but *B*'s total external cost is greatly reduced at 2*a* + 2*b* + 2*c*.

However, from the point of view of society the optimal solution is for production to take place up to the point where the marginal benefit to the firm of an extra unit produced is equal to the marginal external cost to the town. Beyond this point, marginal external cost to *A* exceeds the marginal benefit to *B*. In figures 6.10(i) and (ii) *MEC* equals *MB* at points *Qs* and *qs* respectively. However, point *qs* in figure 6.10(ii) is clearly superior since the net benefit to society is equal to area 2 (that is, 2 + 2*a* – 2*a*) while in figure 6.10(i) the net benefit at *Qs* is only area 1 (1 + 1*a* – 1*a*).

There are essentially three ways in which the level of output *qs* could be achieved: (a) taxation, (b) bargaining and (c) regulation.

(a) Taxation involves the 'polluter pays' principle. It was first suggested by Pigou who showed how the optimal control of externalities could be achieved by charging the polluter a tax equal to the marginal external cost at the optimal level of production (*qs*). Since the tax would become part of the operating cost of the firm, the latter would need to take it into full account when determining the profit-maximising level of output. In the case of figure 6.10(ii), a Pigovian tax given by *st* (per unit of output) would have the effect of shifting *A*'s marginal benefit curve down, parallel to MB_A.

The problem with this approach is that where both the *nature* and *scale* of *A*'s activities may vary, it will be necessary to adopt *two* controls rather than one. With reference to figure 6.10, it can be seen that *both* the level of output and the method of waste disposal (figure 6.10(ii)) must be controlled to achieve *qs*. By itself, setting a tax equal to *st* will not achieve the desired result since the firm would continue to produce (and discharge waste) as in figure 6.10(i) at a level of output slightly below *Qp*.

(b) If there is no impediment to negotiation between the parties involved, it can be shown that bargaining will always produce the optimal solution. In this case MB_A and MEC_B represent the bargaining curves of the two parties. If *A* is liable to pay compensation to *B* then the firm will choose to introduce waste treatment (figure 6.10(ii)), will pay 2*a* in compensation to *B* and retain a net gain of 2 (note: this is greater than 1 in figure 6.10(i)). Although the distributional consequences would differ, it might be possible for *B* to compensate *A* to achieve the same result; *B* would be willing to pay up to 1*a* + 1*b* + 1*c* – 2*a* to secure a level of *qs* output as in figure 6.10(ii). Although this may seem unfair, there may nevertheless be circumstances under which it might appear reasonable – for example, *B* might represent a new housing development and the firm *A* may not see why it should incur additional costs if it had been operating for some time without causing externalities when there had previously been few residents in the area.

In practice, however, negotiation may be virtually impossible if there are many sufferers and polluters or if the source of pollution is unclear.

(c) Regulation could operate if the firm were required firstly to undertake waste treatment (figure 6.10(ii)) and secondly to reduce output (and corresponding pollution) to *qp*. As with the tax solution, this would require full knowledge of *A*'s marginal benefit and *B*'s marginal cost curve, with and without pollution control. The administrative costs of obtaining this information (as well as monitoring discharges) may themselves be quite high and could at worst outweigh any benefits from the scheme. Given the problems involved, a second-best solution may be appropriate; if only the total costs and benefits of production are known, then a total ban on waste disposal would be better than *Qp* output, in figure 6.10(i) (since total costs of 1*a* + 1*b* + 1*c* exceed total benefits of 1 + 1*a* + 1*b*). If more is known about the alternatives, then a requirement that firms should undertake waste treatment (as in figure 6.10(ii) would be better still – giving a net gain of 2 – 2*c* at *qp*.

To sum up: firstly, if negotiation is possible then a tax is unnecessary except where distributional considerations are involved; secondly, where alternative production methods exist then two controls rather than one may be required; and thirdly, if there are substantial costs in imposing a tax, some form of regulation may be preferable.

In practice, environmental control policies are generally developed around Environmental or Air Quality Standards (EQSs/AQSs) or Emission Standards. At present in the United Kingdom, European Community directives set AQSs for lead, sulphur dioxide, smoke and nitrogen dioxide while water quality standards exist for drinking water (nitrate levels) and bathing areas. Examples of emission standards (ESs) exist for classes of alkali and acid works and for cadmium and mercury discharges. Environmental Quality Standards have the advantage of allowing for the fact that geographical differences may mean that disposal of pollutants – and therefore environmental impact – will often vary according to location. On the other hand, this can be criticised as providing a 'licence to pollute' up to certain levels. Finally, EQSs may often require considerable administration and monitoring. Emission standards have the advantage of being easy to implement and of supporting the 'polluter should pay' principle. To some extent, EQs and ESs can in practice be combined to achieve a given environmental objective, and limit values (LV) may require outer limits for both EQSs and ESs to be achieved.

To prevent unnecessary pollution, new firms may increasingly be required to engage in the 'best practicable means' of preventing or counteracting the effect of the nuisance, even where EQSs are not infringed (for example, sulphur dioxide and smoke, cadmium and mercury). In short, the type of control required will depend on a wide range of considerations including damage and nuisance caused, the desired achievement of environmental quality objectives, the ease of dispersion and environmental capacity, and the costs of abatement. However, objectivity and scientific proof are not always easily achieved or obtained given the numerous issues and uncertainties involved; in the words of one specialist (on the problem of lead pollution) "the things we would like to know may be unknowable, so there is some virtue in just getting rid of the problem."[24]

In the case of lead pollution, levels of airborne lead in the United Kingdom have been found to be highest in urban areas, and in the vicinity of motorways and busy main roads, and considerably lower in rural areas. In the United States, where the air quality standard is 1.5 microgrammes per cubic metre, most urban areas were found to be within a range of 0.5–2.0 microgrammes, while most rural sites fell below 0.2 microgrammes,[25] illustrating the urban nature of the problem. Although lead can be ingested from a number of other sources (such as water, paint, dust and industrial sources), petrol emissions are regarded as being a major contributor, and lead emissions from motor vehicles in the United Kingdom have averaged around 7000 tonnes per year in recent years. Given the mounting evidence that even relatively low blood lead levels can cause behavioural problems and affect the learning ability of children, there is surely an urgent need for steps to be taken to remove lead from petrol. Although the European Community is pressing for its swift removal – a move which could also help the introduction of exhaust catalysts to control other exhaust emissions – it is unlikely that this would achieve any substantial reduction from existing vehicles for some time to come.

The complexity of problems brought out by urban pollution can be further illustrated by reference to the findings of several surveys concerning spatial differences in health. In a study in the United States, the concentration of three measures of pollution (sulphur dioxide, nitrogen dioxide and suspended particles) was generally found to increase with city size. The study suggested that major health benefits relating to respiratory diseases and cardiovascular diseases (estimated at more than $1½ billion annually in direct savings on earnings and medical costs) could be achieved from a 50 per cent reduction in air pollution in major urban areas.[26] While no such monetary estimates have been made for the United Kingdom, the results of studies examining (standardised) mortality rates from various diseases, particularly lung-bronchus cancer, show (for 1980–82) that these have tended to be considerably higher in large urban areas as opposed to rural areas; large parts of the cities of West Central Scotland, Tyne and Wear, Cleveland, Humberside, Merseyside, Greater Manchester, West Midlands and Inner London all appear to experience mortality rates more than 20 per cent above the United Kingdom average, rising in some cases to as much as 80 per cent.[27] When compared with earlier studies (for example 1959–63)[28] the overall geographical pattern seems largely unchanged except that there appears to have been a marked improvement in Greater London and the surrounding area, apart from Inner London.

What such studies show is a link between certain aspects of urban living and ill-health relating to diseases where environmental factors (often in combination with other factors) play a recognised role. Unfortunately, given the difficulties involved in separating environmental from other factors (such as income, housing, lifestyle etc.), the exact contribution of the former is often obscured.

In future and under the influence of European Community policy (such as Framework Directive 1984), pollution control is likely to involve a wider range of industrial processes and a greater degree of openness and public accountability. With respect to planning, it has been suggested that firms' confidential discussions with the Industrial Air Pollution Inspectorate should cease to be held separately from the discussions with local authorities regarding planning permission.[26] Pollution and development control policies have been brought closer by a recent European Community directive obliging member states to examine closely the environmental effects or impacts of major construction projects before they are implemented.

Finally, pollution control on a worldwide scale might be implemented through the United Nations. A start was made in 1987 when 21 industrial nations agreed at Geneva to cut their sulphur dioxide emissions (mainly from power stations) by 30 per cent by 1993. The United Kingdom, however, refused to sign the treaty, largely because of cost considerations. Talks on reducing emissions of nitrogen oxides, moreover, broke down since a number of countries, in addition to the United Kingdom, claimed that measures proposed by West Germany and Sweden were too impracticable to implement.[28] It is of note that £600 million will be invested in desulphurisation equipment in three major power stations in the United Kingdom by 1997 and a further £170 million will be spent on reducing emissions of nitrogen oxides at 12 power stations, but these sums almost pale into insignificance when compared with the £13 billion West Germany is committed to spend in reducing pollution from power stations over the same period.[30]

REFERENCES

1. N. Kaldor, 'Welfare Propositions of Economics and Interpersonal Comparisons of Utility', *Economic Journal*, 49 (1939).
2. J. Hicks, 'The Valuation of Social Income', *Economica*, 7 (1940).
3. See R. Lipsey and R. Lancaster, 'The General Theory of the Second Best', *Review of Economic Studies*, 24 (1957); W. J. Baumol, 'On Taxation and Control of Externalities', *American Economic Review*, 62 (1972).
4. See D. W. Pearce, *Cost–Benefit Analysis*, 2nd edn (Macmillan, 1983).
5. W. J. Baumol, *Welfare Economics and the Theory of the State* (Bell & Sons, 1965).
6. O. A. Davis and A. B. Whinston, 'The Economics of Urban Renewal', *Journal of Law and Contemporary Problems*, 16 (1961).
7. J. Vipond and B. Walker, 'The Determinants of Housing Expenditure and Owner-Occupation', *Bull. Oxford Inst. Econ. Stats.*, 34 (1972); M. Ball and R. Kirwan, 'Urban Housing Demand: Some evidence from Cross-Sectional Data', *Applied Economics*, 9 (1977).
8. See C. M. Price, *Welfare Economics in Theory and Practice* (Macmillan, 1977).
9. D. W. Pearce, *Cost–Benefit Analysis*, 1st edn (Macmillan, 1971).
10. (Roskill) Commission on the Third London Airport, *Report* (HMSO, 1970, 1971); C. D. Foster and M. E. Beesley, 'Estimating the Social Benefit of Constructing an Underground Railway in London', *Journal of the Royal Statistical Society*, Series A, 126 (1963); R. Layard (ed.), *Cost–Benefit Analysis* (Penguin, 1972).
11. See D. W. Pearce, *Environmental Economics* (Macmillan, 1975).
12. R. Layard (ed.), *Cost–Benefit Analysis* (Penguin, 1972).
13. A. Sen, 'On Optimising the Rate of Saving', *Economic Journal*, 71 (1961); 'Isolation, Assurance and the Social Rate of Discount', *Quarterly Journal of Economics*, 81 (1967).

14. W. J. Baumol, 'On Taxation and Control of Externalities', *American Economic Review*, 62 (1972).
15. A. C. Pigou, *The Economics of Welfare* (Macmillan, 1920).
16. D. W. Pearce, *Cost-Benefit Analysis* (Macmillan, 1983).
17. R. Arrow and R. Lind, 'Uncertainty and the Evaluation of Public Investment Decisions', *American Economic Review*, 60 (1970).
18. N. Lichfield, 'Cost-Benefit Analysis in Town Planning: a Case Study, Swanley', *Urban Studies*, 3 (1966); N. Lichfield and H. Chapman, 'Cost-Benefit Analysis in Urban Expansion: a Case Study, Ipswich', *Urban Studies*, 7 (1970).
19. E. J. Mishan, *The Cost of Economic Growth* (Staples, 1967).
20. Royal Commission on Environmental Pollution, *10th Report* (HMSO, 1984).
21. R. J. Perriman, 'New Approaches to Air Pollution Control', *6th International Environment and Safety Conference* (1986).
22. *Guardian* (16 December, 1986).
23. R. Turvey, 'On Divergencies between Social Cost and Private Cost', *Economica*, August (1963).
24. Sir J. Gowans, quoted in Royal Commission on Environmental Pollution, *10th Report* (HMSO, 1984).
25. Royal Commission on Environmental Pollution, *9th Report* (HMSO, 1983).
26. I. Hoch, 'Urban Scale and Environmental Quality' in R. G. Ridker (ed.), *Pollution, Resources and the Environment* (U.S. Commission on Population Growth and the Environment, Washington DC, USGPO, 1972).
27. G. M. Howe, 'Does it matter where I live', *Transactions of British Geographers* (1985).
28. G. M. Howe, *National Atlas of Disease and Mortality in the UK* (Nelson, 1970).
29. J. Erlichman, 'UK brings pollution talks to a halt', *Guardian* (5 September, 1987).
30. J. Erlichman, 'Britain shuns first global pact on cutting acid rain pollution', *Guardian* (2 September, 1987).

7

Urban Congestion, Decay and Renewal

There can be little doubt that population increase and urban decay rank among the world's biggest problems. The problems are severe in industrial countries with high population densities. In the United Kingdom, for example, the population increased from 27.4 million in 1870 to 56.3 million in 1986 and with an area of 22.7 million hectares the overall density of about 1 person per 0.4 hectare is one of the highest in the world. For reasons of economic opportunity, over three-quarters of the rapidly growing population have left the countryside since the beginning of the Industrial Revolution to live in towns and cities – urban areas substantially increasing in size. An estimate by Best[1] in 1964, showed that in 1900 about 5 per cent of England and Wales was urban, by 1939 this figure was 8.6 per cent and by 1950 it had reached 10 per cent. It was forecast that by 2000 it could conceivably reach 15–16 per cent.

But even if, as seems likely, population grows more slowly than in the recent past or even falls, there would still be a tendency towards urbanisation. As accommodation standards improve, high density ninteenth-century housing is replaced by either lower density overspill estates, or by relatively low density development within the inner areas of towns. Best[1] estimated that whereas in 1900 24.9 urban hectares were necessary to house 1000 people, in 1960 35.1 hectares were required and by 2000 38.1 might be needed.

Urbanisation was both the result and cause of an increase in GNP. Between 1870 and 1985 the GNP increased from £929 million to £305 547 million or on a *per capita* basis from £35 to £5398. But economic growth is not without its price – a figure largely omitted from GNP statistics. It has caused appalling traffic congestion in our towns and cities, it has brought about the decay of the inner urban areas since 'greenfield' locations have become more attractive for residential populations and more profitable for employers, and its effects have put increased pressure on local government finance.

ECONOMICS AND THE TRAFFIC CONGESTION PROBLEM

Transport plays an important role in determining the scale, nature and form of our urban areas. Although in Greater London the proportion of land occupied by roads is only 16 per cent, in other cities in Britain the proportions are often much higher with the amount of land in central areas devoted to streets and parking rising towards the United States levels of 40 per cent in Cincinnati, 50 per cent in Detroit or 60 per cent in Los Angeles.[2] In addition, railway facilities, airports and docks and harbours make transportation land overall the major urban land use after housing. The efficiency of transport and implicitly the efficiency of the use of land for transportation contribute greatly to the level of productivity, growth and thus the standard of living. Ironically it is a higher standard of living, together with changing social habits and technical advance (permitting more convenient and personal travel over more extensive areas), which produce the problems of urban road transport.

ROAD USE AND DEVELOPMENT

In the years from 1910 to 1986 the number of road vehicles licensed in Great Britain increased very substantially from 144 000 to 21 million. It has been forecast by the Transport and Road Research Laboratory of the Department of the Environment that by 1995 the number of motor vehicles in Great Britain will reach 23 million and by 2005, 27.7 million (double that of 1970). Over 80 per cent of the total will be private motor cars.

Although there was an increase in total expenditure on highways from £312.2 million in 1963 to £3346 million in 1986, its share of gross domestic product (GDP) at factor cost decreased from 1.23 to 1.05 per cent – an appallingly low proportion of public expenditure despite the United Kingdom (by European Community standards) having above-average traffic densities with the degree of overcrowding substantially increasing (table 7.1).

Clearly, road-building and improvements have not kept pace with the growth of motor traffic. There is now less than 1 metre of trunk and principal road (including motorway) for each vehicle in Britain – largely the result of road expenditure being low by international comparisons and low in relation to road taxation (table 7.1).

In densely populated areas, such as inner London, increased investment in roads and/or public transport seems to be necessary. Surveys have shown that these places are at crisis point as far as traffic is concerned and that urban renewal needs to take account of the desire for better mobility.

According to Roth,[3] however, there are four principal approaches to congestion and its effects:

(1) Doing nothing, and allowing congestion to be its own deterrent.

(2) Redeveloping cities to accommodate all the vehicles wishing to use them (assuming public funds are available).

(3) Restricting the use of motor vehicles in inner areas so as to reduce total traffic volumes down to the capacity of existing streets.

Table 7.1 *Some international comparisons of traffic density, taxation and expenditure*

	Vehicles per kilometre			Percentage of state revenue 1985		Road expenditure as a percentage of road tax
	All roads		Motorways and main roads	Taxes incurred by motorists	Road expenditure	
	1975	1985	1985			
Great Britain	46	53	1220	8.1	2.2	27.2
France	22	30	697	13.8	5.1	37.0
West Germany	42	55	679	3.7	2.4	64.9
Italy	50	75	438	22.9	13.4	58.5
European Community (average)*	33	40	611	10.0	4.6	46.0

*The European Community averages for 1985 relate to countires which were members also in 1975.
Source: British Road Federation, *Basic Road Statistics.*

(4) Imposing an economic solution by recognising that road space is scarce and rationing it by a direct form of pricing.

Following the publication of the Buchanan Report[4] in 1963 the second approach became widely considered and influenced transport policies throughout the 1960s. The report proposed the provision of 'urban corridors' to take general and particularly peak-hour and through traffic, and a hierarchy of distributory roads filtering traffic of different sorts into 'urban rooms' or environmental areas. The aim was to ensure that in all places 'environmental capacity' would be realised – that is, the maximum level of permitted traffic would have to be compatible with the environment of the associated area.

Although new road patterns would best achieve these proposals, the existing road network could be temporarily modified by means of prevailing traffic management schemes and urban planning concepts. With limited financial resources, a choice would have to be made between accessibility and environmental requirements, but with more financial availability Buchanan believed that cities could accommodate the increased volumes of traffic forecast provided the urban physical structure were redeveloped.

But the Buchanan thesis was subject to much criticism:

(1) It relied quite heavily on the depreciation and obsolescence of buildings and subsequent urban renewal brought about by massive investment. But given such opportunities for change, it would become possible to opt for a programme of decentralisation – the physical difficulties in accommodating the ultimate traffic level not then occurring.

(2) It may have over-forecast the number of future vehicles in use in Britain. As urban net residential densities rise there is usually a reduction in the proportion of residents owning cars regardless of income groups. However, if substantial decentralisation took place the proportion of car owners would increase, but the *raison d'être* for Buchanan's proposals would cease to exist.

(3) It was questionable whether financial resources would be available to implement the recommendations of the Report except on a very piecemeal basis.

Even so, the Buchanan Report highlighted the fact that transport planning is at the heart of the problems of urban planning. It recognised that transport can do great environmental damage through noise and air pollution and visual intrusion, and that developments in transport (in the form of increased car ownership and declining public transport services) may have contributed to social polarisation. There are two kinds of urban transport costs incurred by the community – direct costs and indirect costs.

Direct Costs

These comprise the initial costs of highway construction, ancillary capital costs of road servicing equipment, loan charges on capital and ancillary costs on such things as lighting, signs, research, administration and policing – and totalled

£3346 million in 1986/87. It can be argued that motorists should at least meet these costs, but although they contribute very large sums each year in fuel tax, value added tax and vehicle excise tax, these payments (£13 755 million in 1986/87) are regarded as part of general taxation. The principle that motorists, by taxation, do not pay specifically or indirectly for the use of roads was established in 1935 with the abolition of the road fund tax.

Indirect Costs

Congestion costs

The most obvious indirect cost is that of traffic congestion. Congestion costs are imposed mainly by motorists upon other motorists and include the costs of time lost in delays and at lower speeds and the costs of higher fuel consumption – for example, when the average speed falls from 32 km/h (20 mph) to 16 km/h (10 mph), fuel consumption can rise by at least 50 per cent. The Road Pricing Panel of the Ministry of Transport estimated in the 1960s that total time-wasting costs per vehicle mile resulting from congestion were 2p at 32 km/h (20 mph) rising to 17½p at 16 km/h (10 mph) and 30p at 13 km/h (8 mph). The costs of delay can be identified as those relating to the class of vehicle involved, to the driver's (and crew's) time, to the passenger's time, and to the police involved in traffic regulations.

The Road Research Laboratory calculated in 1959 that annual traffic congestion costs amounted to £250 million. In the same year C. T. Bruner of Shell-Mex suggested that the probable cost was nearer £500 million. With inflation and the increase in the number of vehicles in the 1960s–1980s the cost now is considerably in excess of £1000 million per annum.

Congestion clearly adds to the cost of public road transport services; a 2 or 3 km/h increase in the average speed of urban buses could produce annual savings of millions of pounds.

In addition to delay, congestion and associated poor road surfaces result in motorists having to incur a high rate of vehicle depreciation, notably because of tyre, brake and clutch wear.

Of course motorists do pay these congestion costs but not equitably nor with any account being taken of the optimum use of road space or the individual's time. If motorists were forced to pay their full share of these costs, congestion might be greatly reduced.

But some congestion costs are clearly not borne in any form by motorists. This is when congestion reduces accessibility to such an extent that central-area land values diminish (as is the case in many US cities). But up to now, non-economic factors such as prestige enable the central areas of British cities to retain their attraction as business centres, though the development of out-of-town shopping centres, geared to the motorist, may have an effect on central-area values in the future.

Environmental costs

Although the burden of congestion affects the community as a whole because of the resultant noise, fumes and visual affliction, the environmental spill-off from motor traffic is not just confined to congested urban streets. Suburban and rural areas can be adversely affected even though roads may be used well below capacity.

Accident costs

Road accidents resulting from congestion or other causes are likewise difficult to value. The 'direct' cost of road accidents was estimated by the Royal Society for the Prevention of Accidents to be £136 million in 1950 and £200 million in 1960. By the 1980s the cost exceeded £500 million. But these costs are partly based on outdated scales of charges laid down by insurance companies regarding ambulance services, treatment and limited hospitalisation.

Opportunity costs

Land and other resources for roads could be used for housing, hospitals, schools and open space. Roads, by having alternative use values, often impose high opportunity costs on urban communities.

Disequilibrium of Demand and Supply

The provision of road space, at a price to the motorist substantially less than cost, inevitably results in excessive demand. Prior to an examination of possible solutions to the problems of excess use, the underlying features of demand and supply are considered.

Demand comprises journeys to work (the largest component of demand), travelling during work, and journeys for shopping or leisure purposes. More specifically there is peak demand – with longer-distance commuting becoming an increasingly important feature; revealed demand – the overall level of demand determined by population size and distribution, incomes and wealth, car-ownership preference and working hours; and suppressed demand – the traffic generated in response to the construction of new roads or the improvement of existing roads.

Supply consists of roads and railway track, and either private or public transport – private car, motorcycle, moped, bicycle or bus, train or tube. But although in mass-commuting the tube is four times more efficient than the bus, and the bus eight times more efficient than the car, the car is more flexible, convenient and comfortable and scores heavily over public transport over short journeys – all compensating the motorist's incurred cost of congestion.

Short-term solutions

Immediate reactions to the problem of disequilibrium have included the more intensive use of short-haul bus services, the adding of extra coaches to commuter rail services and the adoption of new traffic management schemes (such as one-way roads, linked signals and clearways), but the overall gain is usually minimal and at best stop-gap.

Long-term solutions

These have involved large-scale road development to allow for a freer traffic flow. This approach was used widely throughout the 1950s and 1960s, reinforced by the Buchanan proposals, and figured largely in the Greater London Development Plan 1969.

But new road development provides an unrealistic solution because:

(*a*) There would be an adverse environmental impact. The Crowther Steering Group to the Buchanan Report warned that UK cities could not accommodate US-style road patterns.

(*b*) Despite higher speeds, real time-saving may not be reduced as greater distances would be involved. Suppressed demand would soon saturate capacity.

(*c*) Public transport would become uneconomic as diverted demand would reduce revenue, necessitating higher fares or reduced services.

(*d*) The cost of development would be enormous – over £19 million/km in inner areas falling to £5 million in suburban areas. Investment in public transport would be much more cost effective – for example, the initial 18 km of the Victoria Line cost £60 million to develop in the 1960s and has a capacity of 40 000 passengers per hour; 18 km of an urban motorway would have cost £132 million and carried only 10 000 persons per hour (at an average of 1.4 persons per car). Yet public transport usually operates at a loss and will continue to do so until the motorist pays the full costs of his road usage.

In the very long term, excess demand could be eliminated by both strategic and detailed land-use planning. New linear settlements, out-of-town shopping and industrial and commercial relocation would extinguish inward and outward commuter traffic flows. The dilution of peak demand could be brought about also by a radical staggering of working, shopping and leisure hours.

Both in the short and long term, demand must be controlled so as to equate with the supply of transport facilities.

Road Pricing Theory

An economic system allocates factors of production and distributes goods and services so as to maximise social welfare. A traditional way of doing this is by means of the price mechanism with competitive markets and with prices, determined competitively for each product, paid ultimately out of individual consumer incomes. With freedom to enter a market, suppliers produce on a maximum profit basis at a price equalling the cost of the last unit of output (marginal cost). Enough of each item is purchased by consumers to make the marginal benefits from spending an extra unit of income in all cases equal.

But in the case of roads, supply and demand considerations are entirely different. The motorist is influenced essentially by marginal private costs – those which he incurs directly and which expand as congestion increases. He will continue to use road space, however congested, as long as his marginal private costs are less than the marginal private benefits (monetary and non-monetary) which he enjoys through using his vehicle. It must be assumed that his marginal private benefits equal the price he is willing to pay and therefore are equivalent to demand. Marginal social costs equal marginal private costs plus the cost that the vehicle imposes on the rest of the traffic – that is, congestion costs.

The demand for road space is the relationship between the price of a vehicle-kilometre (determined largely by fuel and vehicle taxation) and the quantity of vehicle-kilometres required at that price. As the price of a vehicle-kilometre falls the quantity demanded expands, and as the price rises the quantity demanded contracts. For essential journeys, demand is relatively insensitive to price changes and is inelastic, but in the case of less essential journeys demand is fairly sensitive to price changes and is relatively elastic.

In figure 7.1 marginal private costs (MPC) equal demand D at t, the maximum traffic flow an individual motorist is willing to join. But at this level of flow, marginal social costs (MSC) are considerably higher – the individual motorist clearly not paying the extra cost of congestion that he is imposing on other road users. If the traffic flow was reduced to t_1, then marginal social costs would equal demand. The imposition of a road tax equal to an estimation of the difference between marginal social costs and marginal private costs at t_1 would lead to a contraction of demand from t to t_1 as the price the motorist would be obliged to pay would have risen from p to p_1.

Under such a direct road pricing system, the best use of existing roads would be realised as each motorist would pay the marginal social cost resulting from his use. This would be equivalent to the optimum price and would be independent of the capital cost of the system. The major difficulty in applying this system is in determining the optimum level of traffic. Ideally, the price imposed should reduce the level of traffic to where the revenue collected equals the costs imposed by the vehicle upon the community in general and other vehicles in particular, but trial and error would be inevitable in pricing and establishing the optimum flow. Despite these difficulties direct road pricing was recommended by the Smeed Report[5] in 1964. It suggested that variations from the optimum price might be made with little loss of benefit. If revenue exceeded total congestion costs, a self-financing road expansion or improvement programme would be feasible but, if revenue fell short of total congestion costs, road contraction might be necessary. Only in the long term should revenue equal total congestion costs.

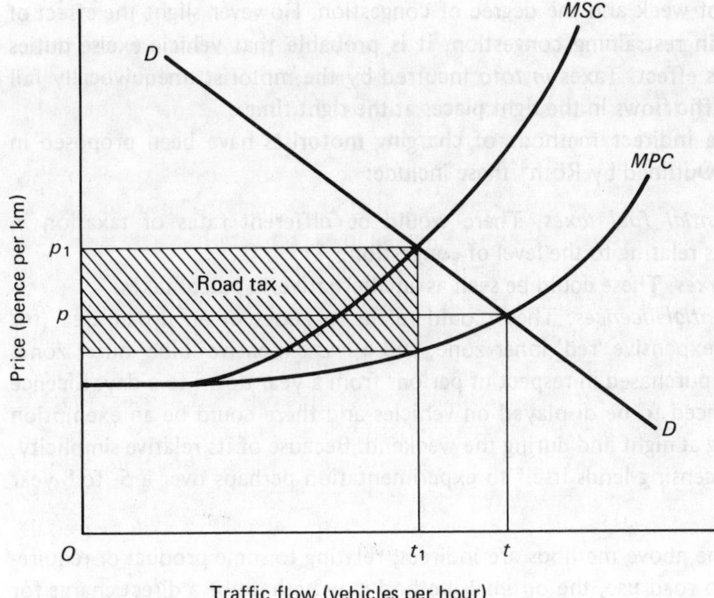

Figure 7.1 *Road tax and costs*

A system of road pricing would thus involve road users paying more directly for the consumption of road space. Road space would be broadly subject to the economic principles on which we rely for the allocation of most of our goods and services. The advantages of this is that it would lead to the more efficient use of existing roads because users would be deterred by higher charges from using congested roads and encouraged by low charges to use uncongested roads; and there would be a built-in criterion for investment, namely profitability. Currently, vehicle and fuel taxation assume as given the existing costs of the road system, and total costs are allocated among users and non-users without there being any reliable guidance as to which sections of the road network should be expanded and which contracted.

Methods of Road Pricing

The current method of taxing motorists (involving vehicle licences, value added tax and petrol tax) fails to cope with current traffic problems in the following ways. It does not discriminate between locations where congestion costs are high or low; it fails to discriminate between times when congestion costs rise or fall; and although more petrol tax is paid on heavy-fuel consuming vehicles than on low-fuel consuming vehicles this is completely independent of location, time of day, or day of week and the degree of congestion. However slight the effect of petrol taxes in restraining congestion, it is probable that vehicle excise duties have even less effect. Taxes *in toto* incurred by the motorist unequivocally fail to control traffic flows in the right places at the right times.

Alternative indirect methods of charging motorists have been proposed in recent years. Outlined by Roth[3] these include:

(a) *Differential fuel taxes*. There would be different rates of taxation in different areas relating to the level of congestion.

(b) *Tyre taxes*. These could be seen as an alternative to petrol taxes.

(c) *Differential licences*. These could relate to zones of an urban area (for example, an expensive 'red' inner zone, and a less expensive 'blue' outer zone) and could be purchased in respect of periods from a year down to a day. Licence discs would need to be displayed on vehicles and there could be an exemption from licensing at night and during the weekend. Because of its relative simplicity, differential licensing lends itself to experimentation perhaps over a 5- to 8-year period.

Whereas the above methods are indirect, relating to some product or requirement allied to road use, the optimal method may perhaps be a direct charge for road use. Direct charging could be by means of one or more of the following methods.

(a) *Toll gates*. Although these are the earliest and simplest method to have been used, in urban areas they can be costly, inefficient, can impede traffic flow and are impracticable where a large number of access points are required.

(b) *Off-vehicle systems*. Identification devices fitted to vehicles would activate a vehicle identification apparatus which would relay information to a central computer station. Motorists would be sent accounts periodically for settlement.

(c) *On-vehicle point pricing*. Meters attached to vehicles would pick up electrical impulses from cables laid across the road at selected pricing points. The meters would be periodically read by the pricing authority and accounts would be settled.

(d) *On-vehicle continuous pricing*. Vehicles would be charged according to the time or distance travelled in a designated pricing zone. The meter would expire after a length of time or distance travelled in the pricing zone.

Both off- and on-pricing systems would be based on a variable schedule – with maximum prices being charged during peak hours and in congested central areas. The point pricing system has advantages. It would not create the same boundary problems inherent in the continuous pricing system; it could be employed for toll collection on bridges and in tunnels; and it would not encourage bad driving habits in an attempt to reduce payable time. The main advantages of the continuous pricing system are the ease of collecting payment (the main administrative difficulty of the point pricing system) and its relevance to motorists living and even driving entirely within a pricing zone – a situation which could not be controlled by the point pricing system. Both private and social costs could be reduced, however, if motorists installed computerised route-guidance systems in their vehicles.

Some Economic Consequences of Direct Road Pricing

The disadvantages of direct road pricing are numerous:

(1) Many critics[6] predict that urban motoring would become the privilege of the wealthy.

(2) As a high proportion of low-income motorists travels exclusively in towns and largely at peak hours, a road tax would be clearly regressive.

(3) It was argued by Richardson,[7] however, that middle income motorists would suffer most. The low-income non-motorist might benefit from cheaper and more reliable public transport, the wealthy could afford the road tax without hardship, but the middle income car owner might wish to continue using his car and incur the burden of the tax.

(4) If the road tax revenue was entirely invested into new and improved roads, congestion might ultimately re-appear. Sharp[8] suggested that motorists would initially trade-off the new tax against reduced travelling times.

(5) If sufficient private motorists diverted their demand to public transport, overcrowded services and higher marginal costs of operation might result.

(6) Private traffic might be forced off congested routes by road pricing and use less busy residential streets as 'short cuts' – thereby spreading environmental costs.

(7) Although it is technically possible to adopt a road pricing system by means of electronic devices, administrators and the police prefer a non-discriminatory system applicable to all sections of the community, and not one which is difficult to enforce or can be interpreted as being unfair.

(8) Continually changing conditions in the view of Munby,[9] would make it necessary to adjust prices – the optimum price being difficult to estimate initially. It cannot be assumed that motorists (any more than non-motorists) always react rationally to changing economic circumstances. Road pricing would result inevitably in under capacity or excess capacity of road space.

(9) A system of road pricing aimed at restricting the number of vehicles entering urban areas would necessitate the development of costly diversionary ring roads or by-passes for the use of through traffic. Often referred to as 'lorry routes' these roads might have no less of an impact on the environment than the existing full-capacity roads of the inner built-up area.

But the advantages of direct road pricing as seen by Hewitt, Lemon, Roth and Walters[10] are no less substantial:

(1) The resulting reduction in traffic in congested areas would produce a freer flow of traffic.

(2) The subsequent increase in average speeds would reduce the costs of delay.

(3) There would be a considerable saving in paid working time of persons travelling during employment, and a saving in fuel – of great importance at a time of high energy costs.

(4) There would be greater productivity from buses and commercial vehicles. In the case of buses there could either be fewer crews and stocks required for the same level of service or existing crews and stocks could produce a higher level of service. It is unlikely that road pricing would lead to an increase in fares.

(5) Road tax revenue would provide local and central government with funds for the improvement of road networks, the subsidisation of public transport or for general purposes.

(6) Provided traffic did not become diffused over the road network and continued using (but at less volume) traditional routes, there could be a net reduction in environmental affliction.

Road pricing has a number of general consequences. Motorists continuing to use road space would incur a higher cost, a cost previously passed on to other motorists. But they would probably attempt to minimise these costs whenever possible by travelling at cheaper times or by cheaper routes, by making fewer but bigger shopping expeditions and by making greater use of vehicle passenger capacity. Road pricing might only be intended to reduce traffic flows by 10–12 per cent, and this reduction might only involve less-essential journeys, the 'second car' trip makers and those middle income commuters ready to transfer from the motor car to public transport as soon as the former becomes more expensive and/or the latter becomes more attractive.

Road pricing would probably not be difficult to enforce – certainly no more difficult than enforcing the 30 m.p.h. (48 km/h) speed limit where it is estimated that only 10 per cent of offenders get caught. But rather than low fines and a low rate of enforcement, high fines could be imposed which would probably deter potential lawbreakers.

Investment

It is all too obvious that since urban roads are frequently congested, a solution to the problems of congestion would involve an increase in the supply of road space, at least on a selective basis but sometimes extensively. In practice, investment techniques are not adequately sophisticated to produce an optimum solution. Conventionally, the future unrestrained traffic flows over the urban road network are forecast, and there is then an attempt to allocate resources and provide facilities to meet this demand. Various *ad hoc* constraints may be proposed where flows would still be excessive.

Investment must take into account present costs and future needs. Although costs (at least direct costs) are predictable, benefits may not be. Information is required on how road development affects traffic speeds, delays, travelling costs, accidents, the environment, property values, commerce and industry – that is, how it affects vehicle-operating costs and indirect costs. Road development is economically justifiable if total benefits exceed total costs.

The economist's role in road investment is to assess the relative costs and benefits of the alternative proposals advanced by planners and highway engineers. An increasingly pursued approach is to undertake a cost–benefit analysis (see chapter 6). With regard to road investment, it was first used in Oregon in the 1930s to help select a route between two points. Although the costs of development were compared with the benefits of savings in fuel, time and tyre wear, there was no consideration of the indirect effects on local economies. Likewise the London–Birmingham motorway was subject to a cost–benefit analysis in the 1950s (after a decision had already been taken to build it). This also ignored the more indirect benefits and costs.

But the main problem in undertaking a cost–benefit analysis, especially in urban areas, is to quantify and value all the many intangibles obtaining to the project. Since the pricing system is dominant, producers generally rely on the cost–profit criterion as a means of assessing investment priorities, but in the case of road development this simpler, less costly and possibly more effective approach requires the establishment of an efficient road pricing system before it can be applied.

Road pricing would result in highway authorities adopting the attitude of a competitive service industry, that is, expanding investment in the profitable sections and reducing expenditure on the less profitable or loss-making sections. In the former, costs borne by the authorities would increase but congestion costs would diminish. Lower congestion costs might then justify a reduction in charges if the savings enjoyed were greater than the development, environmental and other costs. Although profits would be made on some roads and losses on others (the flexibility of road pricing not being perfect) road pricing would indicate the level of demand, identify the locations for development and be very useful in investment decision-making.

To date, no effective solutions have been applied to the problem of urban traffic congestion. Meanwhile, despite increasing energy prices, the shift from public to private transport continues. It is over twenty years since the Buchanan Report was published but no technological answers have been found to solve the problems imposed by cars and highways on people. Architects, engineers and planners are unable to develop towns to accommodate traffic satisfactorily at present and future densities even at unrealistically high costs. Restricting traffic from entering large areas of towns and re-routeing it away is not entirely feasible because of the numbers of vehicles involved and the effect on populations elsewhere. Demand reverting to public transport as it exists today is unlikely to take place (especially with rising fares), and there are no technological developments anticipated which would eliminate the attraction of the private car as a personal mode of transport.

Indirect methods of pricing currently ignore congestion as they do not relate to the price users have to pay to the costs of road use. Although direct road pricing systems seem complex, they would greatly simplify the overall problem of congestion by equating demand and supply. They would also assist in ordering the priorities of use and increasing the efficiency of roads, ensuring a more stable foundation for the operation of public transport services, improving the urban environment and providing a valid means by which public authorities would be able to allocate resources for both road development and related public activities.

There is no reliable evidence to suggest that road pricing would reduce the attractiveness of town centres with regard to commerce or amenity. Road pricing would be probably less detrimental to the economic and social life of the town than current levels of congestion.

Yet road pricing has not been introduced. There have been political reasons for this; the motorists' lobby is very strong and in the public sector there are wide-ranging implications (not just confined to transport) in the concept that the consumer should pay the full marginal social cost for goods and services received. But central government may come around to accepting road pricing. In the 1970s, an official publication[11] suggested that the government was thinking along these lines. But even with political acceptability, it may take until the 1990s before it is administratively feasible for an on-vehicle system to be applied.

Car Parking

At least since the Road Traffic Act 1956, which endeavoured to reduce congestion, local authorities have had powers to prohibit or restrict parking, and consequently (in theory) to restrict the total amount of traffic entering cities. The capacity of parking space (by time of day) is roughly related to the capacity of the road system. Parking restrictions and deterrents such as wheel-clamping are regarded as a first-stage traffic-management measure, something that can be applied before sophisticated methods of road pricing can be evolved.

But they do little to affect the volume of through traffic even during peak hours, they do not affect the total volume of peak-hour traffic, and they encourage motorists to take direct routes into central areas rather than circumferential ones. Motorists may cause congestion when looking for parking spaces; parking is often indiscriminate (it may or may not be close to the worst areas of congestion), much parking space is private under the control of firms or individuals, and parking controls are difficult and costly to enforce.

Users of road space for parking should incur the full costs, both private and social, of doing so. If this is not done the parker is receiving a concealed subsidy at the expense of the community in general and other congested road users in particular.

The absence of an effective price mechanism for parking makes it difficult to assess demand. Roth[12] suggested that the need for parking space might be partly fulfilled by the following methods of allocation:

(a) *Queueing*. A specific amount of parking space is available on a 'first come first served' basis. But it favours peak-hour car commuting; commuters may be the first to find a space and park all day.

(b) *Time limits*. These may be preferable to queueing as they eliminate all-day parkers, but may favour whimsical or frivolous users, and may add to congestion.

(c) *Equilibrium pricing*. Attempts to introduce equilibrium pricing have generally failed because charges have been too low to equate demand with supply. But if the motorist were charged an equilibrium price, congestion would be reduced and he would be meeting the full cost of parking. An equilibrium pricing system would ensure that parking space was filled most of the time, without there being unsatisfied demand at the price charged.

But since there is an absence of a pricing system reflecting the full cost of providing space, there is no economic yardstick to assist authorities in deciding whether parking space should be increased or decreased. 'Rule of thumb' decisions have resulted in unrealistically low parking charges, subsequent congestion and a demand (or 'need') for parking spaces in excess of supply.

Public Transport

From the nineteenth century, public road transport has in many ways been regarded as an 'inferior good'. With the development of the motor car and rising real incomes, travellers have moved away from public to private transport. Congestion has been largely caused by the motor car. The London Transport Executive, referring to recent statistics, proclaimed that if 700 commuters travel to London they could fill 14 buses or 500 cars (or 1 bus for every 35 cars). One major effect of congestion has been that the efficiency and attractiveness of the bus has diminished.

There are no fundamental reasons why public transport should not be able to compete in speed, frequency or convenience with the private car if competition is on equal terms. Present conditions prevent this in the following ways:

(1) Private motorists are not being charged the full price (equal to their marginal social cost) for their use of roads.

(2) The increased congestion on roads and the subsequent rise in bus operating costs have necessitated ever-increasing fares.

(3) At off-peak hours and in outer suburban or rural areas, operators do not undertake marginal cost pricing as it is thought that fares would be intolerably high – cross-subsidisation of unremunerative services being necessary.

But the comprehensive subsidisation of public transport has its advantages:

(1) The present features of road transport tilt the balance in favour of the car and away from the bus. With road pricing applied to the private motorist the balance would become tilted the other way. Although the marginal costs of a car

journey may only be, say, 20 per cent of a bus journey, per traveller it is considerably more – for example, 50 motorists would take up more space and impose higher congestion than 50 passengers on a bus. But the pricing of private motoring might not by itself attract back to public transport more than a marginal number of travellers. Bus services might have to operate at reduced fares, so that there is an absolute and not just a relative price advantage. This could be justified because whereas private motorists would be subject to a new road tax mainly on the basis of their marginal private costs being less than the marginal social costs they inflict on other motorists, buses incur higher marginal private costs (over long stretches of their cost curves) than the marginal social costs they impose on traffic in general. Therefore buses would be eligible for 'negative taxes' or subsidies.

(2) At a time of high oil prices, a re-diversion of demand to public transport could have advantageous effects on the balance of payments.

(3) Subsidies would offset the regressive nature of road pricing by offering an alternative mode of transport.

(4) Generally environmental costs are lower with public transport and a diversion to it would improve the situation.

(5) Reasonable mobility should be facilitated by local and central government for social reasons and the cost should be borne by the community as a whole.

(6) Highly subsidised or even free public transport would be warranted if the savings in travelling, congestion and administrative costs exceeded the extra rate poundage. By the early 1980s the Greater London Council (GLC) and most of the metropolitan counties were implementing cheap fare policies – for example, the GLC reduced London Transport fares by an average of 32 per cent in 1981. Even then only 46 per cent of the fare in London was subsidised, in contrast to 56, 61, 70, 71 and 72 per cent in Paris, Berlin, Brussels, Milan and New York respectively. Although in London, cut fares required a 6.1p in the pound increase to GLC ratepayers, the total increase would have been 11.9p in the pound because of a penalising decrease in the central government's block grant. Despite GLC policy reversing the trend of dwindling passengers for the first time in 20 years and cutting car commuting by 6 per cent, in December 1982 the House of Lords deemed cheap fares uneconomic and hence illegal under the Transport (London) Act 1969 – the Act not taking into account social-cost-benefit considerations. Because of the reform of fare zones, London Transport was legally able to reduce fares in 1983 (by as much as 25 per cent), but at the cost of a 32 per cent increase in rates. Again there was a marked increase in the proportion of commuters travelling by public transport and a decrease in commuting by car.

Under the Transport Act 1983, however, the Ministry of Transport could impose strict limits on the power of the (then) metropolitan counties to subsidise public transport (with inevitable increases in fares), and under the Transport Act of 1985, all bus routes outside of London were opened up for competition from 1 October 1986. Unprofitable services were consequently put out to tender by local authorities with the probability that the bidder requiring the lowest subsidy would be offered the relevant routes. Underlying the 1985 Act was the government's desire to cut public spending by eliminating subsidy as far as possible, but also to extend untrammelled market forces by privatisation and deregulation. Within a year of the Act, 55–70 per cent of the formerly subsidised services were being run commercially, but with service cuts, lost routes, substantial fare increases, job losses and passenger confusion. Metropolitan areas were particularly badly hit. In London (after the abolition of the GLC and London Transport in 1986), the newly established London Regional Transport authority's initial subsidy of £190 million was reduced to £74 million in 1987–88 and to a targeted £59 million by 1988–89 – again with service cuts, lost jobs, and with the possibility of 50 per cent of routes being put out to tender.

The subsidisation of public road transport (except in the case of the abolition of fares) should not be seen as a contradiction to the principles of road pricing but as part of the road pricing system where the basic parameters are marginal private costs and marginal social costs, and where the means of bridging the gap between these costs are taxes or subsidies. Since buses inflict very low congestion, environmental and accident costs on society, the marginal social costs of this mode of transport are often lower than its marginal private costs – and generally decrease with the volume of services (assuming a reciprocal reduction in the volume of motor car traffic). Figure 7.2 shows that if a subsidy were to fill the gap between these costs, bus operators could cut fares from f to f_1 but increase services from b to b_1.

Road pricing (involving both the taxing of private motorists and the subsidisation of public transport) would thus reduce congestion, improve accessibility and eliminate the need for commercial firms to relocate. In short, road pricing would improve the efficiency of the urban economy.

To date, no effective solutions have been applied to the problem of urban traffic congestion. Meanwhile, despite relatively high energy prices, the shift from public to private transport continues. A general trend in public policy initially towards zonal (differential) licensing and ultimately towards comprehensive road pricing and more heavily subsidised public transport may be seen as a solution to the problem of traffic and the environment. But in addition, the very special needs of the elderly and disadvantaged might require additional measures. Access credits have been recommended by a number of organisations[13] to enable the least mobile and less well-off members of society to make use of the telephone or a home computer terminal to acquire information and to order goods for delivery, or to pay fares, road prices or hire taxis. Small, flexible route, minibuses would also increase accessibility and provide an economic substitute for the private motor car or taxi.

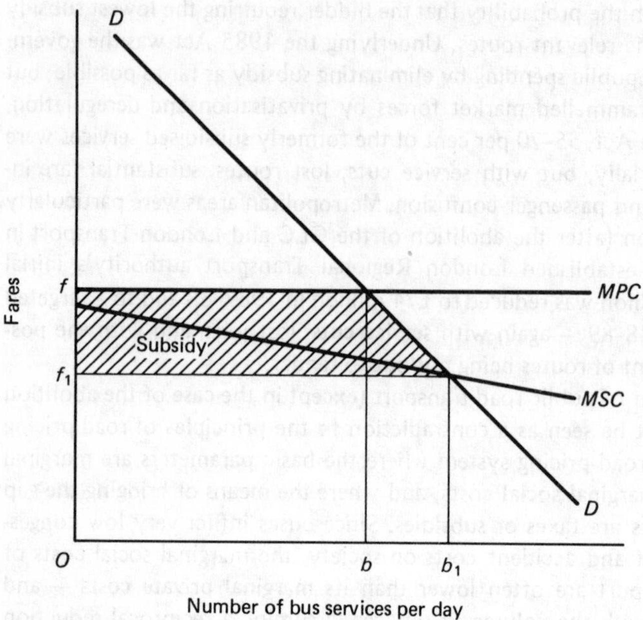

Figure 7.2 *Public transport demand, costs and subsidy*

THE INNER URBAN AREAS

Like the inner areas of many other conurbations in the developed world, those in Britain have decayed. In every major city in Britain population has been in decline throughout much of the twentieth century – Inner London since 1901, Liverpool and Manchester since 1938 and virtually all other major cities since the early 1950s. But until recently, conurbation populations (not just those confined to areas within official conurbation boundaries) have continued to increase – the 'core city' containing a smaller and smaller population both relatively and absolutely – losing population at first to its surrounding suburban ring, then to its outer ring and finally to rural areas beyond. Differential population change has not, of course, been due to significant variations in birth- and death-rates, but to out-migration especially of the higher socio-economic groups (managers and professionals), skilled manual workers and young families. Improved transport technology, increased car ownership, relocation of employment and an increased demand for out-of-town owner-occupied housing have all led to the decentralisation of population to the suburbs and beyond. Inner city manufacturers have not remained competitive. Many have closed down of their own accord, or have been forced to close because of clearance schemes. Others have been taken over by larger organisations and then closed down; many are adversely affected by the lack of a skilled labour force and a poor urban road network; most are affected by cramped sites and old premises (a major disadvantage if a switch from labour intensive to capital intensive production is required); and some are affected by high rates.

Planned overspill has compounded these mainly market forces – although 70 per cent of the loss of manufacturing jobs in Greater London and the conurbations have gone nowhere.[14] From the Barlow Report of 1940, successive legislation (for example, the New Towns Act 1946 and Town Development Act 1952) initiated programmes of planned decentralisation. As a consequence, industrial development in the Midlands, London and the South-east was severely constrained by governments unwilling to grant industrial development certificates (IDCs) in the period 1947–82. For a combination of the above reasons, therefore, the decrease in population and employment in the major cities was substantial – Greater London, for example, losing 500 000 industrial jobs, 1965–80. In recent years, the decrease in manufacturing employment in Greater London has been accelerating, in part because of the application of monetarist policy – different analysts putting the manufacturing job loss at between 215 000 and 500 000 over the period 1979–86.[15]

From the 1940s until the mid 1970s, urban and regional planners believed that declining city populations would produce very real benefits. They argued with conviction that smaller numbers would ease the housing shortage and improve the residential environment; decentralisation would result in fewer commuting problems; more urban open space would reduce crime rates and vandalism; there would be less need for government subsidy; and less overcrowding and more pleasant conditions would improve educational attainment. But none of these results has occurred – quite the contrary. In addition, rates of unemployment in the inner city are so high (upwards of 15 per cent by the end of 1984 – with much higher levels among the unskilled and young), that in the depressed regions it is this, rather than the decline of basic industries (coal, steel, textiles and shipbuilding), that is the principal cause of economic decline.[16]

These disturbing trends could be eliminated by massive investment in the inner city (by the public or private sector or both), and other substantial benefits could accrue. First, there would result a superior pattern of resource allocation. There would be less wastage of land (in otherwise high-cost areas) since densities would be transformed towards an optimum level. Derelict areas would be developed for housing and employment, and overcrowded areas decongested. Some decayed residential areas would be converted into commercial and industrial uses and vice versa. There would also be less wastage of manpower. Reduced unemployment would raise income levels and together with an inflow of middle and higher-income households (with the development of owner-occupied housing and co-ownership) many inner urban areas would be 'transformed' economically and socially. Property values would on aggregate rise and spill over into peripheral areas. Second, there would be considerable social benefits. An improved residential and work environment (and higher incomes) would result in less ill-health, fire damage and crime, reducing the cost of health and fire services and the police. A healthier, higher-paid labour force might increase the level of productivity and lower the rate of absenteeism, and less deprivation would reduce the cost of welfare services and payments. Finally, an improved environment and higher property values would widen the rate base and enable the local authority to provide better services where required. Ironically, areas with poor environments requiring the greatest amount of public expenditures are least able to raise revenue to facilitate it.

But to realise the above benefits, considerable costs would have to be incurred. These include research, survey and planning costs; administrative expenditure; the cost of acquiring decayed property; demolition costs; the cost of public and private developments; relocation costs (both economic and non-economic); and possibly the cost of land value write-down if sites are released for development at below their market value.

By carefully identifying and quantifying the above advantages and costs of renewal investment, cost-benefit analyses could be undertaken to a limited extent, and renewal projects ranked in order of greatest net benefit as a guide to decision-making (chapter 6). Full account would have to be taken of the urban economic base and the effects of the multiplier (chapter 3).

RENEWAL STRATEGIES

Since the Second World War, six principal strategies (each long term) have been employed in the United Kingdom, and each has been modified, upset or abandoned by political and economic change.

(1) *Filtration*. This was based on the out-migration of households and employment followed by the clearance and redevelopment of vacated sites. It was potentially the most system-oriented of the approaches. Out-migration resulted from both planned decentralisation and market forces. Over the period 1946–66 under the New Towns Acts of 1946 and 1959, 21 Mark I and II new towns were designated in Britain. It was intended that, through the medium of development corporations, the new towns would provide overspill housing and employment for the major cities, and geographically concentrate employment to eliminate difficult journeys to work. More recently, from 1967 to 1970, seven Mark III new towns were designated to act as 'countermagnets' of economic activity, to exploit the economies of scale in development and operation, and to meet social needs. From designation to 1985, the population of the new towns grew from 945 900 to 2 094 600, but probably only *one-third* of the increase was due to migration from Greater London and the major conurbations. Under the Town Development Act 1952, a total of 70 town expansion schemes had been initiated by 1980 when the government finally announced the winding-up of all expansion schemes still being undertaken. The expanded towns received even less overspill than the new towns. By comparison with planned decentralisation, the

scale of 'voluntary' overspill – mainly in response to market forces (and environmental considerations) – was enormous.

During the years of planned decentralisation, slum clearance schemes and massive public sector housebuilding programmes were undertaken in the inner cities. In the period 1945–76, 1.24 million dwellings were demolished in England and Wales, but in the inner cities clearance was often followed by the development of high-rise housing at lower overall density. Clearance also had a severe effect on local employment – factories, workshops, retail premises etc. being sacrificed to facilitate housing redevelopment and infrastructure improvement.

(2) *Social planning*. Except possibly for a few years in the late 1960s and early 1970s, governments have regarded this as being secondary to physical and economic planning. Social planning focuses on people rather than on urban space or property, and should first involve analyses of the basic causes of deprivation as a prelude to the application of needs-related policies.

In the 1960s (and emanating from the United States) the social pathology view of urban deprivation emerged in Britain – the Urban Programme (UP) being introduced in 1968 in direct response to the growing concern about race relations, urban poverty and deprivation. Under the UP, the central government was empowered (by the Local Government Grant [Social Need] Act 1969) to award grants of 75 per cent towards the cost of 'approved' projects bid for by local authorities and voluntary agencies (in England and Wales) in areas of 'special social need' (there were separate arrangements for Scotland). In the early 1970s, moreover, the Home Office (considered then to be the appropriate government department to initiate inner city policy), established 12 Community Development Projects (CDPs) – each with an action and a research team – to produce detailed analyses of inner city problems in specific geographical areas and to identify solutions which would require implementation at a higher than local level. Prior to their demise in 1977, CDP teams were claiming that urban deprivation was not the result of social malaise, but the effect of unemployment, inadequate income maintenance, poor housing and a decayed environment; and they called for more public ownership and control of industry, and substantial changes in income maintenance and public sector finance.

In 1974, the Comprehensive Community Programme (CCP) was initiated to tackle urban deprivation by means of both a comprehensive Whitehall approach to urban problems and a new partnership between central and local government. However, since there was a conflict of interest between the Urban Deprivation Unit of the Home Office on the one hand, and the various spending ministries and the Treasury on the other, the CCP 'experiment' achieved very little. The Home Office was increasingly unable to exercise its responsibility for social policy in the inner city.

(3) *The boot-strap strategy*. This involves rehabilitation (often with the aid of grants) and is mainly confined to housing. It does not (or should not) involve the displacement of occupants (chapter 9), and it is often thought that in economic terms it is less costly than redevelopment, although evidence is conflicting. Renewal theory evolved from the basic hypothesis of Needleman.[17] He suggested

that the comparative economics of redevelopment and rehabilitation depends on (a) the rate of interest, (b) the future life of the rehabilitated property, and (c) the difference between the running costs of the new and rehabilitated property. Normally, rehabilitation would be worth while if the present cost of clearance and rebuilding exceeds the sum of the cost of rehabilitation, the present value of the cost of rebuilding, and the present value of the difference in annual running costs. In algebraic terms, rehabilitation would be more economic than redevelopment if

$$b > m + b\,(1+i)^{-\lambda} + \frac{r}{i}\,[1-(1+i)^{-\lambda}]$$

where b = cost of demolition and rebuilding
m = cost of rehabilitation
i = the rate of interest
λ = useful life of the rehabilitated property in years
r = difference in annual repair costs

Needleman extended his hypothesis by taking into account two additional variables – namely, the comparative quality and comparative density of new and rehabilitated housing (normally, new housing would be of higher quality and lower density than rehabilitated property). As Merrett[18] suggests, rehabilitation would be worth while if

$$b > m + b\,(1+i)^{-\lambda} + \frac{r+p+a}{i}\,[1-(1+i)^{-\lambda}]$$

where b = cost of demolition and rebuilding
m = cost of rehabilitiation
i = the rate of interest
λ = useful life of the rehabilitated property in years
r = difference in annual repair costs
p = excess of rent on (higher-quality) redeveloped property
a = annual cost of 'decanting' surplus households from (low density) redeveloped property.

Although Needleman's more comprehensive formula was in general terms incorporated in the Ministry of Housing and Local Government Circular 65/69, Kirby[19] argued that planners may have found detailed formulae time-consuming and unwieldy in calculations. Lean,[20] possibly appreciating that less sophisticated methods were necessary to determine the most appropriate process of renewal, devised the capital value method to compare redevelopment and rehabilitation. This involves a comparison between the costs of redevelopment and the differences in capital values before and after redevelopment, and the costs of rehabilitation and the differences in capital values before and after rehabilitation. If, for example, £18 000 spent on redevelopment increased unit values by £21 000 and £6000 spent on rehabilitation raised values by £9000, then clearly £18 000 spent on rehabilitation would renew three times as many houses as the number supplied by redevelopment (and values would rise £27 000 rather than £21 000).

In the 1970s, a limited amount of empirical evidence in the United States[21] and in Britain[22] seemed to suggest that rehabilitation was cheaper than redevelopment, although in Britain the evidence was by no means conclusive since it was difficult to compare the clearance and redevelopment of a whole area with the rehabilitation of a relatively small number of (often scattered) properties. Nevertheless, the government (particularly after the Housing Act 1969) made rehabilitation a major housing priority (chapter 8).

The above considerations have ignored the question of timing – that is, when should redevelopment take place or when should rehabilitation be undertaken? Even assuming that a site is redeveloped when the economic life of a building has expired (chapter 3), the optimum economic life of a building is not fixed. The capital value of buildings and sites in existing use and the capital value of sites cleared for alternative use continually fluctuate and establish new optima.

The capital value of sites for alternative use will rise if the urban area experiences economic and population growth and benefits from an improved infrastructure. This will shorten the economic life of buildings and sites in existing use and bring forth redevelopment. The value of cleared sites for alternative use will fall if reverse trends occur – a decaying infrastructure alone bringing down values and postponing redevelopment. In figure 7.3 the capital value of a site cleared for alternative use increases from *SS* to S_1S_1 and intersects the capital value of a building and site in its existing use at 80 years – reducing the economic life of the building from the original optimum of 100 years. Conversely, a decrease in the capital value of the cleared site could extend the economic life of the building.

The capital value of a building and site might, however, also change. It could be expected to rise as a result of rehabilitation and/or conversion from, for example, a single family dwelling house into bedsitters, flats or bed and breakfast accommodation. Recently, deconversions of flats and bedsitters into single family freehold or leasehold properties have also increased the capital value of buildings and their sites. If rehabilitation and/or conversion (or deconversion) occurred when the age of the building was 80 years, the economic life of the building could be extended to 120 years where values would again be in equilibrium. Conversely, if the capital value of the property is decreased (perhaps because of the building falling into serious disrepair), there would be a downward shift in the *BB* curve and the economic life of the building would be reduced.

The relationship of the capital value of the cleared site (for alternative use) to the capital value of the building and site (in existing use) is particularly relevant to the problems of the inner city. The inner city contains a high proportion of old dwellings – most of which have been modified over the years. Generally, the capital value of these buildings and their sites has increased to keep pace with the increase in the capital value of sites for alternative uses. Were it not for the conversion of houses into multi-occupied dwellings and other forms of accom-

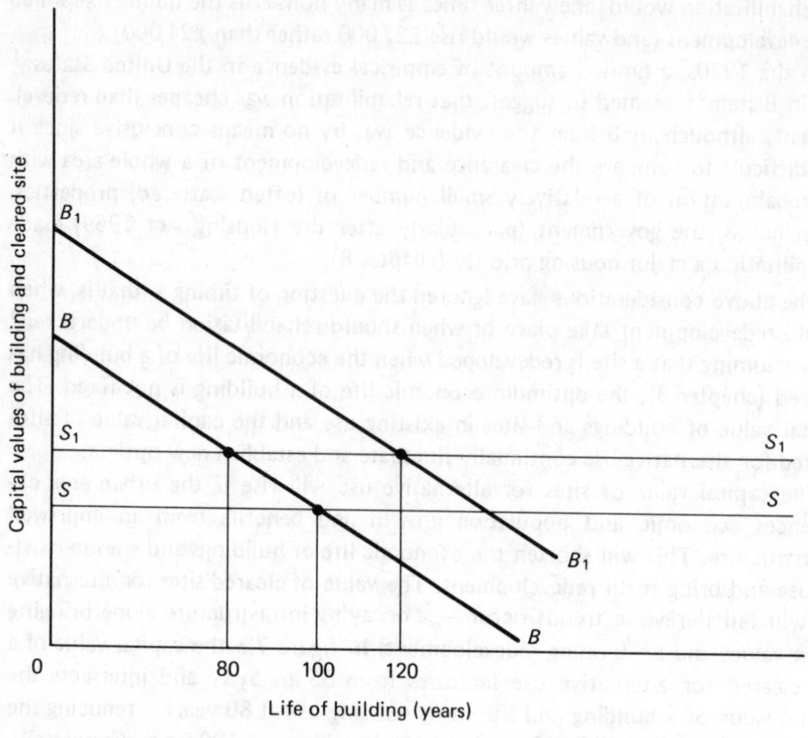

Figure 7.3 *Changes in the maximum economic life of a building (assuming general price stability)*

modation, their demolition would have occurred many decades ago. The inner cities therefore often retain their nineteenth-century image which, except for a minority of buildings of architectural or historic interest, is one of gloom and decay. Yet it is not just the extended life of buildings (brought about by increases in their capital values) that is responsible for much of the inner city being a twilight area. In many cases the capital value of sites cleared for alternative use is much greater than the current or potential capital values of the buildings, but the latter values have been kept artificially low by the effects of legislation. In 1915, 1939, 1965 and 1974 Rent Acts subjected private landlords to rent control or regulation, while tenants were increasingly granted protection (chapter 8). Although these measures should be viewed in the light of problems of housing need and affordability, the direct effect was that buildings which could neither be readily redeveloped nor maintained or repaired for want of an adequate return on investment were kept out of use. But after the Housing Act 1969, improvement grants became increasingly available for modernisation and have raised the capital value of properties. Grants have thus had the effect of retaining in use the older housing stock of the inner city until such a time when redevelopment is feasible.

(4) *Replacement*. Clearance is followed by sound redevelopment schemes. Usually there are many social problems that need to be resolved especially if redevelopment does not occur immediately after clearance, therefore it is essential that, not just for economic reasons, schemes are carefully selected, priorities determined and work sensitively programmed. Development is undertaken by either the public or private sector or by a partnership of both.

In the United States this strategy was introduced by the Kennedy and Johnson administrations as one of their 'Great Society' initiatives following ghetto riots in the 1960s. The federal government set up a Department of Housing and Urban Development in 1965, which in turn introduced the 'model cities programme' in 1966. The programme aimed to concentrate and coordinate the provision of federal resources allocated to the urban areas and to involve local communities in improvement of their physical environment. Development programmes soon came to depend upon private sector investment – for example, the successful Bedford-Stuyvesant scheme in Brooklyn, while being managed by a community-based organisation, was partly funded by Wall Street institutions.

In the United Kingdom, replacement strategy emerged in response to the Inner Areas Studies (IASs) of Birmingham (Small Heath), Liverpool 8, and London (Lambeth) commissioned by the Department of the Environment 1972. In contrast to 'blaming the victim' – the underlying rationale of the Home Office initiatives of the 1960s (see 'Social planning' just discussed), the Department of the Environment acknowledged the conclusion of the IASs which stressed that the economic causes of urban deprivation necessitated a new policy to channel additional resources to the inner cities.

Based on the White Paper, *Policy for the Inner Cities*, 1977, the Inner Urban Areas Act 1978 brought about an increase in public expenditure on the Urban Programme (UP) from £30 million per year (in 1976–77) to £165 million per year (by 1979–80). In addition, the Budget of March 1977 set aside £100 million for a package of construction works in selected inner city areas. Under the 1978 Act, a total of seven partnership, 15 programme authorities and 14 'other' districts were designated in England (table 7.2), and each of the authorities had powers to make 90 per cent loans for the acquisition of land or site preparation, to make loans or grants towards the cost of setting up cooperatives or common-ownership enterprises, and to declare (industrial) improvement areas (IAs). IAs were particularly important components of the 1978 Act. They were to be declared by local authorities to secure a stable level of employment in older industrial and commercial areas. Within them, grants and loans were available for the improvement of the environment, and grants could be obtained for the improvement or conversion of old industrial or commercial property. In 'special areas' within the partnerships, local authorities could make loans interest free up to two years for site preparation, and award grants to assist with rents and to help firms which had incurred interest on loans for land acquisition and the like. Overall, assistance was coordinated by means of inner city partnership programmes (ICPPs) or inner area programmes (IAPs) – the former being produced by teams of civil servants and local government officers in the partnership areas, and the latter emanating solely from programme and other designated authorities.

Table 7.2 *Urban areas designated under the Inner Urban Areas Act 1978*

Areas	Population 1981	Annual UP allocation 1979–80
Partnership authorities		
Birmingham		
Liverpool		
Manchester–Salford		
Newcastle–Gateshead		
Lambeth		
Hackney and Islington		
London Docklands	4 294 184	£66 m
(Greenwich		
Lewisham		
Newham		
Southwark		
Tower Hamlets)		
Programme authorities		
Bolton		
Bradford		
Hammersmith		
Hull		
Leeds		
Leicester		
Middlesbrough		
North Tyneside	4 542 913	£25 m
Nottingham		
Oldham		
Sheffield		
South Tyneside		
Sunderland		
Wirral		
Wolverhampton		

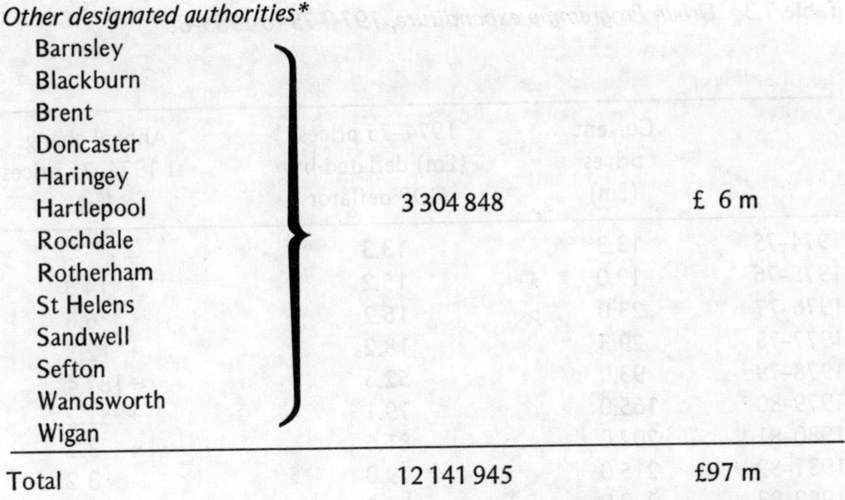

*Other designated authorities**		
Barnsley, Blackburn, Brent, Doncaster, Haringey, Hartlepool, Rochdale, Rotherham, St Helens, Sandwell, Sefton, Wandsworth, Wigan	3 304 848	£ 6 m
Total	12 141 945	£97 m

*In addition, there were 'other designated areas' in Wales: Blaenau Gwent, Cardiff, Newport, Rhondda and Swansea, which in total were allocated £4 million.
Sources: Derived from M. S. Gibson and M. J. Langstaff, *An Introduction to Urban Renewal* (Hutchinson, 1982); and *Town and Country Planning* (September, 1981).

It was ironic that the 1978 legislation was introduced at a time of economic stringency – at a time when the Labour government declared in 1977 that "it could not spend its way out of recession." Although UP spending had increased in real terms up to 1980–81, however, macro-economic policies were being simultaneously adopted to curb the level of aggregate demand. The Conservative administration's 1980 White Paper, *The Government's Expenditure Plans, 1980–81 to 1983–84*, specified swingeing cuts in planned public expenditure with the aim of cutting total public spending by 1984 to a level 4 per cent lower than in 1979–80 (at 1980 prices). Thus in 1981–82 and again in 1984–85 and the following two years, UP spending was cut in real terms (table 7.3). In addition to these reduced injections of resources into the inner city, rate support grants (RSGs) and housing subsidies were being cut in many cities, producing a net withdrawal of funds and a reverse multiplier effect on the local economy (chapter 2).

The provisions of the 1978 Act, however, did not apply to Scotland. Here the onus for urban regeneration fell on the local and regional authorities, and the Scottish Development Agency (SDA) set up in 1976. The SDA was given powers to reclaim derelict land and rehabilitate the environment, build and manage industrial estates, invest in industry, establish new companies and provide industry with finance and advice. Increasingly, the SDA has entered into partnerships with both the private sector and local and regional government (for example, in the East End of Glasgow by the GEAR project) and has helped change the

Table 7.3 *Urban Programme expenditure, 1974–75 to 1985–86*

	Current prices (£m)	1974–75 prices (£m) deflated by GDP deflator	Annual change at 1974–75 prices (%)
1974–75	13.3	13.3	–
1975–76	19.0	15.2	+ 14.3
1976–77	23.0	16.2	+ 6.6
1977–78	29.3	18.2	+ 12.3
1978–79	93.0	52.3	+187.4
1979–80	165.0	79.1	+ 51.2
1980–81	202.0	81.6	+ 3.2
1981–82	215.0	79.0	– 3.2
1982–83	270.0	92.9	+ 17.6
1983–84	348.0	114.4	+ 23.1
1984–85	338.0	106.5	– 6.9
1985–86	338.0	100.6	– 5.5
1986–87	317.0	–	–

Source: Department of the Environment.

image of Clydeside from a region of heavy smokestack industry to one of electronics, advanced engineering and energy-related technology.

(5) *Guiding urban growth through investment*. This method combines the replacement strategy with market forces. Areas are initially ranked according to their renewal potential, related infrastructure might be improved, and private investment is attracted.

This form of strategy was introduced in the United States by the Nixon and Ford administrations in the period 1968–76. It involved direct cooperation between the federal government and private investors. Under a newly introduced 'new towns intown' programme the federal government used its community development block grant to fund urban development in anticipation of complementary private investment, and the Housing and Community Development Act 1977 (of the Carter administration) introduced urban development action grants (UDAGs) to 'lever' finance from the private sector for joint public/private schemes. Under the 1977 Act, city authorities could only obtain UDAGs (for joint schemes with the private sector) if their areas suffered a high level of deprivation, but a fundamental characteristic of the UDAG is that it would have to enable private investors and developers to enjoy a level of return at least equivalent to that obtainable elsewhere. In addition to the above provisions, the federal government, under the Urban Growth and Community Development Act 1977, provides mortgage guarantees to encourage financial institutions to use mortgage-fund capital to finance urban development projects.

In the United Kingdom, with the return of a Conservative government, Urban Development Corporations (UDCs) were designated in the London docklands and Merseyside under the Local Government, Planning and Land Act 1980. It was claimed that UDCs were intended to tackle the problems that local authorities could not or would not deal with alone, and where allegedly the private sector had been deterred from investing. Although becoming planning authorities and having compulsory purchase powers (usurping local authority responsibilities but being largely unaccountable locally), they lacked the powers vested in the New Town Development Corporations (NTDCs) and were not permitted to acquire land except at market value. Nevertheless, the UDCs placed an emphasis on providing an adequate infrastructure, reclaiming and servicing land, renovating old buildings and developing new factories – all in the hope of encouraging substantial development in the private sector. UDCs also provided practical assistance to potential developers and sometimes the offer of finance. The aim was to attract mainly private, commercial and industrial development. Market forces, thought the Conservatives, would be the principal means by which the inner cities would be generated – provided the market was largely unfettered.

A great deal of leverage finance, however, had to be supplied by government. While the London Docklands Development Corporation (LDDC) had attracted over £2 billion of private sector investment by 1987 – a leverage ratio of 4:1 – the Merseyside Development Corporation (MDC) in return for public expenditure of more than £140 million had attracted only £20 million of private funds by mid-1987. New UDCs in Tyneside, Teesside, Sandwell (West Midlands), Trafford Park (Manchester) and Cardiff Bay were created in 1987 – each being allocated up to £160 million over the period 1987/88–1992/93. The government hoped that high leverage ratios would be attained and that by the early 1990s private finance would replace Whitehall funding entirely – for industrial regeneration. In the meanwhile the proceeds from the sale of NTDC assets might be used to provide the funding of the new UDCs (and any smaller UDCs set up in the late 1980s).

UDCs, however, have done little to reduce unemployment in their areas (which remained at over 20 per cent in 1987 – twice the national average); and in the LDDC area, new housing has been largely developed for owner occupation – with land values for luxury riverside development soaring to as much as £7.5 million per ha (by 1987). Public sector housing development is thus squeezed out despite lengthy local authority waiting and transfer lists.

In an attempt to stimulate market forces the government declared – under the Finance Act 1980 – a number of enterprise zones in which the following concessions were made: exemption from Development Land Tax; 100 per cent first-year depreciation allowance on capital expenditure on commercial and industrial buildings; simplification of planning procedures; abolition of Industrial Development Certificates; exemption from rates on all commercial and industrial property; handling of applications for warehousing free of custom duty, plus a relaxed regime for private warehousing; and a major reduction in government requests for statistical information. By 1981, thirteen enterprise zones had been declared – ranging in size from 57 to 364 ha. A further fourteen zones were created by 1984, but not all were in the inner cities (see table 7.4).

The enterprise zone concept is subject to considerable criticism. It is thought that little new employment will be created if the zones attract superstore or warehouse development, and there will be few jobs for the local population if offices are developed. If manufacturing firms move in, employees will probably not receive training and remain unskilled and low-paid. In net terms, land values and economic activity will not increase but merely shift from adjacent areas, causing blighting and higher unemployment on the periphery. Only in the London docklands and Corby have industries been attracted from beyond the immediate vicinity. The Royal Institution of Chartered Surveyors (RICS) have claimed that landlords letting just outside of a zone often receive up to £5000 less in rents on a standard 5000 ft^2 industrial unit than landlords receive inside a zone – higher zonal rents completely offsetting rate exemption. The RICS therefor suggested that the government should give more thought to the impact on surrounding areas if further zones are to be created.[23] But many firms may be deterred from locating in an enterprise zone since concessions may be withdrawn at a later date ('rate holidays' are only initially granted for ten years). From a monetarist point of view the most damning indictment of the enterprise zone concept is the very high cost of job creation. Monitoring progress in the zones, Roger Tym & Partners have shown that in *net* terms only about 5375 jobs had been created by December 1983 at a total cost of £252.4 million or as much as £46 958 per job. The Association of Independent Businessmen also have severe reservations about enterprise zones – believing that the zones emphasise property development rather than the formation and growth of new enterprise, and that their artificial boundaries distort markets and create unfair competition; and the National Audit Office reported that enterprise zones cost the Exchequer £180 million (in 1984–85) and were of dubious benefit.[24] Although the Department of the Environment claimed that 20 000 jobs had been created and 2.9 million m^2 of floor space had been developed in the zones by 1986, the Secretary of State for the Environment conceded that enterprise zones had "been rather expensive and have not given the best value for money."[25]

Although the equivalent of enterprise zones exist elsewhere in the European Community, for example, in Copenhagen, Hamburg and Rotterdam, it must be borne in mind that in these cities public authorities first provided a modern infrastructure prior to releasing market forces. In the United Kingdom such infrastructures are generally absent in the inner city. It must also be borne in

Table 7.4 *Enterprise zones: designations 1981–84*

Designations	Size (ha)	Date of designation
First round		
Team Valley	364	
Swansea	298	
Dudley	219	
Belfast	208	
Isle of Dogs (London Docklands)	195	
Clydebank	190	
Trafford Park	178	April–October 1981
Salford	174	
Speke	138	
Corby	114	
Hartlepool	109	
Newcastle	89	
Wakefield	57	
Second round		
Delwyn	1119	
Milford Haven	147	
North-west Kent	126	
North-west Lancashire	114	
Derry	109	
Scunthorpe	105	
Workington	87	July 1983–December 1984
Middlesbrough	77	
Invergordon	60	
Wellingbrough	55	
Glanford	50	
Tayside	3	
Telford	2	
Rotherham	1	

Source: Roger Tym and Partners, *Monitoring Enterprise Zones: Year Three Report* (Department of the Environment, 1984).

mind that free market forces prevail within the inner cities of the United States and have largely contributed to their decline, and it must be remembered that in Britain many of the problems of the inner cities were themselves caused not by planning, not by central government intervention, but by unbridled free enterprise.

Apart from setting-up UDCs and declaring enterprise zones, the government – in its attempt to unleash market forces – introduced a range of measures to benefit the private sector. The question of land was one of its first priorities. Although derelict land grants (DLGs) became available to local authorities under the Local Government Act 1972, the government extended eligibility to private developers by the Local Government, Planning and Land Act 1980. In the Assisted Areas and Derelict Land Clearance Areas, DLGs of 100 per cent were available to local authorities, and firms became eligible for 80 per cent grants. Elsewhere, both local authorities and firms received 50 per cent grants. Since 1981, the Department of the Environment has given preferential treatment to joint (public and private) schemes, particularly if high leverage ratios can be expected. In 1983–84, for example, DLGs of £32 million were allotted to 48 schemes in England, producing an anticipated £196 million of private sector development. An allocation of £81 million of DLG in 1987–88 can thus be expected to attract private development of over £400 million *ceteris paribus*. Also under the 1980 Act, the Environment Secretary was given powers to direct local authorities to make an assessment of the amount of public land available for development, to register the information with the Department of the Environment, and to dispose of sites to private developers. By the end of 1983, local authorities had compiled 365 public land registers containing a total of 44 750 ha. But from this amount only 3951 ha had been sold and/or brought into use – most of the remainder having little or no development potential regardless of DLG pump-priming.

Urban development grants (UDGs) were probably the most important initiative to emerge from the Department of the Environment in the early 1980s. Like the UDAGs in the United States, their purpose was to promote the economic and physical regeneration of the inner cities by levering private sector investment into such areas. UDGs were to be allocated to private firms via specified local authorities (that is, those designated under the 1978 Act and enterprise zone authorities). The Exchequer would meet 75 per cent of the grant and the local authority 25 per cent. The amount of the UDG was the minimum necessary to make a project commercially viable – any size or type of development being eligible. By 1986, grants totalling £120 million had levered £500 million of private investment, creating 24 000 jobs.

By 1985 it became clear to the government that the private sector might respond better to public sector initiatives if there was a greater coordination in the provision of services. In 1985, therefore, five civil service City Action Teams (CATs) were set up in the partnership areas (of Birmingham, Liverpool, Manchester, Newcastle and London) to bring together officials from the relevant civil service departments and managers seconded from private industry. Their purpose was to eliminate blockages in the provision of services and to ensure a more efficient use of UP spending. Largely in response to civil disorders in Handsworth, Brixton and Toxteth in the summer of 1985, the government set up eight task forces by which ministers in a number of departments became responsible (under the Environment Secretary) for improving the provision of public services in the following areas: North Peckham and Notting Hill (London),

Chapeltown (Leeds), North Central Middlesbrough, Highfields (Leicester), Moss Side (Manchester), St Pauls (Bristol) and Handsworth (Birmingham). In each location, civil servants were allotted £1 million to support existing agencies in providing help for training, regeneration and industrial development. However, although the task forces had started over 100 projects in their first year, only 600 jobs had been created, and at least three task forces managed to spend only one-tenth of their financial allocation – hardly the performance of dynamic management sought by the government. Nevertheless, in 1987 a further eight task forces were set up (in Coventry, Doncaster, Hartlepool, Nottingham, Rochdale, Preston, Wolverhampton and Tower Hamlets) at a cost to the Exchequer of £14 million.

The government's approach to urban problems has been subject to increasing criticism. The Archbishop of Canterbury's Commission on Urban Priority Areas,[26] for example, recommended a complete turnabout of policy and proposed a large increase in the allocation of the rate support grant to the inner cities and an expansion of the UP; while the Town and Country Planning Association[27] proposed that local authorities should again have overall responsibility for the preparation and implementation of inner city renewal strategies. The government, however, continued with its strategy of stimulating private development. Under the Housing and Town Planning Act 1986, urban regeneration grants (URGs) were introduced and were to be paid directly to firms rather than indirectly through local authorities. URGs were intended either to bridge the gap between the cost of development and its value on completion, or to provide temporary finance before any income was received from the development. While URGs were only available for schemes which brought about substantial private investment, priority was given to areas which suffered from a severe loss of employment and where there were large amounts of derelict land or disused industrial and commercial property. Eligible sites had to be in excess of 5 ha, and eligible floorspace more than 23 000 m^2.

Following a Conservative win in the 1987 General Election, the third Thatcher government attempted to reinforce urban policy by giving the Department of Enterprise the responsibility of spearheading the return of business enterprise to the inner cities. Measures needed to be taken to increase the cost-effectiveness of the UP and to reduce the extent of bureaucratic constraint. However, although the Department of Enterprise took over the running of the urban task forces, its inner city budget was miniscule compared with that of the Department of the Environment. In 1987–88, while the Department of Enterprise planned to spend £750 million on regional and industrial support, only about £100 million of this amount would be spent in the inner cities. In contrast, the Department of the Environment planned to spend £525 million specifically in the inner cities (including £230 million on the UP and £125 million on the UDCs) in addition to main departmental expenditure in these areas (on, for example, housing and rate support). The Department of Enterprise, however, could play a major part in urban regeneration if it employed English Estates as an agency to redevelop urban sites and provide small factories and offices. Although English Estates have operated mainly in the Assisted Areas (and own 5000 factories and 508 estates – in 1987), they could become a bridge between the Department of Enterprise and the Department of the Environment. Also, the Department of Enterprise might be able to persuade the Department of the Environment to adopt 'contract compliance' – a practice whereby firms offered aid under the UP would be required to employ a fixed number of local people. After eight years of evolving its particular brand of urban policy, it was still clear that the Conservative administration (often described as the most reactionary government this century) was "prepared to retain or extend urban innovation – despite Treasury proposals for reduced expenditure."[14] (See Postscript, page 344).

There manifestly remains a mismatch between the characteristics of the inner city (large areas of derelict land with outmoded buildings, a high concentration of unskilled workers, an outworn physical infrastructure, fragmented property interests and an uncertain economic base) and the investment criteria of investors and occupiers. Investors in the commercial and industrial sectors require a stream of income, a rental which gives a hedge against inflation, a freehold or long leasehold interest, little onerous management involvement, and a large property in a satisfactory environment. Occupiers usually look for a conventional location, adequate physical access, security, a suitable labour force, and an acceptable working environment. These are generally not available in the inner city. Cadman[28] suggested in 1979 that solutions could be found to the problem of inadequate development if investors were very selective (focusing on the greatest opportunities – in contrast to public authorities which concentrate on the greatest problems); skilled labour and managerial and professional groups were attracted back into the inner cities; there was maximum consultation between the private and public sectors, and between private firms (possible through the medium of chambers of commerce and industry); new agencies were established to promote commercial and industrial development; local authorities and other public bodies released land for development; there was not too much emphasis on manufacturing since this would normally require large sites and these are not usually available; and there was only a little faith in the ability of small firms to regenerate the inner cities – the scale of the task of job creation is too great.

Cadman's proposals have been partly reflected in government policy in the years since 1979. In the 1980s, market forces have been unleashed – Conservative philosophy seeing private investment as the only solution to the problems of the inner city. However, while UDCs and enterprise zones became the principal agencies of urban regeneration, ideologically their purpose was to shift the power balance from the local authorities to central government and to by-pass the normal planning and fiscal barriers. These agencies, together with public land sales, the extension of DLGs, the provision of UDGs and URGs, and the setting up of CATs and task forces, all focused on private profitability; indeed it is possible that the above grants were translated largely into the profits of recipient firms, thereby distorting the market. URGs, in particular, were a cause for concern. Since they were awarded directly by central government, recipient firms were not locally accountable. Both public and private investment decisions, under Conservative renewal strategy, thus not only failed to take into account the cost of job creation, but ignored broad cost-benefit considerations.

(6) *A local government strategy*. By the early 1980s, a number of local authorities began to see the irrelevance of Keynesian policy to the problems of the inner cities, were even more antagonistic to current monetarist policy, and were particularly alarmed at their loss of powers. They increasingly saw the need for a 'bottom-up' (as opposed to a 'top-down') solution to the problems of the inner city. They may also have been aware of initiatives being taken in the United States. Urban authorities since the 1970s had been involved in joint private/public sector development schemes. In Boston, for example, the Economic Development and Industrial Corporation not only helped the city retain and create industrial employment but undertook joint enterprises with the Boston Redevelopment Authority – the city's planning, housing and commercial development agency.

In Britain, therefore, a number of Local Enterprise Boards (LEBs) were set up to provide equity and loan guarantees (to enable firms to borrow longer-term and for more risky ventures than would otherwise be possible), delayed-repayment loans, and 'seed money' for local ventures to attract consequential institutional investment. For the most part, LEBs were funded from the product of a 2p rate levy under Section 137 of the Local Government Act 1972. The largest LEB, the Greater London Enterprise Board (GLEB), was set up in 1983 to help arrest industrial decline in the capital. Over the period 1983–85, it invested £60 million in the London economy – in total creating or saving 2500 jobs at a cost of about £4500 per job. This contrasts with the much higher cost of job creation in the assisted areas and enterprise zones – £35 000 and £47 000 per job respectively in the mid-1980s. LEBs included the West Midlands Enterprise Board, the West Yorkshire Enterprise Board and Lancashire Enterprises Ltd – each of which operated along broadly similar lines to GLEB. Apart from LEBs, many district authorities operate very strident employment and industrial development policies. Sheffield, for example, has used the product of a 2p rate to finance 16 of the city's cooperatives, and has applied a policy of positive discrimination in favour of local firms in the placing of contracts to ensure that the local multiplier is not reduced by 'leakages' out of the area. Compared with the total amount of unemployment in the inner cities, local government initiatives have not created many jobs; for example, unemployment in Greater London, the West Midlands and Sheffield exceeded 725 000 in 1986 but only 9100 jobs had been created over the period 1982–85. However, with more funding and more coordination (perhaps within a regional framework), LEBs and the like might be capable of producing alternative urban strategies more effective than any of the strategies so far employed by central government.

Other alternative strategies could involve: (a) The setting up of an English Development Agency to take over the UP and to provide a framework for private investment. Such an agency, suggested Michael Heseltine, MP,[29] would have a similar role to the Scottish and Welsh Development Agencies and would be responsible for economic activity on inner city land of about 500 ha. (b) Placing an emphasis on shoestring community projects undertaken by the Community Architecture Movement.[30] Underlying this approach is the belief that little is achieved by simply 'throwing money at the problem' and that a bottom-up long-term approach stands the best chance of success. (c) Establishing a National Urban Renewal Agency which would invest substantial funds, say £25 billion, in its first five years – £5 billion originating from the Exchequer and £20 billion from the private sector through the issue of tax exempt revenue bonds.[30] The agency would take over the role of the UDCs and also have powers to approve or disapprove funding for local authority projects. It would be very much a top-down approach since the scale of the problem, in the view of its advocates, requires large-scale investment.

Since this discussion is specifically about urban renewal, it is not relevant here to examine whether or not decentralisation should substitute for any of the above strategies or approaches. Decentralisation as a basis for future policy is considered elsewhere. What is of interest – within the context of decentralisation – is that by the 1980s the decrease in the population of Greater London and the conurbations was slowing down, and by the mid-1980s the population of Greater London was increasing, for the first time in decades. Taking the years 1971–81 and 1981–85, Champion[31] shows that the population of all the principal urban centres (Birmingham, Greater London, Glasgow, Leeds, Sheffield, Liverpool, Manchester and Newcastle upon Tyne) decreased in the two periods by 1.04 and 0.33 per cent respectively (a shift of + 0.17), but the population of Greater London alone decreased by 0.96 and 0.14 per cent over the two periods (a shift of + 0.82). In 1983–84 and 1984–85, however, the population of Greater London *increased* by 0.02 and 0.17 per cent respectively, and even in Inner London there were increases of 0.01 and 0.13 per cent over the same years.

Champion, however, argues that these changes may not necessarily be the outcome of successful urban renewal policy but might have resulted from the recession limiting the creation of new opportunities elsewhere and therefore the extent of out-migration; from the running down of the new towns programme; from the in-migration of the young and/or unemployed from the declining industrial areas elsewhere in Britain; from the depletion of the most mobile segment of the urban population (the skilled manual and managerial and professional groups, for the most part, having already migrated to the outer suburbs or beyond); and from significantly higher birth rates in the inner city than elsewhere. A more stable urban population, however, suggests that there is an increased rather than decreased need for an effective urban renewal strategy, and one which must involve a much greater amount of investment from both public and private sectors than at present. However, to ensure the cost-effectiveness of such investment it is necessary for constructive alliances to be formed between community groups, trade unions, employers, local chambers of commerce and industry, local authorities and central government. It is probable that within the Conservative Party there are substantial groupings that appreciate that a blind adherence to free market ideology will merely sustain the most appalling economic and social conditions for the population of the inner cities.

LOCAL AUTHORITY SOURCES OF FINANCE

In the 1970s, local authorities undertook a large volume of capital expenditure: approximately 40 per cent of housing and most of the community's expenditure on roads and schools. By 1980 total capital expenditure by local authorities was nearly half of the total outlay on capital projects in the public sector. Local authorities were responsible for about 25 per cent of total public expenditure and employed over 2 million people. The rate at which capital expenditure grew was substantially faster than the growth of the economy generally as was the total of local authority debt which steady increased from £6000 million in 1961 to over £43 000 million by 1982.

Two aspects of this finance problem were of special significance: first, the interest charges on borrowing mounted as the outstanding total rose, a trend which in recent years was reinforced by higher interest rates. Loan charges by the mid-1970s accounted for about 20 per cent of current expenditure and were virtually equal to net additional borrowing, exacerbating the problem of obtaining a surplus over current expenditure to help finance capital development. Secondly, local authority borrowing in the market competed with that of central government even if the latter lent to local authorities through the Public Works Loan Board (PWLB).

Local authorities depend on three sources for capital finance: government grants and subsidies, surpluses on current account (the margin of receipts over current outgoings) and borrowings. In the short term, local authorities restrict their temporary debt to no more than 20 per cent of the total loan, and the amount repayable in three months or less to 15 per cent of the total debt. In the long term, the PWLB was established in 1875 to assist mainly the smaller local authorities who lacked the experience to raise funds in the money market. The Board is financed by the Exchequer, and the Treasury prescribes the interest rates to be charged. Up to 50 per cent of long-term capital requirements may be met by the Board with three years as the minimum length of loan at current government borrowing rate plus a management charge. The PWLB is the main source of capital finance to local authorities.

There have been shifts in policy to the extent that local authorities may or may not borrow either from the Exchequer, or through the PWLB, or the market. Access has been encouraged by increasing flexibility and increasing substantially the amounts that may be borrowed. The central government wishes to reduce borrowing by local authorities from the banks and divert it to PWLB to facilitate its monetary targets.

Larger local authorities are able to raise funds by the issue of fixed interest securities which are quoted on the London Stock Exchange. Since 1933 local authorities have borrowed substantial sums by mortgages and bonds.

One other source of long-term finance used to a limited extent by larger authorities has been overseas borrowing. This is subject to Treasury approval and balance of payments constraints but is attractive at times of high home interest rates. The risk is that exchange rates may move against the borrower.

Governments in the United Kingdom have detailed and specific control of local authority capital expenditure and authorities cannot borrow money without the sanction of the appropriate government department. Since 1971 capital expenditure has been divided into 'key' and 'locally determined' services. The former includes services such as housing, principal roads and education, over which central control is exercised and for which local authorities may borrow only in respect of specific approvals. Locally determined sectors include services such as libraries in respect of which a block loan sanction is allocated annually to each authority, which is then free to decide which projects to pursue and how much to borrow within the permitted figure. Since 1981 all capital expenditure has been subject to a national cash limit and this has had a marked effect on local authority activity; for example, the public sector accounted for only 15 per cent of the total starts in 1986.

The reasons for the control of borrowing have changed. Increasingly, there has been concern that local authority capital spending should conform with the government's overall economic strategy and with its patterns of priority. The regulation of local authority expenditure is seen as a useful tool of economic management. The heavy borrowing requirements of local authorities created problems for the Bank of England in seeking orderly financial markets. There have been shifts in policy to the extent that local authorities may or may not borrow either from the Exchequer, or through the PWLB, or the market.

LOCAL AUTHORITY CURRENT FINANCING

Local government revenue expenditure increased in real terms throughout most of the 1970s. As a proportion of GNP between 1965 and 1975 it increased from 8 to 13 per cent, accounting for almost the whole of the rise in the proportion of total public sector to GNP. About 75 per cent of local authority current spending is on social services, principally education and on environmental services; of the balance, over 20 per cent is on debt interest which steadily increased to over £2100 million by 1975.

There are three sources of income to meet this expenditure. Firstly, income from rents, dividends and interest, and from charges for miscellaneous services provided. Secondly, there is grant aid from central government; thirdly, there are the proceeds of the general rate. In the 1970s the share of revenue raised through rates declined and government grants increased in importance. Whereas in 1960 rates accounted for 39 per cent of current revenue, by 1975 they accounted for only 26 per cent. Conversely government grants which in 1960 accounted for 40 per cent of revenue had by 1975–76 reached over 66.5 per cent of relevant expenditure. (In the 1980s, rates rose within limits but grants slumped to about 40 per cent of expenditure by the end of the decade.)

In the 1970s, there was increasing concern that local authorities would be too much under the control of central government since they depended to an ever greater extent on central grants. A major reason for the increase in grant and the government intervention which accompanied it was the confinement of the local authority to a single form of local income – the rate – and the lack of buoyancy in this single source at a time of accelerating inflation and expenditure.

Rates

Rating has a long history as a means of providing revenue for local services. Rates are essentially a local tax paid by occupiers of land and buildings as a contribution towards local services. The rateable value of a hereditament is assessed by the Inland Revenue according to the rental value of the property and the rate poundage; the number of pence in the pound which the occupier must pay on his property is fixed by the local authority. It is calculated by dividing the total sum to be raised by the estimated yield of a 1p rate in the area. For example, with a rateable value of £2 million and £2 million required, the rates would be levied at 100p in the pound.

Between 1970 and 1985 the annual yield from rates increased from £1800 million to £13 796 million – about 10 per cent of the total fiscal revenue and a greater amount than the yield from Value Added Tax and vehicle excise duties combined. From 1945 to the 1980s the rate poundage grew at about the same pace as earnings, but the rate base, the valuation of property upon which rates are levied, and the total yield from rates has not kept up with local authority spending.

This lack of buoyancy has been a major criticism of rates. The method of apportionment of rates depends in essence upon the annual rental value of premises, a criterion based on the historical fact that until this century property was generally disposed of by lettings. Consequently there was an abundance of rental evidence to sustain the valuation lists; this is no longer the case and there has been criticism of the reliance upon rental evidence which may be sparse and unreliable. However, rates have great advantages as a local tax, a fact which is self-evident from their survival:

(1) They provide local authorities with an independent source of income from within their own boundaries and raise a large amount of revenue cheaply and certainly.

(2) The rating mechanism, in spite of complexities of detail, is traditional and well understood. Compared with the income tax system, which provides a complicated set of allowances for the individual, there can be little or no argument about rates liability as such, although there may be considerable argument about an individual assessment against which an appeal can be made.

(3) Since rates are payable on immovable property it is impossible to avoid paying them and therefore local authorities have a stable form of income.

(4) It is flexible; it is easy to alter the poundage and it is economic to collect; collection costs are no more than 1.2 per cent of the total revenue.

(5) Rates are a tax on housing and act as a deterrent to under-occupation of property.

(6) The rate as a variant of a local property tax provides the best test of a person's stake in the locality in which he either lives or works. The property is directly related to the locality in which it is situated. With other forms of taxation, such as sales tax or income tax, problems may arise as to how much of the tax collected can be attributed to the local authority in question.

The great rise in local expenditure has brought to a critical level the demand for an alternative source of local revenue and has emphasised some of the disadvantages of the rating system. The appointment of the Layfield Committee in 1974 to review local government finance was a further attempt to find some means of replacing or substantially augmenting the rating system. The major criticisms of the rating system are as follows:

(1) The value of a house is not a reliable guide to the owner's capacity to pay. In the past it may have been broadly fair since it was based on visible wealth. The Allen Committee (1965) stressed the great distress in paying rates suffered by the elderly not in receipt of social security.[32]

(2) Rates are regressive, taking a higher percentage of the income of the poor than of higher incomes. This criticism has been mitigated since 1966 with rate rebates and supplementary benefits for the poorest sectors of the community – some 4.5 million households in 1976.

(3) Rates are not a buoyant tax and do not grow automatically with rising property values because revaluations take place only quinquennially. The Layfield Report (1976)[33] recommended regular revaluations, preferably every three years.

(4) The reasonable rent basis of valuation for domestic property is largely spurious because of rent restriction and the decline of privately rented accommodation. Valuation officers might use the evidence of fair rents although the statutory definition of a fair rent differs from that of gross value for rating purposes. The feasibility of this approach depends on how professional the rent officer was in his determination of the fair rent. More equitable assessments might be achieved if capital values were used instead of hypothetical rental

values; there is much evidence available and the ratepayer would be better able to understand. The adoption of a capital-value basis may increase the contribution of the domestic as compared with other ratepayers who would continue to be assessed on annual rental values.

(5) Payment requires a conscious effort compared with, for example, Pay As You Earn. Householders may also be deterred from expanding or improving their properties since to do so involves a bigger rate liability.

(6) There is no connection between the use a ratepayer makes of local services and his rates. In the late 1980s, 66 per cent of households either paid no rates, or only paid them in part.

(7) Areas in which the need for social welfare provision is greatest have the lowest rateable value per head, and where needs are less rateable values are high. Thus it is easiest to raise rates revenue where it is least required. Government grants are designed to assist the poorer areas but do not eliminate disparities.

(8) Rates fall unevenly between different classes of taxpayer. Rates for business users can be treated as expenses and deducted from income for purposes of taxation. This relief is not available for the domestic ratepayer; it would be regressive and would give no assistance to those who pay no tax.

In an era of increasing public expenditure, so productive a source of revenue cannot be done away with. The problem may be therefore not so much what alternative sources of revenue may be introduced but how to make the rates more effective. The problem of lack of buoyancy might be partly offset by bringing agricultural buildings and land to full rate liability (they have been derated since 1929). The favourable treatment extended to the various nationalised industries might be terminated. A 'super' rate on industrial and commercial properties has been suggested. A further possibility is that residents of households not already ratepayers should be liable to make some contributions to the costs of local services, although the major administrative costs might negate the extra revenue. Local authorities might also adopt more widely their discretionary power to rate empty property. Since 1966 relatively few authorities outside London have introduced this rate. Authorities could also rate owners of empty sites who presently make no contribution at all to the cost of local services. Possibly the worst weaknesses of rating are not inherent in the system itself but stem from central government policy on broader issues including derating and infrequency of revaluation.

Alternative Sources of Local Revenue

In appraising alternative or concurrent methods of raising local government revenue certain fundamental criteria assist in evaluation.

(a) The subject of the tax should be widely distributed throughout the country.

(b) The tax base should lend itself to variations throughout the country.

(c) The tax should not be disproportionately expensive to administer and collect.

(d) The tax base and its potential yield should be buoyant, both facilitating adjustment over time and providing increases in yield without increasing the rate at which it is levied.

There are possibly two other criteria: when the tax is levied it should be clear which authority is entitled to the revenue and that the yield of the tax should be appreciable in relation to local government expenditure and must permit long-term prediction and budgeting.

There are two possibilities in the search for additional local revenue:

(1) to try to invent entirely new taxes, and

(2) to consider whether any existing national taxes are suitable for local use either with or without adaptation.

Local income tax (LIT)

Proposed by the Layfield Report to augment rates, LIT is related to ability to pay; it is possibly highly productive, comprehensive and complementary to the rating system; those currently evading rates would be required to contribute; and it has built-in flexibility and buoyancy. In Sweden, the United States and West Germany there are effective systems of local income tax closely related to the high degree of local autonomy prevailing. There are, however, several basic problems in applying this in the United Kingdom. If the rating system were to be abolished, the loss of yield would imply an increase of about 13.5p in the £ on basic rate income tax, or 5.5p if domestic rates were replaced. In addition:

(1) Income tax is currently assessed according to the place of employment, which in respect of local revenue collection would necessitate a complete restructuring.

(2) The physical allocation of income, particularly profits, may be an extremely difficult task geographically. Should the company be levied according to the area of its production or its central management? In addition, prosperous areas would tend to become more attractive as they would demand lower taxes; this would extend the existing disparities between areas.

(3) There is a potential time lag between the assessment and collection of taxes which could bring problems for budgeting.

Local sales tax (LST)

Local sales taxes are widely used throughout the United States and in other parts of Europe, including France. Such taxes are simple and productive; being related to economic activity they are both flexible and buoyant with automatic collection from the purchaser. However, the tax would tend to be regressive and involve considerable local disparities relating to the boundary at which it would be imposed. It could give rise to unfair regional competition and tax evasion if levied at different rates in different areas. If the tax rate is much higher in one location than in others, this can have an adverse effect upon the location of economic activity. Prior to 1965, New York City was a sales tax island – there was no sales tax in adjacent New Jersey or in the surrounding counties in New York State. The effect was to divert 25 per cent of the city's retail sales of house furnishings, with serious effects upon employment and retail businesses. It is also likely that administration would be onerous. It has been estimated that a 2 per cent LST would yield sufficient income to reduce central government aid by about one-sixth. As the cost of local government services has been rising at a faster rate than consumers' expenditure, the rate of tax would have to be incrementally increased over time. There are attractions to metropolitan areas, possibly by increasing the level of Value Added Tax, particularly as the tax hits at consumers; this makes non-resident commuters pay for some of the services which they make use of.

Employment and motor taxes

Layfield paid some attention to the practicalities of a local payroll tax and local authorities becoming recipients of motor-tax revenue, but difficulties of administration and equitability ruled out acceptability.

Site value rating (SVR)

A further alternative to the rating system (and as a means of collecting betterment) is site value taxation, as used in Denmark, Australia and New Zealand for example. The essence of SVR is that the site value, the capital value or market selling price of the land as distinct from the buildings on that land, should be rated on the assumption that it was available for the most profitable permissible development. It is argued that SVR is both relevant and fair since land values increase as a consequence largely of community development and growth, not through the actions of individual landowners who receive an unearned increment. It is further argued that as the tax would be on the value of the site it would not penalise improvements as does the rating system. It would encourage development as buildings would not be rated; it would be advantageous to exploit fully all available land; it would encourage the selling of undeveloped land. Unlike betterment levies, SVR would not give owners the opportunity of avoiding payment by keeping land off the market and thus by increasing supply lubricate development. Studies at Whitstable in 1964[34] and in 1973[35] indicate that SVR could be as remunerative as rates. The yield, however, would be recouped differently with proportionately more coming from sources such as agricultural and horticultural land, caravan sites and golf clubs, and probably less from residential and industrial areas. Both reports contended that it was easier to value the site alone compared with the combined value of land and structures.

The disadvantages of SVR are that it might bring about undesirable piecemeal development and some hardship; it also might be more expensive to collect. It would require the use of comprehensive land-value maps (as in Denmark) as precision is desirable; rating on an annual basis would also be necessary to avoid inequitable treatment of site owners. A segment of professional opinion in the United Kingdom rejects the view that SVR would be an improvement on the existing rating system and be better comprehended by the average ratepayer. It is also believed that SVR is more suited to those areas where land is plentiful and not already developed. This view, however, can be disputed. In the United States, in highly urbanised Pennsylvania, a number of cities (Harrisburg, McKeesport, New Castle, Pittsburgh and Scranton) have successfully adopted a graded tax – shifting the incidence from buildings to land, and many other cities throughout the United States are following suit. In Pennsylvania, the effect of the incidence shift has been to reduce the amount of land withheld from the market and to intercept windfall gains for the benefit of the community.[36]

Service charges

In addition, local authorities might extend service charges. In West Germany and the United States, for example, substantial sums are raised from charges paid by users of public services. However, there is a limit to user-charges in the public sector, either because it would be inappropriate for egalitarian reasons to charge for education or social services, or in the case of 'public goods' (such as street-cleaning) where it would be impossible to exclude non-payers from the consumption of the benefit.

In the 1970s to early 1980s there was a general acceptance of the need for reform. In 1974 Mrs Thatcher (as Conservative environment spokesman) pledged to abolish rates "within the lifetime of parliament," but during the period of her first government the 1981 Green Paper[37] went over much the same ground as Layfield, though it suggested that a poll tax of, say, £25–£30 per adult could replace domestic rates if supplemented by either LIT or LST (although the former would add 5p in the pound to the basic rate of income tax and the latter would push up value added tax by 7 per cent). The Green Paper alternatively proposed that either an assigned share of national taxation could be awarded to local authorities or local service charges could be imposed (although there would be limited scope for the latter). A local payroll tax or local duties on vehicles was rejected outright. Any new system of local taxation would have involved high administrative and compliance costs, and would have taken a decade to introduce. It therefore seemed more appropriate to reform rather than replace rates – for example, by switching from hypothetical rental values to capital values as the basis for calculating the rateable value of domestic property. By 1982, however, following a recommendation of the House of Commons Environment Committee, the government abandoned the idea of rate abolition – at least for the time being.

MONETARISM AND RATE CONTROL

In the early 1980s, as an alternative to rate reform, and particularly as part of a monetarist stance, the government attempted to impose severe constraints on local authority spending. Under the Local Government, Planning and Land Act 1980 authorities were penalised if they exceeded either their 'target' or their Grant Related Expenditure Assessment (GREA) whichever was the higher (the target being determined in relation to the council's previous budgets and linked to the government's macro-economic assessment, and, the GREA being worked out from a series of formulae based on census returns and other indicators of local need – the number of children of school age or senior citizens, for example). 'Overspending' was penalised at a flat rate of 15p in the pound – the amount being deducted from the government's local authority grant. From 1983-84, however, local authorities were penalised if their spending exceeded their targets (even if these were below their GREAs). Penalties were increased, rising from 2p in the pound if spending exceeded the target by 1 per cent to 77p in the pound if spending was 10 per cent or more above target. Some authorities, for example, the Greater London Council (GLC), consequently received no government grant at all.

A second form of control was the reduction in the proportion of local authority expenditure met by central government grant. This fell in stages from 61 to 45 per cent (in England), 1978/79–1987/88. The main responsibility for local authority spending therefore shifted dramatically from the taxpayer to the local ratepayer – the government hoping that electoral considerations would impose a constraint on 'high-spending' councils. But the reverse often happened. Many local authorities regarded the maintenance of services as a priority – indeed a statutory duty (an aim not incompatible with electoral considerations). Thus in a period of inflation, local government spending inevitably increased from £11 037 million to £20 550 million (1978/79–1983/84), but in real terms this was an increase of less than 1 per cent per year. Whereas central government spending as a share of national income increased in the same period from 27 to 29 per cent, local government spending fell from 10.5 to 10.2 per cent. By 1983–84 local authorities were nevertheless 'overspending' to the extent of £2.5 billion, having exceeded targets by £750 million in that year alone.

Overall rates increased by 50 per cent (1978/79–1983/84), although they escalated much more in some areas; for example, GLC ratepayers had to incur a 112 per cent increase. But although inflation obviously had an impact, the imposition of penalties and the decrease in the central government grant were often more important factors in determining the increase in rates. Despite this, rates generally rose no faster than direct central taxation over the same period, nor was there any proof that non-domestic rates were 'crippling businesses' or adding to the level of unemployment. Rates account for no more than 1 per cent of industry's costs, and by international standards corporate taxation in Britain is comparatively low.

A third form of control was introduced by the Rates Act 1984. Part 1 of the legislation enabled the government to set a legal maximum on the rates charged by specific local authorities. In 1985–86, 18 large urban authorities were subsequently 'rate-capped' – the list ranging from Lewisham, which had 'overspent' by about 4 per cent in 1984–85, to the GLC, which had exceeded its target by 52.3 per cent. Part 2 of the Act gave the government open-ended powers to limit the rates of every local authority – but it was envisaged that these powers would be rarely used. For the first time since 1601 the level of rates and services were being determined by Whitehall rather than by elected councillors.

Apart from any political consideration, the Conservatives' 1983 election manifesto commitment to abolish the GLC and metropolitan counties was the ultimate attempt to control local expenditure. But although the Conservatives claimed that abolition would save rate- and taxpayers up to £100 million per year, Labour argued that additional costs would amount to £305 million in the first year, falling subsequently to £93 million per annum.

Local government expenditure was thus clearly constrained by monetarism. Not only did this have serious effects upon the national economy since the 'reverse multiplier' reduced demand and raised unemployment, but limitations on local spending had harmful effects on the built environment and local services, consequently creating inefficiencies in the urban economy. In 1986 the need for a reform to the rating system was at last recognised by government.

THE REFORM OF LOCAL GOVERNMENT FINANCE

Based on the 1986 Green Paper, *Paying for Local Government,*[36] plans for the reform of local government finance in England and Wales were announced at the beginning of the third period of the Thatcher government in 1987. The new system, incorporated in the Local Government Finance Act 1988, abolishes rates, and finances local authorities by means of the following four elements:

(1) A *single uniform business rate* will be fixed by central government in London (or Cardiff) and apply to all non-domestic ratepayers in England (or Wales). Its proceeds will be pooled and subsequently redistributed among local authorities on a *pro rata* basis related to the size of their adult population. The rate should amount to approximately £240 per head – equal to the average *per capita* proceeds from non-domestic rates in 1987–88. Thenceforth, it would be indexed to inflation.

(2) Each local authority will then receive from the Exchequer a *standard grant* of about £150 per adult.

(3) In addition, to put all local authorities on an equal footing, they will receive a variable *needs grant*, averaging, say, £140 per adult.

(4) The local authority fixes its own *community charge* (averaging about £220) payable by every adult except the poor (who at the maximum could receive a rebate of 80 per cent); and those in prison, living in hospital or under the age of 19 still at school. Owners of second homes and dwellings empty for more than three months would be charged as if two adults occupied the property, and foreigners would also be liable for the charge. In England and Wales the charge replaces rates on 1 April 1990, although in inner London it will be phased in over 5 years. However, in 1990-91 there will be a *safety net* for each local authority to ensure that its combined income from business rates and grants is about the same as under the old system. The government's reasons for adopting this new form of local taxation (as opposed to retaining domestic rates) was that it would ensure that (almost) every adult would pay the same for local services, it would (possibly) be a better reflection of the cost of these services than rates, and it would (supposedly) increase the degree of local accountability.

Overall, the new system is subject to considerable criticism from many sections of the economy. Firstly, the uniform business rate could have very uneven effects on the local economy. With the revaluation of non-domestic properties in 1990 (and thereafter at five year intervals), southern and prime retail rateable values will rise substantially more than northern and industrial values. This will affect businesses in very different ways since some firms will find that higher values are matched by lower rate poundages, or vice versa, and others will be net gainers or net losers, but, in general, businesses will gain in the North and lose in the South. The Chartered Institute of Public Finance and Accountancy (CIPFA) have estimated that had revaluation taken place in England in the late 1980s, rateable values would have risen five and a half fold, and the accompanying uniform business rate poundage would have been 41p in 1987-88. In this situation, CIPFA claim that in, for example, Slough, office rates would increase by 74 per cent, but would decrease by 42 per cent in Sheffield; in Southampton there would be a 96 per cent increase in shop rates, but only a 27 per cent increase in Liverpool; and in Slough factory rates would rise by 26 per cent but would fall by 49 per cent in Liverpool. Ceilings, however, will be imposed on increases in rateable values at the 1990 revaluation and on annual increases in the business rate over the subsequent five years. Although criticised by the Confederation of British Industry, the new system might become a means of reducing the north-south divide in terms of business expectations – although it remains to be seen how it will operate in the 1990s.

Secondly, the community charge will inevitably be highly regressive. The 1986 Green Paper showed that individuals with gross weekly incomes in excess of £500 would gain from the new system to the extent of £5.84 per week, while those with weekly incomes of less than £100 would lose up to £29 per week. Generally, the gainers would be single-person households and/or those living in high rated property, while the losers would be households with two or more adults and/or those living in low rate property. Regionally, most of the affluent areas of the South and the Midlands would gain, but the North and London (and particularly the inner city areas) would lose – as regional comparisons set out in table 7.5 broadly show.

Table 7.5 *Local taxation in selected areas before and after the imposition of community charges*

District authority	Average rate bill per household 1987–88 (£)	Community charge per 2 person household (£)	Gain or loss (£)
Surrey Heath	519	280	+239
Woking	462	280	+182
Bromsgrove	433	270	+163
Slough	425	298	+127
Worcester	401	300	+101
Redditch	397	306	+ 91
Manchester	492	549	– 57
Liverpool	500	602	–102
Newcastle upon Tyne	479	584	–105
Hackney	765	1382	–614
Lewisham	684	1354	–670
Camden	843	1564	–721

Source: Department of the Environment.

In defending the community charge, the government argues that a flat rate is not unfair since about 50 per cent of local authority current expenditure in Britain is paid for by the Exchequer – in no small part from the proceeds of progressive income tax.

Thirdly, the community charge will be expensive to collect. CIPFA and the Association of Metropolitan Authorities both estimated that the charge will cost up to two and a half times as much as the cost of collecting rates – a major problem being to ensure that everybody liable to pay the charge is registered.

Fourthly, far from increasing the accountability of local authorities to their electorate, the new system will reduce it. In the late 1980s, the rate support grant payable to local authorities in England and Wales was 45 and 65 per cent respectively. When the revenue from the unified business rate is distributed, English and Welsh local authorities will have respectively a further 30 and 20 per cent of their spending met by the Exchequer. English local authorities will then, in effect, be only 25 per cent accountable and Welsh authorities 15 per cent accountable (compared with 55 and 35 per cent before).

Finally, the community charge will have a very substantial but not entirely beneficial effect on the residential property market. It has been estimated that the charge could result in 10 million households being better off by more than £1 billion per year. Taking into account current mortgage interest rates, this sum could be translated into an increase in property values of £12 billion and represent "the greatest distribution of wealth unmatched since the great enclosure of common lands in the eighteenth century."[39] Owners of small, low priced and low rated dwellings would, however, be generally worse off, and the value of their properties could fall (at least in real terms). Since the profit margins on small houses are always slim, builders would tend to cease producing starter-homes and concentrate instead on constructing high value houses where profitability would be much greater.

Scotland's new system, specified in the Domestic Rates etc. (Scotland) Act 1987, was scheduled to take effect in 1989–90. It will be introduced immediately and not phased-in over time. Non-domestic rates will be assessed and collected as before, although each year rate poundages will be indexed to the rate of inflation. A community charge of about £200 per adult replaces domestic rates, and its effects can be expected to be broadly similar to those in England and Wales – and they may become apparent sooner.

REFERENCES

1. R. Best, 'The Future Urban Acreage', *Town and Country Planning*, 32 (1964).
2. C. Doxiadix, *Urban America and the Role of Industry* (United States National Association of Manufacturers, 1971).
3. G. J. Roth, *Paying for Roads* (Penguin, 1967).
4. Ministry of Transport, *Traffic in Towns* (HMSO, 1963).
5. Ministry of Transport, *Road Pricing: The Economic and Technical Possibilities* (HMSO, 1964).
6. M. E. Beesley, 'Technical Possibilities of Special Taxation in Relation to Congestion Caused by Private Users', *Second International Symposium on Theory and Practice in Transport Economics* (OECD European Conference of Ministers of Transport, 1968); L. K. Lemon, 'An Economic Examination of Traffic Congestion in Towns', *Administration* (1972); C. H. Sharp, *Transport Economics* (Macmillan, 1973).
7. H. W. Richardson, 'A Note on the Distributional Effects of Road Pricing', *Journal of Transport Economics and Policy* (1974).
8. C. Sharp, 'Congestion and Welfare: An Examination of the Case for a Congestion Tax', *Economic Journal* (1966).

9. D. L. Munby, 'Management: The Economist's Viewpoint', *Symposium on Traffic and Towns* (Annual Meeting of the British Association for the Advancement of Science, 1971).
10. J. Hewitt, 'The Calculation of Congestion Taxes on Roads', *Economica* (1964); L. K. Lemon, 'An Economic Examination of Traffic Congestion in Towns', *Administration* (1972); G. J. Roth, *Paying for Roads* (Penguin, 1967); A. A. Walters, 'Empirical Evidence on Optimal Motor Taxes for the United Kingdom', *Econometrica* (1961).
11. Department of the Environment, *Urban Transport Planning*, Cmnd 5336 (HMSO, 1973).
12. G. J. Roth, *Paying for Parking*, Hobart Papers (Institute of Economic Affairs, 1965).
13. J. Ardill, 'Transport must face up to the future', *Guardian* (11 December, 1986).
14. P. Lawless and C. Raban, *The Contemporary British City* (Harper and Row, 1986).
15. Confederation of British Industry, *Economic Situation* (CBI, 1977); P. Townsend *et al.*, *Poverty and Labour in London* (Low Pay Unit, 1987).
16. S. Fothergill and G. Gudgin, *Unequal Growth: Urban and Regional Employment Change in the UK* (Heinemann, 1982).
17. L. Needleman, *The Economics of Housing* (Staples Press, 1965).
18. S. Merrett, *State Housing in Britain* (Routledge & Kegan Paul, 1979).
19. D. A. Kirby, *Slum Housing and Residential Renewal. The Case in Urban Britain* (Longman, 1979).
20. W. Lean, 'Housing Rehabilitation or Redevelopment: The Economic Assessment', *Journal of the Town Planning Institute*, 57 (1971).
21. D. G. Bagby, *Housing Rehabilitation Costs* (Lexington Books, 1973). D. Listokin, *The Dynamics of Housing Rehabilitation. Macro and Micro Analysis* (Centre for Urban Policy Research, Rutgers University, 1973).
22. National Community Development Project, *The Poverty of the Improvement Programme* (CDP Information and Intelligence Unit, 1975).
23. A. Taylor, 'Property Market', *Financial Times* (19 June, 1984).
24. I. Wray, 'Enterprise was radical only in its rhetoric', *Guardian* (30 July, 1986).
25. N. Ridley, speaking on 'The London Programme', London Weekend Television, 29 May 1987.
26. Archbishop of Canterbury's Commission on Urban Priority Areas, *Faith in the City* (Church House Publishing, 1985).
27. Town and Country Planning Association, Whose Responsibility?, *Reclaiming the Inner Cities* (TCPA, 1986).
28. D. Cadman, 'Private Capital and the Inner City', *Estates Gazette* (31 March, 1979).
29. G. Andrews, 'Heseltine plan to reverse inner city decay', *Guardian* (28 March, 1987).

30. See M. Pawley, 'City city bang bang', *Guardian* (21 May, 1987).
31. T. Champion, 'Momentous Revival in London's Population', *Town and Country Planning* (March, 1987).
32. *Committee of Inquiry into the Impact of Local Rates on Households*, Cmnd 2582 (HMSO, 1965).
33. *Layfield Committee of Inquiry into Local Government Finance*, Cmnd 6453 (HMSO, 1976).
34. H. Wilks, *Rating of Site Values* (Rating and Valuation Association, 1964).
35. *Site Value Rating – Report on a research exercise carried out in the town of Whitstable to throw further light on the rating of site value as a suitable source of public revenue* (The Land Institute, 1973).
36. P. N. Balchin and G. H. Bull, *Regional and Urban Economics* (Harper and Row, 1987).
37. Department of the Environment, *Alternatives to Domestic Rates*, Cmnd 8449 (HMSO, 1981).
38. Department of the Environment, *Paying for Local Government*, Cmnd 9714 (HMSO, 1986).
39. See *Land and Liberty*, 'How Thatcher boosted price of houses', July–August, 1987.

8

Housing

HOUSING MARKET

The housing market in the United Kingdom is composed of three distinct yet interrelated markets and tenures: private owner-occupied and private rented accommodation, and the public sector which includes voluntary housing, new town and local authority housing. These markets are related through a pattern of flows complicated by contractual obligations, ownership, property rights and Government intervention: from privately rented either to owner-occupation or to the public sector; and from local authority housing to owner-occupation.

The housing market is dominated by the existing stock of buildings which represent a high proportion of the total supply of housing. Relative to the size of stock the net annual addition is small. Supply is therefore relatively fixed even over the long period and prices of the standing stock and its allocation among users are determined primarily by changes in demand conditions. The durability and immobility of housing imposes a brake on the pace of adjustment of supply to changes in demand. In layout and building pattern the market situation is fundamentally one of disequilibrium; since so much of aggregate stock is not of recent construction, its location pattern reflects past distribution of population and economic activity.

House purchase represents a very large capital outlay for the consumer which can rarely be financed out of income, thus borrowing is necessary and the availability of long-term credit is of critical importance in making demand for owner-occupation effective.

In the United Kingdom none of the housing sectors is left free to face market forces. Tax relief and exemption distort owner-occupation, and both private and local authority housing are subject to extensive intervention with marked effects upon supply and demand. Overall, the price system has not been allowed to carry out its function of allocating scarce housing resources between alternative users.

Tenure and Prices

The growth of owner-occupation began in the 1920s and 1930s but the post-war period saw its consolidation as the most important numerical and therefore political factor in the housing market. Favourable government policy, difficulties of finding alternative accommodation, the development of specialist financial intermediaries and an investment atmosphere favourable for property caused the numbers of owner-occupied dwellings to increase from 3.4 million in 1947 to 13.6 million in 1985 or from 26 to 62 per cent of the total stock of dwellings in the United Kingdom (table 8.1).

Table 8.1 *Trends in housing tenure and stock, 1970–85*

	Total owner-occupied		Rented from local authority or new town corporation		Rented from private owners and other tenures		Total stock
	(million)	(% of total)	(million)	(% of total)	(million)	(% of total)	(million)
1970	9.6	50	5.9	30	3.7	20	19.2
1975	10.8	53	6.4	31	3.2	16	20.4
1980	11.9	55	6.8	32	2.8	13	21.5
1985	13.6	62	5.9	27	2.3	11	21.9

Source: Department of the Environment, *Housing and Construction Statistics.*

The growth in owner-occupation was at the expense mainly of the private rented sector. Both the benefits of home ownership and the disincentives of private landlordism (rent control, security of tenure and unfavourable tax treatment) resulted in an average annual loss of rented dwellings of approximately 125 000 in the 1970s. By 1985 only 11 per cent of the total housing stock was privately rented, about 2.3 million dwellings. A decade earlier 16 per cent had been privately rented, in 1951 41 per cent, while in 1914 it had been 90 per cent. The proportion of new houses built for local authorities reached its peak in 1951, with 87.4 per cent of houses erected. Because of economic and political change, council house building decreased rapidly after the mid-1970s and the size of the council stock decreased from 6.8 million to 6 million, 1979–85 – its share of the total housing stock falling from 32 to 27 per cent.

The price of owner-occupied housing has increased steadily (table 8.2). Until 1974 the rate of increase was greater than the rate of inflation, as measured by the retail price index, and between 1971 and 1973 far exceeded this. This apparently inexorable increase encouraged early entry into the housing market as the investment aspects of house purchase were emphasised. Only between 1974 and 1982 was there a realisation that rising house prices in real terms were not inevitable (in fact between the wars prices had fallen).

Generally, the price of new houses will be determined by existing house prices. Because of the durability of buildings the supply of houses is dominated

Table 8.2 *Average house prices and retail prices, 1970–86*

	Average price new houses		Average price all houses		House price earnings ratio	Retail price index increase (%)	Real increase in house prices (%)
	(£)	(% increase)	(£)	(% increase)			
1970	5 180	6.1	5 190	7.0	3.25	6.4	0.6
1971	5 970	15.3	6 130	18.1	3.50	9.4	8.0
1972	7 850	31.5	8 420	37.4	4.29	7.1	28.3
1973	10 690	36.2	11 120	32.1	4.95	9.2	21.0
1974	11 340	6.1	11 300	1.6	4.25	16.1	−12.5
1975	12 406	9.4	12 119	7.2	3.65	24.2	−13.7
1976	13 442	8.4	12 999	7.3	3.40	16.5	− 7.9
1977	14 768	9.9	13 922	7.1	3.34	15.8	− 7.5
1978	17 685	19.8	16 297	17.1	3.43	8.2	8.2
1979	22 728	28.5	21 047	29.1	3.82	13.4	13.8
1980	27 244	19.9	24 307	15.5	3.61	18.0	− 2.1
1981	28 028	2.4	24 810	0.8	3.30	11.9	− 9.9
1982	28 508	1.7	25 553	3.0	3.13	8.6	− 5.2
1983	31 678	11.1	28 593	11.9	3.23	4.6	7.0
1984	34 160	7.8	30 812	7.8	3.29	4.9	2.6
1985	37 304	9.2	31 188	7.7	3.30	6.1	1.5
1986	43 647	17.0	38 121	14.9	3.53	3.4	11.1

Source: Building Societies Association; Department of the Environment, *Housing and Construction Statistics.*

Table 8.3 *Indices of new and existing house prices, house building costs, general index of retail prices (quarter ending 31 December 1973 = 100), 1973–86*

Quarter	Secondhand properties		New properties	All properties	House building (wages and materials) costs	General index of retail prices (all items)
	Modern	Older				
1973 4th Qtr	100	100	100	100	100	100
1974 4th Qtr	104	106	105	105	121	118
1975 4th Qtr	114	116	119	116	149	148
1976 4th Qtr	123	125	131	125	177	170
1977 4th Qtr	132	134	145	135	193	192
1978 4th Qtr	171	171	183	172	209	208
1979 4th Qtr	221	229	236	225	241	244
1980 4th Qtr	235	244	266	241	279	281
1981 4th Qtr	240	243	285	244	302	315
1982 4th Qtr	260	264	302	262	323	334
1983 4th Qtr	293	296	336	294	342	351
1984 4th Qtr	333	341	371	336	360	368
1985 4th Qtr	363	374	427	371	383	388
1986 4th Qtr	410	427	478	422	398	402

Source: Nationwide Building Society: *Housing Trends.*

by the existing stock. The net average addition to stock by new building is relatively insignificant; about 1.2 per cent per year between 1911 and 1986. Thus the supply of houses is relatively inelastic even over a long period; price changes are therefore caused by demand changes. Housebuilders will charge what the market will bear by reference to existing house prices but they cannot always pass on increases in costs to the consumer unless the market is favourable. Consequently there is a close correlation between new and existing house prices (table 8.3) and between housing starts and prices of existing houses. Generally when existing house prices increase at a relatively faster rate there will be an incentive for developers to increase the supply of new houses, other things being equal. The trend will need to be clearly established before the level of new starts is drastically affected. Increases in existing house prices faster than the rate of increase of building costs result in periods of frenzied activity as developers hope to make super-normal profits, as between 1972 and 1973. Periods of falling or merely stable prices have the reverse effect, especially if costs rise at a faster rate; developers complete already started work but drastically reduce new work – as between 1980 and 1981. Because of the nature of housebuilding and the length of time of a typical project, the market may well be into downturn before developers are aware of a change in the situation. The time lag may be approximately 12-18 months dependent upon the size of the project. Thus supply may well overshoot demand on the downturn and be well short on the upswing.

There have been significant regional differences in price and site values; the highest have been in South-east England where site values reached over 35 per cent of price in 1972-73 and approached this percentage again in the mid-1980s. The premium established by these areas reflects the higher incomes and relatively low levels of unemployment, but regional disparities currently restrict rather than encourage household mobility. Households wishing to move to the South-east are aware that they will not only have to pay far more for a house but will need to secure more highly paid (and possibly more highly skilled) employment to be able to afford to move – as regional price and income statistics suggest (table 8.4). Conversely, few households in high price areas are likely to want to move to low price regions (assuming jobs were available) since they would have to forego opportunities for substantial capital accumulation.

Population Trends

Population increase must result in increased demand for housing and changes in the numbers of households are particularly significant. It is new households formed and existing households that move that generate the demand for new houses and put pressure on the stock of existing ones. Households which stay where they are have indirect effects. Those households which are most significant in considering housing demand include newly marrieds, elderly households dis-

Table 8.4 *Regional variations in house prices, income and unemployment, Great Britain, 1987*

	Average house price* (£)	Average income of borrower* (£)	House price/ incomes ratio	Unemploy-ment** (%)
Greater London	59 613	19 136	3.11	
South-east (excluding Greater London)	51 936	15 475	3.36	8.1
South-west	41 329	13 120	3.15	9.5
East Anglia	36 344	12 269	2.96	8.7
East Midlands	29 577	11 445	2.58	10.3
North-west	28 828	11 506	2.50	14.2
West Midlands	28 703	11 022	2.60	12.6
Scotland	27 080	12 747	2.12	14.7
Wales	26 776	10 682	2.51	13.8
Yorkshire and Humberside	25 576	10 714	2.39	12.8
North	25 523	11 524	2.21	15.5

*First quarter 1987.
**Unemployment March 1987.
Sources: Building Societies Association, *BSA Bulletin*; Department of Employment, *Employment Gazette.*

solved, and the formation and dissolution of one-person households. The number of households formed is the result of a very complex pattern of relationships and flows including marriage, death, migration, divorce and elderly households going to live as part of another household.[1]

Between 1951 and 1981 total households increased by 20 per cent with the most significant increase in the 26–30 age group, reflecting the sharp increase in the birth-rate after 1945. Single-person households increased from 11.9 to 23 per cent of total households between 1961 and 1981. The number of marriages substantially increased from the 1960s, reflecting the increase in the percentage of the population in the main marriageable age group and easier divorce. Life expectancy increased, slowing down the recycling of houses as many more elderly households continued in existence. The impact of these factors was to largely increase the demand for small dwelling units, not generallly reflected in the types of housing developed. Between 1951 and 1981 the United Kingdom population increased from 50.2 to 56.3 million while the total stock of dwellings increased from 13.8 to 21.7 million, outstripping the growth in household formation and producing a crude surplus of houses over households – illusory because it conceals serious discrepancies. It takes no regard of the geographical distribution of houses and people, the quality of the housing stock, the splitting of households, the increased demand for second homes, and the need to allow for a vacancy rate to promote mobility. This latter consideration is of increasing importance. In a modern economy, technological change leads to the existence of areas of decline and growth where new industries find favourable locations. There is therefore need for labour to move from areas of decline to areas of growth.

FINANCE FOR HOUSE PURCHASE

The effective demand for owner-occupier housing is critically dependent upon the availability of long-term finance, which in the United Kingdom is provided by a number of institutions including insurance companies, banks and local authorities. The market is dominated by the building societies, whose prime function is the provision of long-term finance for owner-occupation; this dominance is particularly clear in respect of finance for new dwellings. By 1986, building societies had over £116 000 million outstanding loans (76 per cent of all balances) compared with £29 000 million by banks, £3200 million by local authorities and £3000 million by insurance companies. In 1986, a peak year, building societies made 1 232 000 advances, 120 000 on new houses. Because of this dominance (table 8.5) the societies have had important effects on the nature of the housing stock – tending to favour traditionally built modern houses of two to four bedrooms. It may be difficult to obtain a mortgage on unconventional dwellings or conversions. Partly as a result of building society restrictions

Table 8.5 *Mortgages: main institutional sources 1970–86 United Kingdom (£m)*

	Building societies	Banks	Local authorities	Insurance companies	Other public	All
1970	1 088	40	72	32	10	1 245
1975	2 768	60	620	67	133	3 648
1980	5 722	593	454	264	300	7 333
1981	6 331	2 448	269	88	353	9 489
1982	8 147	5 078	555	6	351	14 137
1983	10 928	3 731	–306	126	21	14 500
1984	14 572	2 422	–195	254	–43	17 010
1985	14 711	4 444	–465	200	62	18 952
1986	19 072	7 045	–493	223	93	25 940
Advances outstanding at end of 1986	116 469	29 292	3 186	3 014	1709	153 660

Source: Department of the Environment, *Housing and Construction Statistics.*

there have been little changes in the type or method of construction of dwellings built for owner-occupation.

In deciding whether to grant a mortgage the age, quality, type of house, the likely length of working life and job security are important considerations. Generally mortgages with low deposits and long repayment periods are more difficult to obtain for older properties. Older people usually have to accept shorter repayment periods or smaller loans and therefore need higher deposits or higher incomes to buy houses. Societies are critically concerned with ensuring their reputation as safe investment media. In marginal cases, the non-manual applicant may be better favoured than the manual.[2]

The clearing banks have increased their involvement in mortgage lending beyond their traditional bridging finance. They began to offer a larger volume of loans for house purchase in the early 1980s, increasingly at the upper end of the market and in competition with the building societies. Loans increased from £40 million annually in 1970 to over £5000 million in 1986. North American banks and the Trustee Savings Bank also entered the market, the latter rapidly expanding its activity in 1979–80. Insurance companies have preferred to lend on commercial rather than residential property, thus housebuying loans are normally linked to an endowment policy – with higher repayments than with a conventional building society mortgage. Insurance companies have been significant in the higher mortgage range (above the special advance limit of building societies, £37 000 in 1981) and on new houses, but their overall share of home loans has diminished since the 1960s.

Local authorities may grant mortgages under provisions of the Housing (Financial Provisions) Act 1958. They tend to limit their lending to borrowers unable to obtain a mortgage from a building society either because of the financial status of the borrower or the age or construction of the property to be mortgaged; they also prefer to limit their lending to borrowers within their physical boundaries and also to a strict financial limit. They tend to act as lenders of last resort, mainly for older housing, and interest rates are normally fixed over the whole period of the loan. Public sector cutbacks mean that local authorities will play a lesser role in the 1980s except in financing council house purchase, and recently loans have been less than mortgages.

Building Society Funds

Crucially, the ability of societies to lend depends upon the inflow of funds from savers, which depends largely upon the rate of interest which societies offer in comparison with other competing institutions within the money market. Thus the differential between building society rates and competing rates as indicated by Bank Rate to October 1972, and Minimum Lending Rate (MLR) and base rate since, is of significance in indicating the likely level of inflow funds. Typically, building societies borrow short and lend long but are slow to adjust their interest rates in relation to other short-term rates. This delay in adjusting to general movements in these rates explains how a 'differential' may emerge. The societies are unwilling to alter rates frequently, firstly for administrative reasons. The frequent recalculation of mortgage repayments is a costly and inconvenient process; most mortgage contracts require three months' notice before existing borrowers' rates can be increased. Between 1972 and 1981 banks' base rate changed over 80 times whereas building society rates changed 20 times. Secondly, at times of falling rates, the societies prefer to keep their rates relatively high in order to maintain a large inflow of funds. However, societies do generate a high proportion of their funds for lending through capital repayments and interest credited. Over the period 1970–78, net receipts of new savings from investors accounted for 45 per cent of funds, interest credited 17 per cent and repayments of mortgage principal 38 per cent. Clearly, the ability of building societies to meet mortgage demand is not dependent solely on new savings which they receive from investors.

Although building society rate changes are slow over time, they follow other rates. For example, when MLR is increased a new equilibrium occurs within the money market – building society rates appear relatively unattractive for the marginal investor. Thus funds flow out of societies, less money is available for advances, effective demand for housing falls and properties become more difficult to sell. This situation occurred intermittently from the 1950s, usually at times of economic crisis associated with the balance of payments. The outflow continues until the societies are forced to increase their rates to lenders to restore the original equilibrium. Higher rates to depositors result in higher rates to mortgagors. Effectively, the higher the rate of interest the less capital can be raised by a borrower and the less the effective demand as maximum possible bid price is less. The overall impact therefore of increases in the base rate is a slowing down in the rate of price increase in the private house market and eventually a slowing down in new developments as builders realise that anticipated prices will not be achieved and that they cannot sell completed developments. The reverse process occurs at times of falling interest rates. Thus there is a clear inverse relationship between interest changes and housing starts.

Incomes and Income Elasticity

For existing owner-occupiers, maximum demand, given financial constraints, consists of personal savings, the value of the existing dwelling and the maximum mortgage available. For households who are not already owner-occupiers, maximum effective demand is the maximum mortgage plus any personal savings. Mortgage potential is based on recipient's age, job security and income with a maximum mortgage normally set at between 2½ and 3 times the head of household's gross annual income. With maximum mortgages linked critically to incomes, and mortgages being essential to house purchase, one would expect a fairly stable relationship between average earnings of fully employed men over 18 and house prices with a ratio of average price to income of approximately 3.5. This latter ratio held for most of the 1950s and 1960s, then between 1966 and 1970 dropped to 3.4 before increasing steeply between 1970 and 1973 to 4.95 (rather higher for manual than non-manual workers).[2] Because of the significance of mortgages for house purchase there is clearly a limit to the increase in the price/earnings ratio before some slowing down in house prices occurs to restore equilibrium. This occurred in the housing market between 1974 and 1975. Similarly the relatively low ratio of 3.23 reached in the first quarter of 1985 indicated that house prices were due to rise at a faster rate, which duly occurred in 1986–7. The increase in the number of owner-occupiers means that the many transactions within the housing market are between existing owners rather than households moving in from the rented sector. With a house to sell to partly finance the transaction through the resultant equity, the mortgage becomes marginally less significant and the ratio of price to income may tend to settle higher than hitherto.

The tendency to demand more and better-quality owner-occupier housing reflects the positive income elasticity of demand for housing. Income elasticity has been measured using either time-series analysis in which the available data on housing demand are analysed in relation to income changes over time, or cross-sectional analysis, in which housing demand is examined in relation to families within various income groups in a given period. The latter has advantages in that the time period is too short for other conditions to have changed substantially. In the United Kingdom, permanent income elasticity of demand based on cross-section analysis ranges from 0.6 to 1.0, largely depending on the considerations given to age of head of household and social class. Time-series analysis tends to show higher elasticities probably because of the underlying conditions in the market for housing and in the population structure. Recent work carried out on price elasticity has found values ranging from 0.26 to 0.60 – that is, an inelastic demand.[3] The price elasticity of demand for a dwelling is, of course, less elastic than for housing as a whole.

There has been a consistent increase in the proportion of borrowers with wives working in paid employment whose incomes were taken into account in the granting of a mortgage, although societies are reluctant to give a wife's earnings much weight since the continuity of that income is in doubt. However, by 1973 nearly 57 per cent first-time buyers and 33 per cent of previous owner-occupiers had working wives.[4] Thus the average mortgage repayment as a percentage of average household income was lower than the price/income ratio suggests. The Nationwide Building Society suggested that repayments for normal mortgages represented 22.5 per cent of family income for first-time buyers, reducing to 10 per cent of income after 5½ years (the average life of a mortgage). For all households, average expenditure on housing as a proportion of income increased from 9.5 per cent in 1966 to 14.9 per cent in 1976. By 1980, houses represented 20 per cent of personal sector net wealth. Generally, owner-occupiers tend to spend a higher proportion of their incomes on housing than tenants in either the public or private sector. First-time buyers under 25 required a deposit representing 66 per cent of income by 1978, compared with 50 per cent in 1966 (with the highest figures required in Greater London).[2]

There has, however, been an increased demand for owner-occupation from younger age groups. By 1987, approximately 20 per cent of all mortgages were granted to purchasers under 26 years of age and a further 40 per cent to the 25–34 age group. By the mid-1980s, the proportion of owner-occupied dwellings in the United Kingdom, 62 per cent, was in excess of most other West European countries, although in the United States some 66 per cent of dwellings were owner-occupied. It is of concern, however, that an increasing proportion of owner-occupiers (1 per cent) were affected by mortgage foreclosure in 1987 because of their inability to meet mortgage repayments.

Tax Concessions

A further incentive to owner-occupation has been tax relief at marginal rates on interest payments made on mortgages, although in 1974 this was limited to the first £25 000 borrowed (£30 000 in 1983). In an inflationary period, tax relief often meant that the owner-occupier paid a negative rate of interest (table 8.6). In addition, the steady increase in price emphasised the investment advantages of owner-occupation. If the increase in capital value is included, the effective rate of interest was further reduced. Tax relief on mortgages for owner-occupation was costing over £4000 million annually by the mid-1980s compared with £75 million in 1962–63. It was clearly beneficial to be a borrower repaying in depreciated pounds in order to own an appreciating capital asset which was a fine hedge against inflation. The owner-occupier was also free of capital gains tax (on his main property) at an estimated cost of £3 billion in 1982. Other tax changes favoured the owner-occupier. In 1963, Schedule A, on the imputed net income derived from a dwelling by its owner, was abolished at a cost to the Treasury of £48 million in a full year; the current cost of not having this tax could be more than £7000 million a year.[5] In 1971, stamp duty on mortgages was abolished. In 1973, new housing was zero rated for Value Added Tax. In 1983, thresholds for stamp duty rates were increased.

Mortgage interest relief, general exemption from capital gains tax and the abolition of Schedule A tax have been subject to widespread criticism.[6] It is claimed that mortgage interest relief, in particular, is inflationary since it enables house buyers to bid-up the price of houses higher than would otherwise be the case (see chapter 4, figure 4.1). Conversely, house prices would be reduced if tax concessions were to be withdrawn or reduced.

Mortgage interest relief also provides inequitable assistance. Within the owner-occupied sector it is regressively allocated, and in recent years it has been increasing while exchequer subsidies to local authority tenants have been generally decreasing – the average mortgagor receiving nearly five times more interest

Table 8.6 *Nominal and real rates of interest on loans, 1973–86*

4th Qtr	Average mortgage rate	Basic rate of income tax	Net nominal rate of interest	Increase in RPI (inflation rate)	Net real rate of interest
1973	11.00	30	7.70	9.2	– 1.50
1974	11.00	33	7.37	16.1	– 8.73
1975	11.00	35	7.15	24.2	–17.05
1976	12.25	35	7.96	16.5	– 8.54
1977	9.50	34	6.27	15.8	– 9.53
1978	11.75	33	7.87	8.2	– 0.33
1979	15.00	30	10.50	13.4	– 2.90
1980	14.00	30	9.80	18.0	– 8.20
1981	15.00	30	10.50	11.9	– 1.40
1982	10.00	30	7.00	8.6	– 1.60
1983	11.25	30	7.87	4.6	3.27
1984	11.75	30	8.22	4.9	3.32
1985	12.75	30	9.22	6.1	3.12
1986	12.25	29	8.70	3.4	5.30

Source: Building Societies Association, *BSA Bulletin*: Nationwide Building Society, *House Prices.*

Table 8.7 *Distribution of mortgage interest relief, 1983–84*

Income band	Taxpayers receiving relief (%)	Total relief (%)	Average relief per mortgagor (£)
£20 000 and over	8.5	19.0	830
£15 000–19 000	13.1	16.2	465
£10 000–14 999	33.5	34.3	380
£5 000–9 999	38.7	29.3	280
Under £5 000	6.2	1.2	70

Source: National Federation of Housing Associations, *Inquiry into British Housing*, 1985.

relief than the average tenant's exchequer subsidy in 1985–86 (tables 8.6, 8.7 and 8.8). Furthermore, mortgage interest relief is inefficient since the tax revenue foregone by the Exchequer could finance productive industry rather than lubricate the market largely for existing houses; it has adverse effects on taxation because the foregone revenue has to be made up by higher rates of taxation generally (including income tax); it adversely affects household mobility since it helps to widen regional disparities (particularly boosting house prices in the South-east) and is a disincentive to trade-down; it distorts tenure preferences in favour of owner-occupation (to a greater extent than in many other advanced capitalist countries); it distorts rural values since commuters can easily outbid local labour for a fairly fixed stock of housing; and it fails to protect the poor because the system of relief pushes house prices beyond their means. Critics argue that reform is long-overdue and at the minimum should involve limiting mortgage interest relief to the basic rate of tax.

Table 8.8 *Mortgage interest relief and exchequer subsidy, 1978/79–1985/86*

	Mortgage interest relief		Exchequer subsidy	
	Total cost (£m)	Cost per mortgagor (£)	Total cost (£m)	Cost per dwelling (£)
1978–79	995	200	1258	255
1979–80	1300	265	1274	257
1980–81	1745	335	1393	281
1981–82	1830	350	884	185
1982–83	1915	370	441	92
1983–84	2455	390	350	75
1984–85	3100	500	379	84
1985–86	4250	590	457	105

Note: Exchequer subsidy relates to England only.
Source: Association of Metropolitan Authorities, *Housing Facts*, 1986.

Second Homes

Increasing real income, car ownership and leisure, together with the 'investment' benefits, resulted in an increase in the demand for second homes, which by 1979 represented about 1 per cent of the built housing stock. About 2 per cent of families in Britain owned second homes, much lower than other European Community countries and Scandinavia where there tends to be a higher proportion of properties used primarily for recreational purposes. The demand in the United Kingdom is mainly for homes in coastal and rural areas such as North Wales and the Lake District. Second homes have become a contentious political issue; some have argued that the increased demand from 'wealthy' urbanites forces up prices beyond the abilities of local villagers, others that in the long run there are benefits from the additional rates and purchasing power of the new residents. New purpose-built second homes, in total, are numerically insignificant, more so since 1974 when tax relief on interest payments ended for new purchases. Secondly, the rehabilitation of dwellings as second homes was also constrained when improvement grants for this purpose were stopped in the same year. However, in the late 1980s, easy mortgage credit boosted the second homes market and increasingly squeezed-out indigenous demand in specific localities.

HOUSE PRICES AND THE MACRO-ECONOMY

In recent years, mortgage advances have accounted for an increasing proportion of gross domestic product (GDP) at factor cost – rising from 1 per cent in 1956 to 4 per cent in 1978 and 6.2 per cent (or £18 700 million) in 1985. This, together with the ending of mortgage rationing in 1981 and the escalation of tax relief and exemption, pulled-up house prices dramatically in the mid/late-1980s.

House price inflation (particularly in Greater London and the South-east) was consequently greater than the increase in retail prices. Muellbauer[7] argued that since house prices are a major element in the cost of living of housebuyers, soaring house prices in the period 1984–86 put pressure on the labour market and added 4 per cent to the level of real wages (with even larger increases in nominal wages anticipated over the following two years). Since wage agreements are often nationally based, house prices in the South-east thus influence wage levels throughout Britain. The view that house prices, in effect, determine wage levels could be supported by the notion that people buy the most expensive house they can afford with the largest mortgage they can raise, but then need to earn more to maintain their customary level of consumption and savings.

Congdon and Warburton[8] have similarly argued that there is a link between rising house prices and retail price inflation. Although real house prices tended to rise on average by 2.63 per cent above the level of retail prices over the period 1957–86, occasionally they increased at a faster rate and pulled-up retail prices. It is suggested that the mechanism by which this works is as follows. (a) Housebuyers convert part of the increase in the value of their property into larger mortgages to purchase consumer goods and thereby boost demand and raise retail prices. The Bank of England estimated that equity withdrawal of this sort amounted to £7.2 billion in 1984 (or 3 per cent of consumer spending). (b) The housebuilding industry responds to rising house prices by increasing output. Subsequent wage increases in the industry then inflate retail prices. (c) House price inflation stimulates increased borrowing to invest in housing and this, it is suggested, increases the money supply and hence the rate of inflation.

The Muellbauer/Congdon–Warburton hypotheses have been subject to some criticism. Hamnett[9] has claimed that only a small proportion of equity withdrawal has been diverted into consumption and that most has been returned to the financial system to sustain mortgage lending; and there is little evidence that rising house prices stimulate output or that earnings and wages generated in housebuilding are of sufficient significance to the rate of inflation. Yet, there does appear to be a relationship between house prices and inflation. While the building societies argue that factors other than house prices are the main causes of inflation (for example, rising oil prices and increased Value Added Tax in the late 1970s–early 1980s), they claim that rising incomes cause rising house prices rather than vice versa. It is very likely however, that there is an inflationary 'chicken and egg' relationship. An initial demand change might lead to rapidly rising house prices (as workers find that their additional expenditure on housing only serves to raise the unit cost rather than the quantity consumed), and this causes higher wage demands and, in turn, even higher house prices. If, as new evidence appears to show, widening differences in regional house price trends are producing substantial cost-of-living variations in different parts of the United Kingdom (with the highest prices in the South-east), then high money incomes in high house price regions might frustrate real wage demands in such areas – leading to spiraling money wage demands. If met, such demands could have a significant impact on the retail price index, particularly if they formed the bases of national wage settlements.

Clearly, the Treasury sees little connection between rising house prices and inflation. While this persists, it is unlikely that there will be any radical reform to the current system of subsidising owner-occupation.

PRIVATE RENTED ACCOMMODATION

The decline of private landlordism has been largely due to the comparative advantage in selling vacant properties for owner-occupation, instead of letting, and the onerous task of managing rented housing compared with other forms of investment (many of which were not available in the nineteenth century when rented housing was the norm). The decline of the private rented stock (from 90 per cent of dwellings in 1914 to about 11 per cent in 1986) has also been attributable to several other factors: security of tenure, the tax positions of private landlords, the almost continuous intervention by successive governments in landland-tenant relations, and rent control and regulation. From 1915 until 1974, rent legislation was intermittently introduced to control or regulate rents in the private sector, although in the inter-war period and again in 1957 decontrols were introduced – albeit for relatively short periods of time and specifically in relation to higher value properties (table 8.9).

A Labour Government in 1964 brought an inevitable turn of policy. The Rent Act 1965, consolidated 1968, brought within control all properties with a rateable value of less than £400 in London and £200 elsewhere, most of the houses which had been decontrolled under the 1957 Act. The Act followed upon the Milner Holland Report (1965)[10] and provided security of tenure for unfurnished tenants; tenants protected under the Act were 'regulated' while those protected by previous acts were still 'controlled'. New machinery was set up to fix and review rents for newly protected tenants while new safeguards

Table 8.9 *Legislation controlling rents, 1915–74*

<table>
<tr><th rowspan="2">Year of Rent Act</th><th rowspan="2">Main features</th><th rowspan="2"></th><th colspan="3">Rateable value (£)</th></tr>
<tr><th>London</th><th>Scotland</th><th>Elsewhere</th></tr>
<tr><td>1915</td><td>Rents controlled at 1914 levels</td><td>Not exceeding</td><td>35</td><td>30</td><td>26</td></tr>
<tr><td>1920</td><td>Rent controls continued</td><td>Not exceeding</td><td>105</td><td>90</td><td>78</td></tr>
<tr><td>1923</td><td>Decontrol by possession; letting freed from control when tenant left</td><td></td><td></td><td></td><td></td></tr>
<tr><td>1933</td><td>(a) Decontrol of houses</td><td>Not below</td><td>45</td><td>45</td><td>45</td></tr>
<tr><td></td><td>(b) Decontrol by possession</td><td>Not below</td><td>45</td><td>35</td><td>35</td></tr>
<tr><td></td><td>(c) Decontrol on registration of possession</td><td>Not below</td><td>35</td><td>20</td><td>20</td></tr>
<tr><td></td><td>(d) No decontrol by possession unless decontrolled 1923 to 1933 and registered</td><td>Not below</td><td>20</td><td>20</td><td>20</td></tr>
<tr><td>1938</td><td>(a) Decontrol of houses</td><td>Not below</td><td>35</td><td>20</td><td>20</td></tr>
<tr><td></td><td>(b) No decontrol by possession of self-contained dwellings</td><td>Not exceeding</td><td>35</td><td>20</td><td>20</td></tr>
<tr><td>1939</td><td>Rents controlled</td><td>Not exceeding</td><td>100</td><td>90</td><td>75</td></tr>
<tr><td>1957</td><td>Rents decontrolled owner-occupied dwellings partly let and new unfurnished dwellings. Remaining tenancies had rents fixed at twice their 1939 rateable values</td><td>Not below</td><td>40</td><td>30</td><td>30</td></tr>
<tr><td>1965</td><td>Rent regulation</td><td>Not exceeding</td><td>400</td><td>200</td><td>200</td></tr>
<tr><td></td><td>Rent controlled continued</td><td>Not exceeding</td><td>110</td><td>80</td><td>80</td></tr>
<tr><td>1969*</td><td>Controlled dwellings rehabilitated up to 12 point standard to be decontrolled and regulated</td><td>Not exceeding</td><td>400</td><td colspan="2">200</td></tr>
<tr><td>1972**</td><td>Most controlled tenances to be decontrolled and regulated</td><td>Not exceeding</td><td>400</td><td colspan="2">200</td></tr>
<tr><td>1973</td><td>Rent regulation extended to higher rateable value properties</td><td>Not exceeding</td><td>1500</td><td colspan="2">750</td></tr>
<tr><td>1974</td><td>Rent regulation extended to furnished tenancies</td><td>Not exceeding</td><td>1500</td><td colspan="2">750</td></tr>
</table>

*Housing Act 1969.
**Housing Finance Act 1972.

were introduced to prevent harassment and eviction without court order. Rent was to be assessed and registered by a Rent Officer after application by landlord, tenant or both. It was to be an objective and 'fair rent' although no fixed formula was given to officers in carrying out their assessment. Rent Officers were to have regard 'to all circumstances (other than personal circumstances) and in particular to the age, character and locality of the dwelling-house and to its state of repair'. Any improvement carried out by the tenant, or any damage caused by him, should not be taken into account.

The most contentious aspect of the legislation was that Rent Officers were directed to assume that the supply and demand for accommodation in the locality was equal – this at a time of great housing shortage and where in most urban areas supply was far short of demand. The result of the disregard of the scarcity factor was that rents were fixed at substantially below the market price, providing an additional deterrent to letting as landlords were unsure of obtaining a market return on their investment. On obtaining vacant possession, landlords often preferred not to re-let but to sell for owner-occupation, obtaining a greater price than if the property was sold as an investment. Once the 'fair rent' was registered it was fixed for a statutory two years. The 'fair rent' system placed enormous responsibility on the judgement of the Rent Officer, who often lacked suitable professional qualifications. There was a lack of consistency in rent assessments; appeal was possible to a Rent Assessment Committee which in the majority of cases increased the original fair rent, possibly because landlords made more use of the appeal procedure and employed professional assistance. A further criticism of the system was that Rent Officers paid little regard to inflation in their original registration and the next after three years (up to 1980). The net effect of the 'fair rent' system was that unfurnished accommodation became almost extinct outside the controlled and luxury sectors of the market. In 1971 the Francis Committee[11] reported that in general the system of fair rents was working well, although it suggested a number of modifications. By 1975 the DOE estimated that of all unfurnished tenancies with non-resident landlords, about half had fair rents registered compared with only 14 per cent five years earlier.

The supply of furnished accommodation was less adversely affected as the 'fair rent' did not apply. Rent Tribunals assessed a reasonable rent as they were not specifically directed to disregard scarcity, thus the differential between rent assessed by the Tribunal and the market rent was not so great. Furnished tenants did not have the security of tenure granted to the unfurnished tenant; thus landlords had more incentive to let. However, there was a constant possibility of further legislation to give security of tenure to the furnished tenant. These considerations were justified with the Rent Act 1974 which included all properties with a rateable value of £1500 in London and £750 elsewhere. The furnished tenant of the non-resident landlord was given security of tenure and the right to apply for a 'fair rent'. The Rent Officer too over the Tribunal's functions. Compared with the previous 'reasonable' rents, the new 'fair rents' were often considerably lower – by a third to a half. Inevitably there was a sharp decline in the supply of furnished accommodation and increased difficulty for the young and mobile in finding a home, as landlords preferred to keep their accommodation empty rather than to let and risk the reduction of income and loss of capital. The consequences were particularly serious in cities; about half of Britain's furnished tenancies were in London alone; approximately 10 per cent of London's households were furnished tenants.

An attempt to change housing policy radically was made in 1971 when the Conservative Government published a White Paper, *Fair Deal for Housing*[12] setting out a new system of housing finance for both private and public sectors. The Housing Finance Act 1972 implemented the major proposals. In the private rented sector all controlled tenancies, about 1.3 million, were to become regulated. As recommended by the Francis Committee 1971, landlords and tenants were to agree a rent, and would be free to apply to the Rent Officer for a fair rent. Properties would need to be provided with standard amenities and be in good repair, and the increase would be phased over two years. The government hoped that the conversion to regulated rents would encourage more lettings and prevent deterioration of properties. It was unlikely that this incentive would have proved effective. In any event the government's anti-inflation legislation, 1973, froze rent increases. On the return of the Labour Government in 1974, the Housing Finance Act was repealed.

The major economic effects of government intervention in the rented sector are clear:

(1) The landlord's ability and incentive to maintain premises in good condition is impaired. Many landlords in receipt of controlled or 'fair rents' have found it impossible to meet maintenance charges. Much property degenerates into slums or is at best maintained at a level much below what is economically or socially desirable. Faced with the choice of running property at a loss or allowing it to decay, the landlord may sell. Tenants are also faced with a choice. They can either remain in unsatisfactory rented accommodation or become owner-occupiers – acquire an appreciating asset and benefit from tax privileges. An increasing number have chosen the latter option.

(2) Regardless of the condition of the accommodation, whenever a dwelling has fallen vacant, the landlord usually finds it pays to sell it for owner-occupation rather than to re-let. However, although it is often argued that rent control (or regulation) has resulted in the withdrawing from the letting market of most privately owned houses suitable for owner-occupation or other uses, Harloe[13] has shown that in both Western Europe and the United States the private rented sector has been in decline whether or not it has been subject to control. In most advanced capitalist countries, owner-occupation is the most heavily 'subsidised' tenure and can out-bid all other tenures for a relatively fixed supply of housing or land. The long-term effect of rent control/regulation is shown in figure 8.1. It is assumed that rents are fixed at r_1 (below their market level r), thereby creat-

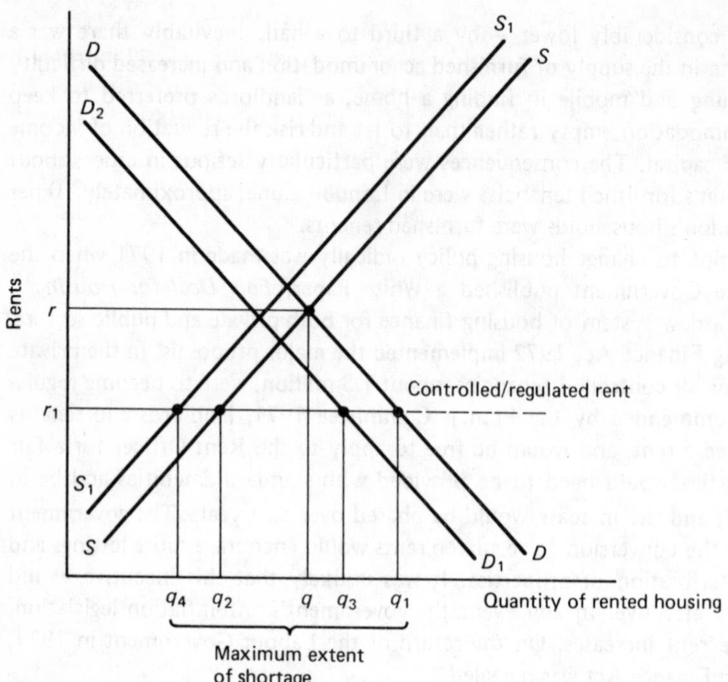

Figure 8.1 *Demand and supply in the controlled sector of the private rented housing market*

ing an initial shortage of accommodation equivalent to $q_1 - q_2$. If landlords sell their properties for owner-occupation, the long-term supply of rented housing will decrease from SS to S_1S_1, but if simultaneously tenants become owner-occupiers the demand for rented accommodation will likewise decrease (from DD to say D_1D_1), the eventual shortage becoming $q_3 - q_4$. However, if demand does not decrease (since there might be a growing number of small households in search of housing) the shortage could be at least as great as $q_1 - q_4$.

(3) The mobility of labour is impeded. Rent restriction involves what is in effect a tax on the landlord and a subsidy to the tenant which he receives only so long as he stays in his existing house. The Rent Acts have reduced the supply of accommodation so that if a tenant wishes to move he may find himself unable to obtain alternative accommodation. The stock of rented property becomes 'fossilised' with a substantial proportion of old and poor-quality dwellings.

(4) Under-use of housing stock. Because tenants cling to their dwellings they prevent the adaptation of housing to changing requirements in size, amenities and standards.

(5) There is a distortion of consumer preference, land-use patterns and allocation of scarce resources.

(6) Landlords have been discriminated against by taxation authorities. A house is considered to last for ever and landlords cannot write down their investment. Even payments into a sinking fund to replace the dwelling cannot be treated as cost. This has led to further distortions within the housing market and further disincentives to letting.

Despite its often generally poor physical quality, largely explained by the succession of adverse legislation, the private rented sector is the only one with a large number of very small dwellings, such as bed-sitters and one- and two-roomed flats. This is very important since approximately 50 per cent of households in 1981 consisted of one or two persons. Thus the sector is attractive for young households, particularly single people, students and couples without children. These groups – the young, the mobile, the newcomers to an area – benefit from the flexibility which is characteristic of the private rented sector. The very arbitrariness of allocation by private landlords may be an attraction to certain groups. Local authorities must observe equitable procedures in the allocation of their housing, which may be superficially fair but fail to provide for special needs or circumstances. The private landlord has a role to play which neither municipalisation nor housing associations can replace. Municipalisation, the process of local authorities buying substandard dwellings from the private landlord, often reproduces existing forms of council housing which does not benefit the marginal groups who benefit from private renting. In any event, municipalisation is expensive and local authorities outside a limited range of central London areas have shown a singular lack of interest in buying up tenanted property. The management problems in providing furnished bed-sit accommodation by local authorities have also not been solved. Similar considerations clearly apply to housing associations who fail to cater for the marginal groups and 'floaters'. Fundamentally, private-rented accommodation may be the only choice for many whose needs are greatest and whose resources are least, short of the availability of suitable public sector housing.

It was largely for these reasons that the Conservative government, in its Housing Act 1980, introduced shorthold tenure. Shorthold was intended to reduce the landlord's uncertainty about letting, since the tenant's security of tenure was to be limited to the period of the shorthold agreement – a period of one to five years. However, the landlord's return on his investment was not improved. The shorthold tenancy in London was to be at a registered fair rent, set by the Rent Officer, which by definition could not take scarcity into account (outside of the capital, market rents could be negotiated). A survey of attitudes to letting which the DOE carried out in 1976 showed that the one change which would be most helpful to landlords would be to allow more realistic rents. Shortholds might have some temporary effect: possibly to persuade landlords to let empty property while they are waiting to sell, but a change of government might make the 'shortholder' a lifetime tenant. The tenure is thus likely to have only a marginal effect on the supply of rented accommodation.

A novel proposal of the 1980 Act was that of 'assured' tenancy. Institutions such as building societies, insurance companies and pension funds wishing to build houses to rent could seek approval from the Department of the Environment to let property at freely negotiated market rents outside the provisions of the Rent Acts as long as building began after August 1980 and the property was not previously occupied. This appeared to be merely a symbolic gesture given the political problems of the private rented sector, and it is unlikely that anything other than a very marginal contribution is likely to arise from this proposal since competitive returns may not be anticipated.

The House of Commons Environment Committee in 1982 critically examined the private rented sector.[14] It concluded that private rented housing compared unfavourably with other forms of investment in terms of risk, liquidity, expected returns on capital and management involvement. Landlords could not expect gross returns in excess of 2.75 per cent in London in the early 1980s, or net yields of more than 1 per cent (after taking into account management, maintenance and tax). To obtain a competitive yield of, say, 10 per cent, rents would need to rise considerably above fair rent levels, putting them beyond the means of most tenants. The tenure also fell short as far as tenants were concerned. It lacked the security of an owner-occupied property, while the average rent allowance was less than 10 per cent of the average relief on mortgage interest. The Committee recommended that the tenure could only be saved from further decline by subsidising both landlords and tenants by tax concessions and other means. However, the National Federation of Housing Associations' *Inquiry into British Housing* (1985) proposed that in order to retain and increase investment in private rented housing, rents should be linked to capital values.[15] Capital value rent would have three components: a basic element to provide a real return of around 4 per cent on capital value, an element for management and maintenance, and (if relevant) an element for service charges. As with the fair rent system, capital value rents would be set by rent officers.

In its third term in office, the Thatcher government attempted to build-on previous policy concerning shorthold and assured tenancies. It hoped that its new measures would bring back into use over 500 000 properties allegedly left vacant because of rent regulation. Based largely on the White Paper, *Housing: The Government's Proposals* (1987),[16] the Housing Act 1988 aims to boost the private rented sector by reducing the minimum period of shorthold to only 6 months and to extend assured tenancies to the remainder of new lettings. Shorthold lettings will be at market rents which take account of the limited period of contractual security of the tenant. Assured tenants, on the other hand, will have security of tenure but rents will be freely negotiated between landlord and tenant and will thus also be at market levels. Existing regulated tenants will (ostensibly) continue to be protected by the Rent Acts, and to deter landlords from forcibly securing vacant possession (to create shorthold or assured tenure, or to sell) the laws on harassment and illegal eviction have been tightened and tenants forced out illegally will be able to claim greater compensation than hitherto.

Critics of the 1988 Act argue that not only will rents rise dramatically, particularly in areas of housing shortages, but under shorthold arrangements tenants will have less protection than before, while assured tenants might have to pay exorbitant rents for dilapidated and unsafe housing. Even regulated tenancies will be under threat since the right of succession at fair rent levels will be reduced, inflicting upon those 'inheriting' the tenure the option of market rents or eviction, and local authorities will lose their powers to apply for a fair rent to be registered. Many tenants will therefore find it more advantageous to buy rather than to continue renting, while others will be severely affected by housing benefits being paid only in relation to specific levels of rent assessed by rent officers on the basis of rules laid down by the Secretary of State for the Environment. Above these levels, landlords will be free to charge any rent the market will bear, with higher-income tenants inevitably squeezing out those in receipt of housing benefits. But even then, landlords may find it more profitable to sell rather than rent.

The 1988 Act, claim its critics, thus gives the landlord a range of incentives and opportunities to secure vacant possession with or without the use of illegal means. Therefore, far from bringing back into the market more than half a million properties, the Act might reduce supply still further until it reaches a core of about 5–6 per cent of the housing stock. If this proves to be correct, homelessness will increase among those sections of the population whose needs have been traditionally met by the private rented sector, and the mobility of labour will be decreased further rather than increased. It is more unlikely, moreover, that the provisions of the Budget of March 1988 will do anything to help in the long term. (See Postscript, page 344).

LOCAL AUTHORITY HOUSING

In the mid-1980s, local authorities were the largest landlords in the country despite fluctuations in the economic and political philosophy of governments. Before 1914, local authorities had built a negligible proportion of houses. With a shortage of houses at the Armistice of about 600 000 and a government pledged to build 'Homes for Heroes', the Town and Country Planning Act 1919 required local authorities to provide working-class housing where the deficiency was not met from other sources. The Act also fixed minimum standards for new housing well above the normal conditions of working-class housing. A succession of Housing Acts related to the subsidy which should be paid to the local authorities for each unit built. Slum clearance received its first assistance under the 1923 Act where the Exchequer bore half the losses local authorities incurred in slum clearance and rehousing. The Housing Act 1930 made local authorities directly responsible for slum clearance; it also made it possible to introduce differential rent or rebate schemes. A 1938 Housing Act made uniform the subsidies and rates contributions for both slum clearance and overcrowding, and by 1939 council housing had grown to about 1.3 million or approximately 11 per cent of the total stock of dwellings. Between 1918 and 1939, local authorities built over a quarter of all permanent houses in Great Britain.

During the Second World War, over 200 000 houses were destroyed while another 500 000 were severely damaged. The result was a physical housing shortage in 1945 of at least 1 350 000, which took no account of obsolete houses that needed replacing. As after the First World War, the government's main weapons were rent controls and subsidised local authority housing on the basis of need rather than ability to pay. Between 1945 and 1951, of 1.01 million houses built in Great Britain 89 per cent were for local authorities. The Housing Act 1946 made subsidies generally available to local authorities the chosen instrument to relieve the housing shortage.

Between 1955 and 1961, subsidies on new buildings to local authorites were reduced to slow down the average annual rate of increase, thus by 1960 only 35 per cent of new building was by local authorities. The subsidy an authority received depended on how many houses it built and when it had built them. Authorities with a large amount of low-cost pre-war housing could, by averaging the lower annual loan-servicing charge of such houses with their more expensive post-war houses, ask a lower rent than others who had built most of their houses after the war. Rural authorities, most of whose houses were built post-war, had to charge higher rents than in urban areas even though incomes in rural areas were usually lower. New Town Corporations, whose houses had been built entirely since the war, were in a similar position. Thus local authority control of rents created wide variety for similar accommodation in different areas. The Housing Act 1961 was a step towards an approach to local authority subsidy based on need. Larger government subsidies went to the poorer authorities and encouragement was given to authorities to charge twice the 1956 rateable value as rent to cover their expenditure including loan financing by introducing a two-level subsidy.

By 1964 there were about 4.2 million local authority houses let at rents lower than the economic level and which failed to cover costs of repairs, maintenance and administration, or loan-servicing charges on an historic basis.

Between 1964 and 1970 with a Labour Government there was an increase in local authority building; throughout this period about half the total completions were by local authorities. The Housing Subsidies Act 1967 introduced a new basis for calculating the Exchequer subsidies to local authorities. This had always been a fixed sum payable for a certain number of years in respect of each house built. For approved new dwellings there was now to be an interest rate subsidy which meant that local authority housing was financed at 4 per cent, half the market rate. This measure attempted to deal with another weakness of the subsidy system, namely that no account was taken of the different rates of interest paid by local authorities on their total debt. The 1967 Act also provided for additional subsidies where blocks of flats of four or more storeys were built.

The change of government in 1970 was reflected in a slump in public housing, by 1973 only 34 per cent of total completions for Great Britain. By this time over 6 million dwellings, 30 per cent of the total housing stock, were owned by local authorities.

The Housing Finance Act 1972 attempted to rationalise local authority subsidies and rents. All existing housing subsidies to local authorities were to be phased out except for a slum-clearance subsidy which was to be automatically provided. A rising cost subsidy was to be payable mainly in housing stress areas, when the costs of providing new housing rose faster than rental income. Otherwise, except for a transitional subsidy each local authority was to pay its own housing costs out of rental income. Thus except in relation to new additions to stock in high-cost areas, local authorities needed to break even in housing for the first time since 1919. Local authorities were to lose their previously unchallenged freedom to set their own rent levels. Fair rents were to be charged for all public authority dwellings bringing them into line with the private sector. It was contended that 90 per cent of the 1970–71 £220 million subsidy had been used to reduce the level of council rents regardless of the needs of the tenants.[12] A system of rent rebates and rent allowances was to operate where there was inability to pay the new rent; subsidies would go to individuals in need. Opponents of this bitterly contested measure contended that the model provisions were insufficient and would result in mass means testing; yet it was estimated that the new legislation would save £200 million annually. The effort was abortive – an economic crisis, a rent freeze and finally the return of a Labour Government ended in major changes: the repeal of the Housing Finance Act and the return to a subsidy system (Housing Rents and Subsidies Act 1975).

The amount of income the average tenant paid as a percentage of household income fell from 17.5 per cent in 1968 to 10.2 per cent in 1975.[17] Council tenants were paying less in real terms for their accommodation at a time when local authority finances were in a critical state. Rental income as a proportion of the Housing Revenue Account fell from 55.3 per cent in 1967–68 to 27 per cent in 1975–76. The share of the Exchequer subsidies increased from 27.8 to 54.0 per cent over the same period. It was clear that council rents would need to rise substantially as local authority improvement schemes were drastically cut back and the housing debt soared to over £16 000 million by 1975.

Following the return of a Conservative government in 1979, a new and radical approach to local authority housing soon emerged. The Housing Act 1980 introduced a new rent subsidy consisting of a 'base amount' (equal to the total subsidy paid in the previous year) *plus* a 'housing cost differential' (representing the increase in the total reckonable housing costs over those for the previous year) *less* the 'local contribution differential' (the amount a government expects the local authority to pay towards housing through increased rents or rate fund contributions). In principle, the local contribution differential gave the local authority the choice between increasing rents or increasing the rate fund contribution, but since it was the government's intention to reduce exchequer subsidies the Department of the Environment had powers to specify the target rate of annual rent increase. This resulted in rent increases considerably in excess of the amount that could be fully met from rate contributions. Over the period 1979/80–1984/85, therefore, exchequer subsidies were reduced from £1258 million to £379 million (or from £255 to £84 per dwelling), while rents on average increased by 128 per cent (from £6.48 to £14.77 per week) compared with an increase in the retail price index of only 50 per cent.

It was argued, however, that rents were still below their economic level – put at about £28 per week by Mr Nicholas Ridley, Secretary of State for the Environment.[18] Mr Ridley suggested that many people in local authority housing could afford economic rents (actual rents having risen from only 6.4 per cent of average earnings in 1979–80 to 8.3 per cent in 1985–86), and that low rents were a cause of the dereliction of much of the local authority stock. The National Federation of Housing Association's *Inquiry into British Housing* (1985)[15] had recommended that local authorities (as well as private landlords) should charge capital value rents, and that subsidies should be related to individual needs rather than to housing – a view shared by the Secretary of State. However, housing benefits in the mid-1980s were already being paid to two-thirds of the 6 million tenants of public sector housing, therefore any substantial increase in rent would further escalate and extend welfare payments.

In 1987 it seemed probable that rents would soon be dramatically increased. The Association of Metropolitan Authorities (AMA) claimed that the government planned to make housing revenue accounts self-financing by no longer permitting rents to be subsidised by rate contributions. Since 80 per cent of local authorities in 1987 did not receive any exchequer subsidy, the loss of rate subsidy would inevitably push up rents in many areas – by as much as 200 per cent according to the AMA. It was ironic that many local authorities in England and Wales (largely in suburban and rural areas) were charging sufficiently high rents that they were able to transfer surpluses on their housing revenue account to their general rate fund – a sum amounting to £61 million in 1987–88.

Local authority tenants not only had to face soaring rents, but increasingly poor management. As Donnison pointed out, local government might be good at meeting needs but "it is . . . bad at meeting demands . . . bad at listening to its customers . . . bad at reparing and maintaining people's homes efficiently."[19] He called for more and more housing to be handed over to housing trusts, cooperatives and associations, while management cooperatives should be set up to run the remaining stock of local authority housing. The Audit Commission in 1986 was equally critical. It claimed that "standards of housing management give cause for concern . . . where money is being spent on growing bureaucracy rather than on better services for tenants."[20]

The Conservative government recognised that problems of housing management had for long caused discontent among council tenants. It also recognised that public sector tenants were aware of both the financial and non-financial advantages of owner-occupation. For electoral and ideological reasons, the government therefore embarked upon a policy of privatising local authority housing – almost regardless of the economic considerations. The Housing Act

1980 thus introduced right-to-buy (RTB) provisions giving tenants of three years' standing the right to buy their homes at a discount of 33 per cent – rising to 50 per cent for tenants of 20 years or more. The Housing and Building Control Act 1984 permitted tenants of only two years standing to qualify for 32 per cent discounts – rising to 60 per cent for tenants of 30 years or more; and, in the case of flats, the Housing and Planning Act 1986 raised discounts to 42 per cent for tenants of only two years standing rising to 70 per cent for tenants of 15 years or more. Altogether over the period 1979–87, over 1 million dwellings were sold-off in England and Wales under RTB legislation – over one-fifth of the total stock of 4.6 million. The 1986 Act also granted local authorities wide-ranging powers both to force recalcitrant tenants to move into alternative accommodation so that their estate or block of flats could be sold-off to private developers, and powers to sell-off complete estates or blocks of flats to private developers with sitting tenants. After the 1987 election, the Conservative government extended privatisation further. The Housing Act 1988 removed limits on the sale of new or substantially improved council houses at full discount under the RTB provisions. The Housing Act 1988 permitted tenants to form ownership and management cooperatives, authorised tenants to invite other institutions to acquire and manage their housing (while tenants wishing to remain with the local authority would be permitted to do so), and gave each local authority tenant individually the right to transfer the ownership of his dwelling to a housing association or any other approved landlord. In the case of very poor housing – for example, in parts of the inner cities – the Act empowered the government to set up housing action trusts (unelected residential counterparts to urban development corporations) to take over the local authority stock, rehabilitate it, and pass it on to owner-occupiers, tenant cooperatives, housing associations or approved private landlords. While the Housing Minister, Mr William Waldegrave, believed that these measures would "wean people off the deadly drug of dependency"[21] on local and central government agencies, housing officials feared that under the 'pick-a-landlord' scheme rents would inevitably rise since economies of scale would be lost if estates were fragmented; and there could also be fewer rights for tenants and an increase in homelessness if private landlordism replaced social ownership.

HOUSING ASSOCIATIONS

Complementary to local authorities in providing accommodation to rent are housing associations. Although with a long history in social housing, these became important under the Housing Act 1961 which set up a loan scheme to help associations both to build new dwellings and buy up older property to rent without profit or subsidy. Some 7000 dwellings were built as a result and in 1964 the scheme was expanded. A new government agency, the Housing Corporation, was established by the Housing Act 1964. It was to promote housing societies (a term which now took on a new meaning) which would provide 'cost-rent' accommodation or 'co-ownership' dwellings. The latter was a comparatively new concept for Britain in that all the society's accommodation was jointly owned by the members; cost-rent schemes have not been popular as the potential rent levels have been unattractive. Both kinds of societies might borrow from the Housing Corporation and building societies.

The statutory definition of 'housing association' in the Housing Act 1957 is a broad one covering societies, bodies of trustees or companies. Fundamentally, both associations and societies are organisations providing housing on a non-profit-making voluntary basis. They can be broadly classified into two categories although there is considerable overlapping. Some look to the Housing Corporation to finance their development schemes, and from January 1973 the Corporation's lending powers were extended to housing associations building to let at fair rents and to those acquiring existing rented property for improvement and conversion. The other group are generally the longer-established associations, some of which began entirely from charitable sources and which increasingly obtained financial support from local authorities.

Housing associations have traditionally filled important gaps in the provision of housing for special groups such as the old or disabled; they also tend to operate in stress areas, providing housing for those in need but who are not eligible for council accommodation. They are often a greater force locally than the national average data suggest. By 1973, housing associations were producing about 15 000 new and improved dwellings per year and were providing approximately a quarter of a million dwellings – about 1.3 per cent of the total housing stock of Great Britain. Until the mid-1970s, new house building by associations although growing in importance, was still small in relation to total output. The movement also had not yet grasped the opportunities offered for the improvement and conversion of existing properties under the Housing Act 1969. In 1973 they accounted for only 1 per cent of total improvements and conversions, a decline on a decade earlier.

The Housing Act 1974 was intended to encourage the expansion of the movement largely under the auspices of the Housing Corporation whose powers of lending and control were greatly extended. Local authorities were to continue to provide support and financial assistance and to collaborate closely with housing associations especially in stress areas. Under the Act, a new subsidy – the housing association grant (HAG) – was introduced. If housing associations needed to borrow from the Housing Corporation to acquire sites, meet development costs and pay the contractor as the building work proceeded, virtually 100 per cent of the loan would be paid-off by a HAG on completion and the grant would be repaid over 60 years. The same provisions applied to rehabilitation although repayments were over 30 years. Housing associations were also eligible for improvement grants. Unlike local authorities, however, housing associations have few, if any, old low-cost housing (producing profit rent) and cannot draw on rate fund contributions. There is thus the facility of a revenue deficit grant to cover rent shortfalls.

Although it is possible for non-registered housing associations to continue to operate with existing loan commitments honoured, clearly the majority of progressive housing associations will wish to register with the Housing Corporation. Records will be open for public scrutiny and there will be an opportunity to collect from a single source comprehensive and reliable information about the voluntary housing movement, its housing stock, current activities and its resources.

Housing associations have two major roles in the future. First to expand their operations in inner urban areas, particularly by acquiring and improving unsatisfactory accommodation and to assist local authorities to deal with the problems caused by the declining rented sector. Under the Housing Finance Act and subsequent legislation, associations were brought within the fair rent and rent allowance scheme. Secondly, housing associations may become a significant force in the provision of new housing, but considerable difficulties remain. The substantial increases in costs during the 1970s adversely affected many schemes and there was also a decline in the number of grants approved for improvement and conversion. Many associations have to cope with decanting and rehousing in order to allow improvements and conversions to take place, and many experience problems caused by rapid growth and in the organisation of building work. The 1974 Act concerning registration, control, finance and subsidy provides conditions in which housing associations can expand and this expectation was justified by the 1974–75 results of the Housing Corporation. During this period it approved finance for 37 000 homes, over twice the number approved in 1973–74 and nearly 40 per cent of total approvals since the Corporation's foundation. Between 1975 and 1979, housing associations completed 95 500 dwellings, approximately 13.4 per cent of public sector completions in the United Kingdom and 6.5 per cent of total dwellings completed. In 1976, alone, there was a total of 35 000 completions – a record. Assocations had over 70 000 improvement grant approvals over this period (13.1 per cent of total approvals).

In the 1980s, however, the housing association movement suffered reversals. Housing association tenants were, in general, offered the right to buy their homes under the same provisions available to local authority tenants. Also, the voluntary sector became adversely affected by cuts in public expenditure. Although the government wished to switch the emphasis in public sector housebuilding and rehabilitation from the local authorities to housing associations, government funding of the Housing Corporation remained static and housing association completions plummeted to only 9700 in 1982–83. In consequence, by 1984, the Housing Corporation and some housing associations began to utilise private sector finance (particularly from pension funds and building societies) to supplement (or replace) HAGs. The North Housing Association, for example (the largest in the United Kingdom with 20 000 dwellings), embarked in 1986 on a £112 million building programme using £100 million from the London capital market and the remainder from its own resources. In general, schemes were developed using assured tenancies (rather than fair rent tenancies) and private sector finance was provided on an index-linked or low start basis (with repayments rising in later years when rental income is increased in line with inflation). These innovations enabled housing associations to borrow more than would have been previously feasible and thus made it possible for the sector to develop viable schemes more effectively than hitherto.

Under the 1988 Act, the government plans to reduce public funding of the housing associations to 50 per cent or less. All new lettings are to be on an assured tenancy or shorthold basis at 'sensible rents' (close to market level), and private capital will be encouraged to provide a major part of the cost of new development and rehabilitation on an index-linked or low start basis (which to a degree will be channelled to the associations via an independent investment agency set up by the Housing Corporation and the National Federation of Housing Associations). Schemes funded in this way will receive grants broadly related to income levels and housing costs in different parts of the country. The housing benefit scheme will continue to be available to voluntary sector tenants.

Housing associations are, to a varying degree, unenthusiastic about the legislation. The creation of assured and shorthold tenancies at near-market rents seems particularly inappropriate in a sector where at least 75 per cent of tenants qualify for housing benefit. But new low-income tenants (just above housing benefit eligibility) are likely to be worst affected by the Act – for example, 'sensible rents' in London could (in real terms) be twice or three times as high as the 1987 fair rent level in the capital.

Because of the fear of higher rents, it is unlikely that many local authority tenants will opt for housing associations taking over the ownership of their homes. If, however, the associations acquire only 10 per cent of the local authority stock, they will not only double their supply of housing but possibly offer tenants a more sensitive and efficient management service. There may, however, be a reluctance on the part of many housing associations to expand their activities if this necessitates adopting more commercial criteria in relation to investment and management, and a breakdown of harmonious relations with local authorities.

Most of the 2700 housing associations in the United Kingdom are small, yet the movement is dominated by a few large associations. A sample survey by the Centre for Urban and Regional Studies suggested that only 14 per cent had 100 houses or more, and these provided more than 90 per cent of dwellings owned by all associations in the sample. Under 20 per cent employed full-time staff.[22] The traditional type of association is still much dependent upon local authority cooperation and assistance, many schemes are jointly run and many units go to applicants on the council's waiting list. Whether this relationship will continue if housing associations take over local authority stock, only time will tell.

SLUM CLEARANCE, REHABILITATION AND RENEWAL

Replacement demand is a function of slum clearance and other houses becoming out of date. With approximately 34 per cent of Britain's housing stock constructed before 1919, at a much higher density than in the inter-war period, any clearance scheme tends to worsen the situation. Density of development between 1881 and 1921 was at about 20 dwellings per acre (49 per hectare), between 1921 and 1941 it was at 13 per acre (31 per hectare) and prior to 1881 at 28 per acre (67 per hectare).[23] Inevitably it is the older stock which will be replaced, thus creating more pressure for local authorities who, since the Housing Act 1930, have been obliged to see that people displaced are properly rehoused. Demolition for slum clearance and for reasons such as road building can be as much as 0.5 per cent of the total housing stock per year. In the century from 1861 to 1961, approximately two million demolitions occurred, of which nearly one million took place prior to 1931.

Slum clearance is the main element in housing loss; it is an 'on going' process, slums can never be eliminated. Clearance is the result of local government action taken with the help of central government subsidies. The real value of these subsidies varies considerably between authorities (depending mainly upon their past building behaviour) and over time. Local authorities have very different attitudes towards slum clearance, depending upon the general housing situation, the quality of local housing and political philosophy. Consequently, the level of slum clearance varies greatly over the country, often being proportionately higher in Scotland than in England and Wales. The rate of slum clearance (table 8.10) has plummeted in recent years, reflecting economic recession as well as cuts in central government expenditure. The Housing Repairs and Rent Act

Table 8.10 *Houses demolished or closed, Great Britain, 1975–85*

	1975–67	1984–85
England and Wales		
Demolished:		
In clearance areas	41 772	6 472
Elsewhere	3 939	1 969
Closed	5 416	1 876
Total	51 127	10 317
Scotland		
Unfit	9 964	1 040
Others	694	783
Total	10 658	1 823

Source: Central Statistical Office, *Annual Abstract of Statistics.*

1954 laid down criteria to define whether a house was unfit for human habitation, including state of repair, stability, freedom from damp, lighting, ventilation, water supply and drainage. Because of the sub-standard nature of stock, demolitions are likely to continue, albeit at a reduced rate; designated slums must clearly be demolished and areas redeveloped even though since 1969 there has been a switch towards rehabilitation rather than clearance.

The number of properties demolished or closed will have effects upon demand for owner-occupier properties, particularly at the older, cheaper end, thereby forcing up prices. This may have a 'ripple' effect through the market as owners of cheap property find that values have increased and that they are able to move to a better class of property. Demand for this better property then increases, giving owners the opportunity to use their higher proceeds to push further up the ladder, assuming mortgage availability; thus all classes of residential property may be affected.

Rehabilitation

After 1945 there was a growing movement towards improving rather than clearing sub-standard dwellings because of the great housing shortage. The 1949 Housing Act gave local authorities powers to pay half the cost of improvement of sub-standard housing in the private sector. In 1959 specific grants for the provision of standard amenities were introduced; these were available to owners of property, public or private, which did not have five basic amenities (bath, wash hand basin, hot water supply, w.c. and a ventilated food store). Additional discretionary grants continued to be available but provided little inducement for landlords of tenanted property. To overcome this, the Housing Act 1964 gave local authorities power to establish improvement areas in neighbourhoods containing dwellings lacking one or more of the standard amenities. Provided it was possible to restore these dwellings to full standard, the local authority could carry out improvement and then charge the landlord. The Act also provided for subsidies towards improvement of dwellings let by local authorities or housing associations.

The Housing Act 1969 saw a major shift towards improvement and conversion. Grants covering half the cost of the installation of standard amenities were made widely available for both owner-occupier and tenanted properties; for the first time funds were available for repair work. Improvement grants were discretionary and aimed at the provision of dwellings by conversion and for improvement other than standard amenities. These would cover half the costs up to a maximum of £1200 for dwellings provided by conversion of a building on three or more storeys, or £1000 for other dwellings. Special discretionary grants were also available for the provision of standard amenities in houses in multiple occupation. The Housing Act 1971 extended grants to private owners in development and intermediate areas to a maximum of 75 per cent of the cost of approved work with a maximum of £1500 per dwelling. Under the 1969 Act and the Housing Finance Act 1972 landlords could convert tenancies from controlled to regulated as a result of improvements. The 1969 Act also made provision for grants for environmental improvement on the designation of general improvement areas (GIAs).

The 1969 Act took its cue from the national sample survey of housing conditions, carried out in 1967.[24] This showed that the dilapidation problem was much worse than had been imagined; at least 1.8 million houses in England and Wales were statutorily 'unfit' and more than 4.5 million lacked basic amenities or were in need of major repairs – about a quarter of the total stock. It also showed that the best conditions were in the South-east, the worst in the North. Dilapidations and deficiencies were most extensive in the privately rented sector, where 60 per cent of all unfit housing and 65 per cent of housing without baths were found, although it accounted for no more than 21 per cent of the total stock. The best conditions were found in local authority housing, with owner-occupier housing in the middle position. A 1971 House Condition Survey showed the extent of improvement. The number of unfit dwellings had been reduced to 1.24 million while 2.87 million still lacked basic amenities; the highest proportion of unfit houses, 51.8 per cent, were rented from private owners. By the end of 1973 less than 2.5 million dwellings lacked basic amenities.[25]

Thus the 1969 Act was a major factor in restoring many properties which otherwise would have remained derelict. There were also several side effects, for example, 'gentrification', the invasion of traditional working-class areas by higher-income households often involving harassment and 'winkling' (persuading tenants to leave). Lower-priced houses were improved and converted, returning to the market at a very much higher price. In areas of acute housing need there was concern that grants were going to developers who were using grants for profit. There was an added incentive for landlords to seek vacant possession to carry out improvements and charge a much higher rent. Thus the less wealthy local population was being driven from inner areas. The massive increase in house improvement work required much skilled labour often drawn from new house-building. It was contended that only about a third of improvement grants benfited the lower-income groups, many went to owner-occupiers who obtained untaxed capital gains as a result of improvements; until the Housing Act 1974 second-home owners were also eligible for grants. Grants have improved the standard of the housing stock and this must be balanced against the reduction of accommodation for lower-income groups (partly because of the operation of improvement grants) who cannot necessarily obtain council housing and are dependent upon the ever-diminishing supply of private rented accommodation.

The White Paper *Better Homes the Next Priority* (1973)[25] placed the emphasis on improvement on 'housing action areas' (HAAs). Measures were proposed to tackle, as a priority, the housing situation within those areas where conditions in human and physical terms were worse; new powers were to be made available to local authorities. A series of broad criteria was envisaged justifying the declaration of a HAA, such as households living at high density per room, many furnished tenancies and houses lacking basic amenities. Typically 400–500 dwellings would be covered although local authorities with substantial resources might be able to tackle larger areas. Special powers included a discretion for local authorities to compel landlords and owner-occupiers to improve their properties to minimum standards, or to act themselves in default, and powers to acquire housing compulsorily. The proposals were largely incorporated in the Housing Act 1974.

Local authorities were to concentrate resources on the worst areas, that is, the HAAs, and were given wide powers to acquire property. The improvement grant system became more selective. Grants of up to 75–80 per cent of eligible expenses were available in the HAAs, 60 per cent in the GIAs and 50 per cent elsewhere (representing payments of £3750–£4500, £3000 and £2500 per unit by 1979). Larger eligible expenses were permitted for conversions. Financial help was also given for essential repairs especially in HAAs. Anyone who obtained an improvement grant and then sold or left a house unoccupied within five years (seven years in a HAA) had to repay the grant at compound interest to the local authority.

But the 1974 Act largely failed to achieve its objective. There was a sharp decline in the number of improvement grants approved in the mid 1970s (table 8.11). Although the recession in the property market, high rates of interest, and the financial difficulties of building firms were all contributory, it is probable that the more stringent conditions of grant approval introduced by the 1974 Act had a major effect on applications. It was particularly regrettable that improvement in the HAAs progressed at a disturbingly low rate, and that although the number of HAAs and GIAs had increased from, respectively, 78 and 964 in 1975 to over 400 and 1200 by 1979, it was doubtful whether they had little more than a 'cosmetic' effect on housing within some of the inner urban areas. It was ironic that proportionately more money was spent on improvement in small provincial towns where it was least necessary than in the inner urban areas of greatest need. Housing improvement expenditure in real terms is seriously lagging behind the formation of new slums. Although there were less than a million unfit houses by the early 1980s, there were over 4 million sub-standard houses which consisted not only of those which were unfit or lacking basic amenities, but also those which required major repairs.

In an attempt to hasten the pace of rehabilitation, the Conservatives, in their Housing Act 1980, made the grant system more flexible giving the Secretary of State powers to fix, for different cases, eligible expenses and grant limits; abolished the five year rule for owner-occupiers; and extended repair grants (the latter being particularly effective). These provisions were introduced at a time when public-sector housebuilding was at a (then) post-war low.

Thus government policy clearly moved away from demolition to renovation as the cheapest way of bringing the quality of housing to a minimum level with as little social upheaval as possible, particularly where many existing houses

Table 8.11 *Renovations with the aid of grant or subsidy, Great Britain, 1971–86*

	Dwellings (000s)			
	Local authorities	Housing Association grant-aided	Grants paid to private owners and tenants	Total
1971	89	5	105	199
1972	137	4	153	294
1973	188	3	207	398
1974	121	4	242	367
1975	62	5	101	168
1976	75	14	83	172
1977	94	20	71	185
1978	106	15	72	193
1979	111	20	82	213
1980	100	18	95	213
1981	79	14	91	184
1982	107	21	135	263
1983	126	18	293	437
1984	123	21	320	464
1985	154	13	200	367
1986	180	13	159	352

Source: Department of the Environment, *Housing and Construction Statistics*.

could be brought up to an acceptable standard as they stood (chapter 7). Certainly the critical economic situation of the mid-1970s influenced policy. So too did the findings of the *English House Condition Survey*, 1981[26] (a survey of housing conditions in Wales produced similar results). Altogether, in England, the total number of dwellings needing repairs of £7000 or more (at 1981 prices) increased substantially (table 8.12), necessitating a £30 000 million backlog in repairs. However, it has been contended that the commitment to a rehabilitation policy "is a vast exercise in putting off the evil day."[22] A commitment to improvement rather than new building is building up problems for the next generation; the housing stock in Britain is the oldest in Europe. But worse still, even this commitment has not been sustained. Although government expenditure on home improvement grants increased from £72.3 million in 1981–82 to £250.6 million in 1983–84, it was cut substantially to £125.2 million in 1985–86. The number of renovations with the aid of grant or subsidy similarly increased at first from 184 000 in 1981 to 464 000 in 1984, and then diminished to 352 000 in 1986. Of equal significance was the Green Paper, *Housing Improvement – A New Approach*, 1985, which proposed means testing improvement and repair grant applications – which by implication suggested *either* further

Table 8.12 *The condition of housing in England 1971–81*

Condition	Number of dwellings (000s)		
	1971	1976	1981
Unfit	678	698	641
Unfit and in disrepair	538	464	475
Fit but lacking one or more amenities	1642	666	316
Fit dwellings with all amenities but with repairs costing (at 1981 prices)			
(i) £2500 to £7000	–	–	2473
(ii) More than £7000	326	395	574

Source: Department of the Environment, *English House Condition Survey, 1981* (HMSO, 1982).

cuts in expenditure on improvement *or* more stringent conditions. The introduction of Value Added Tax in 1984 had already reduced the rate of rehabilitation and means testing would have a further adverse effect on the condition of the housing stock. By the late 1980s, therefore, while rapidly rising house prices and gentrification ensured a substantial amount of rehabilitation in London (both with and without grants), throughout much of Britain, particularly in the low price regions of Yorkshire and Humberside and the North, valuation gaps (the excess of owner-incurred rehabilitation costs over resulting increases in value) deterred home improvement except on a very minor scale.

The 1987 White Paper proposed that improvement grants should be targeted towards the worst housing and to households in greatest need. Houses below a new standard of fitness would qualify for a single mandatory grant while above this standard, grant assistance would be discretionary – related to the cost of necessary repairs and improvement and the ability of households to finance the work from income and savings. To avoid the possibility of windfall gains being realised from grant-aided improvement, discretionary grants would be repayable on a sliding scale where properties were sold within three years and if the selling price exceeded a specific level. Help should be directed to areas of greatest need. Within newly designated Urban Renewal Areas (which would replace GIAs and HAAs), local authorities would be encouraged to undertake a mix of rehabilitation and redevelopment. The implementation of all (or some) of these proposals might well increase cost-effectiveness but without a substantial increase in renewal expenditure it is likely to have but a marginal impact on the condition of urban housing.

In the 1980s, it became increasingly recognised that the stock of public sector housing was in an appallingly bad state of repair. The Association of Metropolitan Authorities (1983, 1984, 1985)[27] estimated that the repair costs to council houses built in the 1950s–60s using non-traditional techniques (such as steel frames and reinforced concrete) would amount to £5000 million, repair costs to council houses constructed in the 1960s–70s using systems building techniques would cost a further £5000 million to put right, and the repair and renovation of council houses built in the 1920s–30s using traditional methods would cost £9000 million to rectify. In total, the £19 000 million needed to be spent on repairs can be contrasted with the government's capital expenditure plans for housing in 1985–86 – £3280 million. It is little wonder that the government encouraged local authorities to sell off the worst of their estates to private developers.

Generally, however, council dwellings have been built to a good standard – major influences being the Tudor Walters Committee 1918, the Dudley Committee 1944 and the Parker Morris Report 1961. The latter was intended to apply to both public and private housing; its provisions were made mandatory in the public sector in 1967 for the new towns and in 1969 for local authorities as far as space and heating standards were concerned. It was not made mandatory in the private sector and thus many privately built owner-occupier houses (particularly starter-homes) did not conform to Parker Morris.[28] Thus, in some respects some council housing is superior to that available in the private sector and certainly in the private rented sector. It was a pity, therefore, that Parker Morris standards were abandoned in 1979.

THE SUPPLY OF HOUSES

At any time the total stock of houses can be clearly defined and measured; however, only part will be available for sale. Households seeking to purchase will consider not only the present total available supply of housing but also how that supply is expected to alter in the near future. Households may usually postpone their demand for a short period if they feel that future trends are more likely to be favourable than the existing situation. Of particular interest is the anticipated net new supply of houses as a function of activity in the housebuilding sector. In fact as we have discussed (page 222) the percentage annual addition to the existing stock is minute. However, generally the smaller the net new supply the faster the rate of second-hand price increases and consequently that of new houses, other things being equal. Increases in the value of established properties enable developers to ask higher prices for new.

The private housebuilding industry is essentially speculative in nature; houses are generally not custom-built but constructed in the expectation of being sold during or shortly after construction. Thus it is very directly affected by government economic policy. With the high risks of the industry, evidenced by bankruptcy figures, builders will generally charge the price which the market will bear. Thus, in 1971–72 prices originally agreed between the prospective purchaser and the developer were revised upwards by the latter during the construction period as demand pressures built up which could not be satisfied by supply. The prospective purchaser was left with the alternative of either agreeing to the new price or losing the house; 'gazumping' became commonplace. Confidence increased within the industry, contractors bought more land and started more houses. However, at other times, the developer was forced to accept a lower price than anticipated, confidence and expectations diminished, and the construction industry generally was depressed. Essentially the developer has been a price taker and not a price maker (although this may be changing with the growth of giant firms). Thus in 1974 there were at least 30 000 unsold new houses on the market, reflecting a change in economic conditions including substantially higher rates of tax and interest. Developers' minimum selling prices were above the maximum bid prices of potential purchasers. Developers' potential profits turned into losses. Confidence declined as developers were unable to pass on sharply higher costs in higher house prices as unemployment increased and disposable incomes fell. Potential purchasers became less willing to take on larger financial commitments. The best years for private housing starts were when mortgage and credit availability were easy and house prices appeared to be accelerating. The poorest years for housing starts were at periods of tight fiscal and monetary policy and rising unemployment. Thus much activity in the owner-occupier and housebuilding sectors is related to changes in economic policy.

The excessively cyclical nature of private sector housebuilding and its relationship with the trade and building cycle has been evident over the last century and can be illustrated from the last three decades (table 8.13). The cycle of activity saw starts move from a peak of 247 000 in 1969 down to 165 100 in 1970 up to 227 400 in 1972 then rapid decline to 105 300 in 1974. Recovery to 1978 was then followed by savage decline to 1980 with the lowest level of starts since the early 1950s. These figures indicate a difference of some 147 000 or 60 per cent between high and low.

The public sector declined sharply from 1955 to the mid-1960s when a Labour Government and New Town building led to a peak in 1967. The end of the 1960s saw decline with the low of 112 800 in 1973. A short recovery peak in 1976 was followed by a sharp decline through to the 1980s with the lowest starts for the sector in the post-war years, total housing starts in 1986 being the lowest since the 1930s.

THE HOUSEBUILDING INDUSTRY IN GREAT BRITAIN

Whereas the Green Paper *Housing Policy: a consultative document* (1977)[29] estimated that it was necessary for a minimum of 300 000 houses to be built per year up to year 2000 to satisfy national housing requirements, the average annual number of starts over the period 1980–84 was only 183 000 (compared with 281 000 per year, 1975–79, or 391 000 per year, 1965–69). It is remarkable that under capitalism, while more and better consumer goods are produced often at lower and lower real prices for more and more people, in Britain there are fewer

Table 8.13 *Houses started, Great Britain, 1950–86*

	Starts (000s)		
	Private sector	Public sector	Total
1950	19.8	184.4	204.6
1955	127.5	185.3	312.8
1960	182.8	126.3	309.1
1961	189.4	122.9	312.3
1962	186.0	137.7	323.7
1963	199.4	168.6	368.0
1964	247.5	178.6	426.1
1965	211.1	181.4	392.5
1966	193.4	185.9	379.3
1967	233.6	213.9	447.6
1968	200.1	194.3	394.4
1969	166.8	176.6	343.5
1970	165.1	154.1	319.2
1971	207.3	136.6	343.9
1972	227.4	123.0	350.4
1973	214.9	112.8	327.7
1974	105.3	146.7	252.1
1975	149.1	173.8	322.9
1976	154.7	170.8	325.4
1977	134.8	132.1	266.9
1978	157.3	107.4	264.7
1979	144.0	81.2	225.1
1980	98.9	56.4	155.2
1981	116.7	37.2	153.9
1982	140.5	53.0	193.4
1983	169.8	48.0	217.7
1984	153.7	40.2	193.9
1985	161.8	33.6	195.3
1986	172.1	31.4	203.4

Source: Ministry of Housing and Local Government; Scottish Development Department; Department of the Environment, *Housing and Construction Statistics.*

houses being built in the 1980s than in recent decades, they are inferior in size and quality to those built in the inter-war or post-war periods and are increasingly expensive. Between 1952 and 1980, whereas the Retail Price Index increased 6½ times, the average price of houses increased eleven fold.

Over the past 25 years, the housebuilding industry has become dominated by a small number of giant firms – 'volume builders' (those constructing more than 500 houses per year) accounting for more than 50 per cent of the output of owner-occupied housing in the 1980s (compared with less than 15 per cent in the 1960s).[30] The top-ten firms alone produced over 53 000 houses (or 28 per cent of the total completions) in 1986. Medium-size firms have either been taken over by the volume builders (often to obtain their land banks) or have been rendered uncompetitive. Volume builders have been able to outbid all others in the acquisition of land, a process aided and abetted by the planning authorities who normally prefer to release blocks of land, rather than single plots, for development.[30]

Apart from public sector contracting, the housebuilding process is largely speculative. As such, there is a high degree of risk and a very high bankruptcy rate. Timing is important at all stages from site purchase, through development, to sales. Most firms depend upon short-term bank credit during building (using the land and part-completed buildings as collateral). When interest rates increase it makes the situation extremely difficult – banks may cut finance to builders early in a squeeze. Private housebuilding thus tends to expand and contract cyclically in relation to the government's macro-economic policy.

To attempt to safeguard themselves against the vicissitudes of the economy, volume builders rely mainly on land development gains (often resulting from infrastructure improvement) and super-normal profits (reflecting their monopoly power) rather than on normal or 'building' profit (that is, the sale price of the dwelling in competitive conditions *less* the sum of wage, capital, material and land costs). There is thus little incentive to improve product quality, to increase productivity and to improve techniques of production.[31] Volume builders 'physically' construct few houses but concentrate instead on land banking (involving the purchase of land when prices slump to facilitate housing development when prices rise) and marketing. Housebuilding itself is undertaken by subcontractors – the number of which increases when there is an upturn in the market and decreases when there is a downturn.

The construction process is thus largely in the hands of the small subcontractor and the results economically are far from satisfactory. Volume builders tend to spread output over a very large number of sites to minimise risk – their subcontractors constructing small batches of dissimilar houses normally with the use of hired plant and equipment, and employing almost entirely casualised labour (individual or gangs of self-employed operatives). Low productivity, retarded innovation, the lack of scale economies, minimal research and development, the absence of training in new techniques and fragmented labour processes all militate against the lowering of unit costs of production.

Duncan contrasts the above characteristics of housebuilding in Britain with housebuilding in Sweden.[31] In Sweden in recent years there has been a high rate of housebuilding, standards have been improving and real costs have been falling. Since local authority land banks provide sites for housebuilding at low cost, and, in return for state housing loans to finance construction, builders have had to sell at prices set by the government, there are few opportunities for builders to realise land development gain and super-normal profit. Instead, they have had to rely on building profits via the construction process itself. There is thus every incentive to increase productivity, improve the quality of the product, develop economies of scale, undertake research and development, ensure that there is proper training in the use of new techniques and employ integrated labour processes.

House Prices and Land Costs

For the country as a whole there is a great deal of land; however, the supply available in urban areas is limited and is further reduced by planning delays, particularly in moving from outline to detailed planning permission. Thus it is not normally possible to substitute housing for other land uses and it may even be difficult to vary the intensity of use.

The quantity of land made available may be further reduced by landowners' own expectations. If they believe that in the future land prices are going to rise faster than other prices they will have an incentive to hold the land off the market and so shift the supply curve. This makes the builder's position difficult. If he holds a land bank he might do better to keep his land stock rather than to build because he expects the price to rise still further in the future. If he holds no land his profit from increased prices might disappear in higher land costs. In a competitive situation builders will bid against one another for the available land up to a level which leaves them a normal profit, and thus the whole price increase benefits the landowner. Thus builders' incentives to expand housing construction following house price increases may be reduced, if not completely removed, by the resulting increase in land prices.

Because land is heterogeneous there are enormous differences in individual plot prices. There is also the role of planning permission in determining prices. Official data show that from 1978 to 1980 prices per plot in England and Wales increased from £2367 to £4460, nearly doubling in these years (table 8.14). During the same period, average house prices rose from £16 792 to £26 131 – an increase of 56 per cent. From 1981 to 1983, however, average plot prices increased by only 28 per cent and average house prices by 15 per cent. In 1983, plot prices as a percentage of house prices ranged from 29 per cent in Greater London to as low as 10 per cent in Wales. By the late 1980s, however, both land and house prices were again increasing rapidly, and nationally plot prices were soaring as a proportion of house prices – exceeding 25 per cent by 1986 (and 40 per cent in parts of the South-east).

But do house prices determine plot prices or do plot prices dictate house prices? While local planning authorities (and some economists) argue that the demand for land and thus its price is derived from the demand for housing, housebuilders (and other economists) believe that the supply of land and thus its cost is a determinant of house prices. As MacLennan suggests, attempts to disentangle the connection between land prices and house prices have been

Table 8.14 *Private sector housing land prices (at constant average density) and house prices, 1971–86*

	Weighted average price per plot (£)	Average price of houses (£)	Plot price as a percentage of house price
1971	1 030	5 510	18.7
1972	1 727	6 920	25.0
1973	2 676	9 630	27.8
1974	2 663	11 140	23.9
1975	1 839	12 124	15.0
1976	1 848	13 132	14.1
1977	1 943	14 343	13.6
1978	2 367	16 792	14.1
1979	3 395	21 455	15.8
1980	4 460	26 131	17.1
1981	4 600	27 910	16.5
1982	5 200	27 914	18.6
1983	5 900	30 943	19.1
1984	6 600	33 416	19.8
1985	8 400	36 295	23.1
1986	10 700	42 319	25.3

Source: Department of the Environment, *Housing and Construction Statistics.*

unconvincing and the relationship thus remains an important research issue.[32] In a report commissioned by the House Builders Federation, Evans argued that a restricted supply of land resulted in both land prices and house prices being higher than they would otherwise be; that, by restricting the supply of building land, planners were forcing up house prices and *either* squeezing-out first time buyers *or* adversely affecting the size of housing units; and that if agricultural land was converted into residential use it would significantly bring down the cost of new housing.[33] Ambrose, similarly, claimed that the planning system adds to Britain's housing problems by being excessively concerned with environmental protection and by "not releasing the 'correct' amount of land in the 'correct' areas as assessed by the housebuilding industry."[34]

In theoretical terms, it can be shown that there is clearly a relationship between the supply of land, land prices and the level of housebuilding. In figure 8.2 the supply of development land *SL* is completely elastic – possibly a result of government intervention (by, for example, public land banking). With an increase in the demand for housing (from *DH* to DH_1), more land is demanded for development (*DL* shifting to DL_1) but, since the supply of land (*SL*) is completely elastic, land is made available at a constant price – facilitating in turn an expansion in the supply of houses (*SH*) from q to q_1 without an increase in house prices. In figure 8.3, however, the supply of land is completely inelastic (for example, as a result of green belt policy). With an increase in the demand for housing (from *DH* to DH_1), more land is demanded for development (*DL* shifting to DL_1) but, since the supply of land (*SL*) is completely inelastic, land supply is not increased and land prices rise sharply, preventing the level of housebuilding from increasing to satisfy the increase in demand. If the supply of development land were to be reduced from *SL* to SL_1 (by government policy or by landowners exercising monopoly power), then land prices would rise even

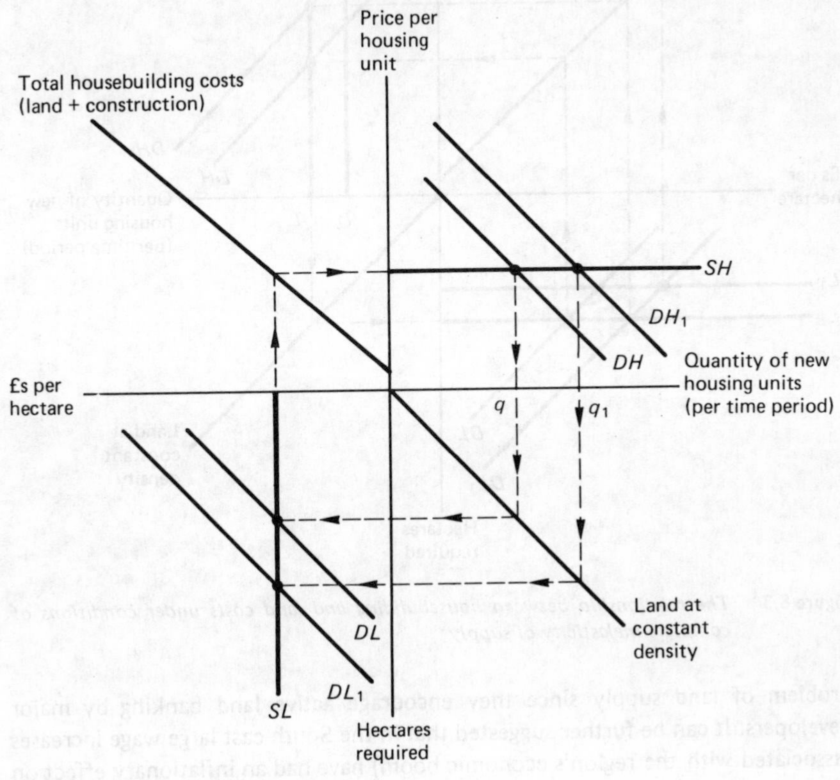

Figure 8.2 *The relationship between housebuilding and land costs under conditions of complete elasticity of supply*

more dramatically and the supply of new housing would be reduced from *SH* to SH_1. Clearly, the reverse could occur if the supply of land were to be increased.

It can, however, be argued that rapidly rising house prices (fuelled by an increase in mortgage credit and tax relief) have pushed up the cost of land since landowners have become aware of the prices builders can charge for new properties. Furthermore, rising house and land prices only serve to accentuate the

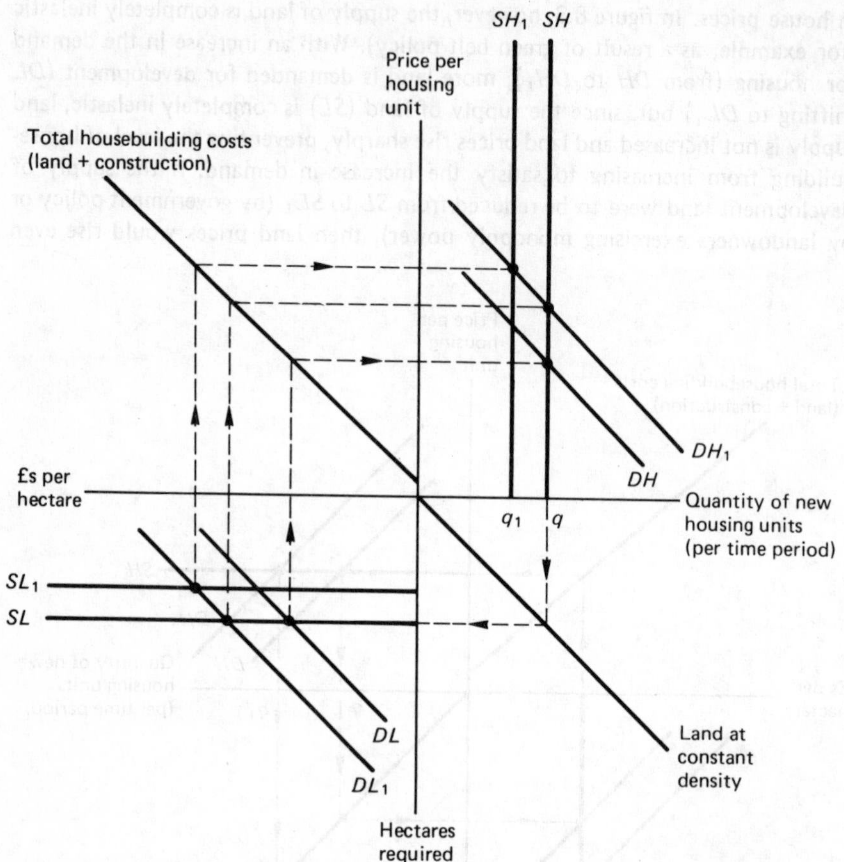

Figure 8.3 *The relationship between housebuilding and land costs under conditions of complete inelasticity of supply*

problem of land supply since they encourage active land banking by major developers. It can be further suggested that in the South-east large wage increases (associated with the region's economic boom) have had an inflationary effect on house prices and hence land prices in recent years – land prices reaching £2.5 million per hectare in the South-east in 1987.

The House Builders Federation are specifically concerned that there is much less inner city land suitable for private building than is generally thought, and that land shortages in the inner city will adversely affect the provision of low-cost housing. This, if it is correct, could have serious consequences since the supply of older private housing is being eroded through gentrification, and the public sector stock is being decimated by 'right to buy' sales and major cutbacks in housebuilding.

Overall, housebuilders lack information about the amount, availability and suitability of vacant land – both in the inner cities and the countryside. Builders claim that they require nationally an extra 2000 ha per year in addition to the 6000 ha allocated by local planning authorities in the late 1980s. Only then, they estimate, could they build 250 000 houses per year – a figure the government currently considers necessary. The extra land, however, according to the housebuilders, would need to be made available in the green belt, but this would be strongly resisted by government on environmental grounds. It is within the South-east that the conflict between housebuilding and conservation is most apparent. Whereas housebuilders predicted that there was a need for an extra 880 000 dwellings in the region in the period 1981–91, the South Eastern Regional Planning Council (SERPLAN) allocated land for only 600 000 new homes. Similarly, Tyler and Rhodes forecast that an extra 770 000 new dwellings will be required during the years 1985–95, but SERPLAN predicted that only 550 000 extra homes will be needed.[35] By the end of this century, therefore, it is probable that local planning authorities will have allocated insufficient land to meet housing demand – with inflationary effects on both land prices and house prices in the region.

In addition to the inflationary effects of land shortages, the slowness of planning consents exacerbates the upward trend in house prices. In the 1970s, Pennance estimated 6 months at least as the average time taken to secure planning permission, while about one in six applicants was refused.[36] The average time between appeal and decision was 36 weeks for those decided by the Inspectorate and 51 weeks for those decided ministerially. In 1975 the Dobry Report[37] recommended changes in procedure to hasten the process, but delays remain much in evidence (in part because of the time devoted to local enquiries) and indicate the extent to which the market is still hamstrung.

Material, Labour and Finance Costs

Since 1945 housebuilding material prices have risen steadily in comparison with prices of materials purchased by manufacturing industry generally. Between 1963 and 1973 housebuilding material prices doubled while those of manufacturing industry increased by approximately 60 per cent. Traditional housebuilding costs are affected more by internal inflation than by international factors; there are exceptions – for example, the price of timber imported from the USSR increased by 102 per cent in 1973 while devaluation in 1967 and the downward floating of sterling after 1971 adversely affected building material costs.

Accurate data on the labour content of cost are difficult to obtain; a particular problem has been the prevalence of labour-only subcontracting among many highly skilled craftsmen (chapter 10). Recorded labour costs in construction have not moved faster than industry in general; hours worked tend to be higher and are more variable to the level of economic activity. However, the relatively small changes in production methods in housebuilding suggest that productivity increases may be less than in industry as a whole.

For most commodities in the long term it is reasonable to expect a stable relationship between the price of the product and its costs of production, with allowance for normal profit. If prices run ahead of costs then output will increase thereby bringing prices back into an equilibrium position with costs. Conversely, if costs run ahead of prices then output will fall, and reduced supply in relation to demand will lead to an increase in prices back to an equilibrium level.

However there is no such relationship between house prices and housebuilding costs. Material, land and labour costs are not major factors in the movement of house prices; with land, developers are unable to pass on increases in costs except at times of rising house prices. If costs rise, other things being equal, developers will either reduce the quantity of houses they build or cut the quality. The reasons are as follows.

(1) There is a long lag in the housebuilding process from site identification to completion. Economic factors may change or new legislation may be introduced which may affect tax relief on mortgage interest.

(2) The shortage of land for housebuilding may prevent an increase in house prices from leading to an increase in the supply of housebuilding land – it may merely increase the price of building land.

(3) Building regulations and NHBC requirements impose costs which might not be recoverable in the price which potential purchasers are willing to pay, because fundamentally the developer is a price taker.

Housebuilders have had to contend with increasingly high interest rates. Most building firms have to borrow to cover construction costs as they do not have sufficient funds to tide them over until they have sold the houses. Increases in interest rates usually coupled with credit restrictions may have a deciding impact on marginal developments; increases are likely to increase builders' costs immediately and by larger than average amounts. Squeezes make building impossible because of builders' inability to raise funds. It is likely that the level of housing starts is determined almost entirely by the availability of funds and the level of sales (which free funds to start new dwellings) which in turn are determined by the availability of building society finance (table 8.15).

In general, the economics of housebuilding are predominantly demand-determined and fluctuations in demand merely serve to compound the inherent difficulties of developers. The operation of housebuilders is essentially determined by financial and structural characteristics quite outside the framework of land and other material supply and costs. In the South-east, however, land supply and land costs might be of at least equal importance in determining the level of housebuilding.

Table 8.15 *Building society loans on new houses, starts and completions in the private sector, 1970–86*

	Building society loans on new houses (000s)	Number of new houses Completed (000s)	Starts (000s)	Loans as percentage of completions
1970	133	170	165	78
1971	165	192	207	86
1972	164	197	227	83
1973	142	187	215	76
1974	102	141	105	72
1975	121	151	149	80
1976	129	152	154	85
1977	122	140	135	87
1978	134	149	157	90
1979	117	140	144	84
1980	94	128	99	73
1981	87	114	117	76
1982	94	124	141	76
1983	111	144	170	77
1984	130	153	154	85
1985	119	150	162	79
1986	120	158	172	76

Source: The Building Societies Association, *BSA Bulletin*.

CONCLUSIONS

Since the early 1970s, successive governments appeared to believe that Britain's housing needs had either been satisfied or were in sight of being satisfied. A crude housing shortage had been turned into a crude surplus, and in broadly defined terms public expenditure on housing had increased.

In 1981 there was undoubtedly a crude housing surplus in England and Wales of 1.6 million dwellings over households – in contrast to a 600 000 deficit in 1966 (table 8.16). However, the 1981 surplus did not indicate the true relationship between supply and need. Included among the 21.1 million dwellings were some 200 000 second homes, while about 128 000 concealed households (such as couples sharing with their parents/in-laws) were omitted from this total. Allowances must also be made for a vacancy reserve of about 800 000 dwellings to facilitate mobility. There were great spatial variations in supply and demand, and an ageing population also produced a mismatch between housing occupied and housing required. There are also qualitative differences. In 1981, there were over 4 million dwellings in a poor condition in England alone,[26] and in 1987 the

Table 8.16 *The number of dwellings and households, England and Wales, 1966–81*

	1966	1971 (millions)	1981
Households	16.9	18.3	19.5
Dwellings	16.3	18.8	21.1
Balance	– 0.6	+ 0.5	+ 1.6

Sources: Department of the Environment, *Housing and Construction Statistics*; Central Statistical Office, *Social Trends*.

Department of the Environment reported that there were "some exceedingly squalid conditions within houses in multiple occupation"[38] – housing which in total accommodated 2.6 million people in England and Wales.

If housing benefit and mortgage interest relief are added to the Department of the Environment's expenditure on housing, then public spending on housing increased from £6002 million in 1979–80 to £10 769 million in 1986–87 (table 8.17). However, both housing benefit and mortgage interest relief are income subsidies and do not directly relate to the provision of housing. If deducted from aggregate public expenditure on housing, then the amount of public spending on housing decreased in cash terms from £4552 million in 1979–80 to £2815 million in 1986–87 – a reduction of 38 per cent (or 62 per cent in real terms).

Table 8.17 *Public expenditure on housing and transfers, United Kingdom, 1979/80–1986/87*

	1979/80 (£m)	1983/84 (£m)	1986/87 (£m)	Change 1979/80–1986/87 (%)
Department of Environment (total housing expenditure)	4522	3140	2815	–38
Housing Benefit*	200	1517	3454	+1627
Mortgage interest relief	1300	2455	4500	+ 246
Total	6022	7122	10 769	+ 78

*Refers to rent allowances and rent rebates.

Source: Treasury, *The Government's Expenditure Plans, 1984–85 to 1986–87* (Cmnd 9143, II); *The Government's Expenditure Plans, 1987–88 to 1989–90* (Cmnd 56, II).

A major result of the net housing shortage and cuts in public expenditure on housing is that the number of registered homeless households in England soared from 57 000 in 1979 to 100 000 in 1986. By late 1987, 11 000 homeless households had to be accommodated in bed and breakfast hotels since local authorities could not provide them with appropriate housing. Council waiting lists, moreover, had increased to 1 200 000 by 1986. Thus, far from there being a large surplus of housing, there is a very substantial deficit – 830 000 in 1981 according to Shelter[39] – a figure almost certainly exceeded by the end of the decade. At the same time as homelessness and council waiting lists reached record levels, it is tragically ironic that there were over 400 000 building workers unemployed (or 25 per cent of the construction industry's workforce). The principal reason for the plight of both the household in need and the unemployed building worker is the low level of housing starts in recent years. In 1986, there were only 32 000 public sector starts in the United Kingdom – the lowest number since 1925 – while private sector starts amounted to 173 000 – markedly below the levels reached in the late 1960s. Total starts were lower than in any year throughout the whole of the 1960s–70s.

It is thus a serious cause of concern that the White Paper, *Housing: The Government's Proposals* (1987)[40] – the basis of the Housing Act 1988 – largely ignored housebuilding and failed to refer to homelessness. Clearly, the government assumed that supply and need are broadly in balance. While fiscal support for owner-occupation continues unabated, the government evidently hopes that it will be able to attract sufficient private capital into the rented sectors to bring forward property lying empty, to rehabilitate public sector housing and (to a very limited extent) to build anew. But private capital will only be forthcoming if rates of return are competitive with other forms of investment. This will either necessitate substantial rent increases (with the poor paying an unacceptably high proportion of their disposable income) or housing benefits will to an extent rise and, in effect, subsidise private capital. As with tax relief to the owner-occupier, housing benefits will almost entirely increase the capital value of property and have a negligible effect on supply. As such, the 1988 Act will do little to tackle the worsening housing crisis.

REFERENCES

1. A. E. Holmans, 'A Forecast of Effective Demand for Housing in Great Britain in the 1970s', *Social Trends*, No. 1 (Central Statistical Office, 1970).
2. G. A. Hughes, *Inflation and Housing* (Housing Research Foundation, 1974).
3. P. M. Hillebrandt, *Economic Theory and the Construction Industry* (Macmillan, 1974).
4. Nationwide Building Society Occasional Bulletin 124, *Who Buys Houses?*

5. Shelter, *Housing and the Economy – A Priority for Reform* (Shelter, 1982).
6. S. Goss and S. Lansley, *What Price Housing? A Review of Housing Subsidies and Proposals for Reform* (SHAC, 1981); A. Gray *et al.*, *Housing Rents, Costs and Subsidies. A Discussion Document* (CIPFA, 1980); B. Kilroy, *Housing Finance – Organic Reform?* (LEFTA, 1978); M. A. King and A. B. Atkinson, 'Housing Policy, Taxation and Reform', *Midland Bank Review* (Spring, 1980); S. Lansley, *Housing Finance: A Policy for Labour* (Labour Housing Group, 1982); Shelter, *Housing and the Economy – A Priority for Reform* (Shelter, 1982).
7. J. Muellbauer, 'How house prices fuel wage rises', *Financial Times* (23 October, 1986).
8. See P. Rodgers, 'Why soaring house prices are a pain in the neck', *Guardian* (21 July, 1987).
9. C. Hamnett, 'Making money from home ownership', *New Society* (27 June, 1986).
10. *Report of the Committee on Housing in Greater London* (The Milner Holland Report) Cmnd. 2605 (HMSO, 1965).
11. *Report of the Committee on the Rent Acts* (The Francis Report), Cmnd 4609 (HMSO, 1971).
12. *Fair Deal for Housing*, Cmnd 4728 (HMSO, 1971).
13. M. Harloe, *Private Rented Housing in the United States and Europe* (Croom Helm, 1985).
14. House of Commons, *The First Report of the Environmental Committee*; session 1981/82 (HMSO, 1982).
15. National Federation of Housing Associations, Inquiry into British Housing, Chaired by HRH The Duke of Edinburgh, *Report* (NFHA, 1985).
16. White Paper, *Housing: The Government's Proposals*, Cmnd 214 (HMSO, 1987).
17. *Financial Times* (21 June, 1975).
18. See D. Lipsey, 'Ridley's home base', *New Society* (7 November, 1986).
19. D. Donnison, 'New drama for a crisis', *Guardian* (11 May, 1987).
20. Audit Commission, *Managing the Crisis in Council Housing* (HMSO, 1986).
21. W. Waldegrave speaking at the Institute of Housing conference, Brighton, 19 June, 1987.
22. F. Berry, *Housing: The Great British Failure* (C. Knight, 1974).
23. P. A. Stone, *Urban Development in Britain: Standards, Costs, Resources, 1964–2004*, Vol. 1 (Cambridge University Press, 1970).
24. *National House Condition Survey, 1967* (HMSO, 1967).
25. *Better Homes the Next Priority*, Cmnd 5339 (HMSO, 1973).
26. *English House Condition Survey, 1981* (HMSO, 1982).
27. Association of Metropolitan Authorities, *Defects in Housing, Part 1* (AMA, 1983); *Defects in Housing, Part 2* (AMA, 1984); *Defects in Housing, Part 3* (AMA, 1985).
28. *Homes for Today and Tomorrow* (Parker Morris Report) (HMSO, 1961).

29. Department of the Environment, *Housing Policy: a consultative document* (HMSO, 1977).
30. M. Ball, *Home Ownership: A Suitable Case for Reform* (Shelter, 1986).
31. S. S. Duncan, 'House Building, Profits and Social Efficiency in Sweden and Britain', *Housing Studies*, 1 (1986).
32. D. MacLennan, *Housing Economics* (Longman, 1982).
33. A. W. Evans, *House prices and Land Prices in the South East – a review* (the House Builders' Federation, 1987).
34. P. Ambrose, *Whatever Happened to Planning?* Methuen, 1986).
35. P. Tyler and J. Rhodes, 'South-East Employment and Housing Study', *Discussion Paper No. 15* (Department of Land Economy, University of Cambridge, 1986).
36. F. Pennance, 'Planning, Land Supply and Demand' in A. A. Walters (ed.) *Government and the Land* (Institute of Economic Affairs, 1974).
37. *Review of the Development Control System* (Dobry Report) (HMSO, 1974).
38. Department of the Environment, *The Physical and Social Survey of Houses in Multiple Occupation in England and Wales* (DOE, 1987).
39. Shelter, *Shelter Election Briefing*, 1983.
40. White Paper, *Housing: The Government's Proposals*, Cmnd 214 (HMSO, 1987).

9

Land Values, Proprietary Interests and Town Planning

In advanced capitalist countries, the property market is an economic mechanism rationing land between competing and occasionally conflicting uses, and is often modified by central and local government requirements. But the market is subject to severe criticism for three principal reasons:

(1) As a means of allocating land between different uses the market may seem to be inefficient, suffering from inherent imperfections – demand and supply overall being rarely in equilibrium (chapter 2).

(2) The pattern of land use and values as determined by the price mechanism disregards the needs of the less profitable, and often unprofitable yet socially desirable, users of land for such purposes as schools, hospitals and public open space.

(3) The financial nature of the property market, with its stress upon private profit, maintains and frequently highlights national inequalities of income and wealth, and usually does so in a way that is a reflection of the 'monopolistic' nature of land-ownership rather than an indication of entrepreneurial ability.

Government intervention is often proposed, largely to replace the market, yet as Wright[1] clearly argued the price mechanism is merely modified by government action within the contexts of town planning, social need and the distribution of income and wealth.

TOWN PLANNING AND PROPERTY VALUES

Since private and public land uses are mutually dependent, and as the value of privately owned land may be increased by changes in the public land use infrastructure, town planning can be seen as a means of increasing the values of private and profitable uses of land.

Yet fragmented and multiple private interests in land restrict private owners from radically altering or enhancing the overall pattern of use, and simultaneously multiple ownership retards the transfer of land to more profitable users and inhibits large-scale redevelopment. Therefore, in this context town planning can be seen both as a means of establishing complementarity of land uses while keeping conflicting uses apart through such devices as zoning, and as a means of speeding up the transfer of land between uses. By creating a climate of greater certainty, the zoning and density control aspects of town planning eliminate some of the imperfections of the property market, and enable land to move more readily to its highest and best use.

Although the report of the Uthwatt Committee[2] stated that town planning could not affect aggregate values but merely shifts or redistributes values from one place to another, since the Town and Country Planning Act 1947 this view has largely lost its credibility. The ability of town planning to increase aggregate values is fully recognised, for example, the granting of planning permission in 1973 for office development in London raised values by over £800 million – a sum which could hardly have shifted from other land uses. But it is equally recognised that although increased property values are publicly created through the planning process they are private realised. Yet from 1953 to 1967, and again from 1970 to 1974, they were not subject to any specific form of betterment taxation.

It is often argued that town planning will lead to a higher level of aggregate land values than would exist in a completely free market situation. This implies that an aim of town planning should be to achieve the long-term maximisation of land values. But increased values (though not necessarily an increased efficiency of use) could come about unintentionally or indirectly in one of the following ways:

(1) Restrictionist policies might cause values to be higher than would normally occur; for example, the prohibition of office development in central London between 1965 and 1970 created scarcity and resulted in rapidly rising rents and capital values.

(2) Taxation can cause values to increase; for example, the 40 per cent levy imposed by the Land Commission Act 1967 raised property prices, not simply because the extent of the tax was added on to the asking price of land, but because the levy caused land to be withheld from the market leading to conditions of scarcity relative to demand (page 290).

(3) Property values are influenced by broad economic trends. Inflation and deflation both bring about changes in value, though not usually at the same rate as changes in the general level of prices or the level of share indices. The wide range of government policies likewise affects value, and it may be difficult to distinguish these effects from the more specific responses to planning legislation.

In most of its manifestations, town planning identifiably affects the working of the property market. In some circumstances town planning might ignore or distort market decisions, leading in consequence to anomalies and the maldistribution of private resources. In other circumstances town planning modifies the conditions of demand and supply, but otherwise allows the market to work more freely than before.

In recent years, however, planning has been undergoing substantial change. Since the late 1960s *process planning* has become increasingly practised, reducing the significance of *blueprint* planning, which had previously developed particularly after the Town and Country Planning Act 1947. Blueprint planning evolved from the technical skills of the architect, engineer or surveyor. Urban problems were viewed largely in their physical context and proposed solutions were similarly physical – involving land-use maps, zoning, density controls, building regulations and planning standards. Although blueprint planning involved a high degree of public intervention, it removed some of the imperfections inherent in the property market. It could have been argued that by imposing a fairly rigid development framework, blueprint planning reduced uncertainty and lessened risk – the 'rules of the game' being clearly defined. In contrast, process planning is more of a continuous and flexible exercise better suited to a largely market economy. Since the Town and Country Planning Act 1968 it has been increasingly recognised that the complex problems of urban structure and organisation cannot be examined, and solutions cannot be found, purely in physical terms. Continual reference to economic and social considerations is necessary. Plans have to be constantly reviewed and adjustments continually made with the aim of avoiding delay and ensuring that policy is relevant to changing circumstances. Whereas blueprint planning provided the framework in which the property market operated, the market very largely provides the framework in which process planning is undertaken. Alterations in the nature of that market (for example, by a greater degree of public sector activity) would call for a response from process planning and possibly necessitate a revision of plans.

MARKET-DETERMINED VALUES AND SOCIAL NEEDS

It is recognised that in the long term, through the interaction of supply and demand, land will transfer to its highest and best use. This will occur because those users or would-be users who are capable of realising the greatest benefit from their use of land will be willing to pay the highest rents or prices, and owners will generally lease their land or sell their interest to the highest bidders. It is often thought that the most profitable use of land is also the most efficient use of land. As efficiency is synonymous with desirability, proponents of a *laissez-faire* free market economy equate the most profitable use of land with the most desirable use of land. This assumed relationship overlooks the importance of social considerations. An uncontrolled market ignores social needs – it only exists to maximise private profit and pecuniary satisfaction. Yet an unfettered market may be no more 'natural' than a society free from man-made laws. All markets are reflections of demand and supply conditions, and intervention to adjust demand and supply can create new conditions of decision-making which can modify land values and land-use patterns. Injected into the market will be social factors and other considerations – often political in nature –

which will alter the relationship between demand and supply and consequently alter rent levels, prices, and the quantities of land used for different purposes. It is very important, however, that the intervening agencies fully appreciate the working of the market mechanism and are able to predict most of the direct and indirect consequences of their intervention.

The best example of the problem of social values is offered by the question of property development and redevelopment. The private developer is only concerned with the feasibility of a particular scheme. He compares those costs he will have to incur (private costs) with those gains he expects to receive (private benefits). Unless he is unusually altruistic, or there is public pressure, he will not be interested in either the costs he might inflict upon the community (social costs) or the benefits which might be gained by the community as a result of the development (social benefits). In the past two decades in central London there has been a plethora of office development. It is unlikely that the developers undertaking such schemes gave much thought to the creation of the additional social costs of traffic congestion and the shortage of resources for other forms of development such as housing; or to the social benefits such as increased local retail trade and rateable values.

When the market mechanism fails to provide socially desirable developments, public authorities may become involved in the development process, but they sometimes find it impossible to evaluate and appraise their schemes by means of the conventional valuation techniques used by private developers. Monetary profit-and-loss criteria are irrelevant to the problem of how to evaluate projects where the price mechanism is not used as an instrument for rationing the end-product between consumers (for example, road construction) or where the end is not essentially profit (for example, a public swimming-pool or a museum).

The economic approach being increasingly used as a means of overcoming these problems is cost–benefit analysis. This attempts to provide a method of evaluation and appraisal intended to indicate not only the private or direct costs and benefits of development, but also the social or indirect costs and benefits. But as an analytical device it is imperfect and is still in the process of refinement; much more research needs to be done. Cost–benefit analysis is mainly used for assessing alternative proposals for development, and has been mainly applied to transport schemes and urban development projects. The best results are usually obtained when cost–benefit analysis is used for deciding between a carefully chosen range of alternatives and is undertaken in the context of a definite set of initial assumptions (chapter 6).

THE PRICE-MECHANISM AND THE INEQUALITIES OF WEALTH

A major criticism of the property market is that it perpetuates the unequal distribution of incomes and wealth stemming from private 'unearned' windfall gains and losses.

The ownership of interest in land usually results in a greatly fragmented pattern of land tenure, and because of the specific locational character of individual sites has brought with it many instances of monopoly. This gives the individual vendor the opportunity to force a hard bargain with a potential buyer. For instance, a developer, having purchased and integrated several parcels of land under one ownership, may find himself having to pay for the marginal site a price considerably above its comparable use value. As the developer is using money borrowed on which substantial interest charges rapidly accumulate, he will consider the value of the site to him in terms of his cost of finance. If he is fully aware of this, the vendor will take advantage of the situation and his own monopolistic position.

The question of land tenure is also seen in the problem of the 'unearned increment'. Land values are not just reflections of their current uses but also of possible future uses. For example, farm output, production costs and prices determine agricultural land values. If, however, it is thought that farmland could be used more profitably for some other purpose, such as housing or industry, then the land will increase in value. The rise in value occurs before the land is transferred to a new and higher use.

The difference between the now higher market value and the current use value is known as the 'development value' (or 'floating value' if there are only expectations of a change in use.) In figure 9.1 the demand for farmland is shown by the curve *DD* and the demand for housing land is shown by the curve D_1D_1. Where these curves intersect the supply line *SS*, the current use and market uses are determined and the difference between them is the development or floating value.

Not all landowners, believing their land to be saleable for development purposes, will be correct in their assumptions about the demand for their land. It is obviously not the landowner who causes the value of his land to rise, but rather the increased demand and the changing nature of demand which causes the value to increase to the level where it is profitable to transfer land from one use to another. Nevertheless it is the landowner who benefits from the enhanced value by making a substantial profit on the sale of his land. This profit is called the 'unearned increment', an income not for work done but for possessing a scarce resource.

Yet land can fall in value. Demand may decrease because of changes in its underlying conditions. Not only might development values be completely eroded but current use values might also fall – in both instances not directly attributable to the action of the property owner.

'Betterment' and 'worsenment' are terms used to describe respective increases and decreases in the value of property, but because values change for many different reasons the terms need to be defined more specifically. In the narrow sense, betterment is the increase in property values resulting from an increase in real national income *per capita*, the effect of the increase in value of adjacent developments, or from inflation – the increased demand for a relatively fixed

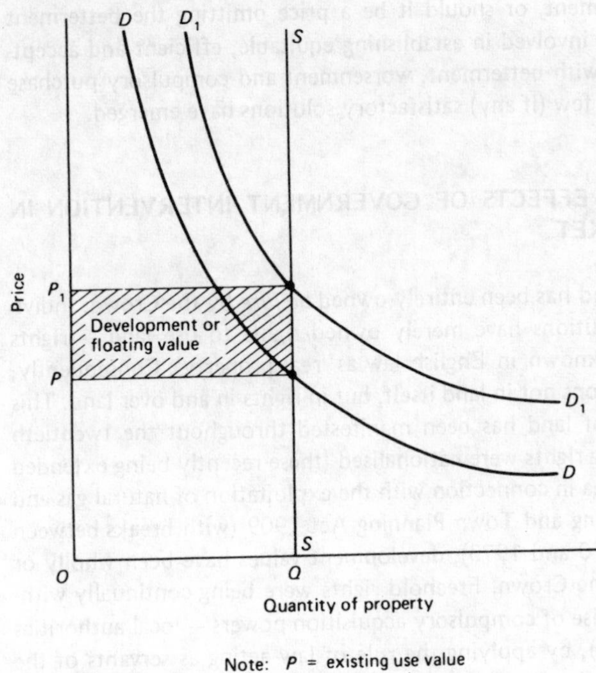

Figure 9.1 *The effects upon value of an increase in demand*

supply of property often causing values to rise at a greater rate than the increase in the general level of prices. Conversely, worsenment in the narrow sense implies falling values due to economic recession – a recession which might only be marked by a slowing down in the rate of inflation rather than a decrease in the general price level. In a broader sense, betterment is any increase in the value of property caused by central and local government policy. This may be manifested directly by the improvement of the infrastructure (for example, by means of better transport facilities) or indirectly through the exercise of planning powers. Development value depends on the granting of planning permission; however, the imposition of use restrictions and density standards also have a favourable effect on property values, if not on the property subjected to these constraints, at least on other properties in the locality. But public works schemes and planning policies may just as likely cause worsenment. Values can also diminish in advance of a planning scheme through the process of blighting. Historically, betterment and worsenment have been subjects of much debate. Philosophically and pragmatically, there have been arguments both for and against imposing taxes on betterment values (and granting compensation for worsenment). There has also been much disagreement over the value at which compulsory purchase should take place – should it be the full market value, which might include a large element of betterment, or should it be a price omitting the betterment content? The problems involved in establishing equitable, efficient and acceptable legislation to deal with betterment, worsenment and compulsory purchase have been immense, and few (if any) satisfactory solutions have emerged.

THE POLEMICS AND EFFECTS OF GOVERNMENT INTERVENTION IN THE PROPERTY MARKET

Since the year 1066, land has been entirely owned *de jure* by the Crown. Individuals and private institutions have merely owned rights to use land – rights which in aggregate are known in English law as 'real property'. Consequently, 'land' deals are transactions not in land itself, but in rights in and over land. This basically 'feudal' view of land has been manifested throughout the twentieth century. In 1936, mining rights were nationalised (these recently being extended over half of the North Sea in connection with the exploitation of natural gas and oil), and since the Housing and Town Planning Act 1909 (with breaks between 1953 and 1967 and 1970 and 1973), development values have been wholly or partly siphoned-off by the Crown. Freehold rights were being continually withdrawn through the exercise of compulsory acquisition powers – local authorities (and other public bodies), by applying the rule of law acting as servants of the Crown. But it has been more than 'feudal law' which has influenced land policy in the twentieth century – Liberal and Socialist thought of the last century and a half has provided the underlying rationale of much of the recent legislation concerning land, and contemporary economic and social trends have been used to justify the measures.

In 1817, Ricardo[3] argued that land was different from other factors of production – it was fixed in supply and was a 'free' give of Nature not capable of being created by man. Demand, rather than any action of its owner, determined the value of land – economic rent being entirely an 'unearned' increment and this Ricardo considered taxable. However, in 1848 Karl Marx[4] drew a distinction between land and property. Initially, he argued, the right of land ownership was based on the owner's personal labour but, as far as the capitalist is concerned, property meant the right to appropriate the unpaid labour of others on the production thereof, with the impossibility of the worker appropriating the product of his own labour. Community or social ownership was a view T. H. Green shared with Marx. Green[5] suggested in 1913 that the desire to own land and property is part of the natural order of things and not just a phenomenon of capitalism. He therefore proposed that control over land and property should be effected through changes in the law of inheritance. This would have involved the creation of leasehold tenure for life with interests ultimately reverting to the State for the purpose of redistribution. The process of inheritance had of course produced a very uneven distribution of property. In 1874 a survey of the Local Government Board showed that whereas 852 438 small landowners owned only 188 413 acres (75 360 ha), as few as 525 peers owned a total of 15 201 164 (6 080 460 ha).

But the rapid growth of towns and the large in-migration of people into growth regions caused economists to be more concerned with the problems of betterment rather than with inheritance. Writing an explanation of the programme of the Land Tenure Reform Association in 1870, Mill[6] argued that the government should be encouraged to claim for the benefit of the State the interception by taxation of the future unearned increase of the value of land, and in California in the 1870s, George[7] (seeing that a substantial in-migration of population was pulling up rents and widening gaps between landowners and the landless) proposed a 100 per cent tax on economic rent. This, he claimed, would restrict the power of land monopoly, remove the incentive to speculate and keep land off the market, and eliminate inequalities arising from the ownership of property. In figure 9.2, with a given quantity of land (q) and a rent of r, the landlord's net income would be only $rn \times q$ since tax revenue ($r - rn \times q$) would be recouped for the benefit of the community. It is of note that the incidence of the tax falls entirely on the landowner since the tax cannot push up the market rent above its equilibrium level at r.

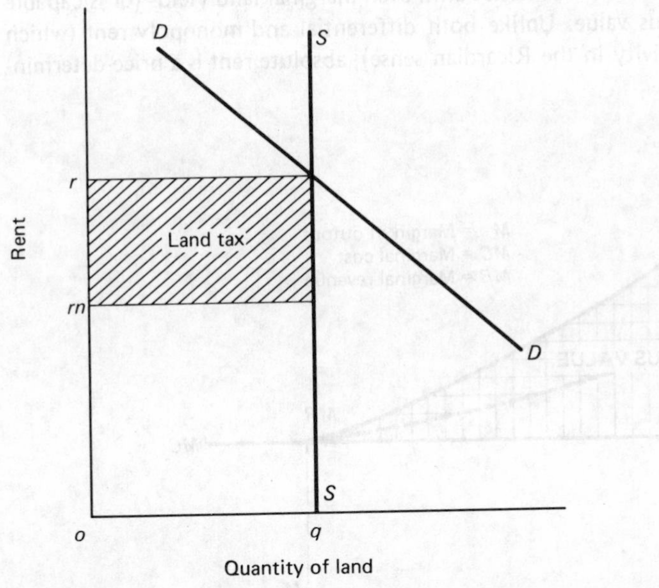

Figure 9.2 *Taxation and the supply of land*

Marxist rent theory is often used to justify the imposition of a land tax. Marx argued that landowners were parasitic since they did not produce value but intercepted part of the flow of surplus value (in the form of rent) which otherwise would have been retained by the industrial capitalist. In *Capital* (Vol. 3), Marx[8] defined three categories of rent – each reflecting a specific form of social relationship. The first category, *differential rent*, arises when *either* a fixed quantity of capital is applied to land of varying fertility or distance from the market (differential rent 1), *or* when different amounts of capital are used on different pieces of land (differential rent 2) – in both cases with marginal wages and marginal interest costs remaining constant. With an increase in fertility or a relocation towards the market, less labour is required and both total and marginal revenue increases and thus more surplus value is produced. Some of the surplus value is retained by the producer as profit, but the rest is siphoned-off by the landowner as rent (figure 9.3). In other situations where there is a decrease in the employment of capital (perhaps because of its improved efficiency of use or because of a greater availability of low-cost natural resources), the amount of surplus value increases and is likewise divided-up by producer and landowner. The second category, *monopoly rent*, is obtained by landowners who let out land for the production of commodities sold under conditions of monopoly. Marx cites an example of a vineyard producing very fine wine which, in the absence of competition, can provide both high profits for the producer and high rent for the landowner. The final category, *absolute rent*, accrues to landowners who withhold land from the market until even marginal land yields (or is capable of yielding) surplus value. Unlike both differential and monopoly rent (which reflect market activity in the Ricardian sense), absolute rent is a price-determinant.

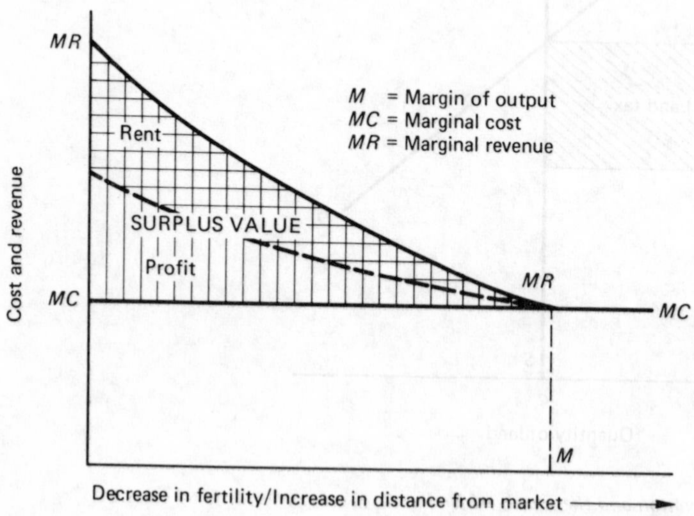

Figure 9.3 *Surplus value, profit and rent*

There are considerable difficulties in applying Marxist rent theory to urban land. As Edwards[9] points out, Marxist analysis is not just concerned with distribution. Although it shows in part the relationship between landowners and tenants, it is also concerned with relations between site-owners, developers, architects, surveyors, planners, construction workers, building-supply industries and financial institutions – relations which not only determine the distribution of surplus value but also what production processes take place. Edwards argues that even when land taxes are applied, there is little long-term threat to the interests of modern landed property (landowners – as monopolists – having the power to deflect the incidence of taxation to other factions of capital and to labour). But regardless of land taxation, the development process narrows down the location and form of new buildings so that, as sources of rent, they become more tradeable commodities – more appealing to tenants and investors than marginal locations and bespoke buildings.

Influenced more by Ricardo and Mill than by Marx, Tawney[10] in 1922 advocated a high level of taxation on large incomes flowing from land ownership. Yet, while believing that land should serve the community, he suggested that this should be achieved by public control since compared with public ownership, it was a preferable way of ensuring that property would fulfil a social purpose.

In twentieth-century Britain, the introduction of town planning legislation has complicated the arguments both for and against governmental intervention in the market pricing of property. The main arguments for intervention in the price mechanism revolve around the inequalities of the planning system:

(1) Since at least the Town and Country Planning Act 1947, land use and land values have been decided largely by planning decisions concerning the granting (or refusal) of permission to develop. Land use and values are thus mainly determined by administrative decisions under the more or less effective control of a democratic political system.

There has emerged a very different pattern of use and values than would have occurred under *laissez-faire* free market conditions. Planning authorities have in fact created incomes and wealth – changes in land values depending greatly upon public policy rather than upon unimpeded market forces. According to Edwards,[9] the planning system has benefited elements of capital by limiting the supply of buildings which would have competed with those already within an area – for example, restrictions on development in conservation areas and in green belts, and on out-of-town shopping, benefit existing individual and corporate interests in both the protected areas and in urban centres. Planning control, moreover, might enable a residential development to be undertaken in locations which otherwise would accommodate commercial uses, while it could facilitate industrial development and agriculture in areas where normally these uses could not compete with housing (figure 9.4).

Goodchild and Munton[11] argue that green belts in particular distort the pattern of land values. Between the inner boundaries of a green belt and an

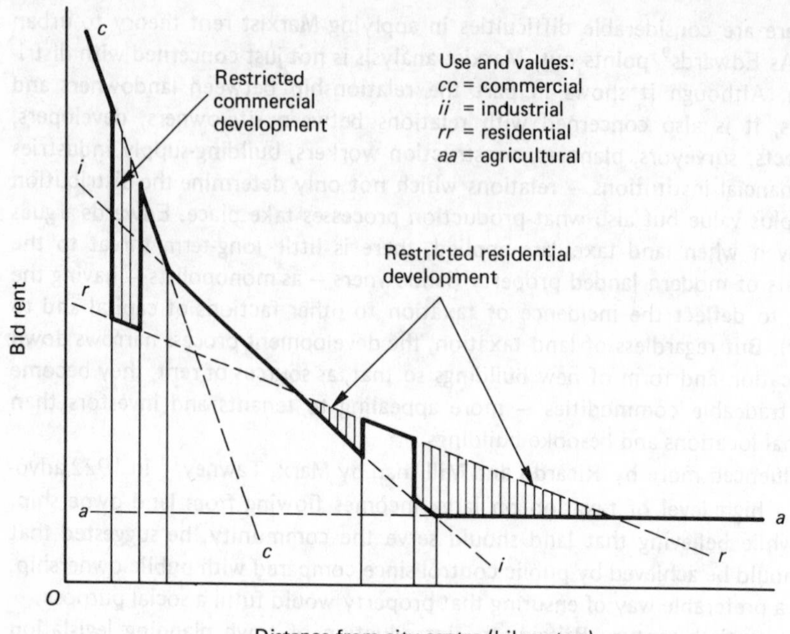

Figure 9.4 *The impact of planning control upon land use and values*

urban centre, residential and other urban values increase because of the artificial shortage of development land, while agricultural values correspondingly decrease; but within the green belt, agricultural values rise since speculative development is substantially constrained (figure 9.5).

Overall, suggests Keogh,[12] local planning authorities should attempt to maximise social returns. If, for example, according to market forces, industrial use can out-bid agriculture over (say) 10 000 ha in the rural–urban fringe, then the local planning authority (taking into account external costs such as lost amenity, environmental affliction etc.) might deem the social value of agricultural land to be higher than the market value of the land, and reduce the amount available to industry to (say) 6000 ha. This is illustrated in figure 9.6 where *DI* represents the demand for land for industrial use, *DA* shows the demand for agricultural purposes, and *DS* indicates the social value of the land.

As part of the process of maximising social welfare, local authorities might attempt to realise 'planning gain' – whereby, in return for planning permission, private developers are willing to donate a proportion of their land for public use. But social welfare is not always an *a priori* aspect of planning. Since future changes in land values are greatly dependent upon public policy rather than on unimpeded market forces, it may be difficult to argue why all of the rental value (or the whole of an increase in value) should accrue to the owner.

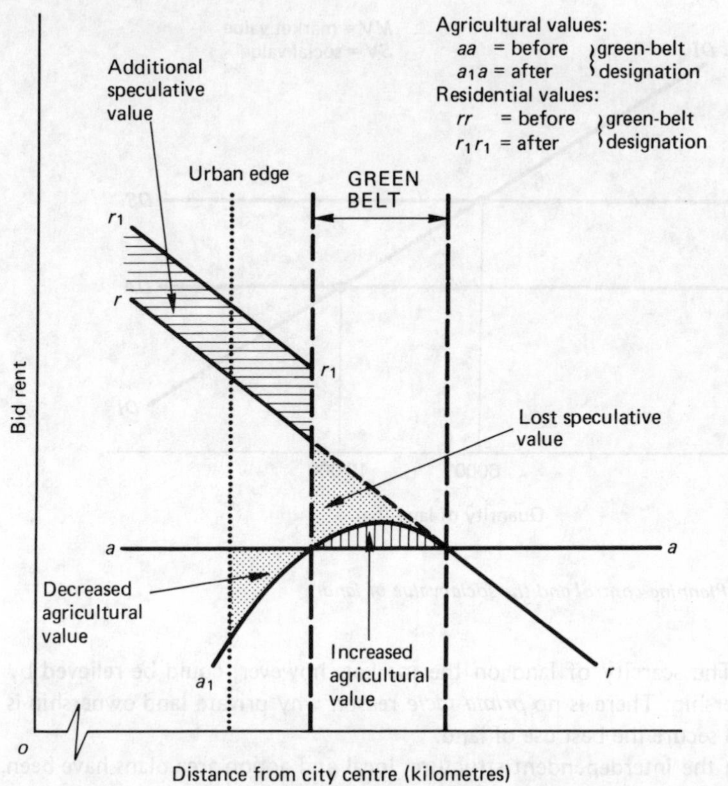

Figure 9.5 *The impact of a green belt upon land use and values*

(2) The working of the price mechanism within the constraints of planning legislation means that local authorities are often forced to pay high market prices for their use of land. Public facilities such as schools, open space or roads are thus expensive to develop or may have been diverted to cheaper but less socially desirable locations.

(3) With market pricing prevailing, local authorities are encouraged to compulsorily purchase economically (though not necessarily socially) 'obsolete' property. They are then compelled to undertake financially viable redevelopment (possibly in partnership with private developers) and largely have to ignore socially desirable renewal.

(4) Comprehensive development and redevelopment involve the ultimate creation of interests at new and higher market values. But local authorities (to the detriment of rate- and tax-payers) are not generally able to realise these enhanced values and the profits which they helped to create.

(5) However justified the government may be in imposing a tax on publicly created values, a high levy would almost certainly result in owners withholding land from the market. But land is practically indestructible and generally fixed

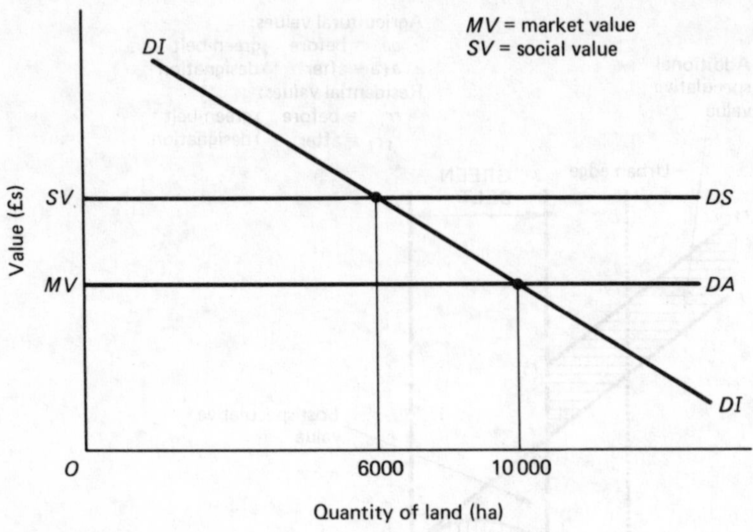

Figure 9.6 *Planning control and the social value of land*

in supply. The scarcity of land on the market, however, could be relieved by public ownership. There is no *prima facie* reason why private land ownership is necessary to secure the best use of land.

(6) When the interdependent structure, local and action area plans have been finalised, there is still the need to allocate land use, or at least to produce a strategy for the future use of land. This is difficult when there is multiple private ownership and when market values prevail. Planning can only become a more effective means of economic and social policy through more substantial control of land.

The arguments against public intervention are similarly numerous:

(1) Development profits are the result and not the cause of land scarcity and high values. Planning authorities have created the scarcity of building land through use restrictions, zoning and density regulations – measures which may not seem appropriate in a country where only about 12 per cent of the land is urban and where population increase has considerably slowed down. It was planning control (and inflation) which resulted in owner-occupiers (comprising over half the total households) experiencing a total increase of £50 000 million in the value of their properties between 1971 and 1973 and an even larger amount in real terms between 1985 and 1987. It has also been planning control which has largely confined retail development to town centres, which in Marxian terms has permitted landowners to siphon-off absolute rent to the ultimate detriment of a low-wage and partially marginalised workforce.[9]

But realising that the planning system is largely instrumental in establishing betterment value, governments, instead of dismantling the restrictive aspects of planning (in an attempt to bring forth a greater supply of developable land), have intervened still further – betterment levies and proposals to nationalise land decrease supply yet again. As Hayek[13] argued in the 1940s, a government's answer to the problems of intervention is yet more intervention.

(2) That betterment should be distributed to the 'community' through fiscal measures rather than be retained by the owner or developer is a *view* which implies that the owner or developer is not a part of that community. But as over half of the housing stock is owner-occupied and the largest part of commercial development provides a return for its investors (the contributors to life assurance companies and pension funds), it can be argued that even without betterment levies a very large part of the community would benefit from property values.

(3) Most planning is prohibitive and negative. It restricts development which would be financially rewarding. Even planning concerned with land use outside the market might pre-empt what could otherwise be market-determined development of a sort consumers prefer. The opportunity cost to the community of the distortion or replacement of the market could be immense. The cost is compounded by the expense incurred in applying for planning permission. In the early 1970s, Pennance[14] suggested that a wait of six months or longer was involved and found that in nearly 20 per cent of cases the applicant was unsuccessful.

(4) No one has (or could) undertake a cost-benefit analysis of the overall effects of town planning. But it is sometimes suggested that it stultifies land use, restricts investment and curbs economic development. It even produces an outflow of funds for investment abroad. There is a feeling that even environmental conservation by tight planning controls fails to benefit society.

(5) Land is heterogeneous and therefore needs a mechanism to allocate sites to the most efficient and most desirable uses. It is the price-mechanism, it is argued, which within legal limits and despite many market imperfections works as this rationing device. Without the price-mechanism, critics of planning argue, there would be a cumbersome, unwieldly, expensive and bureaucratic system with every plot of land subject to an individual administrative decision to decide its use. It was within this context that in 1981 the Property Advisory Group (PAG) criticised the way in which many local authorities traded development approval for planning gain.[15] PAG believed that since the development control process could become distorted (presumably by welfare considerations), it might fall into disrepute, and therefore bargaining for planning gain should be discouraged.

(6) It is argued that land is in fact a commodity like anything else and should not be subject to any special form of taxation or public ownership. Like other products, land is destructible (or it can be rendered unusable) and it is capable of being 'manufactured', improved or moved – more intensive development on a site or reclamation constituting an increase in its supply.

Yet since 1909 a planning machine has evolved. Government departments have been established for the purpose of intervening more and more into land use and the property market. Both centrally and locally staff and financial resources have been accumulated to formulate and apply policies. The planning profession has expanded and its principal institution has gained the 'Royal' prefix. However rational the arguments against public intervention may appear to some, it is most improbable in the foreseeable future that the planning mechanism will be dismantled. It is therefore imperative that one should concentrate on examining some of the weaknesses of planning rather than contemplate its unlikely replacement by an unfettered market.

PLANNING AND THE LOSS AND RECOVERY OF PRIVATE PROPERTY RIGHTS

Under a plethora of measures in the nineteenth century, local authorities could demolish private buildings hazardous to public health and could control and undertake development. But the more important powers (those granted by the Public Health Acts of 1848 and 1875, the Labouring Classes Lodging Houses Act 1868, the Artizans and Labourers Dwellings Act 1868, the Artizans and Labourers Dwellings Improvement Act 1875 and the Housing of the Working Classes Act 1890) were all constrained by the statutory obligation of municipal authorities having to purchase property by agreement or compulsorily at market values, the level of which was generally high as sites were often within the inner areas of cities.

It was in London that some of the biggest hindrances to slum clearance were to be found – the associated social distress being highlighted in the Booth surveys of the 1890s. In 1895, by Act of Parliament, the London County Council was given powers to impose an 'improvement charge' of 3 per cent so as to recoup 'for the benefit of the community' a share (albeit small) of rising property values and to provide an extra source of revenue to facilitate the acquisition of sites for redevelopment. But the levy only remained until 1902, being then abandoned as owners could appeal against assessment and seek arbitration, and could require the LCC to purchase property at the pre-betterment valuation or forego the levy.

The Housing and Town Planning Act 1909 introduced a 50 per cent levy on increases in value caused by the 'making of any town planning scheme' and conversely compensation could be awarded for any injurious effect of a scheme. Although the Act mainly affected suburban development – leaving virtually untouched values within the inner areas of cities – it was a legislative milestone. It introduced the principle that those who benefit from town planning (rather than from their own efforts) should be taxed and those who lose from such planning (rather than from their own mistakes) should be compensated. In the same year David Lloyd George presented his 'People's Budget'. By this he endeavoured to ensure that betterment would be more evenly distributed. In 1911 an increment value duty (on betterment in the narrow sense) came into effect, also an undeveloped land duty, a reversion duty of 10 per cent on the value accruing to a lessor at the end of a lease and a mineral rights duty of 5 per cent on the rental value of all rights to work minerals. With the upheavals of the First World War and the inflation of 1919–21, the levies of the 1909 Act were considered to be both cumbersome and politically unacceptable and were abandoned in the early 1920s. It was left to the physical planning legislation of the inter-war period to embrace what were basically economic issues – betterment, worsenment, compulsory purchase and land values.

Under the Housing and Town Planning Act 1919, county boroughs, urban district councils (with populations over 20 000) and municipal boroughs were compelled to produce planning schemes for suburban development. But only within declared 'interim development control areas' would the 50 per cent levy on betterment (previously introduced) apply – regardless of whether owners had or had not realised the appreciated value. The Town and Country Planning Act 1932 increased the betterment charge to 75 per cent but the levy was only imposed when the market value was realised.

Other methods of taxing rising land values were short-lived. The Finance Act 1931 introduced measures similar to those of two decades earlier but they were likewise criticised for being unwieldly and doctrinaire and were suspended and repealed by the Finance Acts of 1932 and 1934, respectively. Yet planning legislation, though more acceptable, left many issues unresolved.

Local planning authorities lacked both professional staff and financial resources. Because of the difficulties in assessing and collecting betterment tax (shifting and floating values causing intractable problems), authorities were hesitant in producing plans which would also have involved incurring considerable compensation expense. This, together with costly delays in acquiring property under multiple ownership, impeded the production and implementation of plans for the redevelopment of town centres. Town planning depended very much upon local initiative. There were wide variations in the extent to which local authorities drew up plans and attempted to deal with problems of betterment and worsenment.

These problems were recognised by the Uthwatt Committee on Compensation and Betterment (1942). Believing that land values are largely created by community activity it proposed that, in the case of undeveloped land development, rights should be nationalised, and if the land was required for redevelopment it should be purchased by the local authority at existing use value and then leased to a developer at a future use value. Land already developed should be compulsorily acquired when needed for redevelopment at the value appertaining on 31 March 1939; land with building plans prepared for it (but not implemented) should be treated as though it were undeveloped land – its development value being nationalised. In addition, the Uthwatt Committee suggested that there should be a 75 per cent annual tax on annual increases in site values (with valuations every five years) and that central government grants should be available to assist local authorities in undertaking compulsory purchase. It was thought that good town planning would only be possible if local authorities could acquire development land at a price it could afford and it was considered reasonable that betterment should be largely returned to society whose actions had created it.

The post-war Labour government largely based its Town and Country Planning Act 1947 on the principles of the Uthwatt Report although the Act did not differentiate between provisions for developed and undeveloped land. All local planning authorities (then the county councils and county boroughs) were to produce plans for the whole of their areas and these were to be submitted to the Ministry of Town and Country Planning (set up in 1943) for approval. All development (specificially defined) requiring planning permission and development rights were to be entirely nationalised. A development charge of 100 per cent was thus imposed on the developer, who would consequently ensure that all transactions were at existing use value. A Central Land Board was established to collect the levy (the problems of assessing shifting values being eased) and to handle compensation claims for the loss of development value on the enacting day – 1 July 1948. A £300 million fund was available for this purpose. Compensation would also be paid (by local authorities) if planning restrictions reduced existing use values. The Act should have enabled local authorities to have obtained land at a relatively low price, should have permitted them to undertake the 'right' amount of planning and should not have involved them in much compensation expenditure.

But generally the results of the 1947 Act were detrimental to the working of the property market. Different criteria for assessing development values led to much haggling between developers and district valuers, the cash flow of developers was seriously endangered by the levy being payable before development commenced and there was anecdotal evidence that the complexity, uncertainty and stringency of the system prevented or deferred development either by owners withholding land or developers being unwilling to acquire it. Yet the construction industry with limited available resources was working to full capacity, not least on local authority housing and new town development. There was also an increase in activity where there were exemptions from the levy, for example, conversions of houses into flats, small extensions to existing buildings, agricultural improvements and construction involving no change in use. The most severely curtailed development was, of course, that which involved change of use, the end-product of which might have been shops or offices.

In 1951 the Conservatives came to office, and in 1953 and 1954 two Town and Country Planning Acts dismantled many of the provisions of the 1947 Act. The development levy was abolished, the Central Land Board was wound up and the compensation fund for the previous loss of development values was extinguished.

Compulsory purchase, however, continued to be at existing use values. Although confidence was restored to the market, much development was still held back as local authorities (probably because of political expedience) did not always wish to exercise their compulsory purchase powers – compensation at existing use value in relative terms falling further and further below rising market values.

Under the Town and Country Planning Act 1959 the dual market for land came to an end. By re-establishing market prices for compulsory purchase, all land transactions would be determined by the laws of supply and demand. For the first time in fifty years the government 'freed' the property market from fiscal distortions.

Except in green-belt areas (where owners may have felt that their development values were still nationalised), private development became increasingly speculative. From 1953 until the mid-1960s there were very many cases of site values increasing by as much as ten-fold – the development processes and the soaring increase in values being very explicitly described by Marriott.[16]

On returning to power in 1964, the Labour government began formalising its policy on land. In the following year, Lichfield[17] appraised five different forms of land nationalisation: transient nationalisation (the purchase of land at current use value and the creation of new leaseholds); the unification of development rights and values involving a 100 per cent tax on development values (a form implemented by the 1947 Act); the public ownership of land to be developed and redeveloped; the unification of reversion (the state becoming universal freeholder with existing freehold interests becoming leasehold); and complete nationalisation. Except for the last form, each proposal was to a greater or lesser extent compatible with Lichfield's criteria for an acceptable solution to the problems of betterment and the scarcity of development land. Lichfield suggested that in a mixed economy market, forces should be permitted to work and developers' profits condoned (at least in part). But 'unearned' increments should be largely eliminated by public ownership or betterment charges, otherwise values would be prohibitively high for the realisation of planning objectives. Any system of public control or ownership must be understandable, administratively simple and enforceable, and it should not result in a rapid and enormous transfer of assets from the private to the public sector if this would seriously disrupt the economy.

In 1967, something approaching transient nationalisation was introduced by the Land Commission Act. The legislation was intended to ensure that: the burden of the cost of land for essential purposes was reduced; suitable land was available at the right time for the implementation of national, regional and local plans; part of the increased value of land arising from the possibility of changing its use or putting buildings on it returned to the community whose activities helped to create it – while at the same time the market would be left relatively free.

To achieve these aims a Land Commission was established which first had powers to purchase land and to either develop it itself or to make it available to public authorities and private developers. The Commission was equipped with the usual powers of compulsory purchase and could use the normal machinery for appeals and public inquiry. Land would be usually purchased at the market value and sold at the best possible price. A Crownhold would be granted subject to restrictions and with the future development value reserved for the commission. In the case of land for essential housing development, Concessionary Crownhold was created – sites being sold at sub-market prices.

The Commission secondly had powers to assess and collect a 40 per cent levy on net development value, the government believing that there was still enough of the development value left to provide an adequate incentive for owners to sell their land. The levy was payable when the whole or part of the development value was realised. It was with these measures that the government hoped to release sites for development and to redistribute among the community part of the profits accruing to land.

But within the three years in which the Act was in force the Land Commission failed to achieve its objectives. At the time of the Act's repeal, the Commission had purchased only 2800 acres (1120 ha) (although a further 9000 acres [3600 ha] were in the pipeline) and only about 400 acres (160 ha) had been sold. In 1967 it was hoped that the Commission would assess 150 000 deals a year and collect £85 million per annum in levies, but by 1970 a total of only about 50 000 assessments had been made, yielding only £46 million. Even in mid-1971 (several months after the death of the Commission), over £30 million of betterment levy was still uncollected. The resources of the Commission (in terms of its 1000 staff and the £4 million per year allocated to it by the government) were clearly insufficient to handle the complexities of the legislation.

A major criticism of the Act was that, far from bringing down the price of land, it may have contributed to the further soaring of values. But although the observation was probably correct, the generally offered explanation was inaccurate. It had been argued that the 40 per cent levy was merely added on to prevailing prices, but this would have meant that either for some very improbable reason prices before 1967 were at sub-market levels or that the levy could be passed on through higher prices because of a large surge of demand in the period from 1967 to 1970 – but there was no such increase in the level of demand. A more plausible analysis is that prices increased because owners reduced the supply of development land by withholding it from the market as they may not have wished to incur the levy, or they may have anticipated that the Act would prove to be unworkable and thence repealed, or that there would be a change of government and policy.

This analysis is illustrated in figure 9.7. The supply of development land is reduced from SS to S_1S_1, causing capital values to rise from CV to CV_1. Where the demand D_1D_1 was relatively inelastic, capital values increased even more to CV_2.

Neuberger and Nicol[18] estimated that the levy had reduced the supply of development land by 30 per cent, thus the amount of land not put on to the market because of the levy was probably far greater than the quantity acquired by the Land Commission. To some extent the 1967 Act provided safeguards against the withholding of land. It was intended to raise the levy at short intervals from 40 to 45 or 50 per cent to deter owners putting back the date of development, and the Land Commission was expected to use to the full its compulsory purchase powers. But the checks were either not applied or applied very ineffectively. Some of the biggest withholders of land were local authorities, which often obstructed the Land Commission's proposed development by failing to grant planning permission. Ministerial intervention could not always engender local authority support for the activities of the Land Commission, as local government received neither a share of levy revenue nor a portion of the return on establishing Crownhold.

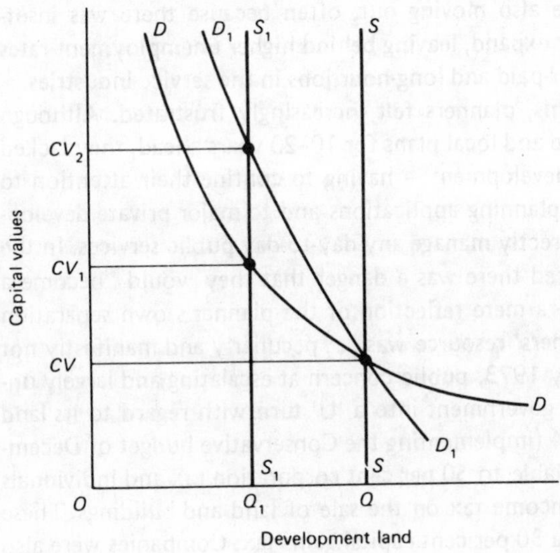

Figure 9.7 *The effect of a reduced supply of development land on capital values*

By 1970 the Land Commission was only just getting into its stride. It may have achieved its aims and objectives given a few more years of life. In the short term it had created uncertainty, it had slowed down development and had induced prices to rise. But during an election year land issues became polarised. Either the Land Commission had to be strengthened, betterment taxation simplified and the levy raised, or the Act had to be repealed as 'having no place in a free society'. After the defeat of the Labour government by the Conservatives in June 1970, the Act was indeed repealed and development land reverted to the free market. No central organisation was reconstituted for the purpose of acquiring land and no new tax specifically on betterment was devised.

The free market in the period 1970–73 produced severe planning problems associated with speculation and land scarcity. The repeal of the 1967 Act, the lifting of the 'Brown Ban' on office development in London, and the raising of the office development permit threshold from 3000 to 10 000 ft^2, all in 1970, heralded a great surge in land speculation. At best, compulsory purchase for 'essential' needs at market value did nothing to recoup for the community a share of the increased values which it helped to create; at worst, public planning policy decisions virtually eliminated public authorities from the market because of inadequate development funds.

In part, the corollary of speculation was land shortage, especially for housing and manufacturing industry. Low and middle-income families were being squeezed out as office and hotel development was inflating site values in central and inner areas, and 'gentrification' led to reduced occupancy in rehabilitated housing. Manufacturers were also moving out, often because there was insufficient space to modernise or expand, leaving behind higher unemployment rates and a narrower range of lower-paid and long-hour jobs in the service industries.

Faced with these problems, planners felt increasingly frustrated. Although they had to produce structure and local plans for 10–20 years ahead, they lacked initiative and control over development – having to confine their attention to the approval or rejection of planning applications and to major private development. They did not even indirectly manage any day-to-day public services. In the way plans were being prepared there was a danger that they would "become a series of vague generalities – a mere reflection of the planner's own separation from reality. Land, the planners' resource was . . . peculiarly and manifestly not the planners' resource."[19] By 1973, public concern at escalating and largely untaxed land values forced the government into a 'U' turn with regard to its land policy. The Finance Act 1974 (implementing the Conservative budget of December 1973) made companies liable to 50 per cent corporation tax and individuals liable to up to 75 per cent income tax on the sale of land and buildings. These taxes in both cases replaced a 30 per cent capital gains tax. Companies were also liable for the 50 per cent corporation tax on first lettings (deemed 'disposals') after material development but only where the rack rent exceeded £2000. The Department of the Environment was given powers to take over (for subsequent letting) buildings which had been empty for two or more years, and local authorities were permitted to rate empty buildings at a 100 per cent plus a surcharge. Both of these latter measures, it was hoped, would deter speculators from withholding property from the market to maintain scarcity and perpetuate the rise in values. But on returning to power in 1974, the Labour administration did not regard this approach as being sufficiently positive.

Based loosely on *Labour's Programme for Britain 1973* and the White Paper *Land*[20] 1974, the Community Land Act 1975 introduced a hybrid method of nationalising land which involved the ownership of land and the unification of development rights. The Act required that initially, and by means of a five year rolling programme, local authorities would have the *power* to acquire all land needed for development over the following ten years. Land would be purchased at market value less development land tax (DLT) – DLT being introduced under the Development Land Tax Act 1976 at 66.66 and 80 per cent. Owner-occupied properties of up to 1 acre (0.45 ha), single house plots producing 10 000 ft^2 (929 m^2), churches and charities, industrial schemes up to 15 000 ft^2 (1393 m^2), agricultural, horticultural, forestry and mining land, and land owned or with planning permission attached on 12 September 1974 were all to some extent exempt from the scheme. Land acquired by local authorities (either by agreement or compulsorily) was to be leased at market values to developers with 99 year leases being established (including 60-year-old rebuilding clauses), except in the case of housing development when the freehold would be sold. The Act was intended to ensure that a substantial part of the development value of land was largely recouped by the community as a whole. The Exchequer initially received 40 per cent of the surplus on land transactions, the local authority 30 per cent and the remaining 30 per cent was shared among other councils. In 1978, the local authority's share was increased to 40 per cent at the expense of the Exchequer.

Eventually, local authorities would be given the *duty* to acquire all development land at current use value (except in the case of permitted exemptions). Effectively, the development value of this land would be nationalised and therefore DLT would no longer be imposed. This long-term provision of the community land scheme was, however, never implemented. The community land scheme (incorporated in the 1975 and 1976 Acts) was thus different from that originally proposed. Under the original scheme, all land was to be frozen at its value on the date of the publication of the White Paper (that is, 12 September 1974), and for the following ten years local authorities could acquire land at that value for development purposes. According to Silkin,[21] this would have stopped land speculation, eliminated land shortages and curbed the escalation of land costs for housing and public services.

The community land scheme was, however, welcomed by the Royal Town Planning Institute, the Town and Country Planning Association and many urban authorities (particularly before the swing from Labour to Conservative in the local government elections of 1976–67). It was thought that plan implementation would be greatly assisted, but it was also believed that the scheme could become a 'builders' charter'. Free from the need to accumulate land banks and identify profitable projects, developers and contractors would be able to enter into a viable partnership with the community. But the community land scheme adversely affected builders if they were accumulating land banks. The retention of a substantial proportion of development value was necessary to recompense builders for development risk but most of this became liable to DLT.

The operation of the community land scheme was tragically similar to that of the Land Commission Act. At no time did it have more than a marginal effect on the purchase and sale of land. Over the three-and-a-half years to May 1979, the

English local authorities acquired about 3600 acres (1458 ha) of development land, and of this sold only 700 acres (284 ha), producing a deficit of over £52 million (this was in contrast to the anticipated net surplus of over £300 million per year for the country as a whole). Although public expenditure was severely curbed in the late 1970s (as deflation followed the Land Commission Act in the late 1960s), local authorities failed to take up the money allocated to them for the scheme, therefore allocations under the White Paper,[22] *The Government's Expenditure Plans, 1978/79 to 1981/82*, 1978, were reduced from £83 million to £54 million (1979–80), and for each of the subsequent two years cut from £102 to £64 million. At a local level there was a lack of political will to implement the scheme. The Conservatives were in control of most county and district councils, and the party vowed to repeal the 1975 Act as soon as it was returned to power nationally. Other councils were reluctant to move into a new entrepreneurial field. The scheme required an extra 12 750 to 14 000 staff (with one-third or more being members of the land professions). Without this full complement of staff, local authorities were unable to operate the scheme as intended and could not fully utilise even the financial resources which were available. But some authorities (especially in areas attractive to developers) were generally opposed to further development. For these reasons, authorities were not induced to establish public development corporations for the purpose of acquiring and disposing of land and preparing it for development. In Wales, in contrast, the 1975 Act gave responsibility for operating the community land scheme not to local authorities but a newly established Land Authority for Wales (LAW). As a public development corporation it was comparatively more successful in selecting, acquiring and reselling land for development than the English local authorities, and it effectively negotiated with local planning authorites.

By 1979, the weaknesses of the community land scheme were recognised. The scheme was particularly ineffective in the inner urban areas where site values reached their peak. Local authorities were thus often inhibited from acquiring land for public development.

Soon after winning the General Election, the Conservatives began to dismantle the community land scheme. The Budget of June 1979 cut DLT from 80 and 66.66 per cent to a single rate of 60 per cent, and raised the threshold from £10 000 to £50 000 (rising to £75 000 in 1984), and the Local Government, Planning and Land Act 1980 repealed the 1975 Act (although the LAW and its role were retained). The demise of the community land scheme marked the end of the third attempt since 1947 to deal with the problem of 'unearned' development profits, and once again the market prevailed – DLT being finally abolished by the Budget of March 1985, although there was little evidence that the tax had reduced the volume of development. Local authorities, however, had by then lost any initiative they might have had in the development process, being forced to pay market prices for land, and under the 1980 Act they became instrumental in the selling-off of public sector land – although at prevailing rates of disposal will take until the end of the century to clear the stock of publicly-owned land in the inner city. It became increasingly clear that by concentrating on the disposal of public sector wasteland the government was putting in jeopardy its inner city policies. It was thus proposed in a publication by the Institute of Economic Affairs[23] (a body normally sympathetic to Conservative policies) that private land which had been vacant for longer than a particular period should be taxed as an incentive for owners to bring it into use – in other words, site value taxation (or site value rating) should be selectively introduced (see chapter 7).

In conclusion, it might be useful to reflect on land policies in two other advanced capitalist countries. In France, land is frequently taken into community ownership by compulsory purchase when it is required for the provision of public services. Within zones of deferred development (ZDDs) (that is, where new town or urban renewal schemes are contemplated), public authorities have pre-emption rights in the purchase of land. Within these zones, the cost of acquisition is minimised since compensation is based on values prevailing one year before the ZDD's declaration. In these cases, and in general, private sector short-term profits are taxed as income and long-term gains are subject to capital taxation (at up to 60 per cent on realisation). In addition, *a priori* ('equipment') taxes are imposed to facilitate the development of infrastructure when an owner either applies for a building permit or sells his property, and a tax of up to 100 per cent is levied on the value of any development in excess of permitted building coefficients (plot-ratios). French land policy thus differed substantially from that employed in Britain throughout the 1980s.

In Sweden, there is also a considerable degree of public intervention in the land market. Local authorities ('communes') have a statutory duty to build up land banks sufficient for 7–10 years' development. Financed on favourable terms from central government, the communes can either acquire land by agreement at approximately current use value or by compulsory purchase at prices appertaining ten years prior to acquisition (with allowances for inflation) – a provision phased-in from 1971. Land might then be used for public sector use or released for private development at low market values (there being an absence of supply constraint), but private developers will be unable to realise any significant speculative gain since, in general, land profits are taxed as incomes and/or wealth, and in the case of housing development prices are regulated (chapter 8). Unlike Britain, where a very large proportion of development gain derives from land, financial returns from the development process in Sweden stem almost entirely from production.[24]

If in Britain a future government wished to adopt a land policy which would facilitate positive planning, it could well base its measures on successful policies employed abroad. In the meanwhile, a relatively free market for land will continue to allocate uses inefficiently, disregard social needs and perpetuate inequalities of income and wealth.

REFERENCES

1. R. H. Wright, 'The Property Market 2', *The Architect and Surveyor* (March/April, 1971).
2. *Report of the Expert Committee on Compensation and Betterment* (Uthwatt Report), Cmnd 6386 (HMSO, 1942).
3. D. Ricardo, *Principles of Political Economy and Taxation* (Penguin, 1971).
4. K. Marx, *A Critique of Political Economy* (Lawrence & Wishart, 1974).
5. T. H. Green, *Lectures on the Principles of Political Obligation* (Longmans, 1913).
6. J. S. Mill, *Programme* (Land Reform Association, 1871).
7. H. George, *Progress and Poverty* (Hogarth, 1979).
8. K. Marx, *Capital*, Vol. 3 (Penguin, 1981).
9. M. Edwards, 'Planning and the Land Market: Problems, Prospects and Strategy' in M. Ball *et al., Land Rent, Housing and Urban Planning: A European Perspective* (Croom Helm, 1984).
10. R. H. Tawney, *The Acquisitive Society* (Bell, 1922).
11. R. Goodchild and R. Munton, *Development and the Landowner. An Analysis of the British Experience* (George Allen & Unwin, 1985).
12. G. Keogh, 'The Economics of Planning Gain' in S. Barrett and P. Healey (eds), *Land Policy: Problems and Alternatives* (Gower, 1985).
13. F. A. Hayek, *The Road to Serfdom* (George Routledge, 1944).
14. F. G. Pennance, 'Planning, Land Supply and Demand' in A. A. Walters *et al., Government and the Land* (Institute of Economic Affairs, 1974).
15. Department of the Environment, *Planning Gain*, Report of the Property Advisory Group (HMSO, 1981).
16. O. Marriott, *The Property Boom* (Hamish Hamilton, 1967).
17. N. Lichfield, 'Land Nationalisation' in P. Hall (ed.), *Land Values* (Sweet & Maxwell, 1965).
18. H. L. T. Neuberger and B. M. Nicol, 'The recent cost of land and property prices and the factors underlying it', Department of the Environment *Research Paper*, 4 (HMSO, 1976).
19. R. Barras *et al.*, 'Planning and the Public Ownership of Land', *New Society* (21 July, 1973).
20. Department of the Environment, *Land*, Cmnd 5730 (HMSO, 1975).
21. J. Silkin, 'A land value scheme that got away', *Town and Country Planning* (January, 1987).
22. Treasury, *The Government's Expenditure Plans 1978/79 to 1981/82*, Cmnd 7049 (HMSO, 1978).
23. M. Chisholm and P. Kivell, *Inner City Wasteland: An Assessment of Market Failure in Land Development* (Institute of Economic Affairs, 1987).
24. S. Duncan, 'Land Policy in Sweden: Separating Ownership from Development' in S. Barrett and P. Healey (eds), *Land Policy: Problems and Alternatives* (Gower, 1985).

10

The Construction Industry in the United Kingdom

The construction industry covers a wide range of loosely integrated groups and sub-markets whose output varies but basically consists of the production, alteration or repair of durable buildings and capital goods involving the use of land combined with other scarce resources – a combination found in other industries, but construction has certain unique characteristics deriving largely from the physical nature of the construction product and its demand.

THE NATURE AND CHARACTERISTICS OF THE INDUSTRY

Much output is large, durable and expensive. Generally, value is high in relation to the income of the purchaser. A house can rarely be purchased out of income nor can a factory out of current profits; payment is either from accumulated reserves or from borrowings. Thus the prosperity of the industry is much affected by changes in the rate of interest and the availability of credit. Demand is wide geographically and much is unique to the requirement of the individual customer. Thus there are few opportunities for traditional building to develop mass production methods which would reduce unit costs. The industry's structure has changed little over the years, its methods of production are still mainly traditional and there are only small signs of technical change. A single contract may account for a large proportion of a constractor's output in any period; this may cause substantial diseconomies in the production process as well as increasing risks.

Repairs and Maintenance

The durability of buildings results in a high percentage of current output in repairs and maintenance – increasing from 27.5 in 1969 to 46 per cent in 1985 (table 10.1), statistics which underestimate repairs and maintenance because of the large volume executed by in-house maintenance workers employed by large firms. Durability results in the existing stock of buildings being very large in relation to annual production; the total supply of buildings is very inelastic even in the long period. Therefore small fluctuations in demand for the existing stock will have large effects on the price of new work.

Repair and maintenance is a sector in which productivity has risen more slowly than in new construction. Inevitably it is heavily labour-intensive, employing over 30 per cent of contractors' labour, and techniques which have improved efficiency in new work are rarely applicable. Capital expenditure per worker per year in construction is probably less than one-half of the average for manufacturing industry, and in repair and maintenance it is substantially less. Mechanisation is uneconomic for all except the largest maintenance operations and returns to modern management techniques dwindle as the scale of operations decreases. The smaller the scale of maintenance work the more intractable are the problems of raising productivity. Small firms, of 25 employees or fewer,[1] carry out over 48 per cent of repair and maintenance in the industry; the smaller the firm the greater the percentage of repair and maintenance work. In addition, the number of firms able to undertake this work is swelled in periods of downturn in demand for new work, particularly housing, and these have little incentive to improve capitalisation.

Site Work

Much construction activity is on site and thus vulnerable to climatic elements against which it is often difficult to provide much protection, at least in the early stages. The development of special plant and protective shelters has reduced these hazards but annual losses of building output are inevitable. Generally, United Kingdom winters are not severe enough for winter building techniques to be economic. The problems of building in winter and the related economic effects are international and many countries, including Canada, Sweden and Austria, have found it necessary to provide economic incentives to avoid these effects.

Management problems on site may be great. Site labour accounts for about one-third of the cost of construction. Much of this is casual employed for one scheme only and often inefficiently employed.[2] Exposure to site conditions reduces the life of plant and in many large contracts it will be written off at the end of the contract. It is less efficiently used than under factory conditions – a factor in the growth of the specialist plant-hire company. Materials and components on site account for about half the total cost of construction – their assembly requires considerable managerial expertise, especially as a project may take five years or more to complete. In fact, management expertise is one of the scarcest resources of the construction industry in the United Kingdom, as in many other countries.

Table 10.1 *Value of construction industry output Great Britain 1970–85 (£ million)*

	New housing		Other new work		Total new work	Total repair and maintenance	All work
	Public	Private	Public	Private (industrial and commercial)			
1970	689	737	1 370	1 230	4 026	1 550	5 576
1971	688	941	1 464	1 384	4 476	1 695	6 171
1972	698	1 218	1 595	1 493	5 003	1 991	6 994
1973	869	1 672	1 950	1 942	6 433	2 547	8 980
1974	1 122	1 467	2 140	2 316	7 046	2 987	10 032
1975	1 482	1 543	2 511	2 465	8 001	3 417	11 418
1976	1 795	1 798	2 748	2 438	8 780	3 765	12 544
1977	1 751	1 867	2 783	2 885	9 285	4 409	13 694
1978	1 786	2 426	2 960	3 497	10 669	5 477	16 147
1979	1 747	2 731	3 285	4 363	12 125	6 659	18 784
1980	1 753	2 652	3 785	5 374	13 562	8 473	22 036
1981	1 222	2 516	3 572	5 044	12 354	9 193	21 546
1982	1 021	2 899	3 671	5 038	12 629	9 911	22 540
1983	1 120	3 729	3 729	4 817	13 396	10 948	24 343
1984	1 077	3 831	3 833	5 452	14 192	12 011	26 203
1985	918	3 848	3 786	6 368	14 921	12 930	27 850

Source: Department of the Environment, *Housing and Construction Statistics.*

The Nature and Determination of Demand

The industry produces investment goods demanded not for their own sake but for their use in the production of less durable goods. This derived-demand for investment goods is unstable, emphasised as 50 per cent of the industry's output is demanded by the government; thus demand (although diminishing) is difficult to forecast as it will depend upon the varying economic and social policies pursued by governments. There are three major categories of demand: commercial and industrial developments whose construction will assist production; social types of development such as schools; and housing, a unique investment good, is also a consumer durable.

Tendering

In addition to the difficulty of estimating total work load for the industry, each construction firm is uncertain about future work loads. Because of the unique nature of so much of its output, the industry fixes its prices largely by competitive tender for individual contracts; tendering is either 'selected list' or 'open'.

Selected list

The selection of tenderers is made from a list or by an open invitation for firms to apply to tender. An objection to selective tendering is that lists may be too long and may not be an accurate reflection of the ability of firms. There is separation between design and construction and the possibility of collusion between firms on the list. Since the Banwell Report (1964)[3] an increasing proportion of public sector work, about 50 per cent of all work, is put out to selective tender, with generally up to eight firms invited to bid. The DOE uses selective tendering for almost all its work, whereas some local authorities, especially the smaller, have been slow to adopt the procedure, preferring the more uneconomic yet superficially more competitive open tendering. Selective tendering is used extensively in civil engineering and almost exclusively in major road contracts.

Open tender

The project is openly advertised and any firm may bid. The major objections are the lack of control of the client over the competence of the builder he is employing and the waste of resources when many firms tender for the same job because the prices for contracts obtained must overall cover the costs of estimating on jobs not obtained. Tendering is an expensive and uncertain process and while in theory open competition should result in the lowest cost for the client, in practice the lowest tender may not necessarily equal the best value. There is evidence that it is associated with less satisfactory performance.[4] Open-tendered projects are least likely to maintain final costs close to contract sums and average time overrun is greater than with projects let by other means. There may be grounds for 'spreading the net' in smaller projects but open competition tends to increase costs and uncertainties. There is also separation of design and construction. Under EEC directives it is possible that open tendering will return for large contracts.

It is not possible to anticipate very far in advance exactly what proportion of tenders will be successful. Research sponsored by the DOE indicated that the tendering success rate of firms is between 17 and 27 per cent by the number of bids.[5] There is therefore a tendency to bid for more contracts than are required, with the risk that at times the number of contracts and actual output will be far less than planned and at other times far more than can be handled efficiently. Thus contractors rarely know even within a relatively short time ahead upon what contracts they will be engaged. It is therefore difficult to plan future work loads so as to secure the most efficient use of resources and wastage is inevitable. The contractor may therefore encounter rapidly increasing costs.

Negotiated Contracts

Most private work is negotiated with a contractor chosen by preliminary tendering or else brought in at the design stage of the project. The involvement of the contractors so early on can lead to improvement in efficiency and savings to the client. It overcomes the separation of design and construction, which is a major disadvantage of tendering systems. A negotiated contract is particularly likely if the contract involves a patented design system or the expertise of a particular contractor. Because public accountability normally requires acceptance of the lower tender, negotiated contracts are less acceptable in the public sector as price may be higher. In 1974 14 per cent of all public building contracts were by negotiation, mainly in housing contracts.

Serial contract or tender

This is a variation of the negotiated contract and is usually negotiated with a firm that has successfully completed a similar contract. Normally there is a legal understanding that there will be a series of like contracts when the first is completed; this is advantageous to the contractor, who can plan a continuous programme of work. Lower costs to the contractor should result in the original price being keener than in normal contracts. Close collaboration is likely between design and construction and both time and cost overrun is less than average. Serial contracting is especially significant for system building and for small to medium-sized repetitive contracts as for housing or schools. Ideally, projects should be within a defined geographical area. Under EEC directive, the negotiation of additional contracts not part of the original competition is not permitted if in aggregate they exceed 50 per cent of the value of the original contract.

Package deals and 'fee construction'

Instead of appointing an architect, the client may go to a company offering a complete service of design and construction. In 1972 about a third of all factories and a quarter of offices were built by package deal[6] – they also represented about 8 per cent of all local authority housing contracts. Since the 1930s, Bovis has pioneered the 'fee construction' system, a radical departure from competitive tendering in which the contractor and client agree on a fee to be charged for management services, while the client meets all construction expenses. The contractor's risks are much lower but, in order to secure further business, he has every incentive to keep down the cost of construction. The system brings a close relationship between the client and contractor but is unacceptable to the public sector as the price for the project is not determined before work commences.

Once a tender has been accepted there is a variety of types of contract. Public sector contracts are let on a firm price when their duration is less than one year. Even in the private sector, the majority of contracts are on a firm-price basis. Thus on most contracts, contractors are assessing their costs over the period of the contract and their price before the contract is executed. This completely reverses the procedure in most of manufacturing industry where the producer has to determine his price only after the good has been produced and costs are known with reasonable certainty. In fact, with inflation in the 1970s, firm price contracts for local authority housing in England and Wales fell dramatically from 88.9 per cent of all contracts in 1970 to 7.2 per cent by 1979. Contracts with fluctuation clauses rose from 11.1 per cent in 1970 to 82.7 per cent in 1979.

Cost yardsticks

These can be used as a method of central control over costs. Although appropriate government departments required that tenders obtained by local authorities for housing work should be submitted for approval, it was not until 1967 that limits were imposed upon such tenders. There is clearly a need for such control; the disadvantage is that the yardstick is not reviewed often enough, consequently it fails to keep pace realistically with rising costs. Designers' time and effort is expended in trying to pare housing schemes to minimum standards and costs; and consequently maintenance costs are likely to be increased. By the 1980s, cost yardsticks were indexed to cost. Cost limits also apply to other public sector projects – for example, educational building and hospitals.

In addition, local authorities tend to be slow payers so that builders often run into borrowing difficulties. A report in 1975[4] commented that in 30 per cent of contracts, final accounts had not been agreed within twelve months of the defects liability period.

THE CONSTRUCTION INDUSTRY AND THE ECONOMY

The construction industry in the United Kingdom is of key economic importance because it is a major client of the government, and because of its size of output, numbers employed, and its contribution to the national stock of investment goods. It has been the subject of report by numerous government bodies. The value of the industry's output in the late 1970s was approximately 12½ per cent of the United Kingdom gross domestic product at factor cost. Net output after providing for depreciation was 6.8 per cent of gross domestic product and new work accounted for about 50 per cent of gross domestic fixed capital formation. The total number of employees in the industry was approximately 7½ per cent of the working population of the United Kingdom. There has subsequently been a decline in the industry's output to 9.2 per cent of the GDP in 1985 and an overall decline in contractors' operative employment, and also in local authority direct labour (table 10.2).

Table 10.2 *Employment in the construction industry, Great Britain, 1970–86*

	Employees in employment				Total (000s)
	Contractors		Public authorities		
	Operatives	APTC*	Operatives	APTC	
1970	882	221	262	103	1468
1971	826	219	252	110	1407
1972	831	224	253	113	1424
1973	863	241	242	116	1462
1974	874	240	233	110	1457
1975	820	240	233	113	1406
1976	788	237	236	114	1375
1977	756	229	230	112	1327
1978	750	231	224	111	1316
1979	770	236	220	113	1333
1980	760	235	215	111	1321
1981	659	226	207	105	1197
1982	619	223	187	95	1123
1983	600	214	183	88	1084
1984	585	214	172	84	1055
1985	556	213	169	84	1022
1986	530	212	160	82	985

*APTC: administrative, professional, clerical, technical staff.
Source: Department of the Environment, *Housing and Construction Statistics.*

According to the Organisation of Economic Cooperation and Development, Britain was bottom of the international league table of net spending on construction and infrastructure in 1985, spending only 6.1 per cent of its GDP on construction (compared with Japan's 17.1 per cent) and 0.7 per cent on infrastructure.

Some 50 per cent of new work (and 85 per cent of all civil engineering work) by contractors is for the public sector, and over half of gross domestic capital formation is for public bodies. Thus the government has a means of direct control over the output of the industry which is consequently directly affected early by any changes in economic policy. Thus its size – of critical importance as an investment goods industry and dependence upon the government as client – provides a key to the interrelationship between the industry and the economy. Changes in the output of the industry are too significant to ignore as they affect the size of the national product and the level of employment both directly and indirectly through the multiplier effect.

Post-war economic management has aimed at balance of payments equilibrium, full employment, economic growth, and control of inflation. These objectives have not always proved compatible and policy has varied. The easiest ways for the government to shift the economy in the direction required all affect construction either directly or indirectly. Interest rates may be increased and credit restricted, making it more difficult and expensive to borrow; taxation may be increased; public expenditure may be reduced. Measures may directly affect construction, projects above a certain value may be controlled or activity directed towards development areas. Changes in government grants, for example, for hotels and house improvements, can cause fluctuations in construction work. An effect of raising home improvement grants was a marked upswing in the repair and maintenance sector.

Effects of Government Policy

An increase in interest rates raises the cost of projects and causes postponement or cancellation of marginal schemes not yet started. Existing projects are likely to proceed but developers' profits are likely to be reduced (depending on the extent of borrowed funds). Future tenders will be increased. The effective demand for buildings will be reduced because at higher rates of interest, borrowers will not be able to raise such large sums. If interest rate increases are sharp or long term, the speculative developer will be hardest hit and overall there will be a downturn in construction activity. A credit squeeze will adversely affect many firms who depend on short-term bank finance during building; banks tend to reduce finance to builders early in a squeeze and not to start financing again until it is relaxed. Larger firms have a better credit rating and have access to alternative funds. The worst affected are likely to be medium-sized firms too big to exist on repair and maintenance work alone, and too small to reap the benefits of a large contract which smooths the work load and is probably heavily dependent on speculative new work. Prospective purchasers may not be able to raise funds and there will be a decline in demand for new work. A reduction in credit availability and a reduction in purchasing power in the economy will reduce demand for other goods and services. Plans for additional or replacement buildings are postponed; manufacturers postpone erection of new factories or offices. Thus there is a lower level of construction activity. Reductions in interest rates and easier credit have the reverse effects.

Cuts in government capital spending are likely to affect the construction industry in the longer or medium rather than short-term as there will be existing work and contracts already signed. Although overall construction activity will be reduced, not all sectors will be similarly affected; this will depend on government priorities – for example, road building may be cut back whereas the housing programmes are maintained. Similarly, tax changes will have varying effects although any increase in taxation leads to lower real income and thus a decline in demand for construction output. Any specific taxes on property or gains from property will adversely affect demand. Conversely, tax concessions for owner-occupiers lead to an increase in demand for owner-occupier houses. The net effects of increased taxation on the industry depend on the way in which tax proceeds are spent. If some of the increased tax revenue is spent on public construction, then the decrease in demand for construction will be less than if none of the tax revenue is used to finance public construction projects.

Contractors have been substantially affected by the fluctuations in economic policy which have contributed to the growth of larger firms and also the increased importance of subcontracting. Until 1969, 'stop-go' policies had not actually caused an absolute fall in the value of output undertaken, probably smoothed by the long contract period on big projects and also by the stability of the repair and maintenance output (table 10.1). As government action affects construction, so a change in construction output will affect employment and hence incomes and ultimately output of other sectors of the economy. The decline in construction activity is, after a time lag, injected back into the system.

A major difficulty in economic management is the problem of timing measures so that the effects of the action occur at the correct time to achieve the desired objective. The problems of using construction as a regulator are that lags tend to be long and variable. If the government reduces its capital expenditure it will not normally cut projects where work has started, the brunt of the impact must be on new orders. The build up of the work load on a contract is at first slow, then increases rapidly and towards the end of the project tails off. Thus if projects are cut, the reduction in the work load is not felt for perhaps a year or longer. This is a critical disadvantage as the major effect comes later and may coincide with the desire to re-stimulate the economy. The effects of the cuts remain for the subsequent year. Also contractors working in the public sector can obtain resources more easily if the cuts coincide with a drop in private sector demand (as is usually the case) because they can work more quickly on outstanding contracts. This can add up to a serious loss of work in the year following public expenditure cuts.

The consequences are serious: long-term programmes are completely disrupted; land already purchased for projects which are cut is held unproductively; design teams are dispersed and staff used less effectively. The repercussions tend to prove longer lasting than the period of the cut itself since programmes lose impetus and cannot be fully reinstated for some time after the restrictions have been withdrawn, and the capacity of the industry to undertake the new work will have been damaged.

Furthermore, it is very difficult to isolate one sector from the effects of the cuts. In December 1973, public expenditure cuts excluded public housing which the government was trying to increase. However, new housing requires, for example, new roads for access as well as shops and recreational facilities. There are also difficulties in switching resources between dissimilar sectors such as civil engineering and housing.

Thus the manipulation of public capital expenditure for medium-term economic management has considerable drawbacks for construction, bringing with it unemployment, a net outflow of trained men, many of whom never return, reduced recruitment and training, and excess material production capacity and and stocks and non-utilisation of contractor's plant together with increasing bankruptcies. The effect of cutbacks under Thatcherism in the 1980s was therefore to disrupt and undermine confidence and damage the industry's overall efficiency (see pages 327-330).

THE STRUCTURE OF THE INDUSTRY AND ITS ECONOMIC ORGANISATION

The structure of the construction industry is largely determined by the nature of the production process – but this, according to Ball,[7] is fundamentally influenced by land rent. Land rent (syphoned-off from surplus value) alters the profitability and feasibility of production methods by *either* reducing the proportion of surplus value available for investment,[8] *or* lowering the profitability of investment,[9] *or* altering the conditions and terms under which investment is undertaken.[10] Ball suggests that while rent does not significantly affect the production process in modern contract building, since it is the client that bears the costs of land and not the contractor, land rent has a major impact upon speculative building. The speculative builder buys up land when the property market slumps to ensure an adequate supply of sites for development when the market picks up. But in recent years (and particularly in South-east England) the market power of the landowner has increased at the expense of the builder since restrictive planning and green belt policy have produced artificial shortage of development land (chapter 8). This, together with the volatility of the property market in the 1970s and 1980s, has forced developers to disperse construction over many sites and/or to concentrate on small standardised runs. Low rates of output and sharp variations in demand therefore have a marked effect on building techniques; casual labour becomes a necessity; and physically fragmented tasks are not amenable to effective management control. Land prices are therefore not just residual in the Ricardian sense but are often synonymous with the concept of absolute rent (chapter 9). To compensate for being squeezed between high land costs and competitive product rises, builders have attempted to maintain their profitability by adopting production methods which are neither conducive to sustained productivity nor to the permanency of a skilled workforce. The effect upon both construction costs and property prices has thus been inflationary in the long-term – to the detriment of both the quantity and quality of building work.

The construction industry in the United Kingdom, moreover, is typified by a large number of small firms with extremely low capitalisation. Although numbers have declined, there are few clear signs of increasing firm size (table 10.3). Much work comprises small projects in repairs, improvements as well as new housing. As there is little scope for technical or managerial economies of scale, this work is best undertaken by locally based firms. Efficiency will depend upon the skill of the operative rather than on the organisation and capital provided by the firm.

Table 10.3 *Structure of the construction industry: number and size of firms, 1973–81*

Size of firm	1973	1977	1981
0–1	29 563	24 915	40 580
2–7	43 962	34 148	54 728
8–13	9 311	7 584	9 161
14–24	6 315	5 070	5 380
25–34	2 364	1 811	1 791
35–39	2 298	1 836	1 721
60–79	743	596	528
80–114	697	563	416
115–299	872	730	598
300–599	246	217	162
600–1199	125	116	82
1 200 and over	80	56	39
All firms	96 576	77 642	115 186

Source: Private Contractors' Census; Department of the Environment, *Housing and Construction Statistics.*

Number and Size of Firms

The fragmentation and numerical supremacy of the small firm is typical of most countries of Western Europe and the United States. In France approximately 200 000 firms employ fewer than 5 men while 50 per cent employ no operatives. Conversely, as in the United Kingdom, few firms employ 500 or more operatives. The typical firm tends to increase in size in countries with a large population concentrated in urban areas.

Little capital or qualification is required for entry into the industry and trade credit is available from builders' merchants. When construction work is profitable and demand is increasing, workers may become 'self-employed' to benefit from the situation. Many small firms have little incentive to remain if work is short and predictably exit from the industry is high – approximately 26 per cent of all bankruptcies in the 1970s were in construction. In 1975, 1522 firms failed with total liabilities of £4½ million, emphasising that it is the low-capitalised medium or small firm that is likely to fail.

Small Firms

Small firms employing 25 or fewer operatives, account for about 90 per cent of the total number of firms (see table 10.4). They are either general builders, specialist engineering and craft-based subcontractors, or plant-hire firms who are more heavily capitalised than the others. The 1971 enquiry indicated that small firms accounted for 23 per cent of net output, 27 per cent of new housing, 9 per cent of new non-housing work and 48 per cent of repair and maintenance. The smaller the firm the greater was the significance of repair and maintenance to the total value of output. The numbers of small firms have held up well. Medium-sized firms, including those not so dependent on repair and maintenance but doing some new work, suffer from their inability to raise finance at reasonable rates in a recession. In the last decade there has been the growth of single-person units not normally included in the industry census. Labour-only subcontracting will be discussed later. Employment by small firms fell from 40 000 to 320 000 over 1970–78 and as a percentage of the total employed from 31 to 27 per cent. In 1978, 28 551 firms employed one or less operatives.

Much of the output of the industry tends to be produced and assembled at the point of ultimate consumption, thus except for large contracts it is uneconomic for contractors to operate over long distances. Many small contractors regard their normal maximum radius as 25 km; the small repair firm may restrict itself to the immediate 8 km. There is a very imperfectly competitive market in which firms will compete largely with similar firms in the same area. The small firm complements the larger because each is serving different markets. Much maintenance work must be handled quickly and the larger firm may not have the flexibility to carry it out. The small firm will carry out new work which the

Table 10.4 *Employment of operatives by contractors, 1973–81 (000s)*

Size of firm	1973	1977	1981
0–1	29.0	24.5	40.5
2–7	157.4	122.0	180.8
8–13	94.1	74.7	91.5
14–24	113.6	90.6	96.3
25–34	68.3	53.0	51.7
35–39	102.1	81.7	76.1
60–79	50.7	40.9	36.2
80–114	65.6	53.3	39.1
115–299	151.8	128.9	105.0
300–599	103.7	89.8	68.3
600–1199	102.4	93.5	65.9
1200 and over	236.2	176.2	124.1
All firms	1274.9	1029.1	975.5

Source: Private Contractors' Census; Department of the Environment, *Housing and Construction Statistics.*

large firm may not want. In new housing it will specialise where it has local knowledge and reputation – an important selling point.

Labour turnover is lower in small firms – many employees remain for long periods; less use is made of labour-only subcontractors and demarcation is rarely a problem, partly because of low trade union membership. The national building strike of 1972 affected larger contracts and sites only. Output *per capita* is lower for small firms because of low capital input, largely a consequence of emphasis on repairs and maintenance, a difficult area in which to increase productivity. However, in overall financial control and pricing the small firm seems decidedly inferior.

Large Firms

While small firms prosper, it is the very large firms (employing over 1200 operatives) who are the most important employers and producers of total output, and who have the highest output per employee (see table 10.4). In 1978, this group accounted for only 0.05 per cent of all firms yet produced 16.5 per cent of total output compared with 21.5 per cent in 1973. Substitution of new materials and processes for labour has improved productivity and benefited the large contractors, as they are most able to take advantage of these developments.

Large firms are better equipped, financed and organised but their number is limited by the nature of the construction process. Difficulties of centralised supervision and management are more acute in construction than in manufacturing industry because firms may be concurrently engaged in work on widely scattered and constantly changing sites. The capacity of individuals to manage is limited and organisations can outgrow the capacity of managements. The greater the size of the firm, the more complex the organisation and the more remote the control and level of incentive on site. The increased costs of non-productive workers as firms grow may offset any savings achieved in the operative labour force or in economies of scale.

Size has advantages because finance may be obtained more easily and cheaply; large buying orders may bring economies in price; there is more economic use of indivisible resources such as specialised skills; risks can be spread over a wide range of contracts; and selling organisations may secure control over markets. The very large contractors cover the whole range of building and civil engineering nationally and overseas.

The size of the largest firms in the industry has steadily increased, largely because of amalgamations between contractors and property development companies. By the mid-1970s there were over 200 publicly quoted construction companies. The larger size of firm reflects the industry's adaptation to changing demand conditions in which the big firm has an advantage; changing cost structures and labour shortages have encouraged mechanisation and system building. Increasing standardisation of components, metrication and dimensional co-ordination have favoured the large firm with sufficient capital and resources to justify expensive plant and managerial skills. The increase in size of individual contracts, often beyond the resources of smaller firms has increased the incentive to form consortia or merge. Institutional involvement in property has brought links between property developers, institutions and contractors. The latter with proven ability to carry out large schemes have benefited because of the availability of finance. This has ensured a continuity of work allowing the very large contractor to survive variations of the construction cycle rather better than the small firm.

Although small contracts predominated numerically in 1978, 0.4 per cent of contracts for commercial building were over £2 million in value and these accounted for about £240 million of work or over a quarter of the value of orders for all commercial work. In public non-housing work, the other sector with very large contracts, 1.1 per cent of contracts accounted for £900 million or approximately 33 per cent of the total orders.

Subcontracting

Increasingly, main contractors have become coordinators of labour, materials and subcontract work. By 1975, £2890 million, about 40 per cent of gross output of civil engineers and builders, was being subcontracted. This trend is due fundamentally to the increasing number and complexities of services demanded in modern buildings and the advantages of specialists in increasing productivity and speed of completion. In addition, the uncertainty of future work load emphasises the advantages of not maintaining specialists but of using them only when required. Only contractors with large financial resources and a steady workload can operate their own specialist departments; these tender for outside work if they are not required by the parent company, thus capital is not tied up under-used. Similar considerations explain the growth of plant hire firms. The continuing shortage of skilled labour and uncertainty of job continuity with general builders has induced many craftsmen to join specialist subcontractors.

The organisation of subcontractors demands managerial expertise, and good communications between the specialist and the contractor. These qualities are often lacking on building sites, causing unnecessary delay, a high accident rate and lower productivity. Efficient organisation of subcontractors requires the main contractor to draw up detailed construction programmes informing the subcontractor well in advance when he is required on site, or informing him of any modification in programme, and to ensure that any necessary facilities are available. Subcontractors may be unable to programme their work efficiently if the main contractor is deficient in this respect.

Where subcontractors are nominated by the architect, because of expertise in specialised areas, they may adopt an independent attitude resented by the main contractor who is often chosen later. The latter prefer to have full control of subcontractors; they contend that the scale of appointment of nominated subcontractors is so great that the organisation of the contract may be jeopardised since it is more difficult to coordinate nominated subcontractors on the site. The practice may also reduce the competitive nature of contracting. There is a potential conflict of interest between architect and contractor; the former may carry the ultimate responsibility for poor quality work as a result of the contractor striking a hard bargain with a subcontractor. The main contractor must accept full responsibility for the organisation of the contract and the work of subcontractors.

A 1968 Report analysed how specialist contractors obtained their work. For large firms, about 60 per cent was by open tender and 23 per cent by selective or serial tendering, and about 17 per cent by nomination. For small firms, 32 per cent by open tendering and 28 per cent by selected or negotiated tender, and 41 per cent by nomination. Various reports have recommended that the main contractor be responsible for as much as possible of the subcontracting. If the nature of the scheme makes it necessary to nominate many specialists at an early stage, then the main contractor should join at this stage and be ready to take responsibility as leader on the production side.

Material Manufacturers

This sector reflects the industry as a whole, ranging widely in size, organisation and location. Generally, the extractive material industries such as sand and gravel quarrying will be located at the source of the material, as will firms heavily dependent upon a key material such as Oxford clay for fletton bricks. Firms producing components are more likely to be located closer to their market. There is a clear trend towards rationalisation; the mass market for many building materials is dominated by a small number of producers, often only one. The development of capital-intensive plant has squeezed the small producer out except where he can compete with the large manufacturer, either because the latter finds it uneconomic to deliver to some parts or because there are specialised products which can be made competitively by less automated methods.

The brick industry illustrates these features. By the early 1980s, the number of firms had fallen to about 200 compared with 900 in 1948. The fletton brick, which comprises about 45 per cent of the industry's output, is based on Oxford clay which requires no additives and is therefore cheaper to produce. London Brick produces about 95 per cent of fletton output from works concentrated in the Midlands. Its monopolist position has brought offical enquiries into the supply and price position from the Prices and Incomes Board and the Monopolies Commission.

The non-fletton industry producing facing and specialised bricks is in comparison widely scattered and comprises some 200 firms from public companies to family businesses. Whereas London Brick is heavily capitalised and automated, many of the smaller brick companies have low capitalisation and employ fewer than 25 men. The small local producer has low transport costs, a big factor in the brick price, and this gives protection within his market. Specialised quality facing bricks, sometimes hand made, are in demand to give interest to buildings.

The fortunes of brick manufacturers are closely tied to housebuilding activity as approximately 70 per cent of total brick output is used for new housebuilding. When housing activity booms as between 1972 and 1973 there is a great demand for bricks. This has led to bottlenecks and long waits in delivery – as the scope for importing is limited. At other periods, manufacturers have faced sharp declines in demand, mounting stocks of unsold bricks and underused capacity – as between 1980 and 1981 when brick works were at only 50 per cent capacity (figure 10.1). Such fluctuations in demand have adverse effects upon manufacturers' willingness to invest in additional capacity at a time of boom. Furthermore, in recessions many smaller, yet regionally important firms go bankrupt, brickworks become derelict and the industry is consequently less able to meet a recovery of demand.

The cement industry is dominated by a few large companies – Associated Portland being the largest producer of cement in the world. Small companies survive because transport costs are important in the cement price. Cement manufacturers are linked with fluctuations in construction generally, but they are less dependent upon one sector than are brick manufacturers and there is also a growing export trade. Sand and roadstone quarrying is dominated by small companies located at the source of material. The glass and plasterboard industries are monopolistic situations. Ceramic sanitary wares include companies among the

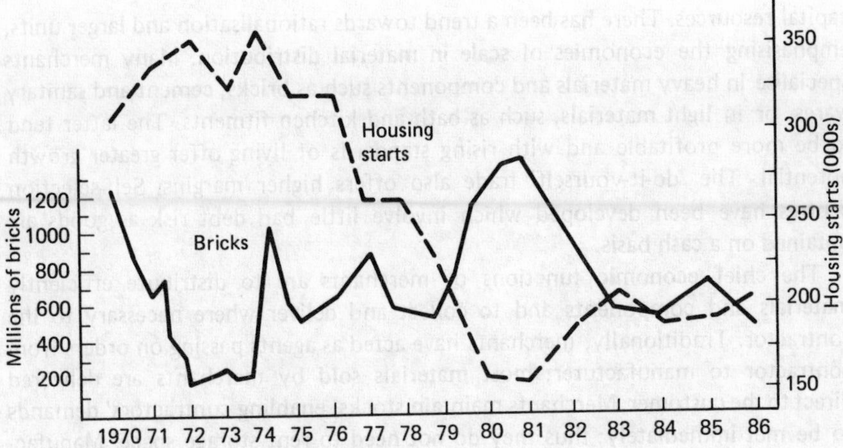

Figure 10.1 *Brick stocks and housing starts*

largest manufacturers of ceramics in the world and about 30 per cent of output is exported. In 1980, the largest cement producer took over the largest ceramics' manufacturer, after reference to the Monopolies Commission. The timber trade has been considerably rationalised and great technological strides have been seen.

Government cutbacks in the economy will vary in effects. A decline in housebuilding starts will affect brick manufacturers immediately, plasterboard and flooring tile manufacturers later. Some materials are exclusively demanded by construction whereas others — for example, glass, iron and steel — are widely used in other industries. The energy crisis and increasing oil costs affected material manufacturers through changing demands. Building regulations' thermal insulation standards were improved to a point where they almost doubled the requirements for roof and wall insulation. Timber-framed housing which could provide substantially greater levels of wall insulation compared with traditional brick construction became increasingly common as many of the larger builders switched to this form of construction. There was stimulus for the brick and block manufacturers to design blocks and bricks with higher insulating qualities. The switch from metals to plastics continued, although higher costs meant that oil-based materials became less competitive. Road builders switched from bitumastic to concrete construction. There was increasing stimulus to changes in house design, in particular to reducing window space, and developments such as solar-control glass to collect the sun's energy and use the fabric of the house to store the heat for later distribution.

Builders' Merchants

The great bulk of building materials, some £2000 million in 1980, is handled by builders' merchants. The merchants are widely located, and vary in size and capital resources. There has been a trend towards rationalisation and larger units, emphasising the economies of scale in material distribution. Many merchants specialise in heavy materials and components such as bricks, cement and sanitary wares, or in light materials, such as bath and kitchen fitments. The latter tend to be more profitable and with rising standards of living offer greater growth potential. The 'do-it-yourself' trade also offers higher margins. Self-selection centres have been developed which involve little bad debt risk as goods are obtained on a cash basis.

The chief economic functions of merchants are to distribute efficiently materials and components and to collect and deliver where necessary to the contractor. Traditionally, merchants have acted as agents passing on orders from contractor to manufacturer; most materials sold by merchants are delivered direct to the customer. Merchants maintain stocks, enabling contractors' demands to be met immediately; thus they do not need to rent storage space. Manufacturers are assisted as merchants deal with the small, uneconomic order, breaking bulk and are thus able to give the purchaser a lower price than would otherwise have been possible. Stockholding also gives the manufacturer a more stable demand. Merchants give technical advice and advance the sale of new materials, especially when the manufacturers provide necessary technical literature. Traditionally, merchants have granted trade credit to builders although, with higher rates of interest, credit control has improved significantly.

Generally the sector is better able to withstand the cycle of construction demand than the material manufacturers, although there is a strong dependence on the level of consumer spending and credit availability. Do-it-yourself and the emphasis on improvement after the Housing Act 1969 have provided a useful base as demand from small builders engaged in renovation has cushioned merchants from the worst effects of any new housing downturn.

LABOUR

The construction industry is labour-intensive, much of it skilled, and there have been persistent shortages in the traditional building crafts since 1945. The industry was one of the first for which a training board was set up under the Industrial Training Act 1964. The prime objectives were to secure an adequate supply of properly trained men and an improvement in the efficiency of training and to share costs more evenly. The Construction Industry Training Board was set up to make levies on firms in the industry and to give grants for approved courses of training. The Act emphasised that demands upon the industry were likely to increase at a time when significant new techniques and methods were being introduced.

The total manpower in the industry is difficult to assess accurately but DOE statistics indicate that numbers employed declined between 1970 and 1986 from about 1.5 million to 985 000, about 6 per cent of the working population.

Operatives employed by contractors declined from 882 000 to 530 000 (in 1986) (table 10.2). Significantly, the number of administrative, technical and clerical workers has increased; construction has become more management orientated in order to increase the output of expensive site operatives.

About 40 per cent of the industry's labour force is under the age of 30, compared with 30 per cent in all industries.[11] There appears to be a clear outflow past 30, emphasising the discomforts of site work and discontinuity of employment. Labour turnover is about twice as high as in industry generally, although there are differences. Employment is relatively stable in many small firms and in the public sector. The greatest turnover is with large civil engineering firms where labour may be employed for one contract only and will not remain stable even for the duration of the contract. A survey by the Institute of Building on personnel policies in the industry in 1974 showed that only 30 per cent of firms employing between 115 and 1199 men had a personnel department and only 50 per cent a personnel policy at all. Unstable employment is associated with high rates of unemployment. The percentage unemployed in construction at any time is usually twice the national average (figure 10.2) and the gap widens in the winter period. The industry's vulnerability to the weather causes much casual

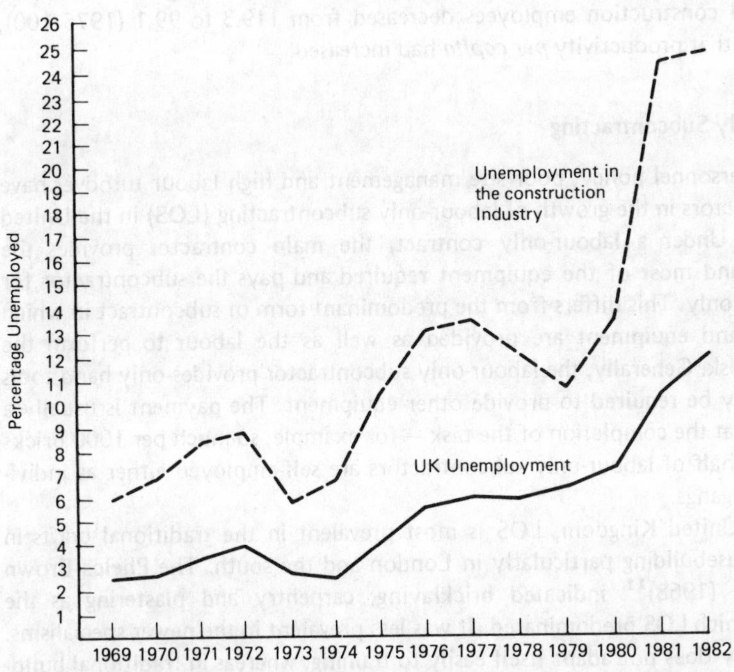

Figure 10.2 *Unemployment in construction as compared with national rates, 1969–86 (source: Central Statistical Office,* Economic Trends; *Department of Employment,* Housing and Construction Statistics)

unemployment. Winter unemployment in the United Kingdom is likely to be about 60 per cent higher than the summer total. Because of the imperfections of the market, high unemployment may exist alongside labour shortages.

About 75 per cent of operatives are employed by contractors, the balance by public authorities. Approximately half are craftsmen for whom apprenticeship or similar training is the usual method of entry. Apprenticeship was reduced from five years to four in 1963 to speed up the intake of skilled men. However, the raising of the school leaving age and a poor public image have adversely affected the flow of new recruits. The fairly clear dividing line which once existed between the craft operatives and other labour has become blurred, especially in small firms, thus reflecting the diversity of building operations and making it impossible to bring in different crafts every time a new material or method is introduced. In larger firms there has been the growth in new skills associated with new technological developments. These have both affected the range of work undertaken by an existing occupation and affected a radical alteration in the work content so that a substantially new occupation is created.

The United Kingdom GDP at 1975 prices increased between 1967 and 1978 by about 170 per cent. Over the same period construction output, all work, measured at 1975 prices, fell from 115.3 to 101.9 with a peak of 122 in 1972. These figures emphasise construction's vulnerability to changes in economic policy All construction employees decreased from 119.3 to 99.1 (1975 100), suggesting that productivity *per capita* had increased.

Labour-only Subcontracting

Lack of personnel policy, poor site management and high labour turnover have all been factors in the growth of labour-only subcontracting (LOS) in the United Kingdom. Under a labour-only contract, the main contractor provides the materials and most of the equipment required and pays the subcontractor for his labour only. This differs from the predominant form of subcontract in which materials and equipment are provided as well as the labour to perform the specified task. Generally, the labour-only subcontractor provides only hand tools but he may be required to provide other equipment. The payment is usually a lump sum at the completion of the task – for example, so much per 1000 bricks laid. Over half of labour-only subcontractors are self-employed either as individuals or in gangs.

In the United Kingdom, LOS is most prevalent in the traditional crafts in private housebuilding particularly in London and the south. The Phelps Brown Committee (1968)[11] indicated bricklaying, carpentry and plastering as the trades in which LOS predominated. It was less prevalent in the newer specialisms. Labour-only does not adapt itself easily to training, whereas in traditional building there is a series of familiar repetitive tasks and methods. Labour-only operatives move from site to site carrying out a limited, fairly uniform range of operations; where there are new and unfamiliar techniques this is not possible.

Full employment and the persistent demand for construction output has resulted in great pressure on resources and particularly in skilled labour. Thus labour-only contractors have had good prospects of continuous employment and tend to earn more than direct employees doing similar work. Generally, payment to labour-only subcontractors is on a 'piece' basis, thus there is a clear relationship between effort and reward; they are able to achieve a greater control over earnings than under a more complicated, bonus scheme. Many employers see LOS as a way of raising productivity through simple forms of incentive. The 1968 Report indicated that 53 per cent of employers believed that LOS productivity was higher than direct labour employed. LOS also provided labour which could not be satisfied elsewhere – for instance, in remote areas where direct labour might not be willing or able to travel. LOS is useful for meeting peak demands for labour, providing an efficient, productive capacity which can swiftly be mobilised without the need to hire and then dismiss direct labour. A crucial incentive to LOS has been the increasing charges on employed labour. These include the Construction Industry Training Levy, Selective Employment Tax (1966–73), redundancy fund contributions, employer insurance contributions, and holiday and sick pay. All these levies and their administration are avoided by the employer whose work is carried out by labour-only, self-employed operatives.

There are also difficulties largely reflecting poor site management. The quality of the work may be more variable although the 1968 Report commented that only 25 per cent of employers thought that quality was worse than that of direct labour. There were complaints of wastage of materials and unfinished work, and also a general impression of neglect of safety precautions, yet there is no evidence that accidents on site are more common among labour-only operatives compared with direct labour. LOS tends to be more difficult to control than direct labour; there may also be more uncertainty as to when the gang might work and lack of cooperation with other subcontractors. There is a wide variety of labour-only subcontractors ranging from the established craft operative maintaining very high productivity and gang leader to the 'fly-by-night' operative with little pride in his work and no standards.

A major criticism of LOS is its effects upon training and apprenticeship. Clearly, men whose aim is to complete a given task as quickly as possible do not want to include a learner in their team or to interrupt their own work to instruct him. There is great concern at the collapse of effective training in the basic craft skills in which LOS predominates. The gravitation of an increasing number of craft operatives towards LOS has substantially reduced the training facilities available in companies which are subject to the Construction Industry Training levy. It is precisely from these tradesmen that trainees would gain their on-site experience. There have been increasing demands for labour-only gangs to include apprentices. Surveys carried out by the National Federation of Building Trades Employers indicate the inverse relationship between the number of labour-only subcontractors and apprentices in the London and Midlands areas and particularly the high proportion of LOS in private housing co-existing with the small number of apprentices.[12]

There are administrative difficulties in dealing with LOS, in particular there is the evasion of taxation and insurance. It has been estimated that the Inland Revenue have been deprived of over £10 million annually. Various attempts have been made since 1968 to control the worst excesses of the 'lump', beginning with the recommendations of the 1968 committee who suggested that all employers should be registered. In 1970, a Bill was introduced to set up a voluntary register for contractors. In 1971, employers were directed to deduct 30 per cent of payments to sub-contractors unable to produce certificates showing that they were *bona fide* with the tax inspector. Registered companies were automatically exempted. In 1977, all building subcontractors were to apply to the Inland Revenue for registration after meeting certain conditions. If accepted, they were issued with a tax certificate – the '714'. It was also suggested that the industry might be policed by an administrative board similar to that in France and Germany.

At best, LOS combines the continuous labour of the specialist subcontractor, higher productivity and flexibility. At worst, it produces faulty work by irresponsible men concerned only with the greatest possible gains in the short run. There is clearly a gap between the industry's collective approach which condemns the practice and the individual companies who exploit it. This duality results in differentials in earnings on the same site and is a consequent source of disputes. However, until firms can offer continuity of employment, improved contracts and better incentives, men will continue to exploit the shortages of skilled craft operatives in the industry.

Regionally, labour-only tends to vary inversely with trade union strength. In construction, unionism is generally strong where unemployment levels are relatively high and where operatives are less likely to negotiate individually from a vulnerable position. Post-war, until the 1970s, the United Kingdom enjoyed relatively low levels of unemployment, a situation conducive to LOS but not to union membership. In addition, trade unionism in construction has been hampered by its fragmented nature. A large number of sites existing for short periods all over the country and the absence of a stable labour force make organisation and negotiation very difficult. Consequently, unions have pressed for the control and registration of LOS; however, their ability to force employers to dispense with labour-only has been reduced by the overall labour shortage in the industry and particularly in the skilled trades. Trade union membership tends to be low compared with manufacturing industry although it increases with the size of firm. The 1968 Report indicated that 78 per cent of businesses with fewer than eight employees had no union members; conversely 34 per cent of companies with 300 or more employees had 90 per cent or over union labour. The report also confirmed that trade union membership was high in the North of Britain, less organised in the South and Midlands and that the greater the value of the contract the greater the proportion of trade union operatives. Thus in the national building strike of 1972, it was the larger sites which were primarily affected.

The growth of LOS and the fragmentation of building work are not the only reasons why trade union influence is weak in the construction industry. Since 1979, direct labour organisations (DLOs) were expected to show a return of 5 per cent on capital employed, while subsequently the Direct Labour Act 1981 compelled local authorities to put out for tender all but the smallest jobs. Yet DLOs were required to adopt accountancy procedures which showed an anticipated profit or loss on *each* of their activities. Under these conditions, DLOs found it difficult to secure work in the face of competition from the private sector not tied to the same constraint, or were wound up by the government for consistently not complying with official requirements. Since DLOs were highly unionised, a substantial reduction in their activity weakened trade union influence within the construction industry.

A further reason for the weakness of trade unionism in the industry is the lack of unity. There are four main unions in the industry: the Union of Construction and Allied Trade Technicians (UCATT) (with over 200 000 members out of a total 'eligible' workforce of nearly 700 000); the Transport and General Workers (TGWU) (representing about 100 000 unskilled operatives); and the Amalgamated Union of Engineering Workers (AUEW) and Electrical, Electronic, Telecommunications and Plumbing Union (EETPU) both with comparatively small memberships within the industry; yet there is all too often an absence of cohesion in philosophy, policy and tactics – particularly with regard to the problem of LOS.

Although LOS has been an anathema to trade unions since it is associated with (in their view) the unacceptable exploitive nature of piecework, UCATT has recently showed signs of being willing to allow its members to work with *bona-fide* subcontractors – for example, UCATT (and the TGWU) signed an agreement in 1987 with the newly formed Federation of Brickwork Contractors (a grouping of bricklaying subcontractors operating in the South-east of England).[13]

TECHNICAL DEVELOPMENTS IN THE CONSTRUCTION INDUSTRY: SYSTEM BUILDING

As traditional building costs have spiralled, so increasing consideration has been given to switching from conventional methods to system or industrialised building. This latter embraces many facets, combining aesthetic value and user satisfaction with economy of materials, factory production and quality control methods entailing the maximum use of off-site prefabrication. New materials and techniques will be used including the use of dry processes, increased mechanisation of site processes, improved management techniques, the correlation of design and production, and better organisation and training of operatives on site, using new skills or fully rationalised traditional methods. Ultimately, more parts of a building will be in their final form when erected so that much site work becomes an assembly of factory-made components.

The advantages of industrialised over traditional building are economies in time and labour. The DOE has reported it possible to reduce the time required to build a house from over 2000 man-hours to 1300 when there was a series of large contracts each of about 500 houses.[14] Saving in construction time is effected by a division of labour between factory and site, using them as a single production line; by protecting labour from variable site conditions; by producing better quality and more complex components under controlled factory conditions free from factors which limit productivity on site; by reducing the number of operations and mechanising a high proportion of them; and by increasing the scope for modern management techniques, permitting complex operations to be organised smoothly. Quick completion brings an early return in rent, reduces site supervision, and enables capital to be released for further work.

Industrialised building (and to a lesser extent traditional) will be more economic the larger and more repetitive the contract. The costs per unit of a manufactured product will fall as the production run is extended, although after a point the rate of reduction in costs falls off. In Finland the costs of doors fell by 14 per cent when the production run was increased from twenty to fifty, but only by 5 per cent when increased from 200 to 500.[15] The more times a system is used the more economic it is likely to be.

The manufacturer given a large order over an extended period can invest in new machinery, plan his production flow efficiently and thereby reduce waste. Fixed costs spread over a long run of production reduce unit cost. The contractor benefits, being able to programme more accurately, increasing efficiency and making continuous use of site labour. The designer benefits and techniques of briefing may be systematically developed for the programme more thoroughly than could be possible for each individual building.

Similarly, in very large single projects more time is available to analyse and solve user's requirements. As a result, architects' output can be greatly increased. The repetitive nature of system building allows the quantity surveyor more time in positive advice to architect and client. Cost planning becomes more accurate.

Although systems demand the development of new skills, notably in the site assembly of prefabricated components, the pressure upon the traditional crafts is reduced. However, the differential advantage in wage rates of skilled as against unskilled workers is smaller in the United Kingdom than in most other countries so there is less incentive to use techniques which replace skilled by unskilled workers. Also, labour costs of site workers are generally less than those of factory workers. Thus there are less advantages in transferring work away from the site. Systems do reduce the amount of site labour, total man-hours may be less than 50 per cent of the traditional figure. Seeley[14] estimates the labour requirements per dwelling using traditional building as about 1800 site man-hours; in industrial building from 700 to 1300 per dwelling, depending on the buildings and systems. Difference between labour requirements for conventional and system building is likely to increase in tall buildings because these are better suited to industrial techniques.

Thus, increased mechanisation can speed up production and may result in reduced costs of construction, for example, on small sites the use of power tools or larger cranes and fork lift trucks; on all sites the extensive use of prefabricated components which have eliminated many of the time-consuming 'wet' trades. In addition, the developments in organisation and materials in non-traditional building have stimulated the industry and represent an important gain.

Yet mechanisation of the industry has not proceeded as rapidly as might have been expected. Fundamentally, system building is only economic when high productive efficiency more than offsets additional factory overheads, and this will depend upon a high and stable demand to justify the high initial capital input. This stability has been absent in the United Kingdom, aggravated by a local government structure which until reorganisation comprised some 1500 housing authorities. The average local authority contract was for fewer than 50 houses, and well over 80 per cent of local authorities had annual programmes of fewer than 100 dwellings.[14]

In addition, the total costs of a building constructed by industrialised methods are not determined by factory costs alone. Problems may arise fixing prefabricated parts on site because factory tolerances are much stricter than those on site. This has led to serious conflicts between the use of traditional methods and the installation of prefabricated components. Many of the potential advantages of prefabrication can be lost by poor design details, leaving awkward work to be carried out by traditional methods. Also, site handling costs for the largest prefabricated components are high. There is need for expensive capital equipment and highly qualified personnel.

Industrial building may have lowered the aesthetic quality of the built environment, and may have reduced the expected life of buildings and increased the maintenance liability of buildings erected. Economic use requires the minimum departure from standard design; thus the client has to accept a more restricted choice than with traditional building.

The difficulty in achieving economy by use of the system building lies in the small proportion of the costs of the dwelling in which economies can be achieved in this way. Economies are largely limited to the structure itself and to services in walls and floors – probably no more than a quarter of the total costs. Moreover, to prefabricate and save on labour it is necessary to use precision materials and plant which are more expensive than traditional methods. Basically, in the United Kingdom the cost relationships are less favourable to systems than in many other countries. Traditional building is based on the brick which dimensionally may not be very accurate; it favours small building units and does not lend itself to factory prefabrication. It is also very cheap compared with basic materials available in many countries.

Local Authority Housing and Industrial Building Costs

The DOE publish statistics on the cost of construction of local authority dwellings, but no clear-cut picture emerges. Tender prices for industrialised houses and bungalows in 1964 were 10 per cent higher than for traditional building, flats of two to four storeys were 8 per cent more expensive; but by 1971 the advantage had moved to industrial dwellings, and traditional methods were more expensive by 5 per cent (although flats were 11 per cent higher by traditional methods). This advantage was held by industrial building through to 1978. Flats in five storeys or more (high rise) were cheaper by industrial methods than traditional even in 1964, and were about 18 per cent cheaper by 1971; yet by the second half of 1973 traditional methods were cheaper, primarily reflecting the lower demand for high rise developments and therefore lower economies of scale. These figures are difficult to interpret because they reflect tenders approved rather than actual costs, and they also do not indicate whether the contracts were profitable. By 1975, in all sectors except houses and bungalows, industrialised building was cheaper than traditional. By 1978 there was a dramatic switch in cost advantage to traditional.

The amount of industrialised building (table 10.5) was relatively small in the early 1960s and costs using more capital and less labour were higher than dwellings built using traditional methods. However, between 1964 and 1967 as more resources were shifted to public housing, industrialised dwellings started increased from 28 000 to 66 000. By 1967, industrialised building was used in 42 per cent of public sector starts, over half in high rise flats. From 1968 to 1971, industrialised dwellings fell from 38 to 19 per cent of public sector approvals. Consequently, industrial building became less competitive with traditional, even for high rise blocks of flats. Whereas in 1967, 20 000 high rise flats had been built using industrialised building methods, by 1972 it had dropped to less than 1 per cent of public sector approvals.

High rise, in which industrialised systems have played such a dominant role, never recovered from the shock to public confidence caused by the Ronan Point disaster, May 1968. In addition there were growing doubts about the social and economic aspects of high rise housing. In fact, by this date high-rise blocks were already in decline. There were three total weaknesses in the high-rise block, one of which existed from the start while the others developed with the programme. The first was the inadequacy of the lift services. In council blocks, lifts were always on the extreme limit of allowable expenditure. They were neither fast nor large enough; provision was basically inadequate and they broke down often. The second fault was basic: as demand outstripped supply with the rapid post-war growth in population and new households, housing managers were forced to house families with small children for which the blocks were totally unsuitable. The third failure was in management and maintenance. The rapidly growing council housing stock was outstripping both. The fate of the notorious block of flats in Liverpool known as 'the piggeries' – rendered uninhabitable by vandalism and the collapsing social framework characteristic of the deprived urban area and ultimately sold for a token sum to private enterprise – epitomised the failure of this attempt to cope with the problems of post-war housing.

The overall decline in public sector housing from 146 000 approvals in 1965 to 55 435 in 1972 (Great Britain) adversely affected system building. There was also a decline in the use of industrialised methods for low rise building, indicating local authority preference for traditional methods (table 10.5). Although the Labour Government in 1974 indicated that more resources would be diverted to local authority housing, the economic recession of the early 1980s severely affected all public spending, and housing expenditure as a percentage of total government expenditure declined from 10 per cent to less than 5 per cent by 1980.

Table 10.5 *Dwellings built by non-traditional methods: local authorities and New Towns in England and Wales, 1965–79*

	Total	Percentage of all dwellings
1965	25 527	14.4
1970	55 701	41.3
1971	38 314	32.7
1972	24 557	26.2
1973	17 660	22.3
1974	24 536	24.7
1975	25 792	21.0
1976	23 780	19.6
1977	19 697	16.2
1978	10 313	10.7
1979	4 566	6.3

Source: Department of the Environment, *Housing and Construction Statistics.*

The biggest impact of systems outside local authority housing has been in schools, and by 1973 systems accounted for 44 per cent of all major projects started. In hospital building, progress has been slow.

Any system depends upon the extent of its market to be profitable. Most of the early systems were 'closed' systems whereby components were designed for use together in similar schemes, thus the market for a particular system was relatively restricted. Only a few of the many hundred systems evolved really succeeded, and the number has been drastically reduced but still numbers over 50. Open systems have evolved whereby components can be bought off the peg and put together in any scheme and so provide the designer with a wider range of choice. The future of open systems depends upon the development of a mass market for prefabricated components, which has been limited by the non-standardised demand for construction output and lack of policies to rationalise demand and long-term building programmes of public authorities.

In 1964, the National Building Agency was established to provide assistance in the use of industrialised methods. It disseminates information about existing industrial housing methods, advising on systems and bulk ordering – enabling a large number of small demands to be collated into a satisfactory programme. Fundamentally, production must be of a sufficient scale to allow the spreading of capital costs and sometimes expensive teething troubles. Costs may be initially higher than traditional but systems such as CLASP for schools have shown that industrial building can produce substantial economies over traditional methods provided there is sufficient size and continuity of contracts.

Perhaps the most radical prospect for the 1980s is a good factory-delivered house. If the costs are right, the potential benefits of quality, a more structured factory environment and avoidance of disruption by weather are obvious. The 'volumetric' house has been produced for sale. The houses are built timber-framed in four sections with all the plumbing, electrics, heating and internal finishes incorporated. Each house takes ten days to build the sections in the factory, one day to fit the sections together on site and then two days to brick-clad the house. Production cost is reported slightly higher than site assembly, but this is offset by interest savings.[16] Other houses have been produced that are traditional in appearance using a concrete panel structure, and they have been used on a local authority build-for-sale scheme.

Metrication and Dimensional Coordination; Computer Applications

Industrialised building may be boosted by metrication and dimensional coordination with all components related to a common set of dimensions ultimately on an international basis. Great progress has been made in the public sector in the United Kingdom where approximately 90 per cent of work is dimensionally coordinated compared with 55 per cent in the private sector. All new work for government departments since the beginning of 1973 has been designed in metric units, dimensionally coordinated where possible. As the use of standard units grow so prices should fall, with the greatest savings from standardisation being in the most complex components. The system will allow interchange of parts and flexibility in design, and assist manufacturers in stockpiling to even out production over time. Increasing standardisation of components may be expected to accelerate the process of concentration in the industry.

In construction, computers are widely used for accounting purposes. While some large firms own computers, many make use of computer bureaux. Major contractors have been increasingly concerned with the development of computerised management control systems embracing the whole building process from tender to completion. An essential part is the analysis of each project into its constituent activities which form the basis of tendering. During the contract, requirements for cash and other resources can be predicted and the deviation of costs and performance from what was predicted can be measured, enabling remedial action to be taken. One great benefit is expected to be cheaper and more accurate tendering for contracts.

Construction Overseas

The EEC has yet to provide a market for the United Kingdom construction industry. In-built restrictions in the various countries are very great and there is little prospect of any fundamental change in the near future. The total capacity of the construction industry of the nine EEC members is between 6 and 10 per cent of GNP of the countries concerned, and its labour force of approximately 23 million accounts for approximately 10 per cent of total labour.

Some steps have been taken towards harmonising conditions in each country within the basic principles of the EEC that barriers, both fiscal and social, should in time be removed between the constituent states. Freedom of movement of labour and equal opportunities for employment imply that EEC nationals have a right to employment in any member state. Harmonisation has not to date extended to the question of mutual recognition of qualifications in such areas as architecture and civil engineering. In the case of the quantity surveyor, there is no equivalent profession in Europe outside the United Kingdom, although some of the basic training is incorporated in other disciplines. This is an opportunity of which many United Kingdom consultant quantity surveyors are aware, and there has been some development towards the spread of this profession by firms opening up offices in centres such as Brussels and Paris. Elsewhere, professional education and practice differ considerably between the countries. For example, in West Germany and the Netherlands, the education and qualifications of architects and engineers are closely related while in France they are completely separate. A further difficulty has been that the EEC approach has been to equate academic study as a measure of equivalence and professional qualification. Since the United Kingdom joined in 1973 there has been more pressure for more weight to be given to practical experience in relation to academic study.

Since the formation of the EEC, there has been no significant increase in inter-community construction work brought about by its existence. There has been no great influx of work on a competitive basis. Clearly, the practical advantage lies with local companies for general construction work. The barriers against change are appreciable. Safety standards, technical differences and language all play their part, thus the relatively low significance for British contractors of the EEC.

EEC Directive 71/305 (1971) was the first practical step in the direction of giving contractors in each country at least the same opportunity of knowing what work was available for bidding. Projects with a value of over one million

Units of Account (approximately £415 000) must be advertised in the *Official Journal of the European Commission*. Generally, only when this procedure has been followed and failed to get any response is the client free to adopt other negotiation if he chooses.

There may be possibilities for increasing work not within the EEC itself but with associated states eligible for financial aid through the European Development Fund; these include a number of Commonwealth territories in Africa and elsewhere. The more highly complex schemes may well depend upon international participation involving multi-national consortia well suited to the expertise and financial resources of the largest United Kingdom contracting companies.

Outside the EEC, total overseas contracts undertaken by United Kingdom contractors increased dramatically from some 5.3 per cent of all United Kingdom output in 1972 to over 15 per cent by 1975. In 1975–76, some 80 United Kingdom companies won contracts worth over £1400 million, with the six largest taking two-thirds of the business. In addition, there was £1135 million value of work outstanding and the construction industry was able to make a contribution (including overseas earnings of surveyors, engineers and architects) of more than £350 million to the balance of payments.

The dominant factor in the mid-1970s was the sharp fall in home construction demand coinciding with a great oil-financed demand overseas for construction on a massive scale. In the oil-producing countries there were national plans on a vast scale in which construction projects constituted well over half. For example, Saudi Arabia's second five year plan called for spending of £63 000 million over the period from 1975 to 1980, of which 60 per cent was to be on development. The Middle East was thus the major growth area with £600 million of new orders in 1976, mainly in civil engineering projects. Europe outside the EEC, North and South America and Australia were other important areas. United Kingdom contractors with well established reputations had much to offer in consultancy skills, manufacturing technology and project management.

By the mid-1980s, however, United Kingdom companies looking overseas for markets found demand had severely slumped. Contracts won in 1985–86 were 37 per cent below their peak value in 1982–83 – largely a result of falling oil revenues and the depressed Middle East market.[17] Although only a small number of United Kingdom companies undertake overseas contracts (10 firms handling as much as 90 per cent of the work), depressed demand overseas in the mid-1980s encouraged construction activity to shift back to the United Kingdom – increasing the degree of competition in the relatively comfortable home market.[17]

Contracting activity overseas is dependent upon factors such as political stability, security of payment, local taxes and contract law, and the extent of competition. Tendering is expensive and complex and is likely to deter smaller companies. The United Kingdom Construction Exports Advisory Board has been formed to stimulate more effort by contractors in export markets. For large firms, overseas work is seen as a useful cushion against recession in the domestic market. It has also encouraged joint ventures and multi-national consortia working.

Comparisons between construction projects in the United Kingdom, in Europe and in North America indicate the following features. The total time that elapses from the inception of a scheme to its completion is considerably longer in the United Kingdom than in other countries. The preliminary stages of design, pricing and application and grant of planning permission in the United Kingdom are more complex and more time-consuming than elsewhere. Also greater uncertainty exists for the applicant as to whether or not the requisite permission will eventually be granted. Unit costs in the United Kingdom are comparable with European countries but costs in North America were significantly lower. Because of longer programme times, the final development costs of projects are greater in the United Kingdom.

Conclusions

The major problems facing construction are the continual pressure of land costs and the cyclical nature of demand for its output; the economic policy objectives of governments have frequently conflicted with stability in the industry; also there are fluctuations in demand for construction output outside the control of government. Allowing that fluctuation will inevitably occur, the aim of the government and the industry must be to alleviate, as much as possible, the undesirable effects of these fluctuations. But both government and industry failed to do this. Under Thatcherism in the 1980s, the downturn in council house building, public sector contracts in general and new industrial and commercial work was particularly severe. There were fewer council houses built in 1986 than in any other peacetime year since 1923, and in 1986 public-sector housebuilding was accounting for under 10 per cent of the total new work of the construction industry by value compared with 20 per cent a few years earlier. Unemployment in the construction industry (already having risen from 60 000 to 160 000, 1972–79) escalated rapidly to 366 000 by 1982. One in eight of the unemployed in Britain were redundant construction workers, and the labour force of the industry shrank from 1 587 000 to 981 000, 1973–83. There was a danger that there would be too few craftsmen available either to build new houses or to rehabilitate dwellings on the scale needed when economic recovery came. All sectors of the industry were affected – private firms, direct labour organisations, architects and planners. Even the normally resilient fields of repair, maintenance and improvement, were not immune. Taking into account administrative and professional manpower, unemployment in the industry (broadly defined) reached 480 000 by 1982.

The industry suffered from severe under-capacity. The National Federation of Building Trade Employers claimed that fewer than 20 per cent of firms were operating at full or near capacity in 1981 – the industry consequently suffering from the loss of skilled workers, a decline in the number of apprenticeships, a low level of investment in new plant, extensive de-stocking and closures in the building supply industries.[18] It was probable that if capacity was not protected, future increases in demand (coupled with shortages of skilled labour and materials) would be severely cost-inflationary. Yet capacity was under threat. In the early 1980s the bankruptcy rate increased substantially, and even in 1982 when a slight upturn in housebuilding was apparent, there were 26 per cent more bankruptcies than in 1981. There was much concern within the Group of Eight (a pressure group representing management, the professions and unions within the industry) that since employers were becoming insolvent in increasing numbers, there would be very little left of the construction industry to respond to increased demand when the recession of the 1980s was over. Because of this scenario, both the Building and Civil Engineering Development Committee and the Social and Economic Committee of the European Commission recommended that government should introduce policies which would have a stabilising or expansionary impact on construction, so that the industry could plan ahead and increase its level of investment and training.

It is doubtful, however, whether the construction industry could expand without direct-labour organisations playing a substantial role. Under Thatcherism in the early 1980s this was impossible. As part of the government's philosophy of minimising public expenditure and ostensibly supporting private industry, severe restrictions were placed on direct labour. Direct labour was expected to show a return of 5 per cent on capital employed (far in excess of the return the private sector could have expected in the early 1980s). The Local Government, Planning and Land Act 1980 put an obligation on local authorites to put out for tender all except the smallest jobs, rather than negotiate terms with their own direct-labour organisations; required these organisations to adopt accounting procedures which showed a profit or loss on each of its activities; and warned the organisations that if they were consistently unsuccessful they would be wound up. The emaciation of direct labour was an invitation to the private sector to become increasingly obligopolistic or monopolistic, and it was ironic that while the Conservative Government voiced support for competition, the 1980 Act cut out Labour's proposal to permit direct-labour organisations to tender on the open market beyond their local authority boundaries.

With the increase in minimum lending rate to 17 per cent in November 1979 (and with base rate remaining above 10 per cent until 1983) Conservative monetarism, far from helping the construction industry, decimated much of it. The government failed to appreciate that the construction industry could help pull the rest of the economy out of the recession (believing instead that an eventual recovery in the economy would assist the construction industry). Construction (especially housebuilding) is very labour intensive, creating more jobs for any given volume of capital expenditure than most other activities. The industry also relies heavily on purchased materials. Any increase in investment therefore – in, for example, housebuilding – has a multiplier effect on employment 'down' and 'up the line'. Shelter estimated that for every £100 million spent on constructing new dwellings, 5600 man years would be created for on-site operatives and 3000 new homes would be built. An extra 1850 man years work would be created for architects, surveyors and clerical staff, and a further 7450 man-years for labour 'up the line' – for example, in building supply and transport.[18] The Trades Unions Congress calculated that there was an employment multiplier in the construction industry of two (for every one extra person employed in construction, one extra job would be created elsewhere).[19] The creation of this amount of employment would save the Treasury up to £82 million (in terms of reduced unemployment pay and supplementary benefits, and extra tax revenue), therefore the net cost of building 3000 new homes would be only £20–£30 million extra on the borrowing requirement. On this basis, the gross cost of employing an additional 150 000 construction workers (on public sector work) would be £2000 million, but the net cost could be as low as £400 million. Overall, increased public expenditure on housebuilding would not only increase or improve the supply of housing and safeguard the capacity of the construction industry, but would also reduce the level of unemployment substantially and reflate the economy as a whole.

There is also the need to adopt a system of decasualisation to raise the status of the building worker and to provide additional security in an industry which has made widespread use of casual labour. Better working conditions, reasonable pension schemes and more stable employment would weaken the hold of the 'lump'. In the public sector there is a need for reform of cost yardsticks, particularly housing. There is also a strong case for more flexible attitudes to such developments as 'non-specific' buildings in which the main dimensions and positions of vertical supports allow for a wide range of accommodation. This system approach is equally fundamentally dependent upon a stable long-term demand.

The importance of the construction industry to the national economy has been stressed above. Its importance to the urban economy is even more crucial. Undoubtedly, the construction industry was showing distinct signs of recovery by the mid-1980s. In 1986, output increased by 2.5 per cent (compared with a drop of 14 per cent, 1980–82), while the average return on capital increased from 4.8 per cent in 1982–83 to 9 per cent in 1986–87 in real terms.[19] But with a substantial decline in public sector contracts and reduced opportunities overseas, the industry became increasingly dependent on an overheated private market at home, with the associated risk of being eventually squeezed by deflationary policies. The imbalance in construction activity was thus a major cause for concern, particularly in view of the depreciation of social capital.

The Charter for Jobs[20] estimated in 1987 that £93 million needed to be spent on infrastructure investment – an injection into the economy which could produce 1 million jobs over six years. Of this sum, at least £30 billion was needed to remedy defects in the housing stock, £1.7 billion was required for hospital building, £500 million was needed for maintenance work on schools, and other large sums were required to repair water mains, sewers and roads. Britain was bottom of the international league table of spending on construction and infrastructure in the mid-1980s, and its built environment was facing a renewal crisis of enormous proportions. The urban economy was yet again showing all the signs of private affluence and public squalor.

REFERENCES

1. P. M. Hillebrandt, *Small Firms in the Construction Industry*, Committee of Inquiry on Small Firms, Research Report No. 10 (HMSO, 1971).
2. U.K. National Board for Prices and Incomes, *Pay and Conditions in the Building Industry*, Report No. 92, Cmnd 3837 (HMSO, 1968).
3. Ministry of Building and Public Works, *The pacing and management of contracts for building and civil engineering work* (HMSO, 1964).
4. *The Public Client and the Construction Industries*, The Report of the Building and Civil Engineering Economic Development Committee (HMSO, 1975).
5. E. Lea, P. Harvey and P. Spencer, *Efficiency and Growth in the Building Industry*, sponsored by the Department of the Environment, 1972.
6. P. M. Hillebrandt, *Economic Theory and the Construction Industry* (Macmillan, 1974).
7. M. Ball, 'Land Rent and the Construction Industry' in M. Ball *et al.*, *Land Rent, Housing and Urban Planning – A European Perspective* (Croom Helm, 1984).
8. D. Massey and A. Catalano, *Capital and Land: Landownership by Capital in Great Britain* (Edward Arnold, 1978).
9. M. Ball, 'Differential Rent and the Role of Landed Property', *International Journal of Urban and Regional Research*, 1 (1977); B. Fine, 'On Marx's Theory of Agricultural Rent', *Economy and Society*, 8 (1979).
10. B. Fine, 'Land, Capital and the British Coal Industry Prior to World War II' in M. Ball *et al.*, *Land Rent, Housing and Urban Planning – A European Perspective* (Croom Helm, 1984).
11. *Committee of Inquiry under Professor E. H. Phelps Brown* (1968).
12. *Manpower Study 1974* (National Federation of Building Trades Employers, 1974).
13. I. McNeill, 'New facade for building's bad practices', *Morning Star* (11 March, 1987).
14. I. H. Seeley, *Building Economics* (Macmillan, 1974).
15. P. A. Stone, *Building Economy: Design, Production and Organisation – a Synoptic View* (Pergamon Press, 1966).
16. A. Henney, *New Housebuilding in the 1980's – Prospects and Problems of Housing in the 1980's* (The Building Societies Association Conference, 1980).

17. D. Turner, 'The construction industry in Britain', *Midland Bank Review*, (Autumn, 1987).
18. S. Hilditch, 'Build Houses. Build Hope', *Roof* (November/December, 1981).
19. Trade Union Congress, *The Reconstruction of Britain* (TUC, 1981).
20. Charter for Jobs, reported in *Guardian* (8 June, 1987).

Index

Postcript

In March 1988 The Conservative government took two policy initiatives which it hoped would hasten the pace of inner city regeneration and help to revive the private rented housing sector. In its *Action for Cities* it announced a new Urban Development Corporation for Sheffield; a doubling of the area of the Merseyside Development Corporation; two new City Action Teams for Leeds and Nottingham; and a City Grant which would replace the Urban Development Grant and Urban Regeneration Grant and be paid directly to developers. Other measures included an intensified drive to bring unused and under-used public sector land on to the market; additional help for small businesses; and extra provision of premises for new businesses in rundown inner cities. Critics argued, however, that very little extra public expenditure was involved; that the cash allocations had to be contrasted with the £20 billion cut in the rate support grant (1979–88); and that attempts to regenerate local economies without entering into effective partnership with local authorities was doomed to failure.

The spring Budget of 1988 was the second initiative. It extended the Business Expansion Scheme (BES) to individuals who invested up to £40 000 per annum in approved unquoted property companies supplying houses for rent under assured tenancy arrangements (eligible properties had to have a maximum value of £125 000 in London and £85 000 elsewhere. Individuals qualified for tax relief on their investment and companies were able to raise up to £5 million under the scheme. While the BES, however, might increase the number of rented properties in the short term (benefiting investors and landlords more than tenants since rents will need to be high to provide a competitive return), in the long term supply could diminish. Since tax relief is intended to cease in 1993, many individuals might seek to withdraw their investments, while landlords will become increasingly interested in realising capital gain – both situations resulting in the selling-off of properties for owner-occupation. In addition, the reduction in the upper rates of income tax to a maximum of 40 per cent will inevitably increase the demand for owner-occupied housing at the upper end of the market which will not only increase urban and regional disparities in house prices but also compound the advantages to landlords in selling-off. It is thus very probable that neither of the above initiatives of March 1988 will be successful.